John Engler:

The Man, the Leader & the Legacy

JOHN ENGLER

The Man, the Leader & the Legacy

★

GLEAVES WHITNEY

Sleeping Bear Press

Sleeping Bear Press is an imprint of Gale Group, Inc.

Sleeping Bear Press
310 North Main Street
P.O. Box 20
Chelsea, MI 48118
www.sleepingbearpress.com

Printed and bound in the United States.

10 9 8 7 6 5 4 3 2 1

Library of Congress Cataloging-in-Publication Data on file.

I'm a Franklin D. Roosevelt Democrat, so John Engler's philosophy is not mine. But he is as honest as he is aggressive. He keeps his word. And he's been extremely effective. He has had more control over the legislature than any other governor I've worked with. On issue after issue, he has done things that no other governor had the courage to do.

FRANK KELLEY[1]

John Engler has unseated more state officeholders than any politician since World War II and, very possibly, in all of Michigan history. That is truly a remarkable achievement.

BILL BALLENGER[2]

The remarkable thing about John Engler is the breadth of his leadership. Arguably he is among the greatest party builders in Michigan history. Arguably he is the only governor in the U.S. who doesn't need a policy division—he is out in front of his policy team on almost every issue. Arguably he is among the most skillful legislators who have ever worked in the Capitol. Arguably he has as clear a set of principles as any public figure in Michigan. Most successful governors can get by with two or three of these attributes and do quite well. John Engler has them all. He is the complete governor.

MARK MURRAY[3]

[1]*Frank Kelley, interview with Gleaves Whitney (hereafter GW), October 1, 2002. Kelley offered a similar quotation in David S. Broder, "Conservative Leaves Progressive Legacy: Michigan Governor Led School Finance Reform Seen as Model of Equity, Innovation,"* Washington Post, *July 28, 2002, p. A4.*
[2]*Bill Ballenger, interview with GW, October 2, 2002.*
[3]*Mark Murray, interview with GW, September 25, 2001.*

★

To three who will lead in the 21st century—

Ian, Alasdair, and Andrew

★

Table of Contents

Part II
Governor: 1991-2002

Part III
What Kind of Legacy?

★

Acknowledgments

I wish to express my appreciation to many colleagues who set aside their work to help me with mine. While space limits my ability to name everyone who helped, there are no limits to my gratitude.

First and foremost, I should like to thank Governor John Engler, whose cooperation made this book possible; he is the inspiration behind the perspiration. I hasten to add First Lady Michelle Engler, who has always been gracious with her time, memories, and insights. Having known the First Family for 11 years, I can assuredly attest that they are "first" in much more than the strictly official sense.

Heartfelt thanks also to Richard McLellan and the Cornerstone Foundation for their encouragement and support since the work's inception.

For help with the innumerable tasks involved in pulling together a book of this complexity, many thanks to my research assistant, Josh Nunez; the manuscript could not have been completed under deadline without his hard work. The administration archivist, Christopher Kelley, sifted through thousands of internal documents and made valuable discoveries. One of the leaders in our Communication Division, John Nevin, was generous with his insights and research. My work has benefited from many other colleagues in the governor's office, especially Rusty Hills, Sharon Rothwell, Susan Shafer, and John Truscott. Further assistance was given by a dedicated corps of colleagues at the Library of Michigan and in offices throughout state government. In many ways they helped retrieve important parts of the public record.

A team of college interns also contributed, and I am grateful to these outstanding members of the rising generation: Melissa Bierman, Sarah Crone, Janet Daig, Daniel Ferrill, Elena Gill, Eric Groenendyk, Chad Groenhout, Joshua Knicely, Amber Luttig, Kyle McGrath, Julia Murray, Gabriel Nunez, Lisa Prentice, Victoria Rariden, Benjamin Rawson, Charity Reed, James Risner, Amy Robertson, Kelly

Roland, Janell Roth, Anthony Soloman, Jessica Strattard, and Ian Whitney.

It especially pleases me to acknowledge two people who do not live in Michigan but who have closely followed Engler's gubernatorial career—my dad, Fred Whitney, who must have sent every clipping about the governor from the *Orange County Register* and *Los Angeles Times*, and my late mother-in-law, Martha Doak, who assiduously dispatched clippings from the Fort Collins *Coloradoan*.

Then there are the women and men—more than 150 in all—with whom I corresponded or consulted or interviewed: Republicans and Democrats, liberals and conservatives, journalists and analysts, allies and opponents, family and friends. Their words constitute the heart of the book. Acknowledged in the text and notes that follow, these individuals were generous in sharing their stories, sending their clippings, and offering their insights. I must also mention the half-dozen people whom I interviewed off the record; they spoke on condition of anonymity yet still contributed in important ways. I thank you all.

A documentary biography can only succeed to the extent that individuals and organizations grant permission to reprint source material. For access and permission to use his personal papers, many thanks to John Engler. For permission to reprint articles, op-ed pieces, and book passages, I am grateful to the *New York Times, Wall Street Journal, National Review, Economist, Washington Times, Detroit Free Press, Detroit News, Lansing State Journal,* Booth Newspapers, *Oakland Press, Flint Journal, Holland Sentinel*, (Mount Pleasant) *Morning Sun*, (Mount Pleasant) *Daily Times News*, (Alma) *Record Leader, Clare Sentinel, Big Rapids Pioneer*, Donovan Reynolds, Simon & Schuster, and University of Nebraska Press. For permission to reprint photographs, I am grateful to John Engler, the White House, Annette Kirk, *Detroit News, Detroit Free Press,* Gannett News Service, *Lansing State Journal, L'Osservatore Romano*, Michigan Senate, and State of Michigan's Department of Military Affairs.

Many thanks also to the leadership of the Gale Group, especially Ben Mondloch and Scott Smith, and the staff at Sleeping Bear Press, particularly Brian Lewis, Jennifer Lundahl, and Vivian Collier, for helping midwife this manuscript into the world.

My toughest editor-critic deserves praise for the love with which she can administer the *coup de grâce* to a bad word, overwrought sentence, or imprudent passage—thanks, Louise.

For any excellence in this work, I am indebted to many. For any weaknesses, lapses, or errors, I needed no outside help.

Gleaves Whitney

What a piece of work is a man!
How noble in reason! How infinite in faculty!
SHAKESPEARE

★

Introduction

This book is the first full-length biography of John Engler. A first draft of history, it can best be described as a *documentary biography* that attempts to order the vast written, spoken, and visual record of a man who has spent more than three decades in the public arena. That record is engaging in its own right—of importance to anyone who seeks to understand Michigan and even U.S. political history from 1970 to 2002. The work can be approached as a fairly intimate biography of a very private man, for the stories and impressions of more than 150 people are distilled in these pages. Or it can be viewed as a portrait of leadership, for Engler headed up two branches of government during 19 years of his career. Or it can serve as a survey of the public record of one of America's most innovative, accomplished governors.[4]

Who is John Engler? Talk to enough people, and you'll encounter three different perceptions.

There is the Engler of the sympathetic public, the same public that three times elected "Governor John" to lead their state. They emphasize that he has been in the vanguard of American politics since 1991. That he is one of the most effective chief executives in Michigan history. That he "made" the modern Michigan Republican Party. That he cut taxes 32 times. That he sliced through the Gordian knot of school finance. That he took the national lead on welfare reforms. That he fought for more public school choice and accountability. That he slowed the growth of state government. That he worked to decrease abortions. That he would make a first-rate vice president—or president. As one admirer bluntly put it: "John Engler is probably the greatest gov-

[4] *For complete details of the Engler administration's accomplishments, see the links at www.michigan.gov.*

ernor in Michigan history—and great governors make great presidents: Theodore Roosevelt, Franklin Delano Roosevelt, Ronald Reagan...."

By contrast, there is the Engler of his harshest critics—"King John" to them, or worse, the "Butcher of Beal City." They respect his political agility but insist that he is consumed by the desire for power. That he is a calculating political machine. That he is Machiavellian. That he is ruthless about getting his way. That he cares not one whit for Detroit, children, or public schools. That he looks for every opportunity to slash arts funding and environmental protection. That somehow he is not quite fully—human. "I think he lacks soul," one person said. "I doubt that he has the capacity to be moved by nature or human artistic creativity."

Finally, as though hermetically sealed from the other two perceptions, there is the private John Engler, the inner man revealed only to his family and closest friends. They know that he has a generous heart. That he is a devout Catholic who unfailingly goes to Mass. That deep down he is shy. That he is fiercely loyal to his friends. That he loves to read to his three daughters. That he agonizes over the plight of children in failing schools. That he has worried unceasingly about Detroit. That he will drop everything to console the sick and suffering.

Three distinctly different views of John Engler—is there an "image problem" here? In one sense, not at all. Engler has won 20 races straight in a very tough state. He has one of the best electoral records in the U.S.; most pols would die to have such an unbroken record of success. How can a guy who has never lost an election have an image problem? More than that, at his side are Michelle Engler, his charismatic wife, and their three winsome daughters—golden-haired triplets, no less. The public sees Engler happy and smiling and solicitous of the "four ladies" in his life. They make a beautiful family.

And yet—and yet—there *is* an image problem. Engler is a public man with a public record going back more than three decades. People close to him are dismayed by what political opponents, reporters, and editorial writers have said on the record. One top aide (formerly a political operative on the East Coast) opined that there is not another major American political leader today for whom the "disconnect" between perception and reality yawns so large. "There are many paradoxes surrounding John Engler," this aide said. "Maybe the biggest paradox of all is that the most public man in the state is the most private man in the state. People just don't know who he is. That has sometimes made it hard to sell his policies."

Another longtime aide reflected: "There is a stark contrast between who

John Engler is in public and who he is in private. If the public understood what a devoted husband and father he is and saw all the little things he does that engender loyalty in the people who work with him, they would have a much different picture. Reporters would, too, and many of their stories would have a different slant. Everybody knows he's smart—he has a brain as big as Montana. But what they don't see, which we do, is that John has a heart as big as all Texas."

The aide then confessed, "I have to say I love the guy. I feel a real sense of love for and loyalty to him. He is a father figure, someone I can depend on. This is a man I would die for—I would take a bullet for him."

A remarkable statement, this. But not a unique one.

Of course, there are not three John Englers; there is only one. The discerning observer realizes that he is neither the Machiavelli of detractors nor the marble statue of campaigners. The truth is more complex, more interesting. The purpose of this documentary biography is to bridge the gaping canyon between public perception and private reality. It is not a conventional biography, however. The story in these pages is told not by a single narrator, but by scores of people—by those who have had the opportunity to watch Engler, write about him, live with him, and work with, for, and against him. The book is their words, their observations, and their insights. Everyone from the mother who bore him to the Democrats who bear him has a say.

The interviews, indeed, have been with a distinguished and diverse lot: former U.S. presidents, governors and ex-governors, Ivy League professors, nationally syndicated columnists, judges, legislators, teachers, think tank experts, lobbyists, journalists, editorial cartoonists, party leaders, Engler's family, friends, staff, and his college professors. It must be said: their contributions have made the project an historian's paradise. After all, interesting people know Engler—they have strong feelings about him—and people who feel passionately tell good stories. If I have any regrets, it is that time and space prevented my including even more stories in these pages.

This book has been three years in the making. The research involved conducting more than 150 interviews; sifting through some 10,000 newspaper articles, editorials, and op-eds; gleaning the best editorial cartoons and photographs; and reviewing an endless Niagara of e-mails, memos, government reports, and speeches. The writing centered on developing headnotes and bridgenotes around the source material to keep the story moving.

The work is divided into three parts. Part I covers Engler from the day he was born to the day he was inaugurated as Michigan's 46th governor. Part II spans his 12 years in the governor's office. Part III offers evaluations from a number of perspectives—analysts and reporters, Democrats and Republicans, opponents and friends.

Which brings me to an important juncture. In the spirit of full disclosure, readers should know three things. First, the book was my idea, not Engler's. I sold him on the project with difficulty, and only after months of lobbying. Second, it is an authorized project, meaning that Engler agreed to cooperate with my research efforts. He did not, however, determine its contents. Third, I have worked for Engler 11 years and currently serve as his chief speechwriter and historian. More than that, I regard him as a friend. If that association raises red flags, readers should be aware that the work includes passages by opponents as well as allies, Democrats as well as Republicans, liberals as well as conservatives. The aim has not been to generate hagiography but to create an accurate rendering of a complex man.

Historians observe that there are three reasons to justify a biography. Either the person (1) made history, or (2) participated in something historically significant, or (3) represents a type among an historically interesting group of people. Taking care to avoid overstatement, I think John Engler has made his mark by all three criteria. First, observers of all stripes agree that Engler has decisively changed one of the nation's major industrial states. Through the skillful use of powers granted him by the Michigan constitution, Engler has governed with vigor. He has dominated policy, modernized state government, administered programs, vetoed legislation, appointed judges, filled boards, and framed public debates. As two *Detroit News* reporters noted: "Gov. John Engler has had more impact on the lives of Michiganians over the past decade than any other single person, and his deep imprint will be evident well into the new century."[5]

Second, Engler participated in something historically significant: a powerful wave of conservative governance whose epicenter was Ronald Reagan's election in 1980 and whose shock waves reached out to the 104th Congress in 1995-1996. Two writers have called this conservative movement a "revolution at the roots."[6] This revolution—perhaps better regarded as a counter-revolution since its inspiration was the American founding—was animated by freedom. Its champions did not regard government as evil, but neither did they think government should usurp civil society. Their goal was to make American govern-

[5]*Charlie Cain and Mark Hornbeck, "Policies Seal Name for Engler,"* Detroit News, *April 9, 2001, p. 1A.*
[6]*The term comes from the title of a book by William D. Eggers and John O'Leary,* Revolution at the Roots: Making Our Government Smaller, Better, and Closer to Home *(New York: Free Press, 1995).*

ment smaller, better, closer to the people, and thus more responsive to them. The attempted sea change was in part successful, in part frustrated; democratic politics is an arena of compromise; total victory is as rare as complete annihilation. But to the extent that it was successful, some credit is due to Engler, whose vision, leadership, and achievements made a difference in Michigan and on the national stage.

Third, Engler is a type—an outstanding type—among an historically important class of individuals: American governors who were in office in the 1990s. In part, it was historical circumstance that made the governors significant. With the fall of the Berlin Wall in 1989 and the collapse of the Soviet Empire in 1991, the Cold War ended. For one brief decade (until September 11, 2001), Americans turned away from foreign affairs. With the spotlight on domestic concerns, governors moved to center stage and contributed significantly to public policy. What kept them in the spotlight was sheer talent and political acumen. In the 1990s, not Washington but the states became the arena of action—especially those states with powerful governor-reformers. In their respective "laboratories of democracy," governors challenged the assumptions, programs, and defenders of the Great Society. They championed federalism and sought to wrest money and power from Washington. It is no wonder that this class of governors would also serve as a White House farm club in the 1990s. Commentator William Kristol notes, "The '90s were an extraordinary time for American governors. John Engler and Wisconsin Governor Tommy Thompson were especially courageous. In leading their states through a tough recession [in 1991-92], they did more to legitimize conservative policies than anybody else. Certainly they laid the groundwork for governors who followed in their footsteps. One chief executive benefited from Engler and Thompson more than any other: George W. Bush. He was elected governor of Texas in 1994—after Engler and Thompson had already run the gauntlet. These two Midwestern governors helped make it possible for George W. Bush to seek the presidency."[7] The rest, as they say, is history.

John Engler has remarked that he has no interest in writing a book about himself, and historians would observe that it is too soon to write a conventional biography of a person still in office: not enough time has elapsed to put the subject in perspective. So why this documentary biography? Because it is

[7] *William Kristol, interview with GW, October 21, 1999.*

not too soon to interview the people with whom Engler has worked, and to sort through the huge volume of material generated by his career. Nor is it too soon to look at the man's remarkable capacity to lead. Whatever readers think of him—whether they love him or loathe him—John Engler has been a man of consequence. The aim of this book is to help readers understand who he is and what he has done.

Throughout this undertaking, my work has been buoyed by the words of James Madison, inscribed at the entrance of the Library of Congress:

"A popular Government, without popular information, or the means of acquiring it, is but a Prologue to a Farce or a Tragedy; or, perhaps both. Knowledge will forever govern ignorance: And a people who mean to be their own Governors, must arm themselves with the power which knowledge gives."[8]

[8]*James Madison, letter to W. T. Barry, August 4, 1822; in* The Writings of James Madison, *ed. Gaillard Hunt, vol. 9 (New York: Putnam's Sons, 1910), p. 103.*

A note to readers about the format of this book. Because this is a documentary biography, it weaves a variety of source material into the text—John Engler's private papers, oral interviews, contemporary newspaper articles, editorials, letters, and book passages. Italicized headnotes and bridgenotes introduce speakers, sources, and topics. Footnotes provide citations for further research.

For convenience, some of the more frequently encountered names follow.

Who's Who

Abraham, Spencer	chairman of Michigan Republican Party (1983-1994), U.S. Senator (1995-2001), U.S. Secretary of Energy (2001-)
Andrews, Chris	*Lansing State Journal* reporter
Avery, Susy (Heinz)	Republican activist, senior Engler administration aide, state GOP chair
Ballenger, William	state representative (1969-1970), state senator (1971-1974), Republican, political commentator and editor of *Inside Michigan Politics*
Barks Hoffman, Kathy	Associated Press reporter, Lansing bureau
Bell, Dawson	*Detroit Free Press* reporter, Lansing bureau
Bennett, William	U.S. education secretary, served in Reagan and Bush administrations
Bertram, David	Engler campaign worker and administration aide
Binsfeld, Connie	schoolteacher, state representative (1974-1982), state senator (1982-1990), Engler's lieutenant governor (1991-1998)
Blanchard, James	U.S. representative (1975-1982), governor of Michigan (1983-1990), U.S. ambassador to Canada (1993-1996), Democratic gubernatorial candidate (2002)
Brandell, Jim	aide in first gubernatorial campaign and in administration
Bray, Tom	*Detroit News* columnist and editor
Broder, David	*Washington Post* columnist
Bush, George H. W.	41st president (1989-1993)
Bush, George W.	43rd president (2001-)
Cawthorne, Dennis	served in the Michigan House with Engler, House leader (1975-1978), Republican
Christoff, Chris	*Detroit Free Press* reporter, Lansing bureau
Crandall, Jerry	Engler's chief of staff in the senate majority leader's office
Davis, Matt	*Detroit Free Press* reporter
DeVos, Betsy	Republican activist, businesswoman, chaired the Michigan Republican Party (1996-2000)
Dodak, Lew	Democratic speaker of the Michigan House (1989-1992)

Doyle, Dave	past chairman of the Michigan Republican Party
Ellis, Art	past Central Michigan University president, director of Department of Commerce, and superintendent of public instruction during Engler administration
Engler, Agnes (Neyer)	John Engler's mother
Engler, Hannah	daughter of John and Michelle Engler
Engler, Madeleine	daughter of John and Michelle Engler
Engler, Margaret (Maggie)	daughter of John and Michelle Engler
Engler, Mathias John	John Engler's father
Engler, Michelle	John Engler's wife (married 1990)
Ford, Gerald R.	38th president (1974-1977), formerly of Grand Rapids, Michigan
Gizzi, John	political editor, *Human Events*
Gnodtke, William	staff in House of Representatives (1971-1982), friend of John Engler, Republican
Gobler, Linda	lobbyist, Engler friend, wife of Dennis Schornack, president of Michigan Grocers Association
Gonzales, Sue (Engler)	sister of John Engler
Griffiths, Martha	state representative (1949-1952), U. S. Representative (1955-1974), Blanchard's lieutenant governor (1983-1990)
Haas, Mark	economist, director of Michigan's Office of Revenue and Tax Analysis
Haveman, James	Engler's director of the Department of Community Health
Hillegonds, Paul	Speaker, Co-speaker of the Michigan House of Representatives, Republican
Hills, G. J. "Rusty"	Engler's director of communication and public affairs, then chairman of the Michigan Republican Party (2000-2003)
Hollister, David	state representative (1975-1993), mayor of Lansing (1993-), Democrat
House, Colleen	state representative (1974-1976, 1983-1986), Republican lieutenant governor candidate (1986), John Engler's first wife (1975-1986)
Huckabee, Mike	governor of Arkansas, Republican
Hunt, Jim	former governor of North Carolina, Democrat
Kelley, Frank	attorney general of Michigan (1961-1998), Democrat
Kirk, Annette	wife of Russell Kirk, member of President Reagan's National Commission on Excellence in Education
Kirk, Russell	man of letters from Mecosta, author of *The Conservative Mind*, lived in Engler's senate district (died 1994)
Kost, John	headed Senate caucus policy staff, and senior aide in first term of Engler administration

Kristol, William	Vice President Quayle's chief of staff, editor of the *Weekly Standard*
LaBelle, Bart	businessman from Mount Pleasant, early Engler supporter
Laughlin, Pat	Lansing lobbyist, friend of Engler in the 1970s and 1980s
Listing, Barbara	president, Right to Life of Michigan
Mallett, Jef	editorial cartoonist
Mandersheid, Les	Engler's College of Agriculture advisor at Michigan State University
McAlvey, JefF	Engler's senate staff, legislative director in Engler administration
McConnell, John	speechwriter for Vice-Presidents Dan Quayle and Dick Cheney
McLellan, Richard	attorney, led Engler transition team in 1990, close Engler friend and confidant
Mehan, G. Tracy	director of Engler's Office of the Great Lakes
Mervenne, Anne	gubernatorial campaign aide, staff member in gubernatorial administration
Michaelson, Mark	director of Engler's constituent services during first term
Miller, Art	state senator (1977-2002), Senate minority leader during Proposal A, Democrat
Miller, Gerald	Engler's first director of the Department of Social Services, later the Family Independent Agency
Milliken, William	governor of Michigan (1969-1982), Republican
Molloy, John	Engler's professor at Michigan State University
Murphy, Jill	Engler senate staff and administration official
Murray, Mark	state treasurer, budget director, director of the Department of Management and Budget, acting director of the Family Independence Agency, and special policy advisor to the governor
Nevin, John	Engler's first chief speechwriter, later deputy director of Communications
Newman, Andrea Fischer	Engler's friend, fundraiser during first gubernatorial campaign, University of Michigan regent, Republican
Owen, Gary	Democratic speaker of the House (1982-1988) when Engler was Senate majority leader
Peltomaa, Dave	first lieutenant in Michigan State Police and head of governor's security detail
Pero, Colleen	legislative staff, senior campaign aide, senior administration aide, wife of Dan Pero, introduced John and Michelle in 1989
Pero, Dan	Engler campaign manager (1990 and 1994), longtime friend, husband of Colleen Pero
Pluta, Rick	Lansing reporter

Pollack, Lana	state senator (1983-1994), Democrat
Porteous, David	Reed City attorney and Michigan State University trustee, has known Engler since the early 1970s
Posthumus, Dick	high-school rival, college classmate, helped manage Engler's first campaign for the Michigan House, later state senator (1982-1998) and lieutenant governor (1998-2002)
Prechter, Heinz	close friend of Engler's, businessman, Republican activist, died 2001
Quebbeman, Marsha	Engler aide in Senate, during campaign, and in administration
Reagan, Ronald	40th president (1981-1989)
Redick (Wilson), LeAnne	deputy campaign manager in first gubernatorial campaign, director of Engler's Washington office
Reed, Lawrence	founder and president of Mackinac Center for Public Policy, Midland
Roberts, Doug	former Democratic staffer, state treasurer twice under Engler
Romney, George	governor of Michigan (1963-1968), Republican
Roosa, Bryan	Engler aide in the Washington office
Rothwell, Doug	beginning April 1993, director of Michigan Jobs Commission and its spin-offs
Rothwell, Sharon	Engler administration chief of staff in second and third terms
Schornack, Dennis	Engler senate staff, unofficial policy director in gubernatorial campaign, "white papers" editor, and senior administration aide, husband of Linda Gobler
Secchia, Peter	businessman from Grand Rapids, U.S. ambassador to Italy (1989-1993), longtime friend of Engler
Shields, Tom	Engler friend and ally, founder and president of Marketing Resource Group, Inc.
Short, Al	longtime leader at the Michigan Education Association and lobbyist during Proposal A
Siglow, Rachel	executive assistant to Governor Engler
Skubick, Tim	dean of Lansing reporters and commentators
Smith, Sid	early supporter of Engler's from Mount Pleasant
Stieber, Carolyn	Engler's political science professor at Michigan State University
Strange, Russell	State Representative (1957-1970), Republican, defeated by Engler in the 1970 primary, died in 2001
Swift, Brian	Engler aide in the northern Michigan office
Taylor, Cliff	attorney, supreme court justice, longtime friend of Engler, husband of Lucille Taylor
Taylor, Lucille	Michigan house and senate staff, director of governor's legal department, wife of Cliff Taylor

Toepp, John (Jack)	state senator (1967-1978), Republican, defeated by Engler in 1978, died in 1979
Torreano, Gail	chief of staff for Engler during senate years, president of Ameritech Michigan
Truscott, John	Engler campaign aide, administration press secretary
Viventi, Carol	Engler's first hire when state representative, deputy chief of staff in Engler's first term
Whitbeck, William	attorney, helped lead transition, senior Engler aide during first term, chief judge of Michigan Court of Appeals
Whitney, Gleaves	Engler's chief speechwriter and historian
Wolfram, Gary	Hillsdale College professor and economist, worked with Engler in the senate and then served as deputy treasurer
Woodworth, Patti	first term director of Department of Management and Budget
Young, Coleman	state senator (1964-1974), mayor of Detroit (1974-1994), died in 1997
Ziegler, Hal	state representative and senator in the 1970s, Republican

PART I

Years of Preparation:
1948-1990

Life is a romantic business.
It is painting a picture, not doing a sum—
but you have to make the romance, and it will come to the
question of how much fire you have in your belly.
Oliver Wendell Holmes Jr.

★

Chapter One
Childhood: 1948 - 1966

The times

In 1948 Michigan was in the economic vanguard. General Motors, Ford, and Chrysler were on the verge of assembling a record six million cars, more than the rest of the world combined.

After the lean depression and war years, consumerism was in full swing again. In 1948 the long-playing record was invented. The Polaroid Land Camera was launched. And two brothers named Richard and Maurice opened the original McDonalds restaurant featuring their "Speedee Service System" and selling 15-cent hamburgers and 10-cent fries.

Also in 1948, the state's most illustrious boxer, Joe Louis, retired after having fought 25 title bouts. In the Rose Bowl Michigan crushed Southern Cal, 49-0.

That year saw the Cold War heat up. Communists took over Czechoslovakia. President Truman ordered the Berlin Airlift to save the three Allied sectors of the divided city. Congress reinstated the draft. And Time *magazine editor Whittaker Chambers led reporters and investigators to the famous pumpkin patch where evidence against Alger Hiss had been secreted.*

The world was in the dawn of the atomic age. Perhaps summing up the mood of the era was W. H. Auden's collection of poems that won the Pulitzer Prize in 1948; the title piece was called "The Age of Anxiety."

The Engler family calls this the "four generations photograph," taken in the summer of 1949: baby John, his father Matt (kneeling), his grandfather John Engler (standing), and his great-grandmother Hannah Engler. SOURCE: *John Engler*

*

The Engler family and their land

John Mathias Engler was born on Columbus Day—October 12, 1948. He was the first child of Mathias John Engler and Agnes Neyer Engler. His father Matt was three-quarters Irish and one-quarter German. He was from a farming family that had settled in the Mount Pleasant area. John's mother is 100 percent Austrian. Her ancestors came to America from Tyrol and Voralberg. She grew up in the village of Beal City, just a few miles northwest of Mount Pleasant. Both sides of the family were Roman Catholic.

Matt and Agnes had seven children—3 boys and 4 girls. They raised their children in the same region in which they had grown up, Isabella County, about 70 miles north of Lansing. During most of John's childhood, the Englers lived four miles south-southeast of Beal City on a 500-acre farm. The land has a quintessentially Midwestern look—a gently rolling patchwork of field and forest. It is sometimes called "stump country" because loggers came through in the 1800s and clear-cut vast expanses of native oak and white pine trees.

The Engler farmhouse was on West River Road, near the North Branch of the Chippewa River. They rented an additional 400 acres. Their farm had painted fences and a red barn. Agnes Engler loved the farm. "It was a wonderful home," she said, "a real showplace." [9]

The Engler farmhouse and barn on West River Road, c. 1950. SOURCE: *John Engler*

*

The Brandell family grew up near the Englers. A future aide to the governor, Jim Brandell, observes:

John grew up on a farm with a big red barn that had their name on it. The house isn't far off the road, maybe 50 feet. The house and barn look like all the other farms you see in the Midwest, mile after mile.

With John's family, what you see is what you get. John's parents, Matt and Agnes, were the kind of people you would like to have as your neighbors. They were not ostentatious. They were not braggarts. They were just a good, solid, Midwestern family.

John is more like his father than his mother. He's more reserved than she is. Agnes is more gregarious.[10]

[9] *Agnes Engler, interview with GW, July 18, 2002.*
[10] *Jim Brandell, interview with GW, February 16, 2001.*

*

Dick Posthumus would be one of John Engler's greatest political allies through the years. He also knew John's father Matt.

I knew Matt Engler very well and liked him a lot. On the positive side, Matt was go-get-'em; on the negative side, a bull-in-a-china-shop. He was hard driving, willing to take risks, and used to throwing the long ball. He had the cattle feeder instinct.

John Engler gets a lot of his attributes from Matt.[11]

*

Another political ally, William (Bill) Gnodtke, reflects on John Engler's early influences.

Matt could talk politics with you until the sun came up, just like John. John's political philosophy grew out of his upbringing. His parents' happy marriage, their close family, the conservative German stock, the close-knit community, the hard work every day on his farm in rural Michigan—all these made John who he is.[12]

*

Childhood

These are some of Agnes Engler's favorite stories about her first child.

As a toddler, John liked to go out to the chicken coop. He would cause havoc and make the chickens fly around. One Sunday—it was in August and I was pregnant with Jim—I was looking for John in the chicken coop but didn't see him. I was standing in the kitchen door calling for him. No answer. Then I happened to look down the road a quarter of a mile, and I saw John walking right down the middle of the road. In his training pants.

Even though I was pregnant, I ran as fast as I could to catch him, because he was approaching a rise in the road, and cars would sometimes fly down that road. When he saw me coming, he started to run.

"John! Where do you think you're going?" I demanded when I scooped him up.

"To Grandma's to get a cookie."

That boy had a mind of his own from the start!

When he was two, I used to tell everyone that he was going to run for president someday. Of course, I didn't mean it literally. But he was so smart. I used

[11] *Dick Posthumus, interview with GW, February 7, 2001.*
[12] *William Gnodtke, interview with GW, August 2, 2002.*

John with his father Matt in their living room. SOURCE: *John Engler*

to think he knew everything I was going to say before I'd say it. He could answer me before the words were even out of my mouth.

When John started kindergarten he would take the bus in the morning. The first day the bus came for him, the driver opened the door and said, "Come on, Butch. Get in."

He said, "My name is John, and you can call me that."

John can be very funny. He was funny from an early age. I've heard news people say he doesn't have a sense of humor. I say, "You don't know him. His sense of humor is very dry."

He was a pill—too smart for his own good. When he was in elementary school, I got a call one day from a Dominican nun, Sister Ramon. She wanted to talk to me.

When we sat down to talk, she told me, "I've taught school for 12 years, but I don't know what to do with John. It's not that he's bad. He's not sassy. He's very polite. But I've never had anyone like him. He finishes up his assignments so fast and tries to go around telling all the other children how to finish theirs. I have a real problem on my hands."

I said I'd talk to him. But I knew that wasn't the end of it, so I told Matt, "If Sister calls again, you go talk to her."

Sister did call again, and it was Matt's turn to see her. He suggested that she solve the problem by giving John extra assignments to work on, and maybe a good book to read. Well, that did it. She challenged him and kept him busy with his own work. It's what he needed.

Later she told me, "He's got a brilliant mind, but we have to steer him in the right direction."

One time a teacher said to John, "You talk too much in class. I am going to move you."

John looked right back at her and said, "Why don't you move the other children. I like where I'm sitting." He said it very politely.

John got up at six every morning. He had to go to the barn to feed the cattle. After he would come back and shower, he'd read the newspaper. He loved reading the newspaper. He'd read it every day before he got on the school bus. Sometimes he would forget the time and miss the bus, and then I'd have to drive him to school.

The Church was an important part of John's upbringing. Our family went to

John's 2nd-grade class at St. Philomena's in Mount Pleasant. He is sitting in the second row from the left, third seat back. SOURCE: *John Engler*

Mass every week at St. Joseph the Worker in Beal City.

We don't lie in our family. I never allowed it, because if you start lying, soon you'll be stealing. Once when I thought I caught John lying, I took him by both shoulders and shook him till his head almost fell off, and I told him never to lie, never to me or to anybody else.

I think one of the great qualities he's retained throughout his life is his honesty. John does not say something unless he means it. I think he inspires honesty in others.

John, age seven, celebrates first communion in the Catholic Church.
SOURCE: *John Engler*

John didn't date much. After he got his driver's license, Matt and I used to ask, "John, do you want the car tonight?"

"No." He wanted to stay home and read, even on Friday and Saturday nights. A lot of his classmates drank. He wasn't interested in partying and drinking.[13]

*

David Bertram was Engler's driver during the first gubernatorial campaign. He recalls:

One of John's teachers at St. Philomena told me that he was a very good but difficult student. Difficult in that he would challenge his teachers and even try to correct them. Literally, if he could have, he would have taken over the classroom.[14]

*

Family friend Mary Ellen Brandell shared some of her research into John Engler's childhood with a Mount Pleasant audience shortly after the community's "favorite son" became governor. Agnes Engler has corroborated these stories.

John demonstrated creativity at an early age. His favorite pastime was reading. According to family members, he took pleasure in telling wild bedtime stories to his younger brothers and sisters. They recall exciting journeys through fantasyland by sharing in the imagination of their older brother.

[13] *Agnes Engler, interview with GW, July 18, 2002.*
[14] *David Bertram, interview with GW, July 11, 2002.*

Not only was he creative, but apparently he had aspirations to become a sea captain. He and his brother built a raft and had visions of sailing down the Chippewa River. However, by the time the raft was finished, it was so big they borrowed a tractor to get it into the water. They nicely got it launched—and it sank to the bottom. That was the end of the vision of becoming a sea captain.

John demonstrated his work ethic as early as his elementary school years. He was always a willing baby-sitter. He did everything from taking care of his siblings to working at the Isabella County Fair and acting as an inventory clerk and stock boy at Gould's Drug Store to earn spending money.

Unlike most young people during their high school years, John spent little time socializing. Apparently he attended only two dances: once in his junior year and once in his senior year, which was at the insistence of his mother.

Based on a report to me from his parents, when John left home and went away to college, he asked that his bedroom be preserved. He used the example of George Washington and Abraham Lincoln. Apparently even at the age of 17, he had a sense of future greatness. However, much to his dismay, there was a large protest from his young siblings, and his bedroom was turned over to the next in line.[15]

John Engler quips that his room was occupied before he got as far as Mount Pleasant.[16]

*

John's sister, Sue (Engler) Gonzales

John loved to read the newspaper. At breakfast, he and Dad would fight over which section of the newspaper they'd read first. If John was hogging a section, Dad would tell him to go get ready for school.

Every Saturday the boys and girls had to do chores. The girls had to pick up not just their bedrooms, but the boys' rooms, too. We thought that was unfair. Since we were raised in a household where you had to have good arguments to get your way, one Saturday I said to my dad, "It's not fair that we have to clean up after our brothers. The boys should pick up after themselves."

[15]*Excerpts from Mary Ellen Brandell, "Introduction of 1991 Outstanding Citizen," speech to Mount Pleasant Area Chamber of Commerce, February 16, 1991.*

[16]*John Engler (hereafter JE), note to GW, October 22, 2002.*

John, 15 months old, catches up on the news. SOURCE: *John Engler*

My father agreed. The boys and girls would be treated equally. Starting the next Saturday, the boys had to clean up their own rooms. My dad taught us fairness.

I never realized until much later how different our household must have seemed to our friends. We always ate dinner at 6:00 when the news was on. Our dad would always watch the news. He would say to us, "If you're quiet, you might learn something." When he wasn't watching the news, he'd be talking politics. We were all expected to know something about politics.

Recently a friend told me, "Going over to your house was not like going over to others'. Most houses with a lot of kids are absolutely chaotic around dinnertime. But at your house, dinner was always at the same time and there was always a political discussion going on.[17]

*

The politics

One of Michigan's preeminent historians, Willis Dunbar, wrote that voters in the Great Lakes State found themselves drawn to a young candidate for governor in 1948. He traveled across the state in his trademark old car. Before and during the campaign, he revealed "talents that made him one of the most formidable and effective campaign-

[17] *Sue (Engler) Gonzales, interview with GW, August 5, 2002.*

ers in Michigan history." Intellectually brilliant, he nevertheless had the populist touch —an "amazing ability," according to Dunbar, "to establish a true rapport with the workingmen." Remarkably, this same governor was elected and re-elected when the opposing party was able to carry the White House. For most of his time in office, "the Michigan Republican organization enjoyed unusual power...." Moreover, "His appointments were excellent; there was hardly a breath of scandal during his dozen years as governor." He would prove to be one of Michigan's strongest, most effective chief executives.

The man Dunbar describes sounds like future Governor John Engler. Actually it is G. Mennen "Soapy" Williams. A Democrat, Soapy Williams was first elected governor in 1948, three weeks after Engler was born. He was only 37 years old. He would go on to serve a total of six two-year terms. Thus Soapy would have been the dominant Michigan governor during Engler's childhood—a household name even in Republican Isabella County, where Engler grew up.[18]

*

Education reform: first lessons

Sue (Engler) Gonzales

Our dad served on the local school board for 20 years. He had to fight the teachers' union more than once. Talking to Dad, John learned how the system worked and why education reform was so hard.[19]

*

Lucille Taylor, a friend and future senior aide to Engler, recalls this story.

Education reform was a part of John Engler's heritage back in Beal City. Before he even left home, he observed that public schools were very different based on the amount of local property tax revenue that supported the school.

John lived in the Beal City school district. The boundary between the Engler farm and Murphy farm was the dividing line between the Beal City and Mount Pleasant school districts. John likes to tell the story about the Mount Pleasant school bus stopping and turning around—sometimes on the Englers' property—but without picking up John. He was required to go to the high school in Beal City. He got a good enough education there, but I don't think his mother and father were happy about the lack of choices. This experience contributed to John's view that reforms were needed in the educational system.[20]

[18] *Willis F. Dunbar and George S. May,* Michigan: A History of the Wolverine State, *rev. ed. (Grand Rapids: Eerdmans, 1980), pp. 629-31.*

[19] *Sue (Engler) Gonzales, interview with GW, August 5, 2002.*

[20] *Lucille Taylor, interview with GW, September 27, 1999.*

*

4-H: a GOP farm club

John Engler's agrarian background is essential to understanding who he is as a man and a leader. Art Ellis, a longtime Engler ally from Mount Pleasant, captures his friend's essence:

John Engler is an intellectual stuck in a farm boy's body.[21]

*

Dennis Schornack, a close friend and senior aide to John Engler, observes:

John was a farm kid from Beal City, a member of 4-H. No pun intended, but I think 4-H was a "farm club" for the Republican Party in Michigan back then. They still are. I think John got a lot of his skills organizing a caucus and a party from those early experiences in 4-H.[22]

*

John meets Dick

Dick Posthumus also grew up on a farm. As kids, he and John lived about 60 miles from each other. Dick describes his first encounter with John when they were high school students competing against each other. They disagree to this day over who won a timed parliamentary contest.

John would have been a senior at Beal City High School, and I was a sophomore at Caledonia High School, when we first met in 1965 or '66. That year my school was hosting the Future Farmers of America [FFA] regional leadership contests, and we were each chairman of our team.

One of the contests was a parliamentary procedure contest. In this contest, each team was given a series of tasks that it was supposed to perform using actual parliamentary procedure maneuvers to solve their given problem. The teams were allowed eight to ten minutes to finish the given tasks, and early and late finishes were penalized. Usually, it was the home team that provided the timekeeper. Independent judges were brought in to score the teams. Therefore, at the tournament that year we provided the timekeeper. Unfortunately, he was using a 30-second stopwatch instead of a 60-second stopwatch, and no one noticed prior to the start of the parliamentary procedure competition. So he was counting revolutions instead of minutes, and after eight revolutions he stood up. But instead of it being eight minutes, it was only four. The judges thought that it seemed somewhat odd how fast the rounds

[21] *Art Ellis, interview with GW, January 3, 2001.*
[22] *Dennis Schornack, interview with GW, November 15, 1999.*

were going, yet no team complained, so they went on.

Then a team came to the judges and asked why the contest was so fast. One of the students went over to the timekeeper and figured out the error. The judges, however, decided that it was too late to make the first teams redo the competition or to allow the next teams to have the correct amount of time. It was decided that the remaining teams would have only four minutes, just like the first few teams.

Well, John Engler brought his team into the room and made the decision that his team would stick to the original time frame—8 minutes. Typical John Engler! His team did not care when the timekeeper motioned that time was up because they were entitled to their full 8 minutes! So during the contest, he and his team kept going until they had accomplished all that they had set out to do.

My team's turn came, and we obeyed the timekeeper. As a result, we came in first and John's team came in second. To this day, he argues that his team only lost the contest because we provided a bad timekeeper![23]

*

Defeat

When John Engler played center for his high school football team, the Beal City Aggies, they lost 19 games in a row. It was defeat that taught him lessons that he could later apply to politics.

When I was a junior at Beal City High School, we had a coach who was a great cheerleader, but we had a pretty lousy team. We didn't win a game. Didn't even score a point. In short, our coaching was just awful.

But by my senior year, we changed coaches. And he changed the program. We began to score points. We broke our 19 game losing streak and we began to win. And over the years, Beal City has built one of the best Class D football programs in the state. It was great coaching and teamwork, not great cheerleading and self-promotion, that made Beal City strong.[24]

*

Dan Pero, a close friend who managed two of Engler's gubernatorial campaigns, points out:

When John's team lost game after game after game, he didn't just sit back and take it. Even as a kid in high school he had a strong will to win and developed

[23]*Dick Posthumus, interview with GW, February 7, 2001.*
[24]*John Engler, "Declaration of Candidacy for Governor," speech draft 11, February 6, 1990, p. 11.*

a great tactical mind. He would tell the coach what plays to call. I think John would have run the team if he could have.[25]

*

High school yearbook

"He makes haste slowly."[26]

That is the epigram under John Engler's senior picture. Under a nearby page titled "Prophesy," there was this statement regarding Engler's political future:

"Now out west we see John Engler visiting his huge cattle ranch. Next year, John will try to take the presidential office away from Anne. Good luck, John!"[27]

*

John Engler reflects on his childhood faith

Detroit Free Press *reporter Dawson Bell interviewed John Engler and asked him about his faith. The following is an excerpt from a taped (but unpublished) interview.*

DAWSON BELL: We all know you're a lifelong Catholic; you were raised Catholic. Has your faith changed over time, or your relationship with the Church?

GOVERNOR ENGLER: I grew up in a family where faith was important. When I was home we attended church, and we did it as a family. My parents didn't lecture to us, but it was made very clear that this was important to them. It was a central part of their lives and as kids, it was a central part of our lives as well. I believe that my parents transmitted their strong set of values to their children and I hope to do the same with my daughters.

I continue to practice my faith, not only observing the traditions of the faith and the responsibilities of being a Catholic, but also paying attention to the teachings of the faith. My relationship with God has been very steady. I have never gone through a period of non-believing. I knew people who were religious but when they went away to college they came home without any faith. I didn't go through any of that at all.[28]

[25]*Dan Pero, communication with GW, 1994.*

[26]The Spotlight, *Beal City High School yearbook, 1966. Thanks to Carrie Smith Bleise, superintendent's secretary, Beal City Public Schools, for providing this.*

[27]The Spotlight, *Beal City High School yearbook, 1966. The student offering this "prophesy" is named simply Ken. The reference is to Anne Young, whom a classmate predicted would run for president. Amusingly—considering that John Engler eventually married a Texan—another student predicted that Engler would have a woman help him out in the Lone Star State. Many years later the story circulated that Engler "wrote in his Beal City High School yearbook that he would one day be president." [See, e.g., Associated Press, "MSU Junior Sets His Sights...,"* Detroit News, *January 13, 2000, p. D7.] Clearly Engler did not write that, but it shows the power of the written word, even when wrong.*

[28]*JE, taped interview with Dawson Bell, February 1995.*

*

Reporter Kathy Barks Hoffman summarized Engler's early life.

John's senior picture, Beal City High School, 1965-1966. SOURCE: *John Engler*

Back when John Engler was on the Beal City High School football team, he played center—the offensive lineman who hiked the ball and protected the quarterback.

Engler admits the Aggies in tiny Beal City, about 10 miles northwest of Mount Pleasant, weren't very successful. But pluck and hard work finally paid off. "We broke a long losing streak my senior year," he says, adding, tongue-in-cheek: "We sowed the seeds of future greatness."

His mother, Agnes Engler, says Engler has never been afraid to go after what he wants, even if the odds are against him.

"He's very, very determined, and when he sets his mind on something, he doesn't leave a stone unturned," she says. "I always used to tell him, you can do anything you want to do if you're willing to work for it."...

Growing up near Beal City on the family farm with his six younger brothers and sisters, Engler got used to working for what he wanted. Like most farm kids, he was driving tractors by the time he was 10, and helped care for the family's herd of beef cattle.

"From an early age, I was sort of this little kid who had to be responsible for these big animals," he says. "I still take a lot of ribbing from my brothers and sisters because they had grand champions (at the 4-H fair) and I had none. That was a lesson that hard work didn't always pay off."

Tom Reed, a former county extension agent who knew the Engler family well, said it's Engler's farm background that has stood him in such good stead in politics.

"The ag community is a very close-knit kind of family. You learn from that that you need to listen closely to the people, and that's what John has done," says Reed, now vice president of MLE Marketing, a regional livestock cooperative.

"In his position as governor, you would think he would be an extremely busy man, but I have never seen him at a time where he wouldn't listen, look you straight in the eye, stand there and make sure he understood the message."

Engler's taste for public service came from his father, Matt, who served on the school board for 20 years and was active in community affairs.

"If you talk to anyone in Mount Pleasant or Beal City, there's probably no one who set a better example for family and community involvement than his dad," says Dan Pero, a close Engler friend who ran his 1990 and '94 gubernatorial campaigns.

When his father ran for a state House seat in 1968, his son helped him out. And though he knew nothing about campaigns, the young Engler thought there had to be a better way.

So he went back to his classes at Michigan State University, read some books, took a government course and teamed up with another student to write a paper on how to run a campaign in his home district.

Two years later, at the age of 21, he ran his own campaign against the same man who had defeated his father—and won.[29]

[29] *Kathy Barks Hoffman, "Campaign for Governor: Engler Tries for Third Term, Runs on Experience,"* Holland Sentinel, *October 4, 1998, p. A9.*

There lurks, perhaps, in every human heart a desire of distinction,
which inclines every man to hope, and then to believe,
that nature has given him something peculiar to himself.
SAMUEL JOHNSON

★

Chapter Two
College: 1966 - 1970

John Engler entered Michigan State University in September 1966. He majored in agricultural economics. His advisor in the College of Agriculture was Les Mandersheid, who taught applied statistics.

John struck me as more of a people person than a book person. He was busy with extracurricular activities on campus so didn't have time to be an academic nerd. In fact, he was not at the top of his class academically. But he was very personable and very perceptive of those around him. He could read people well. He knew what they wanted and needed. In later years this skill would help him lead. When John was in the legislature and in the governor's office, he could bring people with opposing agendas to the table and help forge a win-win compromise.[30]

*

John Molloy also taught Engler at MSU.

John was in my social science class in Bessie Hall. I remember there were 54 students in the class. Certain kids stood out. They actively participated, read the textbook, and argued the points that were raised. John was one of those students. He sat near the front, and I specifically remember that he frequently raised his hand. That was different because some students didn't bother with

[30]*Les Mandersheid, interview with GW, September 28-29, 2002.*

that courtesy. They would simply blurt out whatever they had to say. John was more polite than his classmates, and brighter, too.

One of the things that set John apart was his interest in politics and philosophy. He was active in class, the type who would read a textbook and argue the points raised, unlike some other students who were more interested in grades than in what they learned. John would come to your office and talk to you about a point you had made in class. I remember he stopped at my office once and asked about conservative writers: Clinton Rossiter, Peter Viereck, Russell Kirk. It was unusual: a young man in the late '60s who was genuinely interested in conservative thought.

John also had a mischievous streak. He asked questions on a point that he really didn't want to debate out of firm or deeply held convictions. Rather, he was interested in seeing what you'd say. It caused some people to misinterpret his views. The first time the governor ran for re-election [1994], a story came up that he favored legalized prostitution as a student. I know where that came from. We had a discussion in class about a book, *Crimes without Victims*. The book presented libertarian approaches on a number of issues, and John asked, "What's wrong with legalized prostitution?" I told him and the class what was wrong with it from my perspective, and we talked about that a little bit.

Later, John came into my office and said, "I don't want you to think that I'm in favor of legalized prostitution. I'm not. I just wanted to see what you'd say."[31]

*

At Michigan State University, Engler lived in an all-male dorm, East Shaw Hall. Above the hall's grill was a line attributed to the British statesman and political philosopher Edmund Burke. It obviously impressed him, for in later years, Engler would recite the line from memory:

"The only thing necessary for evil to triumph is for good men to do nothing."[32]

*

1968 dress rehearsal

John Engler was between his sophomore and junior years when his father Matt challenged Representative Russell Strange for the 100th House district seat. In the summer of 1968, the 19-year-old helped his father out in the campaign. On Tuesday, August 6th,

[31]*John Molloy, interview with GW, May 22, 2002.*
[32]*GW, personal papers, July 1998 and July 2002.*

Matt Engler lost the primary. But the election did two things. It put the name "Engler" before voters in the district, and it served as a dress rehearsal for John Engler's 1970 challenge to Strange.

1968 Primary Election for the 100th House District

Russell Strange	3,991 votes (43.3%)
Matt Engler	2,978 votes (32.3%)
Lloyd Walker	2,257 votes (24.4%)[33]

*

The local newspaper covering the election reported:

During the campaign, [Matt] Engler accused Strange of establishing a "sham residency" in Mt. Pleasant while living in Lansing, but it was in Mt. Pleasant that Strange took a commanding 2 to 1 edge over Engler.

Mt. Pleasant voters [responded] to Strange's campaign emphasis on experience and service....

[Matt] Engler said he was "beaten in Isabella County where we knew we had to win. We ran a little better than expected in Montcalm, and we were extremely happy with the Beal City vote. We ran a hard campaign, and we accept the decision of the voters."[34]

*

Agnes Engler

Strange was a do-nothing legislator. He didn't even answer his letters. Matt thought that the district deserved better representation and that Strange needed competition.

John helped his father out a lot in that race. He did the scheduling for his dad's campaign and organized handing out literature. Matt could have won, but a man from Greenville entered the primary and divided the opposition against Strange.[35]

*

On being in college in the '60s

Dawson Bell captured this reflection in a taped interview with Engler.

I think when you go away to college there is a freedom to try things. I didn't

[33]Michigan Manual, *1969-1970 ed. (Lansing: Department of Administration), p. 446.*

[34]*No author, "Strange Defeats Engler, Walker for GOP Nod," (Mt. Pleasant)* Daily Times News, *August 7, 1968, front page.*

[35]*Agnes Engler, interview with GW, July 18, 2002.*

drop out and become this counterculture figure because I was too busy. I had to work all the way through college. I didn't have the luxury of resources where I could do a lot of things. I wasn't even able to go to Florida for spring break, because I was working. Although I had saved up money working different jobs through high school and had worked at Michigan State, when I graduated I was still in debt.

The great adventure I had in college was the summer of 1969. I was able to patch together enough money to go overseas and study in London for the summer. I even went to see the Rolling Stones play in Hyde Park.[36]

*

John Engler

My parents paid for my first term of college; I paid for the rest.

When I went to Britain, I traveled every weekend. During my final five weeks overseas, I traveled around the Continent with a backpack.[37]

*

College friends

Despite their high school rivalry, Dick Posthumus and John Engler became friends in college.

In this world there is a higher authority that leads you in directions—or sometimes actually kicks you in a certain direction!—because when I was a freshman in college I met John again. I was president of the state association of Future Farmers of America [FFA]. One of my responsibilities was to speak to agricultural groups around the state. One night I was speaking to the Michigan Cattle Feeders at the Boom-Boom Room, a restaurant in Frandor [a shopping center between Lansing and East Lansing].

After I finished speaking the president of the association came up to me and said, "My name is Matt Engler, and I think you ought to meet my son. His name is John. He's a student at Michigan State. You're studying agricultural economics, and he is studying that, too."

At the time, the name seemed unfamiliar and I made no connection back to the high school parliamentary contest. "Well, what dorm is he in?" I asked.

"East Shaw Hall. He's the president of the dorm."

"You're kidding! That's the dorm I live in."

[36] *JE, interview (taped) with Dawson Bell, February 1995.*
[37] *JE, note to GW, October 22, 2002.*

So it turned out that of all the 40,000 kids, of all the places on campus, he happened to be the president of the dorm where I lived my freshman year of college.

I looked him up and we began talking and soon we became friends.[38]

*

The term paper

During his senior year at Michigan State, John Engler enrolled in Carolyn Stieber's class, Political Science 303. The term John was in her class, Stieber came out with a book titled The Politics of Change in Michigan. *Engler and a classmate co-authored a now-famous term paper whose title, "The Change of Politics in Michigan," was an obvious play on the book's title. The 25-page paper detailed how a challenger could beat the Republican incumbent who represented Engler in the Michigan House of Representatives. The opening of the term paper announced:*

This paper is a preliminary step in an attempt to unseat one of Michigan's representatives, Russell Strange of the 100th Representative District.

Why are we attempting something of this order? Primarily because we feel that Representative Strange has ceased to be responsive to the needs of his district.

In the body of the paper, the authors analyzed Strange's strengths and weaknesses. They maintained that hard work, knowledge of issues important to constituents, and old-fashioned campaigning would enable a challenger to beat the incumbent. Engler summed up:

The above has been a hopefully objective view of a conservative Republican.[39]

*

Carolyn Stieber gave the paper an "A-" and later reflected on her student and the paper.

John is a student I will never forget. His is a paper I will never forget—one of the most interesting papers I ever received. I had never before read a paper that had this degree of quality, this degree of thought. It was also the first and only paper that I ever shared with a colleague. I wondered at the time if John himself were preparing to run. I thought that if any student could succeed, John could.

My colleague told me, "I agree that it's a good paper, but it takes a somebody to beat a somebody, and he is just a kid."

[38]*Dick Posthumus, interview with GW, February 7, 2001.*

[39]*John Engler and Thomas Plachta, "The Change of Politics in Michigan, or the Strange 100th," unpublished term paper, May 28, 1970. The words "conservative Republican" did not appear in the first draft but were put into a revision of the paper.*

Sure, but that kid won the election, and the rest is history.[40]

*

John Engler

I originally wrote the paper thinking that our county treasurer, Ron Demlow, would run against Strange in 1970.[41]

*

Andrea Fischer Newman, a friend and fundraiser of Engler's, observes:

When the other man decided not to run, John seized the opportunity. He thought, "I'll run instead." I think he just fell into that first race.[42]

[40] *Carolyn Stieber, interview with GW, June 4, 2002.*

[41] *JE, note to GW, October 22, 2002.*

[42] *Andrea Fischer Newman, interview with GW, August 3, 2002.*

Vengeance is mine. I will repay, says the Lord.
OLD TESTAMENT

★

Chapter Three

The Campaign That Launched a Career: 1970

Early in life John Engler knew the disappointment of defeat. His steers never won a grand championship.[43] His parliamentary procedure team lost the competition to Dick Posthumus's team. His football team got clobbered 19 games in a row. And in 1968 his father lost in the primary against Russell Strange, the incumbent in the 100th House district.

In 1970, at the age of 21, Engler was looking to finish up his bachelor's degree at Michigan State. He was also looking for meaningful work. When Ron Demlow decided not to run against Russ Strange, the college senior decided to challenge the seven-term incumbent himself. He wanted to avenge his father.

John had written the term paper on how to beat Strange. Now he sought a capable individual to manage his campaign. In January Engler found himself in the same economics class as Dick Posthumus, a sophomore. He respected Posthumus—after all, he was state president of Future Farmers of America. He also knew that his father liked Posthumus. Years later Posthumus recalls:

We had a class together called Land Resource Economics. About the middle of the term [February 1970], Engler approached me and said, "I think there is an exciting chance to win an election up in Mount Pleasant. I am putting together a paper showing how to do it, and I would like to have you get involved in the campaign. You ought to think about it."

At first I wasn't interested in getting involved. But later I read a draft of

[43] Once, in college, when Engler had just returned from London and was broke, he helped his sister prepare a steer that took first place. [Source: Agnes Engler and Sue (Engler) Gonzales, interviews with GW, July 18 and August 5, 2002.]

John's paper, written for Carolyn Stieber's class. In the paper he described how through hard work and a smart strategy you could win the Republican primary. I thought that it was an impressive paper; it really could be the game plan for beating the 14-year incumbent.

During the summer of 1970 there was a slight downturn in the economy. Since I did not have a summer job, I thought, "Well, why not?" And I signed on to help manage John's campaign. I would coordinate Montcalm County and another friend would coordinate Isabella County. A month into it, John's friend quit. So I ended up managing the whole campaign. I wasn't even old enough to vote![44]

At the time John Engler announced his candidacy, people were surprised, and some even thought it was a joke. When asked why he ran, one of the first answers he had was, "Because I thought I could do a better job than Representative Strange and I just wanted to see if I could beat him."...

In 1968 Matt Engler had run in the Republican primary against Representative Russell Strange from Mt. Pleasant. A three-man race ensued as a Greenville resident [Lloyd Walker] also became a candidate. It was bitterly fought with accusations of half-truths, questions of legal residency, and some undertones of religious bigotry [since Strange did not support parochiaid]. Through all of this, the incumbent was able to muster enough votes to win. But, he left many scars behind which would haunt him again.

One of these was with John Engler, the 19-year-old son of the 1968 challenger. He felt Russell Strange had to be beaten and could be beaten. Having caught the "political bug" in the 1968 campaign, the younger Engler decided to challenge the incumbent himself.[45]

*

John Molloy reflects on his student's political ambitions.

I remember one awkward visit that I had with John in my office. Looking back now, I laugh about it. He told me that he was going to run for the House of Representatives, and I didn't take him seriously. Actually, a lot of students run for office, but of course most of them aren't like John Engler. He was very serious about it; he was confident that he would get elected; and the whole time I was thinking, "Sure, Kid."

[44]*Dick Posthumus, interview with GW, February 7, 2001.*
[45]*Dick Posthumus, "Political Resources in a Campaign for State Representative: John M. Engler—100th District," unpublished term paper, March 9, 1971.*

He asked me to help him with his campaign, but I told him that I couldn't do it. Now, I realize that I probably didn't take him as seriously as I should have.[46]

*

John's advisor, Les Mandersheid, was struck by the young candidate's stealth.

John did a good job keeping his intentions under wraps. I heard that he was going to file only the day before. I was told, in the strictest confidence, "Don't say a word until after 4:00 tomorrow afternoon."[47]

*

Agnes Engler

One of the things John learned from Matt's race was this: If you're the underdog, do not attract attention to yourself too early. He remembered how his father would have won if that third candidate [Lloyd Walker] had not also entered the race. So John decided to keep a low profile until the last minute. He turned in his forms to the Secretary of State just 15 minutes before the filing deadline.

Russ Strange was also there, at the very same time, and John later said Strange's hand was shaking so bad he could hardly sign his name. He knew he was in trouble because Matt's son was taking him on.

I told Matt, "You know, I think John's going to win."

Matt said, "He's too young."

"Matt, he's *going* to win." He was working so hard—I just knew that he was bound and determined to win.[48]

*

Dick Posthumus

Our campaign headquarters was this old student ghetto house right on the edge of Central Michigan University. Headquarters was downstairs; upstairs we had two bedrooms and a bathroom that did not have a shower. John would work and sleep upstairs. Every day he would map out what happened during the day and what we were going to do the next day. Every night around midnight, John would say, "Ah, let's go to bed." I would be lying in the bedroom next to John's and I could hear him talking. He would talk about what was

[46]*John Molloy, interview with GW, May 22, 2002.*
[47]*Les Mandersheid, interview with GW, September 28, 2002.*
[48]*Agnes Engler, interview with GW, July 18, 2002.*

going on and what we had to do the next day. Sometimes, I could hear him talking until 2:00 in the morning and all of a sudden he would fall off to sleep. Then he would be up at 5:00 in the morning running again.[49]

*

Bill Gnodtke

When I worked on the House Republican staff, I observed both Matt's campaign in 1968 and John's campaign in 1970. Both of them were hard workers. During the '70 election, people familiar with the 100th district were saying, "This guy John Engler is everywhere." That was because his signs were all over the district. He went to all the parades. He went door-to-door. He worked the same people his father had in 1968. John and Dick put together an outstanding campaign.[50]

*

David Porteous, of Reed City, was a freshman at Michigan State University in 1970. He tells of a kind of Road to Emmaus experience.

During my freshman year at Michigan State I was hitchhiking on U.S.-27, going from East Lansing to my hometown of Reed City. A car stopped and offered me a ride. The driver was also a student at MSU. We started talking about a political campaign he was involved with. He said that an MSU student was running for a House seat, but that he had to knock off the incumbent in his own party first. I was thinking, "An MSU student is too young to do that." But he said they had a plan to beat the incumbent. The plan was to go to the county clerks and look at voter lists. They would see who actually voted in primaries. Their strategy was to reach out and focus on the people who voted. They were confident they could win.

The driver who picked me up: Dick Posthumus. The candidate whose campaign he was running: John Engler.[51]

*

John Engler

I was 21. My own campaign was the first election I was old enough to vote in.[52]

[49]*Dick Posthumus, interview with GW, February 7, 2001.*
[50]*William Gnodtke, interview with GW, August 2, 2002.*
[51]*David Porteous, interview with GW, September 21, 2002.*
[52]*JE, interview with GW, August 26, 2002.*

*

Election Day

Dick Posthumus

It was a close race; we won by 159 votes. The night of the primary we were in that old house, the one in the student ghetto. We were just students; we didn't have much money. There is one thing that I will never forget about that night. We had this tough old farmer taking in the vote counts. He kept saying, "You know, it doesn't matter how close it is, as long as there are more plusses than minuses."[53]

A night to remember. Candidate Engler checks election returns in his first race as young campaign volunteers look on. Mount Pleasant, August 4, 1970. SOURCE: *John Engler*

*

John Engler

That tough old farmer was Bob Hafer, who contributed the first $100 to my first campaign.[54]

*

For John Engler, August 4, 1970, would be a day to celebrate victory.[55] There would be many such days in his career. In terms of number of ballots cast, Engler won his first election by the slimmest margin, 159 votes (but not by the slimmest percentage).

1970 Primary Election for the 100th House District

John Engler	3,498 votes (51.2%)
Russell Strange	3,339 votes (48.8%)[56]

*

There was an eerie déjà-vu quality to the results, as one newspaper article noted.

'70 LIKE '56 IN 100TH DISTRICT
AS ANOTHER 21-YEAR-OLD WINS

In 1956 the 100th District elected a state representative to the legislature at

[53]*Dick Posthumus, interview with GW, February 7, 2001.*
[54]*JE, note to GW, October 22, 2002.*
[55]*For newspaper coverage of the victory, see, e.g., Dave Hanson, "Youngster Upsets Strange in House Race,"* Lansing State Journal, *August 5, 1970, p. A6.*
[56]Michigan Manual, *1971-1972 ed. (Lansing: Department of Administration, 1971), p. 496.*

the age of 21: Russell H. Strange of Mount Pleasant.

In the primary, a 21-year-old Republican named John M. Engler ... defeated Strange for the nomination.

Each man at the time of nomination was the youngest person ever to receive it, for Engler is one month younger than Strange was....

Thus history comes full circle....

Engler got a piece of luck: on July 15 Strange suffered a back injury in a boating accident, and was immobilized for the rest of the primary campaign—never reaching Montcalm County to campaign.[57]

*

Les Mandersheid

When I picked up the newspaper the next day and saw that John had upset Strange, I was pleased. In all honesty, I had not expected him to win; it's hard to beat an incumbent. But in retrospect there were three things going for John. First, he knew Representative Strange's record better than Strange did—he had studied it and lived it. Second, he had name recognition since an Engler—his father—had been on the ballot two years earlier. Third, he and Dick Posthumus put together a tremendous campaign, outworking their opponent and using a lot of energetic students mostly from local high schools but also from Central Michigan University. All these things helped John pull off an upset.[58]

*

After managing Engler's campaign, Posthumus took an independent study course at MSU under Carolyn Stieber's direction and wrote a paper analyzing how Engler had won the primary. He attached Engler's paper as an appendix to his own. Interestingly, Dick Posthumus has kept both papers in his desk ever since he was first elected to public office in 1982. Why?

"I suppose I keep the papers in my desk for sentimental reasons. This was how I got here," he says, riffling through the pages.[59]

*

[57] *Bud Vestal, "'70 Like '56 in 100th District as Another 21-Year-Old Wins,"* Flint Journal, *August 11, 1970.*
[58] *Les Mandersheid, interview with GW, September 28, 2002.*
[59] *Dick Posthumus, interview with GW, February 7, 2001.*

Democrats for Engler

The retired president of Central Michigan University, Charles Anspach, wrote these encouraging words to the young candidate.

My compliments to you on the excellent campaign that you conducted and the large number of friends that you have made as a result of the campaign. In fact, it may interest you to know that several Democrats, one of whom is quite active in the party, told me they will vote for you.[60]

*

Agnes Engler recalls this exchange before the general election:

A teacher in the district—I think the head of the local MEA—asked John, "If we give you our money and our votes, will you vote the way we want you to?"

"No, I don't owe anyone anything, and I don't intend to start."[61]

*

The times

In 1970, American troops invaded Cambodia, and National Guardsmen fired on student demonstrators at Kent State. President Nixon delivered speeches addressing "the great Silent Majority." American women, on the 50th anniversary of suffrage, took to the streets in support of the Equal Rights Amendment. New York allowed "abortion on demand." Earth Day was inaugurated, and Apollo 13 was launched into space. The Beatles broke up, Janis Joplin and Jimi Hendrix died, and a 21-year-old named Garretson Beekman Trudeau went national with the Doonesbury *comic strip. The top films of 1970 were* Patton, M*A*S*H, *and* Woodstock.

*

General election

John Engler won his first general election by a comfortable margin, garnering almost 60 percent of the vote.

1970 General Election for the 100th House District

John Engler	12,728 votes (59.2%)
Joseph DeBolt	8,759 votes (40.8%)[62]

*

[60] *Letter from Charles L. Anspach to JE, October 13, 1970. Anspach was president of Central Michigan University.*
[61] *Agnes Engler, interview with GW, July 18, 2002.*
[62] Michigan Manual, *1971-1972 ed. (Lansing: Department of Administration, 1971), p. 551.*

The local newspaper reported:

ENGLER NEW REPRESENTATIVE

Said Engler after the election, "This is a tremendous victory and ... I am anxious to begin serving the people in Lansing."

Commenting on the outcome of the election, DeBolt said ... "Our analysis of the Mt. Pleasant returns tentatively indicates Catholic defections in Democrats over parochiaid.... As far as I am concerned, there is no Democratic Party in [Isabella] county. It needs to be rebuilt."[63]

*

There is a biblical expression about certain people being without honor in their own land. Agnes Engler recalls this exchange in Beal City shortly after the election:

A man named Pattison, a counselor and teacher at Beal City High, was talking to Harry Hauck. Pattison was surprised John won the election. He said, "Well, John may have won the state rep seat, but he won't go any further. A kid from Beal City won't go far at all."

"What? He could be our governor someday," said Harry Hauck.

"Never. No kid from Beal City will ever be governor."[64]

[63] *"Engler New Representative," (Mt. Pleasant)* Morning Sun, *November 4, 1970.*
[64] *Agnes Engler, interview with GW, July 18, 2002.*

Blessed is he who has found his work;
let him ask no other blessedness.
THOMAS CARLYLE

★

Chapter Four
Representative: 1971 - 1978

In 1970 at the age of 22, John Engler became the youngest person ever elected to the Michigan legislature. He entered public service when a majority of Americans believed that government was basically good. This belief would soon be severely eroded after the Watergate scandal surfaced in 1972—during Engler's freshman term. Watergate would bring down Republican President Richard Nixon in 1974—during Engler's second term.

Engler formally entered the 76th Legislature on January 13, 1971. There was divided government in Lansing. Although Republican William Milliken controlled the governor's office, Democrats dominated the House, 58 to 52. Republicans and Democrats were evenly split in the Senate, having 19 members apiece.[65]

John Engler's first hire was Carol Viventi.

Right after John was elected Jerry Roe asked me if I wanted to interview with some of the new members, and that's when I interviewed with John. My interview consisted of John saying, "You know, I hear that you are a really bright person, so why don't you come work for me?" All I could think was, "What? I don't even know what the job is yet."

So then I had to fill out an application and John peered over my shoulder. There was a question: "Which party do you belong to?" and I checked "Democrat." He said, "You can't do that!" He made me erase it, and I changed it. Right then and there!

[65]Michigan Manual, *1991-1992 ed. (Lansing: Legislative Service Bureau), p. 345.*

Chief Justice Thomas E. Brennan swearing in freshman Representative John Engler, in the Capitol, January 1971. SOURCE: *John Engler*

Then he went to London, and he called me collect and said, "Show up on January 2 and they will tell you where your office is." So I showed up, and on his desk there was a stack of accumulated mail, along with resumes of people who had 20 and 30 years of experience. He again called collect from London, and I felt obligated to tell him that he was receiving resumes from people who were much more qualified than I was. I had no clue what I was doing—and he had no clue what he was doing.

"You and I are going to learn together," he told me.

I don't think he wanted someone with experience. He didn't want someone in the office telling him what to do.[66]

Right away I noticed that John had the habit of completely disappearing. I was always trying to find him. What he was doing was going around to everyone in the Capitol and introducing himself. He was finding out about every office in the building. He was just so curious. He wanted to know what every-

[66] *Carol Viventi, interview with GW, December 2, 2000.*

body did. Right away he found the important offices and staff: the Legislative Service Bureau, the bill drafters, the research people. He knew everything about the place within the first couple of months of taking office. All this, while he was trying to figure out what his job was as a legislator.

Very early on he made a statement to the press that he was going to be the governor someday. It was in that first year, 1971, and it was reported in the press. But it was meant to be taken lightly, because he was the youngest member of the legislature and in the minority party. People thought it was a joke.[67]

*

Mastering the issues and the process

Undaunted by the problems plaguing Republicans nationally, Engler during his first term in office served on as many committees as possible—Colleges and Universities, Mental Health, Insurance, and Youth and Student Participation. In addition, he was one of 10 young legislators in the nation to attend the White House Conference on Youth. Back in Lansing, one of the more interesting bills he sponsored would have created a unicameral legislature in Michigan.[68]

Following is Representative Engler's first recorded speech in the Journal of the House. *He criticized the Democratic majority and expressed concern over government spending, property taxes, and tax increases—all themes that he would pursue into the governor's office two decades later.*

Mr. Speaker and Members of the House:

House Bill No. 4236 is the first of 13 budget bills that will come before us this year. I voted "no" because I feel passage of this bill at this time is premature and unwise. It is imperative that we establish a budget level with adequate means of financing that level. To proceed on a piecemeal basis is to build a piecemeal budget that will undoubtedly need an increased level of taxation. I am unwilling to blindly march down this dangerous path. I am concerned about our level of spending, about property tax reform, and about probable tax increases. Until the Democratic majority begins to show a sincere awareness and sharing of this concern I shall very likely continue to vote "no."[69]

*

[67] *Carol Viventi, interview with GW, December 2, 2000.*
[68] *"John Engler for State Representative," political advertisement,* Central Michigan University Life, *November 3, 1972.*
[69] *Rep. John M. Engler,* Journal of the House of the State of Michigan, *July 12, 1971, p. 2042.*

John Engler wrote out his first high-school commencement speeches in longhand. Only five years out of high school, the young representative delivered the addresses when there was much national discussion over the 26th Amendment, giving 18-year-old citizens the right to vote. The amendment had been passed by Congress on March 23, 1971, and would be ratified July 1, 1971.

Face up to the fact that you are already involved in politics—in the art and science of government. Decisions are going to be made with or without the influence your participation can mean in the decision-making process. And you're going to have to live with those decisions.

Can you afford not to be concerned with the future? That's where you're going to spend the rest of your life.

Does it make sense for young people to leave the decision-making process to their elders? Who is going to have to live the longest in the world with those decisions?

Many of you may remember a speech Robert Kennedy made shortly before his death in which he used a quotation from George Bernard Shaw: "Some people see things as they are and say, why? I dream things that never were and say, why not?"[70]

*

Doug Roberts began his career working for the Democrats and observed this about Engler:

John Engler was elected and showed up in January of 1971. I showed up a year later and went to work on the Democratic side for the House Taxation Committee. I remember finishing a piece of legislation that I was working on and sending it to the floor. Unbeknownst to us, there was a drafting error in the bill. We didn't catch it. But somebody did. He was a young representative on the other side of the aisle. His name was John Engler, and he actually read the bill.[71]

*

Another pattern that would be established early on would be enmity between John Engler and the Michigan Education Association. Pat Laughlin, who worked for the MEA in the 1970s, explains.

Matt Engler was a traditional Farm Bureau guy. Matt had no use for union

[70] *JE, high school graduation speech, Cedar Lake, c. June 1971.*
[71] *Doug Roberts, interview with GW, December 2, 2000.*

advocacy in education. From his point of view, the union movement did not help educate children. He especially did not like tenure.

John Engler was his father's son. He was not enamored with tenure either. One of the first bills John supported in the legislature was to repeal the teacher tenure act, which at the time was an MEA rallying cry.

In those days, the MEA did not take John Engler seriously. In their minds, he was a farm boy from Beal City—a nondescript freshman legislator from a nondescript part of the state. He was uninformed, just another Republican Neanderthal.[72]

*

Lucille Taylor shared her first impressions of John Engler:

The first time I reported for duty in the House, a receptionist pointed out a representative walking down the hall. She said, "That is our newest and youngest member of the legislature. He just arrived here out of college." It was John Engler.

My first impressions of him were that, though he was young, he was not willing to wait his turn. He was always thinking about how to make Republicans the majority in the House. He wanted to change the agenda. It seemed he had amendments on every bill. Often he did not clear those amendments with the party leadership, so many times he wouldn't even get the votes of his own caucus. But he never gave up.

Early on, he thought about how to get more Republicans elected, and how to recruit candidates for every office and every race. He was active in going out and trying to persuade individuals with some skills to run for office rather than waiting passively and taking what came their way.

Some people found these attributes annoying. But they had to acknowledge that if John Engler worked on an issue, he was doing a better job than everyone else. People could either ignore that fact or use it to their advantage. Many older and wiser heads chose the latter course and put him in charge of tasks that needed to be done. I don't think they were ever disappointed.[73]

*

Bill Gnodtke

In the Michigan legislature in the '70s, Republicans were in the minority. It

[72] *Pat Laughlin, interview with GW, July 3, 2002.*
[73] *Lucille Taylor, interview with GW, October 20, 1999.*

became especially bad after Nixon's troubles. Republicans were getting run over by Democrats. John wanted to change that.

In the early '70s I remember him saying to me—it's as vivid as though he said it yesterday—"Bill, if I ever get into a position where I can help the party and other candidates, I'll do it." What he meant was that he wanted to have enough stature to make a difference, to recruit strong candidates, to endorse people with the ability to win, to raise money for them, and to help in any way he could.

So from the very start, right after he got to Lansing, John was on the lookout for seats that Republicans could win. He would look at the numbers in marginal districts where he figured a Republican could win. He would get involved in the district, help recruit a good candidate, help raise money for them, attend legislative dinners (unlike Governor Milliken), and work hard to make it possible for the candidate to cross the finish line a winner.

In fact, John would have rather won his own race by 55 percent instead of 65 percent, if it meant that he could bring two, three, or more candidates into the legislature with him. The reason his race with Odykirk in 1976 was so close was that he was working so hard in other districts.

It was wonderful, the way John was always working for the good of the party, sometimes at his own expense. People don't appreciate how much he did for the GOP from the start.[74]

*

Seeking a second term

Because of reapportionment, Engler had to square off against a Republican, Dick Allen, in his quest to be re-elected to the state House. Dennis Cawthorne, who served in the Michigan House with Engler, recalls:

In 1972 the right-to-life movement was just getting legs around the country. It is interesting in retrospect. Dick Allen, a Republican, was the most pro-choice representative in the House. Speaker Bill Ryan, a Democrat, was ardently pro-life. Because of reapportionment, Bill Ryan saw a golden opportunity to get rid of Dick Allen. To do that, you had to draw the lines in a way that would give John Engler the upper hand in the race. As I recall, the district was redrawn in such a way that Dick Allen's house on one side of the road was in one district, and his mailbox on the other side of the road was in another district! Ironically, this is how the Democrats helped further John Engler's career.[75]

[74] *William Gnodtke, interview with GW, August 2, 2002.*
[75] *Dennis Cawthorne, interview with GW, September 25, 2002.*

*

The Beal City candidate received the endorsement of the Mount Pleasant newspaper.

The race in the 89th District for the Republican nomination August 8 comes down to a choice between two incumbent legislators, both of whom point to impressive records.

Rep. John Engler and Rep. Dick Allen are virtually fighting for their political lives in this race, with no thanks to a reapportionment plan which has thrown both together, face-to-face and toe-to-toe....

We have generally agreed with the voting record and stands of Engler. He may not be the party leader that Allen is at this point, but we think he is very definitely a legislative leader at this stage of his career and if given another term, he would only strengthen that position....

What Engler may lack in experience (that comes with age), he makes up for in terms of sincerity and his commitment to work for the people of this area. His first term record proves this.

We believe in keeping a local man in the running for state representative and John Engler fills the bill on that score for the Republicans. He is sincerely interested in maintaining the strength of local government and we think voters should support him on August 8.[76]

*

As this newspaper article noted, Rep. Engler backed an MEA petition drive because he thought that it would address much-needed property tax reform.

State Representative John M. Engler (R-Mount Pleasant) has joined Governor Milliken, the Michigan Farm Bureau and other officials in endorsing and supporting the Michigan Education Association petition drive to put the question of property tax reform on the ballot, and announced that he was launching a month long campaign in the 100th District to discuss the issue.

"In my opinion, property tax reform is the number one issue in the state today. The question affects virtually every citizen in the state, from the schoolchild who deserves an opportunity to an adequate education, to the property taxpayer who deserves the assurance that he is paying his fair share in proper taxes, no more and no less. The MEA petition drive to prohibit the use of property tax as the major financial support for our state's schools is the first step in achieving these goals....

[76]*"Support Engler in GOP Primary," editorial,* Daily Times News, *August 3, 1972.*

"To assist the MEA in their cause, I am launching a month long campaign in the 100th District to discuss the MEA proposals, answer any questions area residents may have concerning the petition drive and collect signatures on the petitions."[77]

*

Another newspaper article highlighted Engler's commitment to property tax relief.

"Property tax relief is a goal that has been mentioned for 10 years probably and one that has been sought after in the legislature," Engler said....

Many people feel the property tax is no longer a fair tax, said Engler. "There used to be a time when the property a man owned was pretty consistent with that man's ability to pay taxes; this isn't true anymore."[78]

*

In the 1972 primary, a strong showing in Isabella and Montcalm counties enabled Engler to beat Allen and advance to the general election.[79]

1972 Primary Election for the new 98th House District

John Engler	5,499 votes (53.0%)
Dick Allen	4,870 votes (47.0%)[80]

*

Robert Mitchell, then the deputy chairman of the Democratic State Central Committee, wrote this about young Representative Engler.

We are extremely concerned and we hope that you will send to Lansing in '73, a new state representative. We have nothing against youth; we have nothing against males, but the young male you sent to Lansing is voting a hard-line Republican vote. He is extremely partisan and unwilling to listen to the other side.

If you call yourself anything other than "quite conservative," John Engler is not representing you. Although he is young and makes a nice image, we urge you to take a good long look at his philosophy and the way he conducts himself.... I am convinced that he is not going to get a second term in Lansing.[81]

*

[77]*"Rep. Engler Backs MEA Petition Drive,"* Daily Times News, *May 6, 1972.*

[78]*"Tax Issues Keynote Debate,"* Central Michigan University Life, *October 26, 1972.*

[79]*"Strong Isabella Vote Gives Engler Victory,"* Detroit News, *August 9, 1972; JE, note to GW, October 22, 2002.*

[80]Michigan Manual, *1973-1974 ed. (Lansing: Department of Management and Budget), p. 532.*

[81]*Robert Mitchell, "Send New Rep in '73: State Dems,"* Daily Times News, *March 10, 1972.*

After winning the primary, Engler easily won re-election against his Democratic opponent. In other elections, President Richard Nixon beat George McGovern in a landslide, while Michigan voters rejected an effort to overhaul the state's system of school financing by replacing local property taxes with a higher state income tax. A companion proposal, which would have permitted the legislature to adopt a graduated income tax, was even more soundly beaten.[82] *Michigan voters also rejected a liberalized abortion law, leaving intact the 126-year-old state law that prohibited abortion except "to preserve the life" of a pregnant woman.*[83]

1972 General Election for the 98th House District

John Engler	18,342 votes (62.2%)
William Joyner	11,147 votes (37.8%)[84]

*

Local newspapers reported:

STATE'S YOUNGEST LEGISLATOR RETURNS FOR HIS SECOND TERM

At an age when many young men are still searching for a place in life, John Engler is starting his second term in the Michigan legislature.

A 24-year old bachelor, Engler has defeated two tough incumbent Republican opponents to win and maintain his seat. He's still the state's youngest legislator and one of the youngest in the country.

He seemed to shock everyone but himself in the old 100th District in 1970 when he ousted Rep. Russell Strange, a veteran of seven terms in the legislature, in the GOP primary.

Before graduating from Michigan State University in [December 1971], Engler had written a paper on defeating Strange.

"When I defeated Strange by 160 votes, everyone was surprised we beat him, but we weren't. I wanted to be able to run to win," Engler said.

Engler said that he first became active in campaigning when his father ran against Strange and Lloyd Walker, mayor of Greenville, for the seat in 1968. He worked three weeks on that campaign.

Engler attributed his initial victory to a good organization, including fellow students from Michigan State plus some rank and file Republicans. He also says Strange underestimated him.

[82] *William Grant, "School Tax Revision Rejected,"* Detroit Free Press, *November 8, 1972.*
[83] *Paul M. Branzburg, "Liberalized Abortion Loses by 3-2 Margin,"* Detroit Free Press, *November 8, 1972.*
[84] Michigan Manual, *1973-1974 ed. (Lansing: Department of Administration), p. 580.*

"The element of luck is there also. Politics is a game of variables," Engler said.

After Engler beat Strange, he won his seat with 60 percent of the vote over Democrat Joe DeBolt, a sociology professor at Central Michigan University.

After the legislature was reapportioned in 1972, he defeated Republican incumbent Richard Allen of Alma in the primary. He then beat Democrat William Joyner of Mt. Pleasant with 63 percent of the vote in the general election.

"The reapportionment plan didn't change the district very much although it is a little more homogenous. It's a freeway district," he said.

After being around Lansing for two years, Engler says he's somewhat surprised that he is often tagged as a conservative.

"Although I don't like to put labels on people, I am very conservative in some areas, such as fiscal management," he said.

Engler points out, however, that he has supported the age of majority law, drug reform legislation and environmental legislation, all usually considered liberal causes....

Engler said he expects that school financing reform will be the most important issue handled by the legislature in this session.[85]

*

Challenges

SCHOOL FINANCING TOP PRIORITY

State Rep. John M. Engler (R-Mount Pleasant) told ... Isabella County taxpayers last night that the problem of educational financing in Michigan will be the most important problem before the legislature this year....

Engler said the image that Michigan is a poor place in which to do business because of the lack of tax incentives and unemployment and work compensation laws must be changed to attract more business.[86]

*

John Engler was gaining a reputation as a fiscal conservative. He wrote the following in a local newspaper:

The House of Representatives must accept much of the blame for the Congress-like approach to budgeting which is much in evidence this year. We are required by the Constitution to adopt a balanced budget each fiscal year.

[85] *"State's Youngest Legislator Returns for His Second Term,"* Clare Sentinel, *January 31, 1973, p. 8.*
[86] *Rick Burnham, "School Financing Top Priority: Engler,"* Daily Times News, *February 22, 1973.*

It is now apparent that without substantial reductions in many areas of proposed expenditures that the budget will not balance. When this is the case the legislature must awaken to its responsibility and make some difficult political decisions.

The first test will come possibly this week on the state aid to schools. Despite distinctly partisan overtones, this issue is shaping up as a battle of philosophies. The philosophy of spend now-tax later vs. the philosophy of the reasonable and balanced budget. The fight over state aid has been brewing for several weeks now....

If the leadership of the House cannot control the wild spending impulses of its membership in order to pass reasonable budget bills then the governor will have to use the most powerful weapon he has—the veto. I would urge him to do so if the spending levels of the budget bills do not come down. It is high time that some of my colleagues realize that government cannot solve all of the problems in this state in one year and concentrate on doing the best job possible with available revenues. The thought of a tax increase in 1974 as a result of legislative irresponsibility in 1973 is abhorrent to me.[87]

*

With troubles plaguing the Nixon administration, Engler also wrote on the need to restore confidence in government.

Governor Milliken presented last week his Special Message to the Legislature on Ethics and Election Reform. He minced no words when he said, "Democracy could not continue to function unless public confidence in its institutions and its political system is restored."

Confidence in government and politicians is at a new low. Restoration of this confidence is believed to be, by the governor, myself and hopefully a majority of the Michigan legislature and citizenry, our most urgent task. The continuing revelations and events of Watergate, the felony conviction of a state senator and judge in Michigan, the resignation of the vice-president, the recent indictment of a Democratic New York congressman, this litany of sins against the public trust could go on and on. Public tolerance of arrogance, misrepresentation and downright dishonesty is ending....

This fall session will provide a key to the future of political reform in Michigan. The governor has said, "The iron has never been hotter." I believe

[87]*John M. Engler, "From the House,"* Daily Record Leader, *May 21, 1973.*

that's true, but the real question is: will anyone be burned in 1974 if no reform is forthcoming?[88]

*

Engler was also pursuing measures that would make Michigan's economy more competitive.

ENGLER HONORED

State Representative John Engler (R-Mt. Pleasant), a member of the House Republican Task Force on Economic Development, was officially recognized today for his efforts in developing a plan to promote economic development in Michigan. The report developed by the Task Force won national honors this fall at the Seattle, Washington, conference of the National Conference of State Legislative Leaders.... The Economic Development Package titled "A Blueprint for the Seventies" recommends, among other things, that Michigan begin reorganizing state operations to bring new activities in the area of attracting industry and to assist it in selling products.[89]

*

1974 general election

Engler won his re-election bid, as did Governor Milliken, but in the wake of Nixon's resignation, it was a terrible year for most Republican candidates. In Michigan Democrats won control of the state legislature for the first time in a decade, taking a majority in the Senate and tightening an already firm grip on the House.[90] *One of the Democrats who won a congressional seat was a young Democrat from Pleasant Ridge named James Blanchard.*[91]

1974 General Election for the 89th House District

John Engler	11,427 votes (53.9%)
James Dickinson	9,785 votes (46.1%)[92]

*

A House in the House

Also in 1974, a newcomer appeared among Michigan representatives, Colleen House of Bay City. A Republican, she won in a Democratic district. She and John Engler

[88] *John M. Engler, "From the House,"* Daily Record Leader, *October 31, 1973.*
[89] *"Engler Honored,"* Gratiot County Herald, *December 20, 1973.*
[90] *Roger Lane, "Dems Control Legislature for First Time in Decade,"* Detroit Free Press, *November 6, 1974.*
[91] *Remer Tyson, "Blanchard Crushes Huber in 18th District,"* Detroit Free Press, *November 6, 1974.*
[92] Michigan Manual, *1975-1976 ed. (Lansing: Department of Management and Budget), p. 519.*

would marry in 1975. Both were intensely involved in politics, and they were soon regarded as one of Lansing's "power couples." They had no children. In 1986, Colleen would run for governor and lieutenant governor. They were divorced later that year, and their marriage was annulled in 1989. Several years later:

Colleen House told the [*Detroit*] *Free Press* ... that she has nothing bad to say about Engler, adding, "I've voted for him every time he's been on the ballot."[93]

*

1 Engler equals 6 Democrats

John Engler was as aggressive as he could be in the minority. It was widely reported:

House speaker Bobby Crim, D-Davison, is reputed to have said: "I'd give up six (Democratic) seats to get rid of him."[94]

*

Spencer Abraham, a good friend and ally of Engler's, eventually chaired the Michigan Republican Party and served in the U.S. Senate. He reflects on Speaker Crim's statement:

From day one, John Engler was a thorn in the side of Michigan Democrats. Nothing better shows this than Bobby Crim's comment about giving up six seats—if it meant that Engler could be beat. Bobby Crim understood who John was and what he could do. It was a prophetic comment, because neither he nor fellow Democrats would ever have the satisfaction of beating John head-to-head.[95]

*

Next step: taking over the Republican Party

Although a Republican, William Milliken was never regarded as a conservative. The longest-serving Michigan governor once said, "My father was a great progressive liberal. He took positions that were considered to be quite un-Republican. And I guess I tend to do the same."[96] It was inevitable that Milliken and Engler would clash. The question was when ... and how.

Earlier we saw Engler's paper on how to knock off an incumbent. Now he trained his

[93]*Colleen House quoted in Public Sector Consultants, "Legislative and Political Week in Review," April 19, 1996.*
[94]*Pat McCarthy, "Embattled GOP Struggling to Hold State House Seats,"* Battle Creek Enquirer & News, *October 3, 1976.*
[95]*Spencer Abraham, correspondence with GW, October 2002.*
[96]*Hillel Levin, "Milliken: The Man You Never Knew,"* Monthly Detroit *magazine, February 1982, p. 49; quoted by George Weeks,* Stewards of the State, *2nd ed. (Detroit:* Detroit News; *and Ann Arbor: Historical Society of Michigan, 1991), p. 129.*

sights audaciously on a bigger target—the Republican Establishment, the good old boys surrounding Milliken. How could the party be rejuvenated and become Michigan's majority party? Others were dreaming big, too. Engler's close friend Colleen (Meeuwenberg) Pero explains:

I was in college when I started working at the Capitol in March of 1974. That's when I met John. He had had Carolyn Stieber as a professor, and in 1976 I took a class from her, too. My paper was on how to take over the Republican Party. I interviewed all the county chairs and district chairs and looked at the number of people who showed up at the conventions. I found out that with a little effort, you could take over the party in a number of counties. John had also been thinking about how to take over the Republican Party from Milliken's people—and not just thinking about it, but doing it, when the time was right.[97]

*

Engler on Engler in 1976

As he prepared to run for the last time for a House seat, Representative Engler put out a press release, excerpts of which follow:

"I have been actively involved in major policy decisions. Winning and losing is part of the legislative process. Like others, I have had my share of victories and defeats. However, I have never sat silently on the sidelines and compromised my principles."

Engler is proud of the fact that he is independent.... "I feel my independence is a necessary and tremendous asset," Engler commented. "When I vote on an issue, I am free of secret commitments. I get the facts from the district and in Lansing, and I vote according to my principles and convictions as to what is in the public interest."

Certain lobbyists and interest groups don't always like Engler's approach to decision-making; however, according to Engler, that might be an advantage.

"I feel the major problem in Lansing today is that there exists a special and unhealthy relationship between many elected officials and varied powerful interest groups. At some point these politicians cease to represent the total public interest, and choose instead to represent the private special interests.

"I am trying to change this system," Engler said. "I don't believe candidates for public office have to go 'hat in hand' seeking campaign assistance and funds from these powerbrokers. I pledge that in my campaign this won't be done."

[97]*Colleen Pero, interview with GW, August 5, 2002.*

In keeping with his past campaigns, Engler indicated his campaign this year will again be a "people to people" campaign, and will include certain voluntary guidelines.

"My campaign will be one of citizen involvement. As in my past campaigns, people of all backgrounds, ages, and occupations will play important volunteer roles. Interest groups, lobbyists and political action committees will be allowed no role in my campaign. I want to be able to continue voting on issues in Lansing free of any obligation to any special interest group.

"I will accept contributions only from individuals, and only in amounts of less than $100.01 per individual. I will not accept contributions from interest groups, lobbyists and political action committees."[98]

*

1976 general election

In 1976, America's bicentennial year, Engler successfully ran for re-election in the 89th House District—it would be his fourth and final term as a representative. Also in 1976, Michigan voters rejected Proposal C, which would have limited state spending, and they crushed Proposal D, which called for a graduated income tax.[99] *On the national scene that Tuesday, Jimmy Carter won a cliffhanger, taking the presidency away from President Ford in the wee hours of Wednesday morning in one of the closest elections in modern times. Engler had supported President Ford, a fellow Michigander.*[100]

1976 General Election for the 89th House District

John Engler	16,510 votes (52.4%)
Bill Odykirk	14,818 votes (47.0%)[101]

*

Engler in the '70s

In October 1971, Lucille Taylor was hired to join the Republican policy staff of the Michigan House of Representatives, and she had the opportunity to observe the young legislator.

Nothing in John Engler's public life has occurred by accident. Look at his career. In January, 1971, he came to the House of Representatives as a freshman legislator. Even as a junior member of the House of Representatives—and in

[98]*Press release from State Rep. John M. Engler's office, May 2, 1976.*
[99]*Hugh McDiarmid, "Tax and Spending Limit Beaten,"* Detroit Free Press, *November 3, 1976.*
[100]*Associated Press, "Carter wins Cliff-Hanger,"* Detroit Free Press, *November 3, 1976.*
[101]Michigan Manual, *1977-1978 ed. (Lansing: Department of Management and Budget), p. 597.*

the minority party—he displayed certain characteristics that have been evident throughout his public career. For example, John was better versed on the rules of the House than any of his colleagues. John also read the bills, which is something that he continues to do even in his role as governor. In addition, he understands the process by which state government works. He excels at process in the way some individuals excel at athletics. He understands the subtlest nuances, knows how to use rules advantageously, and has an excellent sense of timing. This puts him so much further ahead than most of his colleagues. In fact, I think that it annoyed his colleagues, already during his freshman term.[102]

*

Dennis Cawthorne was House Republican leader in the 1970s. He recalls:

One of the interesting things about John Engler's House career is that he never really held a leadership position. He spent those eight years observing, absorbing everything he could, and learning the legislative process.

John did not sit quietly at his desk with his hands folded, however. He would get crosswise with some of Governor Milliken's people. And he became particularly adept at needling the Democratic majority. John's caustic comments about them would elicit catcalls. The Democrats did everything they could to make life miserable for him. And John returned the favor. That is why Bobby Crim made his caustic remark about gladly giving up six Democratic legislators if he could just get rid of one Republican—John Engler.

But it's important to understand that John was not a conservative ideologue. He was pragmatic, only a little more conservative than our caucus.[103]

*

Hal Ziegler served in the Michigan Senate when Engler was in the House. He observes:

John Engler was always very independent. Back in the '70s, most of the money came from the party, not from lobbyists, PACs, or special interests. Therefore the pressure to vote a particular way on a bill came from the party, not the lobbyists.

But John was one of these guys who read the bills and sometimes took a position that was at odds with the caucus. He was his own man. He read the fine

[102] *Lucille Taylor, interview with GW, October 20, 1999.*
[103] *Dennis Cawthorne, interview with GW, September 25, 2002.*

print. He actually thought through the policies for himself.

And I'll tell you this: he was ahead of most people. He really got into the legislative process. A lot of us didn't do this. I don't mean we were bad legislators; we just didn't delve into it 12 hours a day, seven days a week. But John Engler did, and that put him ahead of most other legislators.

Whether you agreed or disagreed with everything that John Engler did, there's one thing you can't disagree with. He's unique among politicians in that he does what he says he will do. This trait confounded not only his enemies, but also surprised his supporters. Such follow-through was virtually unheard of.[104]

*

Bill Whitbeck would be a strong Engler ally. This was his first impression.

Bill Gnodtke and his wife bought a house out on Clark Road, and Bill decided to start having volleyball parties, and that was the first time I ever met John Engler. (I have to say that John is the worst volleyball player I have ever met.) I recall one time sitting on Gnodtke's front porch. All of us were drinking pop, and John wanted to talk issues. All the rest of us were talking about the Detroit Tigers and other nonpolitical things, yet John always wanted to discuss the issues. "What do you think about this bill?" "What do you think about that policy?" He never stopped thinking about the issues; he was always working. He took his job very seriously.[105]

*

Aspiring to the Senate

Gleaves Whitney had this exchange with John Engler:

GLEAVES: Why did you challenge a powerful Republican and run for the Senate seat when you did?

ENGLER: It was either up or out. I didn't want to be a minority Republican in the House anymore.[106]

*

Dennis Cawthorne

If you were a Republican, the House was the Dismal Swamp: there was little chance Republicans would be in the majority. However, I was surprised that

[104] *Hal Ziegler, interview with GW, February 1, 2001.*
[105] *Bill Whitbeck, interview with GW, December 2, 2000.*
[106] *JE, interview with GW, September 4, 2002.*

John Engler decided to get out of the House when he did to take on Jack Toepp. At that time, I was House Republican leader, and Toepp sought me out and asked me to discourage Engler from running against him.

"I can't do that," I said. "You'd better be prepared to batten down the hatches because John is one tenacious campaigner." But deep down I was skeptical that John could win that race. Jack Toepp was not ripe for defeat. He was floor leader of the Senate Republicans and not unpopular with his constituency. Also, considering the large geographic extent of the district, Toepp as the incumbent had the media advantage.

John could have easily waited four years when there would be a new apportionment plan, and have better odds of winning. In 1978, he was defying the odds.[107]

*

Joanne Emmons, who herself would represent this area in the Senate, knew the district well.

It was dicey for John to take on Jack Toepp. But what drove him was that he was tired of being in the minority in the House. The Democrats held the majority for so long, they thought they owned the House. When you are in the minority in the House, you don't even talk. But in the Senate, even if you are in the minority, you at least can get your name on the board and talk.[108]

*

Carol Viventi

When he was running against Jack Toepp, I kept reminding him that he had a perfectly safe seat in the House. His answer was, "I have nothing to lose." And that was always his attitude. He has never been defeated. He took on Russ Strange with nothing to lose. He ran year after year, and always came out victorious.[109]

*

A student of politics, Jami Sue DaDan, offered this contemporary assessment of the candidate aspiring to a Senate seat.

John Engler is known for his ... willingness to stand up on tough issues and to

[107] *Dennis Cawthorne, interview with GW, September 25, 2002.*
[108] *Joanne Emmons, interview with GW, September 25, 2002.*
[109] *Carol Viventi, interview with GW, December 2, 2000.*

party bosses. This is evident from his attempt to dethrone state party officials at the 1977 Michigan Republican Convention when he led the fight to unseat state party chairman William McLaughlin.

John himself spent a whole year laying the base for the campaign: getting support from key individuals throughout the districts [*sic*], mapping the strategies in the media, a mailing program, and grass roots organizations. John was never seen by this staff during the actual campaign period of June, July, and August, due to his excellent groundwork. John Engler masterminded his decentralized campaign organization months before the election, so during the summer, all that was left was to meet the voters....

Some potential problems acknowledged by Representative Engler.... Due to Engler's bad relationship with the state GOP committee, a possible threat from party executives existed in the form of an endorsement of another candidate and/or through financial or political contributions.[110]

*

Al Short, who worked for the Michigan Education Association in the 1970s, comments.

John took on some tough challenges in the 1970s, but nothing like the Senate race that he would win in 1978. He took on Jack Toepp, someone in his own party, and the fact that he had enough gall to take on someone like that showed how brave he was. Jack didn't take him seriously. He just saw this kid going out and working hard to get votes, and didn't really give much thought to it. In fact, Jack spent more time in Lansing than he did in his own district. It was John Engler who was out shaking hands, getting to know people and, in turn, getting people to know him. He was out finding the people who would vote for him. All of his hard work paid off.[111]

*

In the Senate one of John Engler's constituents was Russell Kirk, regarded as one of the nation's preeminent conservative thinkers from the 1950s to the 1990s. During his first campaign for the Senate seat, Russell and his wife Annette Kirk invited candidate Engler to address a gathering in their home. The following is Russell Kirk's impression of the young candidate.

We were introducing him to Mecosta County Republicans. We had a gather-

[110] *Jami Sue DaDan, "An Analysis of the Campaign Organization to Elect John M. Engler to the Michigan State Senate," unpublished paper, May 26, 1979, pp. 6-7, 45.*
[111] *Al Short, interview with GW, February 26, 2001.*

ing of 20 to 25 in our drawing room. The speech he gave was well reasoned—he always had a practical knowledge of politics. But his delivery was rather faulty and uncertain. My wife, who was formerly a teacher of speech and dramatics, severely criticized his delivery. Some improvement ensued.[112]

*

As the primary neared, the Mount Pleasant Morning Sun *opined.*

UNIQUE RACE IN MID-MICHIGAN

A lot of eyes across the state are on the primary race for the 36th Senatorial seat between Republicans John Toepp, Cadillac, and John Engler, Mount Pleasant.

One unique twist that hasn't been publicized much is the fact that it is the only state race where two incumbents are facing each other in the primary.

Engler had been the State Representative for the 89th District prior to leaving that post to run a campaign for the 36th Senate seat. Toepp is the incumbent in the 36th Senate District.

Both have been actively campaigning and on Aug. 8 a lot of eyes will be on the results of that race, which is expected to be a close one.[113]

*

TIME TO CHOOSE FOR '78 PRIMARY

The John Engler-Jack Toepp race was expected to be one of the closest in the state when the two Republicans both filed for the office currently held by Toepp several weeks ago. It hasn't disappointed anyone.

Both candidates have some solid points and detractors can find problems with each. Generally, both are highly qualified and committed to serving their constituents. Both have a good voting record in many areas (the Michigan Chamber of Commerce rates both 100 percent) and both have strong support.

In Engler there is energy and drive associated with a young politician who has already had remarkable success. He would bring in a new aggressiveness to the job and possibly fight some battles differently from the current representative. He has made many sound decisions and has shown a receptiveness to input from his area.

Toepp deals from a position of strength on the merit of his experience on the job and positions that he has attained in the Senate. He has been generally

[112] *Russell Kirk, interview by Donovan Reynolds (video taped), c. February 1991.*
[113] *"Unique Race in Mid-Michigan," editorial,* Morning Sun, *July 29, 1978, p. 4.*

well-liked around the district and built up an impressive record in many areas.

An endorsement? It's a tough one. Engler may represent the *Morning Sun* area better because of residence and ties here, but Toepp also has good qualifications and could continue to do the job. It boils down to an individual decision on the part of each voter.[114]

*

John the Giant Killer

The final tally in the 1978 primary election for the 36th Senate District seat:

John Engler	12,118 votes (54%)
Jack Toepp	10,362 votes (46%)[115]

*

After Engler beat Toepp, observers started noticing a distinct pattern. This twenty-something fellow from Beal City was able to take on—and defeat—popular incumbents in his own party.

Again, Engler faced long odds and doubters. Toepp was the Republican Senate floor leader and a member of the powerful Appropriations Committee, which controls the state's purse strings. Toepp had recorded comfortable wins in his last two elections.

Engler won by 1,756 votes. A third incumbent had been slain, and the nickname, "John the Giant Killer" caught on.[116]

*

Having knocked off Toepp in the primary, Engler crushed Democratic opponent Don Jones in his first bid for a senate seat. It was the largest percentage by which he ever won a general election. That same Election Day, Michigan voters returned Milliken to the governor's office for a third term,[117] and selected a new U.S. senator, Carl Levin, over Robert Griffin, who had represented Michigan in the Senate since the mid-1960s.[118] 1978 was also an important year for ballot issues. Michiganders got caught up in the tax revolt sweeping the nation but only narrowly adopted the Headlee Amendment, limit-

[114]*"Time to Choose for '78 Primary," editorial,* Morning Sun, *August 3, 1978, p. 4.*
[115]*Election Results, 1978 Primary, Department of State, Election Division, RG 85-57, State Archives of Michigan, Lansing.*
[116]*Roger Martin, Nolan Finley, Charlie Cain, et al.,* The Journey of John Engler *(West Bloomfield: Altwerger & Mandel, 1991), p. 11.*
[117]*Hugh McDiarmid, "It's Milliken Again, and Sen. Levin,"* Detroit Free Press, *November 8, 1978.*
[118]*William J. Mitchell, "Detroit Democrat Thanks Griffin for Fair Campaign,"* Detroit Free Press, *November 8, 1978.*

ing state government's ability to tax.[119] *By contrast, a student voucher amendment was roundly rejected.*

1978 General Election for the 36th Senate District

John Engler	60,422 votes (67.2%)
Don Jones	29,538 votes (32.8%)[120]

*

From a local newspaper:

ENGLER WINS EASILY

As expected, Republican Engler won the 36th State Senatorial District handily, easily outdistancing Democratic challenger Don Jones, also of Mount Pleasant.

The win cemented Engler's position as the political heir to the seat formerly held by 12-year Senate veteran John Toepp of Cadillac, whom Engler narrowly defeated in a hard-fought primary earlier this year.

Engler, 30, will enter the state Senate January 1 as one of a crop of aggressive new faces determined to make their mark in the legislature's upper house.

Engler will return to the state House of Representatives later this month to "get things wrapped up."... Once he makes the move, he expects to see a great deal of jockeying for leadership positions, and "I hope to play a role in that," Engler said.[121]

*

Bill Ballenger entered the Michigan Senate the same year Engler entered the House. He comments on his colleague's canny political skills.

John Engler and I were elected to separate chambers of the legislature in the same year—1970. He was 22 and I was 29. We liked to refer to ourselves (especially in Montcalm County, where our districts overlapped) as the youngest pair of legislators representing common territory in the entire United States of America. We even opened a district office in Greenville together, paying the rent out of our own pockets because the people in those parts were so chagrined that they didn't have a native serving in Lansing, being forced to rely on legislators from Beal City and Ovid. Between us, John and I covered every Monday and Friday afternoon in Greenville, but we never got the flood of con-

[119] *Billy Bowles, "Headlee a Toss-Up,"* Detroit Free Press, *November 8, 1978.*
[120] Michigan Manual, *1977-1978 ed. (Lansing: Department of Management and Budget) p.552.*
[121] *"Engler Wins Easily,"* Big Rapids Pioneer, *November 8, 1978.*

stituents coming to see us that we thought we would. John said, "I always felt like the Maytag repairman." After a year we closed it down.

In those days, John was just feeling his way in the State capital, as you might expect, and once the reapportionment maps were finalized he had to prepare for still another primary struggle against an incumbent—this time his colleague, the more moderate Richard (Dick) Allen of Ithaca. That was the focus of John's attention, and when he prevailed in a very close race in 1972 it reinforced his image and reputation as a cagey, relentless campaigner capable of pulling off shocking victories when few thought he had a chance.

John Engeler contemplating his the next move.
SOURCE: *John Engler*

You can't overestimate the impression John's success as a candidate had on other politicians, including me. No matter your degree of success in your own races, you always had grudging admiration for anyone who could knock off an incumbent, either in his own party in a primary, or in a general election. John did it twice, in his first two attempts—something that was unprecedented in recent Michigan political history. Then he did it a third time, in 1978 when he defeated Republican incumbent state Senator Jack Toepp of Cadillac. That made it three times in the space of eight years! (Finally, of course, he upended Democrat James Blanchard in 1990 for governor.)

Suffice to say that John Engler has unseated more state officeholders (4) than any politician since World War II and, very possibly, in all of Michigan history. That is truly a remarkable achievement.[122]

[122]*Bill Ballenger, interview with GW, October 2, 2002.*

The man who is swimming against the stream knows the strength of it.
WOODROW WILSON

★

Chapter Five

Senator in the Minority Party: 1979 - 1983

The times

During the eight years John Engler served in the House, and the first four years he served in the Senate, Michigan's governor was William Milliken. Through much of the '70s and early '80s, the state was battered by storm after economic storm—and conditions just seemed to worsen. These were the years when many residents left Michigan for work in sunbelt states; the jobs-section of the Houston Chronicle *was circulating on the streets of Detroit; and many Michiganders sardonically remarked, "Would the last one to leave Michigan turn out the lights?" As Milliken opined in a televised economic report during his last year in office, "Since I have been governor, there have been four national recessions. But Michigan has not been hurt as much as it hurts now."*[123] *Not long afterward, the newspapers carried this news:*

"Gov. Milliken, a moderate Republican who has often been assailed by conservative members of his own party, is not running for re-election...."[124]

*

Enter John Engler

Peter Secchia, a steadfast Engler ally and friend, remembers the young senator's determination.

John Engler knew what was wrong with this state: we needed a better eco-

[123] *Milliken quoted in Weeks,* Stewards of the State *(1991 ed.), p. 126.*
[124] *David Kushma, "GOP's Aim: Swing State to the Right,"* Detroit Free Press, *July 4, 1982, p. B1.*

nomic climate. And he knew what was wrong with Republican Party leadership: it was weak and would never have control. Early on, I think he decided to do something about that.

Back in the early '80s, Engler told me that Republicans needed to get control of the state Senate. So we formed a finance committee that Jay Van Andel chaired. Milliken got wind of this, called us into his office, and told us to disband because we were a threat to the governor's good old boys.

Engler just ignored him. Flat out ignored him. Engler did what he had to do, and within a few years achieved the majority in the Senate. Engler is fearless—he doesn't suck up to anybody.[125]

*

Rusty Hills, who would eventually become one of Engler's great media strategists, recalls his first encounter with the young senator.

The first time I remember meeting John Engler, he had just been elected to the Senate and I was a reporter for Channel 6 [WJIM then]. I was walking through the Capitol and ran into Bill Sederburg, a senator at the time, and he was with this fellow wearing a tam-o'-shanter. Bill said, "Let me introduce you to a man who is going to be governor someday: John Engler."

I looked at this guy wearing the tam-o'-shanter and, honestly, Bill's words went in one ear and right out the other. I thought, "Yeah, right." John hardly said a thing.[126]

*

Gail Torreano came from the Mount Pleasant area. She met Engler in 1970 and worked intermittently in his Senate office in the early 1980s, serving as his chief of staff.

In 1980 John approached me and asked if I would run his Senate office. He said that we would be working on three goals:

1. to help make the Senate Republicans the majority;
2. to help him become Senate majority leader;
3. to help him become governor.

Put these three goals in perspective. In 1980 he was still serving his first term in the Senate. He was low man on the totem pole. He was just 1 of 14 Republicans—there were 24 Democrats then—so he was very much in the minority. But he didn't hesitate. He planned far in advance, and he was certain of himself.

[125] *Peter Secchia, interview with GW, July 12, 2002.*
[126] *G. J. "Rusty" Hills [hereafter Rusty Hills], interview with GW, February 12, 2001.*

Never doubt that John Engler can achieve a goal he sets his mind to. He is the most tenacious person I've ever known.[127]

*

Reagan Revolution

The 1980s began with the U.S. economy sputtering. In April 1980, President Carter conceded that the nation was in the grips of a recession. Unemployment and inflation were high and hitting Michigan residents hard. For many workers, the best news was that Congress had approved a $1.5 billion loan to the ailing Chrysler Corporation.

During the Republican presidential primary, John Engler initially supported Howard Baker, who came in third in the New Hampshire primary, behind Ronald Reagan and George H. W. Bush. After Baker dropped out of the race, Engler supported George H. W. Bush. When the Republicans held their convention in Detroit in mid-July, Reagan was easily nominated and selected Bush to be his running mate. Engler was 100 percent behind the GOP ticket.

Reagan and Bush's victory on November 4 registered the rise of a more conservative American electorate. As Reagan cruised to re-election and 1984, and Bush to victory in 1988, it was apparent that many liberal positions were losing ground with the majority of Americans. There was a notable change in the way such topics as education, welfare, and government's role were debated.

Engler, who by 1980 had been identified as one of the more conservative members of the legislature, would benefit greatly from the political tone set during the 12 Reagan-Bush years. He would map out ambitious political goals and sharpen his leadership skills during the decade.

*

Dennis Cawthorne

John was somewhat conservative but never a conservative ideologue. In fact, in 1980 he and I supported Howard Baker. John was not a Reaganite.[128]

*

Low point to turning point

But before Engler achieved his ambitious goals, he went through a political trial by fire. His close friend and confidant Richard McLellan recalls:

I talked to John about the lowest point in his career. "John," I said, "I'd bet

[127] *Gail Torreano, interview with GW, September 24, 2002.*
[128] *Dennis Cawthorne, interview with GW, September 25, 2002.*

the lowest point for you was when [Senate minority leader] Bob Vander Laan removed you from the Appropriations Committee." John had been the chairman of the Michigan Senatorial Trust, a fund set up to support good candidates for the Senate. John gave the money to young, motivated, committed candidates who had a chance to win primaries. In the good old days of Vander Laan, the sitting Republican senators would just give money to themselves—it was incumbent protection.

Vander Laan alleged that John had misspent the money, and he sent a letter containing those allegations to the former prosecuting attorney in Ingham County, Leo Farhat. They were either going to bring a suit or get John prosecuted for misspending the money. Being on the Appropriations Committee is a big deal; being removed from the Appropriations Committee is an even bigger deal.

So John and I went to Beggar's Banquet [a restaurant in downtown East Lansing] and sat there for about six hours and went though everything that he had done—all of the committees, all of the money, all of the candidates, everything. Then I wrote a letter to Leo Farhat and pointed out, "You may not like what John Engler has done, but he was the chairman of the campaign committee and he had the authority to spend the money. Everything he did was consistent and lawful under current campaign spending laws."

That was the end of it. Nothing happened. Vander Laan was wrong, but this incident didn't do any further political damage to John Engler.[129]

*

Pat Laughlin, a lobbyist and friend of Engler's, reviews this critical test in Engler's life.

John Engler and Dick Allen had an up-and-down relationship. Dick was a pro-choice Republican from Alma. John was a pro-life Republican from Beal City. In 1972, they were thrown against each other because of reapportionment, and Dick lost.

Dick had long harbored ambitions to run for Congress, and in 1980 he got his chance. He was fearful that John would run against him, since John had already beat him once. So they met to work out a deal. Now, John had no intention of running for that seat, but Dick couldn't assume that. John made all the right moves to express interest in it. He did not discourage his name being bandied about as congressional timber. John, being the wheeler-dealer that he is, sought to get something for it. They cut a deal: Dick would give up his

[129]*Richard McLellan, interview with GW, December 2, 2000, and October 1, 2002.*

appropriations seat, and John would not run for Congress. In fact, John would support him.

In November Dick ran against a Democrat, Don Albosta. Problem was, he lost even though it was a "Republican" seat. Dick however still retained his state Senate seat, and now he wanted his Appropriations seat back. John wouldn't give it back. A deal's a deal.

Unbeknownst to John, Dick went to [Senate minority leader] Bob Vander Laan and said he wanted his seat back. After session, there was a caucus and John got euchred—he lost the vote 9 to 1 and got booted off the Appropriations Committee.

John walked out of that caucus numb. I bumped into him right after the meeting. He was so low he had to reach up to touch bottom. Here he had been in the legislature for 10 years. He had been a constant source of irritation to the Milliken people. He had beaten three Republican incumbents [Strange, Allen, Toepp] but still was getting no respect. He had to be thinking about a career change. "I have support among conservatives," he complained, "but the Milliken moderates run everything."

I had never seen John so down or so vulnerable. As we were walking out of the Capitol, I put my arm around him as a gesture of friendship and support.

A lesser man would have thrown in the towel at that point. But John was tireless, relentless. He finagled to get himself appointed chair of the Senate Republican Campaign Committee. He was very smart about it. He went out and identified open seats where a Republican was retiring or could win marginal swing seats. He recruited quality candidates like Dick Posthumus, Connie Binsfeld, Dan DeGrow, Doug Cruce, and others who shared his vision. After recruiting viable candidates, he went to people in strategic positions to raise money. I was one of them, being president of the Michigan Beer and Wine Wholesalers Association. He targeted money on these campaigns. The net result in 1982: the Republicans did not take the majority, but they won 18 seats, which was only 2 seats from a majority. John had a significant hand in electing almost a dozen of the senators. As a result, he got their commitment to vote for him to be minority leader.

It's an amazing story. John went from being defrocked of his membership on the Appropriations Committee to being the Senate minority leader. All in less than two years.

He transformed defeat into victory. Now he had a forum, a bully pulpit. He became the leader of the loyal opposition in the Senate. And—once Bill Milliken retired [on January 1, 1983], he was able to become the leader of the party. That's an amazing story, too. He got his longtime political ally, Spence Abraham, elected chair of the Republican Party, which at that point was broke and deep in debt. By the early '80s John was becoming the political leader of the Republicans as well as their legislative leader. He was not yet 35 years old.

Then, in 1983, he would have a chance to take his leadership to the next level when two Democratic senators were recalled, and two Republicans elected in their place. By 1984, Engler would have a 20 to 18 Republican majority. In just a few years, John went from being a nothing in the minority to the leader of the majority. He is a political Horatio Alger. Politically he went from rags to riches.[130]

*

Bill Gnodtke

John had a tough time in the early '80s. One day in May or June of '83, I was out on the porch of the Republican State Committee building on Walnut Street. It was the lunch hour, and Matt Engler happened to be walking by. We started talking. Matt said, "You know, when John got knocked off the Appropriations Committee, he came home with his tail between his legs. It's the only time in my life that I ever saw him so down. I told John, 'Englers don't quit.'"

It was wonderful advice from a father to a son. John did bounce back. In November of '82, his caucus elected him minority leader. And then in '83, after the recall of the two Democratic senators, Serotkin and Mastin, John was chosen to be Senate majority leader. He went from the back bench to the front bench in an amazingly short time.[131]

*

1982 gubernatorial campaign

Governor William Milliken, in office from 1969-1982, was the longest-serving governor in Michigan history. Deciding not to seek re-election, he cleared the way for a new Republican to emerge. Establishment Republicans wanted Lieutenant Governor Brickley to advance, but Dick Headlee beat him out, owing to the support of Young Turks like John Engler. Headlee had led Michigan's tax revolt in the late 1970s and had a popular constitutional amendment named after him. During the 1982 gubernatorial campaign, Engler chaired the Headlee for Governor Committee. Headlee's opponent

[130] *Pat Laughlin, interview with GW, July 3, 2002.*
[131] *William Gnodtke, interview with GW, August 2, 2002.*

would be James Blanchard, a four-term congressman and avowed political junkie from the age of ten, when he campaigned for Democratic presidential candidate Adlai Stevenson.[132] *Blanchard's win would begin to set the stage, eight years later, for the show-down with Engler.*

*

Jerry Crandall would serve as Engler's chief of staff in the Senate.

I got to know John Engler during the Headlee campaign for governor in 1982. It showed me a lot of Engler's character. He was one of only two senators to support Dick Headlee in the Republican primary; only two would stick their necks out. Of course, after Headlee won the primary, a bunch of other Republicans came on board, but John Engler did it first.

In retrospect, it is easy to see how the Headlee campaign and John Engler's involvement in it set the stage for the Republican takeover of Michigan. 1982 was a year when Democrats did well across the country. But Headlee was one of just two Republicans who came close to winning the gubernatorial race that year. Engler took note of what resonated with Michigan voters.[133]

*

1982 general election

Engler easily won re-election to the state Senate in a year when a Democrat, James Blanchard, defeated Dick Headlee to capture the governor's office. Michigan had not had a Democratic governor in two decades. Martha Griffiths, a 70-year-old former congresswoman who came out of retirement to run with Blanchard, became the first woman to be elected the state's lieutenant governor.[134] *Democrats maintained control of the state House and Senate. It was the first time in 20 years that the governor's office and both legislative houses were controlled by the same party.*[135]

1982 General Election for the 35th Senate District

John Engler	45,035 (60.4%)
Donald Zinser	27,893 (37.4%)[136]

*

[132] *See Weeks,* Stewards of the State *(1991 ed.), pp. 132; and Kathleen Gray, "James Blanchard: Heeding a Call to Service,"* Detroit Free Press, *May 17, 2002.*
[133] *Jerry Crandall, interview with GW, March 30, 2001.*
[134] *James N. Crutchfield, "1st Democrat Governor in Two Decades,"* Detroit Free Press, *November 3, 1982.*
[135] *David Kushima, "Democrats Lead State House and Senate Races,"* Detroit Free Press, *November 3, 1982.*
[136] Michigan Manual, *1983-1984 ed. (Lansing: Department of Management and Budget), p. 466.*

Minority Leader Engler: an emerging force

Charlie Cain of the Detroit News *reported on the implications of the '82 election for Engler.*

ENGLER NAMED STATE SENATE MINORITY CHIEF

Sen. John Engler of Mt. Pleasant, a conservative lawmaker who co-chaired the Headlee for Governor Committee, will become Senate minority leader when the new legislature convenes next year.

Engler, 34, was elected to the post by fellow Republicans yesterday to succeed the retiring Sen. Robert Vander Laan of Kentwood. He survived challenges by Sens. Ed Fredricks of Holland and Robert Geake of Northville....

Considered an excellent campaign strategist, he has defeated three incumbent lawmakers during his brief career....

As a result of last week's election, Republicans narrowed the Democratic lead in the 38-member Senate from 24-14 to 20-18. In addition, the incoming Senate will be more conservative, Engler said.

With a Democrat winning the governor's office for the first time in 20 years, the Senate minority leader [Engler] will now speak for the Republican Party, according to the outgoing Vander Laan.[137]

*

Democratic Senator Lana Pollack recalls her early impressions of John Engler.

I met John Engler in January 1983. I was a freshman senator; he was the Republican caucus leader. We started out (I thought) with an appropriate balance of power because I was in the majority party and chairing subcommittees on Appropriations, and he was in the minority. I frankly found him unimpressive in every way—not particularly dynamic or attractive—but reasonably pleasant. I lacked understanding of his talent and drive, as well as the potential he held as minority leader in a closely held chamber during an economic downturn of historic proportions. I do remember hearing that the Milliken folks thought John Engler was arrogant and self-promoting. But overall I didn't think he was important enough to spend any negative energy on. How wrong I was.[138]

*

David Hollister was a Democratic representative.

When Engler and I were in the House, I could ignore him: he was just

[137] *Charlie Cain, "Engler Named State Senate Minority Chief,"* Detroit News, *November 11, 1982.*
[138] *Lana Pollack, interview with GW, July 30, 2002.*

another one of the 110 people who didn't carry any power. And—he was marginalized even by his own party. You had to deal with a moderate Republican caucus in the House, and the politics had to be played with them. John wasn't part of that equation.

But when he moved over to the Senate, he positioned himself to be part of every deal that was made. That's when John became a force.[139]

*

Dennis Schornack worked on Engler's senate staff.

As the Senate minority leader, John Engler was very different from the speaker of the House, Gary Owen. Whereas Owen was loud and crass, Engler was cool and calm. Owen would pound the podium, get red, rant, and rave. Engler was just the opposite—his coolness drove Owen nuts. The two were polar opposites.[140]

*

Gary Wolfram, an economics professor at Hillsdale College, would join Engler's staff.

After John won minority leader in 1983, Saul Anuzis called me and said, "Engler is going to start a first-rate policy staff. It's going to be more than a dumping ground for old staffers who lost their job. John wants a true policy staff. We need an economist. Do you want to come up here and interview?"

After meeting with John, I decided that joining his policy staff was something I wanted to do. When I started, I learned that Engler had visited with Margaret Thatcher. Their discussion had changed his philosophical view of how things should be done. She had started with public policy analysis and explained why a change of direction was needed. And that is what John wanted from me. I was going to give the Senate what I thought was the right thing to do from an economist's perspective. I had the freedom to decide what I thought was the best policy on any given issue. I was told that I didn't have to deal with any of the repercussions on the funding side; his staff dealt with that.

Sure enough, at one point Dick Posthumus told his colleagues in the legislature, "You guys vote your conscience. I'll worry about the money."

I thought to myself, "This is amazing." I never expected government to be like that. We were still the minority party. We didn't have the Senate or the

[139]*David Hollister, interview with GW, March 29, 2001.*
[140]*Dennis Schornack, interview with GW, November 15, 1999.*

House or the governor's office. Yet the caucus was making their decisions based on what was right, not on the politics of the moment.

I never felt that John was going to tell me to tread lightly. John has confidence in himself, and he has confidence in the people he hires. He's not afraid that a staffer is going to upstage him. He said, "I hire good people who are going the direction I want to go." Not everybody can have a strong staff like that, which is why not everybody can be as successful as John can.

Contrast this with the Democrats. A big reason the Democrats didn't keep their majorities is that they didn't let their staff do what they needed to win.

We did, and we won. We won more fights—even though we were in the minority—because we had better ideas, better policies, and greater knowledge of the law.

Before I started to work for John Engler, I didn't realize what a big difference there is between the academic and "real" worlds.

Academics generate ideas, but we never expect them to happen. We don't worry about making them a reality. Once I publish an article in a journal, I can forget about it and go to the next idea and publish that idea somewhere else.

As a politician, John Engler had to have a very different approach. He was definitely an idea guy, always open to new ideas, but he wanted good ideas to be implemented. He would say, "OK, that's a good idea. Now let's figure out a way to *do* it!" John Engler was a person who made things happen.

Working around him changed the whole perspective of my academic career. I realized that it was important to get ideas implemented rather than simply throw them around and expect things to happen by themselves.[141]

*

John Kost would join Engler's staff.

My allegiance to John began in 1982 when he was the Republican minority leader and I was working for House *Democratic* staff. I'd had the opportunity to work with brilliant Democratic legislators like Bill Ryan and Bobby Crim, but never had I seen anyone as smart as John.

The next year I was working for him.

John was not what you'd call a "fun" guy to work with in the conventional

[141]*Gary Wolfram, interview with GW, February 13, 2001.*

sense of the word, but the work was intellectually stimulating, so in that sense it was fun. To watch him and to understand how his mind works is almost frightening. He is really smart. His brain works in creative ways—you never know where he is going to go. But despite his seemingly off-the-wall questions, you have confidence that he knows where he is headed. From his questions, you can tell that he was thinking many steps ahead—like a chess master.

In 1983, as minority leader, John was already planning his run for governor. Back then, it wasn't really an issue whether the income tax hike would pass, because we didn't have the votes to stop it. The issue was how to let it pass with the maximum political damage to the Blanchard administration to assure that we could unravel the guy's political future.[142]

*

Jill Murphy worked for John Engler in the Senate.

Back in the early days, before the advent of the car phone, John used to drive down from Mount Pleasant to Lansing most days. During the drive down US-27, he would dictate correspondence and other tasks for us to take care of. These drives must have been harrowing. Later that morning, you'd listen to the tape, and in the background you would hear cars honking at him. You would hear the newspaper rustling—yes, he would be reading the newspaper while driving. You would also hear him pause to put in his contacts while driving over the speed limit. He drove so fast the Isabella County sheriff deputies used to call him "Air Engler."[143]

*

Jerry Crandall

John always knew what he was doing, but he had a tendency to keep the big picture to himself. Even if you did get pieces of the puzzle, there were always at least one or two pieces missing. In my view, the only guy who ever had all the pieces to John Engler's puzzle was John Engler. He had fantastic vision and foresight.[144]

*

[142] *John Kost, interview with GW, February 20, 2001.*
[143] *Jill Murphy, interview with GW, June 17, 2002.*
[144] *Jerry Crandall, interview with GW, March 30, 2001.*

Art Miller, a Democrat, served on the Michigan Senate.

John did the smart thing. When his party was in the minority, he further prepared himself to lead by going to law school. He had his law degree in hand when Republicans became the majority.[145]

*

Fatal tax hike

At least one Democrat had a faint heart for Governor Blanchard's income tax hike. Engler aide Anne Mervenne explains:

Back in November 1983, when we were still in the minority and Blanchard had been governor for less than a year, we were headed for a tax hike. It was one of the weirdest days in politics that I have ever witnessed, because Joe Mack said he was having a heart attack, and we didn't know if he was faking it to get out of voting for the tax increase or if he was truly sick. The Democrats had him literally voting for the tax hike on a stretcher, as he was getting ready to go to the hospital. Every vote counted that day, and they wouldn't let him go to the hospital until he voted.[146]

*

Recalls

When Governor Blanchard and the Democratic-controlled House and Senate passed a 38 percent state income tax increase in March of 1983, public outrage was mobilized; anti-tax groups mounted or threatened recall campaigns against the governor as well as 17 Democrats and 1 Republican in the legislature. The tax-hike blunder would give Republicans an unparalleled opportunity to win back control of the Senate. John Engler pounced—but behind the scenes. The Detroit News *chronicled what happened.*

SEROTKIN RECALLED BY 2-1 MARGIN IN MACOMB COUNTY

State Sen. David Serotkin of Mt. Clemens was recalled from office by Macomb County voters in a second, stinging repudiation of Gov. James J. Blanchard's 38 percent income tax increase.

Serotkin yesterday became the second lawmaker in Michigan history to be ousted from office. His defeat followed by just eight days the recall of State Sen. Philip O. Mastin of Pontiac....

Mastin and Serotkin—both first-term Democrats—were dumped because they voted for Blanchard's tax hike last March.

[145] *Art Miller, interview with GW, September 25, 2002.*
[146] *Anne Mervenne, interview with GW, February 1, 2001.*

Serotkin's defeat plunges Democrats into an 18-18 tie with Republicans in the Senate and could give Senate control to the GOP if Republicans are elected to fill the two seats in special elections in January. Pieces of Blanchard's economic program pending in the legislature are seriously jeopardized as a result of the current Senate tie.

The Serotkin recall also could reinvigorate threatened recalls in 16 other legislative districts....

At least 16 other lawmakers—and Blanchard himself—have been threatened with recall as a result of the controversial tax increase.

The specter of recall has virtually halted action in the legislature because lawmakers are hesitant to vote on controversial issues for fear the "wrong" vote will trigger a recall campaign against them....

While Macomb County voters decided his fate, Serotkin and fellow Democrats at the Capitol caucused throughout the day, debating whether to redraw legislative district boundaries in a desperate attempt to retain their control of the Senate. Ultimately, they hurried the redistricting bill out of committee. The action drew a violent response from Republicans.

Senate GOP Leader John Engler of Mt. Pleasant, throwing a stack of bills across the committee table, accused the Democrats of an "arrogant abuse of power."

The bill would create a new district in predominantly Democratic Wayne County and, according to Senate Majority Leader William Faust of Westland, should assure 21 Democratic seats the next time senators are elected—in 1986.

Many political observers believe Republicans will capture Mastin's seat in a January special election. If Serotkin is replaced by another Democrat the Senate would be deadlocked 19-19 and Lt. Gov. Martha Griffiths, a Democrat, would hold the tie-breaking vote.

If Serotkin is replaced by a Republican, however, the GOP will have a 20-18 Senate majority—its first since 1974—and that is why Democrats frantically tried to pass a reapportionment bill last night.

Although the state Republican Party denied complicity in the recall campaigns, some Democrats were convinced that the GOP was involved. The Macomb County Republican Party donated $5,000 to the Serotkin recall effort.

Ironically, Serotkin was a Republican until 1977, when he changed parties.

He won the $31,000-a-year Senate seat last November by a narrow margin. He considers the district a "swing" seat—meaning it could go either Republican or Democratic....

After the last defeat, Serotkin switched parties and became a Democrat, explaining that the GOP "was shifting from the Gerald Fords to the Ronald Reagans and I wasn't happy with that." [147]

*

John Engler

When he was a Republican, David Serotkin was my seatmate in the House.[148]

*

Lana Pollack

David Serotkin, one of the targets of the recall, told me that he was sure that while Allen Cropsey was the foot soldier behind the recall campaigns, John Engler was the general, the brains behind this bold assault on Democratic senate leadership.[149]

*

Art Miller

The talk in the Democratic caucus had been, "There's no way senators will be recalled." But it started to happen and then everybody got nervous, including Governor Blanchard, who was extremely vulnerable. If Republicans had really wanted to, I think they could have wrestled the governorship away from him.

John was a good Senate leader because he had a disciplined Republican caucus that hung together. He was also visionary and could see how the times were changing: anti-taxes, anti-welfare, pro-life.

Some of the Democrats, by contrast, held on to old ideas too long and it cost them the majority.[150]

*

A scholar and friend of Engler later remarked, perhaps with some irony, that it was a reform associated with the Progressive movement—citizen recall—that helped create the major turning point in Engler's career.

This was the catalyst eventually boosting John Engler to the governor's office.[151]

[147] *Charlie Cain and Joanna Firestone, "Serotkin Recalled by 2-1 Margin in Macomb County,"* Detroit News, *December 1, 1983.*

[148] *JE, note to GW, October 22, 2002.*

[149] *Lana Pollack, interview with GW, July 30, 2002.*

[150] *Art Miller, interview with GW, September 25, 2002.*

[151] *William P. Browne et al., "Inescapable Partisanship in a Ticket-Splitting State," in* Michigan Politics and Government: Facing Change in a Complex State *(Lincoln: University of Nebraska Press, 1995), p. 196.*

For myself I am an optimist—it does not seem to be much use being anything else.
Winston Churchill

★

Chapter Six
Senate Majority Leader: 1984 - 1990

The new Republican majority

Until late November of 1983, Democrats controlled the Senate 20 to 18. A major turning point in John Engler's career came during the eight days from November 22 and 30, when two Democratic senators who supported Blanchard's income tax increase were recalled. Suddenly the Senate was tied 18 to 18. When special elections were held on January 31, 1984, the two Republicans won. In a remarkably short time, the Senate had been turned upside down. The GOP now enjoyed a 20 to 18 advantage and controlled the chamber for the first time since 1970. On February 2, 1984, the Senate Republican caucus selected John Engler to be majority leader. The Detroit News *reported:*

GOP WINS GIVE CLOUT TO ENGLER

What a difference a day makes. Just ask state Sen. John Engler.

On Tuesday, the Mt. Pleasant Republican was Senate minority leader—a man who had some difficulty getting much respect around the Democrat-dominated Capitol.

But things changed dramatically after two lopsided Republican victories in Tuesday's Special Senate elections....

Engler, a plumpish 35-year-old, consummate politician, is about to be elevated to the top spot in the Michigan Senate. Now that Republicans control the upper chamber by a 20-18 margin, Engler is expected to face only token opposition today when Republicans elect the majority leader.[152]

[152]*Charlie Cain, "GOP Wins Give Clout to Engler,"* Detroit News, *February 2, 1984, pp. 1A, 2A.*

*

Jeff McAlvey joined Engler's Senate staff and reflects on the majority leader's ascent.

John Engler rose so fast in the Senate because he had incredible focus. By February 1984 the Republicans were thrilled to be in the majority, and the class of '82 that he had helped get elected were excited by his leadership. But some of the other members were not so sure. He had run against Bob Geake to be minority leader, and Geake was a little bit off the reservation. And although they were in the same class—the class of '70—Harry DeMaso wasn't a fan of his because Harry had worked for the Blanchard tax increase. They fought a lot, so they had a sometimes rocky relationship. Connie Binsfeld wasn't always with Engler, either. She chaired the public health committee and sometimes would go off in directions that Engler wasn't comfortable with.

So it was remarkable to watch how John Engler would work with each one of his caucus members and help them grow. A lot of them were puppies. Very young legislators, they had never served in the majority, so chairing a committee was a new experience for them. Engler was always asking them to come up to his office after hours. He met with all his caucus members. He was very good about working with each one of them individually and helping them with their issues, teaching them what it meant to be the majority caucus. Sometimes he would encourage. Sometimes he would nudge. Sometimes he would chastise.

We were very purposeful, under Engler's direction, to schedule time each week with members alone, to make sure that he got through the entire caucus once a month. He spent time with each caucus member at least once a month.

Politics was his passion. He was always in the Capitol. There were very few nights when I left that he had already gone home.

John Engler also succeeded as majority leader because he was very strategic. He always has been. Gary Owen used to say that Engler was always four steps ahead of him. And he was. I've never seen anybody figure out the end game so well.[153]

*

Engler attracted talent

Jeff McAlvey

In early 1984, when I was offered a job in Engler's office, a woman who was a friend and staff member in the legislature called me and said, "I hear you are considering working for John Engler. Don't do it. Nobody can work for him. He's a tyrant. Don't do this to your family."

[153]*Jeff McAlvey, interview with GW, May 29, 2002.*

I did not take her advice. I worked for John Engler for 14 years. He is a political genius, he is my mentor, and he has taught me just about everything I know about politics.[154]

*

Doug Roberts

John was majority leader in the Senate, and they were looking for someone to head up the Senate Fiscal Agency. I got a call from a gentleman named Dan DeGrow, who wanted to know if I would be interested in the job. I said no.

Then I get a call from the majority leader himself, and I said, "Senator, is this the same thing as Senator DeGrow wanted?"

He said yes.

I said, "Senator, I'm not trying to play games. I have too much respect for elected officials to do that. I just don't think I want the job."

He said, "All I want to do is talk." (Whenever John Engler says that, it's a problem—he's so persuasive.)

So of course I went to talk to the Senate majority leader. At the time I was the deputy in education. I made it clear to him that I wasn't sure that things would work out. A few months passed and he saw me again, and he asked if he could talk to me again. I told him sure, but if we were to meet, it would have to be in a bar or something, because people knew that we had met the previous time.

Well, I obviously ended up working for him, and it speaks volumes about his character. Once he makes up his mind about what he wants, you need to either get out of town or say yes, because he always gets what he wants. But in retrospect it would have been a great mistake had I said no. You just can't argue with the man, because you will never win.[155]

*

Dennis Schornack

I was offered a job to work for the majority leader and be the legislative assistant. When John called me up and offered me that job, I jumped on it. It was a great opportunity to work with the leader. But everybody kept telling me these horror stories about John, about how he treats the people who work for him terribly. But I said to myself, "I'll take that risk to go work

[154]*Jeff McAlvey, interview with GW, May 29, 2002.*
[155]*Doug Roberts, interview with GW, December 2, 2000.*

for the leader." As it turned out, he has been one of the finest people that I have ever had the opportunity to work with, or for.[156]

*

Engler's success as a legislator

Because Republicans held a narrow 20 to 18 advantage in the Senate, Engler learned in this environment how to forge deals with Democrats. Jeff McAlvey:

One of the things John Engler taught me—and he would say this to me over and over—"Look, in the end, we've got to do a deal. So don't get so far out that we alienate the folks we have to deal with. And also remember that tomorrow they may be our allies on another issue. So don't ever make it personal."

I always thought that that was one of the remarkable things about John Engler. Everybody sees him as a dogmatic conservative. But he is a very practical man who, in the end, wants to get the job done.

That's why he works so well with Democrats like Bob Emerson. Bob is one of the most liberal members of the legislature, but a very practical liberal. And Engler is a very practical conservative. So they could sit down together and get the job done. That's the measure of a legislator—getting something done.[157]

*

Dennis Schornack

John Engler is the most organized person I have ever met. In the Senate, he was able to lay out horizons for every committee under his jurisdiction for months and months into the future. He was able to control the legislature's agenda, not just the Senate's agenda, by sheer force of organizational work and an ability to frame an issue in a politically attractive, almost irresistible way.

There were only a couple of issues in which it came down to a pure 20 to 18 vote—one or two times in which it was pure politics and each caucus voted along strict party lines. I can think of dozens of meetings in which we needed to change the opinion of senators. John liked to create a situation in which Democrats were afraid to vote "no" on the final version of the bill.

He was always able to pull it together. He led by taking the common elements in everyone's position and knitting them together into a whole, then finding what compromises were needed to get the final vote.[158]

[156] *Denny Schornack, interview with GW, December 2, 2000.*
[157] *Jeff McAlvey, interview with GW, May 29, 2002.*
[158] *Dennis Schornack, interview with GW, November 15, 1999.*

*

Lucille Taylor

During the years that John Engler was Senate majority leader, we had a Democratic governor, a Democratic House, and a Republican Senate. It was a difficult situation for a Republican leader to be in. The role of the Senate leader was twofold. It was the leader's job to inject some Republican or conservative ideas into the larger framework. But he also had to deal with 18 Democrats. This is where John Engler's knowledge of the rules, his wonderful negotiating skills, and his ability to build up the party were really honed. He could not afford to make a mistake. He had not one vote to spare.[159]

*

Connie Binsfeld, who served in the House and Senate with Engler before becoming lieutenant governor, comments on the ingredients that made him such a skillful politician. Among other things, his optimism struck her.

One of the things that should be said about John is that, when we were in the smallest of minorities and we suffered a defeat, he would never say, "*If* we got to be in the majority, we would do this and this." He never said *if*. He would say, "*When* we get to be the majority."[160]

*

Jerry Crandall

Nothing fazed John Engler. When he wanted something, he would think it through, far into the future. If there were a temporary setback, he wouldn't give up. He would deal with it and keep working to get closer to the ultimate result. He always found a way.[161]

*

Joanne Emmons

John Engler used to say, like Russell Kirk, "Politics is the art of the possible." When I was frustrated with a bill, he would say to me, "You get a little bit as often as you can. Every time you are offered something instead of nothing, and it moves you in the direction you want to go, you take it. Then you come back for more a later day.

[159] *Lucille Taylor, interview with GW, October 20, 1999.*
[160] *Connie Binsfeld, interview with GW, January 23, 2001.*
[161] *Jerry Crandall, interview with GW, March 30, 2001.*

One of John's strengths is his patience. I think the reason he wanted to run things was so he could be in a position to hang on to his position, and hang on, and hang on, until everybody else gave up. He used to say to me, "Patience, Joanne. Patience." He knew the longer he waited, the more others would give. After the deal was finalized, he would say to me, "We got so much more than I ever thought we could get." Why? Patience. He was always the last man standing. Patience is a wonderful tool in the legislature. I've learned that from John.

When I got to the legislature, I soon discovered that it was John Engler who was in charge. Not Jim Blanchard. Not Gary Owen. But John Engler. When you went to see the majority leader on the Senate floor, you had to stand in line. I don't ever remember that happening with [later Senate majority leaders] Dick Posthumus or Dan DeGrow. The reason there was a line to see John was that he was absolutely pivotal to every decision.[162]

*

School finance conundrum

Al Short of the Michigan Education Association speaks of his meetings with Engler.

When Engler was the majority leader, I would often talk to him about school finance. During our meetings he would get angry and say, "Al, you're not speaking for all MEA members; you're speaking for rich school districts." There were districts that had $12- or $13,000, and they formed their own "out of formula" lobbying group. The president of the MEA at that time was from a very wealthy district in the out-of-formula association. All those years John would continually tell me, "You don't represent most people. You don't talk about the people from my area, Mount Pleasant. You are controlled by the wealthy school districts." The problem was—it was true.[163]

*

1986 Campaign

In 1986, Wayne County Executive William Lucas won the Republican nomination to challenge incumbent James Blanchard. Engler's first wife, Colleen House, ran for lieutenant governor on the Republican ticket. Lucas, an ex-Democrat, aspired to be the nation's first elected African-American governor. It was not to be. Lucas was crushed,

[162] *Joanne Emmons, interview with GW, September 25, 2002.*
[163] *Al Short, interview with GW, February 26, 2001.*

and Blanchard coasted to re-election with 68 percent of the vote, the second largest landslide in Michigan history.[164]

COLLEEN PERO: I remember John calling me in Texas in 1985. He said, "We are going to have the first black Republican governor in the U.S.—in Michigan!"

I said, "What? Who is it? Who's going to vote for him?"

"Bill Lucas and all the Republicans will," said John.

I wasn't so sure.

RICHARD McLELLAN: John and Spencer believed that conservative Republican Catholics would vote for him because he was conservative and Republican and Catholic, and that blacks would vote for him because he was black. They were wrong on both counts. Lucas had never run in a tough election, so he wasn't a great campaigner. Blanchard won 82 counties—all but Ottawa.[165]

*

Jeff McAlvey

John Engler poured his heart and soul out for Bill Lucas in '86. That same year, he was up for re-election. The Democrats recruited a credible candidate, Jerry White, the prosecutor of Midland County, a former Republican who changed parties and ran as a Democrat. We had done a poll in December of '85, and Engler's numbers were not very good. His re-elect numbers were below 50 percent, and his positives were pretty low because he did not spend much time in the district. He was the majority leader. He didn't go home much. Also, in the previous redistricting [1980] he had lost Traverse City and now had Midland, where the people did not know Engler well. They were a bit arrogant and wanted their senator to come from Midland, not Mount Pleasant. So Engler never played well there. Because of that, he didn't like to go to Midland.

The Democrats knew the numbers were not very good; they thought they had a chance to go after Engler.

So we sat down with Tom Shields and Mark Pischea at MRG [Marketing Resource Group] and Engler made it clear, "We've got to put together a plan where I don't need to go to the district very much."

We called it the "smoke and mirrors campaign." We raised a ton of money, but Engler did not spend more than five days in the district between Labor

[164] *Weeks,* Stewards of the State *(1991 ed.), p. 134.*

[165] *Colleen Pero, Richard McLellan, interview with GW, February 3, 2001.*

Day and Election Day. We would surrogate for him and say, "The senator has to be somewhere else tonight." Audiences would assume he was somewhere else in the district, but he never was. Engler would be campaigning for Republicans in other districts. We spent a ton of money on media in places like Grand Rapids, which would build up his name recognition for the 1990 campaign.[166]

*

Blanchard: "A Lucky Boy Wonder"

Governor Blanchard won a second term by one of the largest margins in Michigan history, shattering William Lucas's dreams of becoming the nation's first elected black governor.[167] The Democratic governor was quoted by a reporter as saying that he had been very lucky to have the Republican opponents he did: "Headlee and Huber," a smiling Blanchard observed, "they've made me what I am today."[168]

*

Final electoral results for the 35th Senate District

John Engler	40,204 votes (59.2%)
Gerald White	27,683 votes (40.8%)[169]

After the election, Engler was unanimously chosen by his caucus to continue on as Senate majority leader.[170]

*

1990 will be the year

Human Events *editor John Gizzi recalls a conversation in which Engler revealed his strategy.*

It was a cold morning soon after the election. John, Jerry Crandall, and I were at the Hyatt-Regency in Washington, DC. John told me, "This is my last term in the Senate, Giz. In 1990 I'll either run for governor or U.S. Senator."[171]

*

The opposition

Gary Owen was the Democratic speaker of the House from 1982-1988, when Engler

[166]*Jeff McAlvey, interview with GW, May 29, 2002.*
[167]*Susan Goldberg and David Kushma, "Historic Try by Lucas Crumbles,"* Detroit Free Press, *November 5, 1986.*
[168]*Tim Jones, "A Lucky Boy Wonder Becomes Luckier Still,"* Detroit Free Press, *November 5, 1986.*
[169]Michigan Manual, *1987-1988 ed. (Lansing: Department of Management and Budget), p. 499.*
[170]*JE, interview by GW, October 3, 2002.*
[171]*John Gizzi, interview with GW, October 2, 2002.*

was minority then majority leader. Here are his reflections on Engler's Senate years.

John Engler was not conservative. He was not ideological. He was not dogmatic. He was not guided by philosophical principles. Or, to put it another way, his philosophy would change depending on his constituency. That's why he supported the legalization of marijuana when he was in the House: his constituents were students at Central Michigan University. In the legislature, he was very pragmatic, very flexible. Whatever the situation, he could adapt to it, and at times that made him very difficult to deal with.

Jack Welborn—you knew where he stood: far right. Dick Posthumus—you knew his policies were based on his background: Dutch Reformed. Engler never had that philosophical bent.

When John Engler was elected in 1970, Democrats controlled the House. John saw a succession of strong, powerful Democratic speakers like Bill Ryan and Bobby Crim. He saw how they ran the House, which is no easy thing to do. Compared to the Senate, which is a "gentlemen's club," the House is more rancorous. There is more debate. Members are more opinionated. There is more animosity. I think John looked at the powerful leadership tradition of Democratic speakers in the House and tried to take that legislative model over to the Senate.

But John had a tough time there, even with his own caucus. The Senate Republicans were fragmented. Many were strongly opposed to him. He did not deal from a basis of strength. As a result, he was not effective as majority leader. That is not necessarily a reflection of John, but of the difficult situation he faced in his caucus.

I think where John was a lot more successful was in building up the Republican Party. His strength was to work tirelessly on behalf of the party. He devoted a lot of time making the party more unified, more partisan, more conservative. He worked hard to pull together people who had the same objective he did: to make the Republican Party the majority party in the state. He benefited from Ronald Reagan. He rode the wave that swept Reagan into office. He co-opted the grass roots enthusiasm for the president and used it to his advantage. In the process, he made a lot of enemies among the old guard Republicans who were far more liberal than Reagan. John generated a lot of animosity among people like Bill Milliken, animosity that I think has lasted to this day. He was younger and more committed than the old guard.[172]

[172]*Gary Owen, interview with GW, July 8, 2002.*

*

Pat Laughlin explains why John Engler was able to set the agenda in the late 1980s.

Speaker Gary Owen was a brilliant tactician. He was truly John's equal. A mastermind. They had different styles, but otherwise they were very similar: creative, intuitive, resourceful. When Gary was out of the way [from 1989 on], John Engler took off. It wasn't widely recognized how brilliant John was until Gary left public office for the private sector.

Blanchard perceived himself to be a big fish in a small pond. But he was no match for Engler. At first he did not take seriously Engler's political sophistication and institutional memory. It was Gary Owen who carried the water for Blanchard. So when Gary left, Blanchard's political flanks were exposed and he was left without the heavy artillery.

When Jim Blanchard tried to match wits with John Engler, he lost. Engler constantly outsmarted him and went on to become the greatest governor Michigan has ever had.[173]

*

Dawson Bell

Gary Owen used to say that John didn't always tell the truth. The truth is that Gary didn't always understand what he was agreeing to. John was always willing to negotiate a deal in which the other side didn't understand what they were agreeing to, but that is very different from lying. It's just John's way of saying, "If you aren't prepared, if you haven't done your homework, then you are at a disadvantage."[174]

*

David Hollister, a self-avowed liberal Democrat, served in the Michigan House of Representatives from 1975 to 1993.

Over the years, John and I developed a respectful but adversarial relationship. I have always considered him a smart son of a gun. John is always three to five steps ahead of everybody else with his strategy. So when you take him on, you'd better know what you're planning to do. And don't try to bluff because he will call your bluff.

My biggest problem with taking on Engler was that my caucus was afraid of him.

[173]*Pat Laughlin, interview with GW, July 3, 2002.*

[174]*Dawson Bell, interview with GW, February 27, 2001.*

When John Engler was Senate majority leader, our [Democratic] leadership didn't like him. We would swear, cuss, and bluster over human services. I would always have to negotiate away what I really thought was the right thing to do, because we didn't have a party that had an identity, and we had no leader to articulate what we were doing. Blanchard was a moderate Democrat; he didn't support liberals in the House. Blanchard wouldn't fight for us. I had more personal conflict with Blanchard than I did with Engler.

We knew that Engler could manipulate power. He was smart enough to win the public relations battle on welfare. He would accuse people of being a "welfare-mom supporter" or a "bleeding-heart liberal." He was able to frame the debate very effectively. He could be manipulative—though he was not deceitful.

John used his role as majority leader to build a constituency in the Capitol press corps. They may not have liked him as an individual, but they liked his strategy. Engler was a masterful chess player. He was always five steps ahead of everyone else. He was always frank about it and would always tell people exactly where he wanted to be.[175]

*

Dennis Schornack tells of this encounter between Engler and Blanchard.

John Engler never shut off communications even with people who were his worst critics or opponents.

There is a very funny story about an accidental meeting on an elevator with Blanchard. It was back in 1989. John and I were in the elevator in the Capitol building. When the doors opened, there was Blanchard. He saw John and the color drained from his face.

We all noticed the hesitation Blanchard felt, whether to get on the elevator or not. He could have chosen not to get on, but there were other people standing around. Blanchard must have decided that it would have looked very childish for the governor not to get on the elevator on his way to the office just because his archenemy was in it.

So Blanchard stepped in. But you could see that he would have passed out if he could have. The tension was so high, it was palpable. It was such a stunning nonverbal reaction: the draining of the color from his face, the tight lips, and not even a single glance at Engler.

John was amused by it. He said, "Good morning, governor."

[175]*David Hollister, interview with GW, March 29, 2001.*

But Blanchard ignored him completely and turned to his aide to mumble something. I recall standing there and being wowed by how strong John Engler's personality was to produce such an impact on the governor. We were still a year and a half from the election at that time.

There was no pleasantry at all. Blanchard got off the elevator without a word. We continued on up to our floor, and John turned to me and deadpanned, "I don't think he was very happy to see me, do you?"[176]

*

Marsha Quebbeman worked in Engler's Senate office. She observes:

Martha Griffiths and John had such respect for each other, and the two really got along. It shows how bipartisan John was—he could work with the opposition. John could always talk to Lieutenant Governor Griffiths, but it wasn't so easy with Governor Blanchard.[177]

*

Engler rebuilds the GOP

Many political observers believe that one of the most significant achievements of Senator Engler was to rebuild a moribund Republican Party in Michigan. In 1980 Republicans around the nation were ascendant. They had elected Ronald Reagan to the presidency and had taken back the U.S. Senate.

Michigan Republicans were another story. By 1982 the party of Milliken was in free fall. That year they failed to win a majority in either the House or Senate; they lost the governor's office to Democrat Jim Blanchard; and they did not hold a majority on the Supreme Court. This, in the state that claimed bragging rights for having given birth to the GOP in 1854.

Engler was chosen by his caucus to be Senate minority leader in November of 1982. That made him the highest-ranking Republican in the state. He would remain the highest-ranking Republican in Michigan for the next two decades. From day one, he made it a priority to rebuild and reenergize the Michigan GOP. It was not a smooth ascent; the Lucas debacle in 1986 illustrates. Yet in a few short years he achieved remarkable goals on behalf of his party, becoming minority leader in 1982; taking over the Senate in 1983; winning the governor's race in 1990; taking back the House in the '90s; sending a Republican to the U.S. Senate in 1994; building a majority on the Supreme Court; and dominating reapportionment after the 2000 census. In 2002, as

[176] *Dennis Schornack, interview with GW, November 15, 1999.*
[177] *Marsha Quebbeman, interview with GW, February 23, 2002.*

Engler's gubernatorial career came to a close, Milliken observed, "John Engler is a remarkable leader. He has shaped the Michigan Republican Party in his own conservative image."[178]

Much of Engler's success was obviously due to his own hard work and strategic talents. But it was also due to the able people he put in positions of responsibility. One of his greatest lieutenants in these years was E. Spencer Abraham, a graduate of Michigan State University and Harvard Law School, and a founder of the Federalist Society. By the mid-1980s, Engler was crediting Abraham with successfully rebuilding the Michigan Republican Party. The following is an excerpt from a memorandum Engler wrote in preparation for a meeting with Vice President George Bush. It says as much about Engler's goals for the party as it does about Abraham's chairmanship.

SPENCER ABRAHAM

Republican State Chairman of Michigan. Age 31.... He has been chairman of the Michigan Republicans since 1983. Credited with rebuilding the Michigan Republican Party and uniting its diverse membership into a cohesive unit, Spence is recognized as one of the outstanding state chairmen in America. He is acknowledged as a tactical and organizational wizard and helped to introduce computerized, targeted campaigns to Michigan politics....[179]

*

1988 presidential primary

Michigan Republicans still talk about the 1988 presidential contest. The primary was hotly contested by George H. W. Bush, Pat Robertson, and Jack Kemp. Robertson, a TV evangelist and head of the Christian Coalition, posed particular problems to the GOP establishment. Early in the primary season he blitzed Michigan with his "invisible army" and took over the GOP's Central Steering Committee. Up to the eve of the Republican Party convention in Grand Rapids, Robertson counted on having 44 of the 77 delegates behind him. It appeared that Vice President George H. W. Bush would suffer a humiliating defeat at the beginning of the primary season.

John Engler, a staunch Bush ally, was determined to help the vice president come out on top in the Michigan primary and in the November election.

*

[178] *William Milliken, interview with GW, November 7, 2002.*

[179] *JE, memo to Ron Kaufman, May 3, 1985, p. 1; the meeting with Vice President Bush took place four days later at the Detroit Athletic Club.*

Peter Secchia, who was vice chairman of the GOP in 1988, was amazed at Engler's strategic skill throughout the presidential campaign.

When we won the state's nomination for Bush in 1988, John was the strategic genius who put together the game plan. That was a nasty race. The people who were working for Pat Robertson thought they were working for God. We were not working for God—so from their point of view we were working for the other side. Guess who that was?

Pat Robertson almost pulled off an upset. He put skilled people heavily Democratic in districts that could be easily picked off by new Republican leadership. His people claimed they had a majority of the delegates. After he lost the nomination Robertson declared that he was coming to Grand Rapids to fight the convention's decision.

We had to act quickly. We gaveled the convention closed while Robertson was still at the airport. (They took us to court because of that and I think eventually won—five years later. A little too late since Clinton was president.)

In August of 1988 the Republican National Convention met in New Orleans. I was vice chairman of the Republican National Committee. John Engler wanted to make sure Pat Robertson's people were on board with support for Bush. So he suggested to me that Pat Robertson's delegates be allowed to be seated on the floor of the convention. Remember, this was a minority delegation. It was the first time a minority delegation was ever allowed to be seated on the floor. I had to fight hard to acheive this for John. But John knew it had to be done so that the Robertson people would get behind Bush candidacy.

What's interesting about this is that John Engler was ignoring his own political situation. He was jeopardizing his relationship with the state Bush delegation that didn't want the Robertson people seated on the floor of the convention. But he was thinking of the party, putting the needs of the party above himself. The national organization supported this.

In November Bush won Michigan with the help of the Robertson people. We pulled it off because of John Engler's strategic genius. James Baker later thanked me for the victory. I said, "Don't thank me. Thank John Engler."

Later, when I was appointed ambassador to Italy, I said to many people that I indirectly owed that appointment to John Engler because of what he did in the '88 primary.[180]

*

[180] *Peter Secchia, interview with GW, July 12, 2002.*

Second Front: Medicaid funded abortion

While John Engler was fighting to keep the Michigan Republican Party unified, he was also leading the effort to end Medicaid funded abortions.[181] *The* Detroit Free Press *reported:*

ABORTION VOTE GOES FOR THE BAN

After a 10-year battle over state-paid abortions for poor women, Michigan voters Tuesday appeared to give a major victory to the anti-abortion movement....

Approval of Proposal A would enact a state law passed in 1987 that forbids the use of state money for Medicaid-funded abortions except to save the life of the mother.

The ban won widespread support from Republicans (63 percent to 37 percent) and independents (53 to 47), while losing among Democrats (56 to 44), according to a preliminary survey of about 2,000 voters from all over the state....

Tuesday's referendum came after 17 legislative attempts since 1978 to stop abortion funding were vetoed by Govs. William Milliken and James Blanchard. The law enacted by Proposal A cannot be vetoed.

"There is a sadness that this had to happen," [Barbara] Listing said, "that Michigan was involved in funding the deaths of 175,000 unborn children just because of the philosophy of two men."

Passage of Proposal A would make Michigan only the second state to ban state-funded abortions by referendum. Colorado, the only other state to do so, voted Tuesday on a proposal to rescind the measure....

Michigan took over Medicaid payments for abortion in 1978 after Congress passed the Hyde Amendment, banning the use of federal funds for abortions. Since then, the state has paid for about 175,000 abortions at a cost of about $57 million.[182]

*

Master of the Senate

A number of people observe that John Engler's mastery of politics in the Michigan Senate was like Lyndon Johnson's mastery of politics in the U.S. Senate. John Gizzi:

[181] *Dawson Bell, "Debate on Abortion Ban Still Rages: Sides Say the Issue Is Not a Matter of Morality or Money," The* Detroit Free Press, *November 4, 1988, p. 3A.*

[182] *Dawson Bell and Patricia Chargot, "Abortion Vote Goes for the Ban,"* Detroit Free Press, *November 9, 1988, p. 1A.*

I've been reading Caro's *Master of the Senate*, and I am struck by the similarities between John Engler and Lyndon Johnson. Both had a consuming love of politics. Both knew how to play the game in the best sense of the word. Both could see politics as blood sport. And both were risk-takers. Having spent their adult lives on the public payroll, both were willing to give up one office to seek a higher office at a time that it seemed a faraway goal.[183]

*

Mark Michaelson worked for John Engler in the Senate.

I like to describe John as the Republican Lyndon B. Johnson because he was the master of policy and a very thoughtful legislative strategist. In the Michigan legislature, John was the center of majority strategy. He was the guy who engineered legislative maneuvering, set budget policy, and closed the sale. The speaker would come over to his office and talk to him. It was obvious that John was the biggest shooter in the room.[184]

*

A scholarly perspective from William Browne, Kenneth Verburg, Richard McAnaw, and Noelle Schiffer:

Engler, who became majority leader in 1984, was Blanchard's chief political nemesis for the remainder of the decade. Presiding over the senate, Engler became the focus of Republican power in state politics and the front-running Republican candidate for governor. He used the political tools at his disposal to elevate the importance of the entire chamber. Often he did the unheard of, trampling on what were thought of as gubernatorial prerogatives. Engler, for example, put the governor on notice by having a committee reject, without a hearing, two gubernatorial nominations that required senate confirmation.[185]

*

The Senate majority leader: up close and personal

Jerry Crandall

When I became John's chief of staff we were all working long hours. I was usually in by 7:00 or 7:30 in the morning, and I was home about 6:30 or 7:00 at

[183] *John Gizzi, interview with GW, October 2, 2002.*
[184] *Mark Michaelson, interview with GW, February 28, 2001.*
[185] *William P. Browne, Kenneth Verburg, et al., "Legislative Quandary: Leaders of Followers?" in* Michigan Politics and Government: Facing Change in a Complex State *(Lincoln: University of Nebraska Press, 1995), p. 116.*

night. Sometimes if John was in the office I would work until 7:30 or 8:00. John was even busier; he was going, going, going all the time.

John's thinking was organized but his personal space was not. His desk was always piled with papers. He didn't want staff messing with his stacks of papers. There weren't many days when you could see his desktop. On Mondays he would bring in a stack of newspaper clippings from the Saturday and Sunday papers. Often he would hand you a newspaper story on a particular issue and say, "Put that in the file for six or eight months down the road." He was always thinking ahead.

When I first started as his chief of staff, I noticed that John was constantly generating new ideas. So I'd drop everything I was doing and start to work on his latest idea. You'd get it done—but then you'd discover, in some cases, that you'd never hear about it again. So I created a three-stack approach to working with him. I started putting things in a stack on my desk. If I heard about an issue a second time, I'd move it to the second stack. If I heard about it a third time, that was serious; that would go to the category of "Get it done fast." After a lapse of time, I'd push the entire first stack off the desk and into a file, just in case he wanted to go back to an old idea.

John had a fantastic capability of looking at information, digesting it, and moving on. He would ask you to reduce any issue to one page of background. If you gave him two or three pages, he'd give it back to you—very much like a professor rejecting an assignment. So if a meeting was at 10:00, he'd look at the one page that you gave him for a few moments, then walk into the meeting and perform as if he'd been studying the issue all his life.

John Engler was a conservative pragmatist. He was very different from some of the other Republican members in this respect. Their approach was, "Give me the whole loaf, or give me nothing." John thought, by contrast, "If I can't get the whole loaf, I'll take half of it, declare victory, and worry about getting the rest of it next time."

As a pragmatist, John Engler thoroughly understood that politics is the art of compromise, so he followed the rule, "Get what you can get, when you can get it," to advance his conservative philosophy. John always wanted to keep the ball moving forward.

John never wanted to go to Washington because he had too much to do in

Michigan. He really had no interest in the U.S. Senate because he didn't want to be just 1 of 100 individuals.

However, he used to love to go down to Washington to meet with President Bush. He would get invited to dinner, and when he'd come back to Lansing, he would be so easy to deal with. He would be on such a high after a dinner, meeting, or social event in Washington.

To get what he wanted in the legislature, John would push the envelope. He was always willing to go as far as the constitution would let him go, right up to the line. He might even lean over the line. But he would never cross the line ethically or legally.

John was very close to his father. Matt Engler had run for public office, and I think that he contributed considerably to his son's political philosophy. Before Matt got cancer, he'd stop by John's office once a month or so. He'd come in to say hello. If John wasn't there, he'd sit down and shoot the breeze with the staff.

Matt and John had many things in common, and it was very tough on John when Matt got sick. If a call came from his dad, John would drop everything. If he sensed his dad needed him, he'd take off immediately.

There are two types of people: one who rises to the top by beating down everybody else, and one who rises to the top by outworking and outperforming everybody else. John Engler is the latter type. In the Senate, when John knew what he wanted to do, he made sure that he was always a step ahead of everybody else.

When the Capitol was undergoing renovation, John would sometimes come over to my office and say, "Hey, let's take a walk." He wanted to see how the reconstruction was progressing. So we would walk up into the catwalks. He was just so curious. He wanted to know everything that was happening because it was all part of history. He loves history.

John absorbed politics: he ate, drank, and slept politics. He was also a voracious reader. He read books in addition to newspapers. He would trade books with people in the office. But I have to say this: there was a definite division between John's political life and his private life. In the seven or eight years that I worked with him, I only received two calls from John while he was at home. It wasn't often that we bothered him at home either.

Every morning when John came to work he passed by the women of the office: the scheduler, the receptionist, and the secretary. On occasion John would come into the office with bouquets of flowers in hand; he would pass them out to the women as he walked past. He would do this to cheer everyone up.

If he traveled somewhere he would always bring back souvenirs. When he went to China, he brought back many things. The gifts he gives are always thoughtful; they are directly connected to the person and their particular interests.

After a few years in the Senate, John indicated that he was no longer interested in being the Senate majority leader. He was bored.

People would ask me, "You work with him. What do you think he is going to do?"

I'd tell them I thought he wanted to be governor, but I really couldn't be sure, because there was so much that he could do and do well. Once I sat down and listed what I thought were his options. The list was long, but when I got to the bottom, I drew a line and wrote, "Bored." I definitely knew there would be a change in his job title. It was just a matter of time.[186]

*

Saving a lamb named Fluffy

Jill Murphy

When John was in the Senate, he used to go to the county fairs in his six counties and buy the best-of-show from a 4-H'er. Some years it was a pig, other years it was a lamb, etc. He would then have it butchered and the meat given to charity. One year, a little girl who had heard that he did this every year wrote him a letter telling him about her lamb, Fluffy, that she was raising for 4-H. She even sent a picture. We thought that since this girl had taken the initiative to write, he should buy her animal—BUT—in the minds of us city girls, you can't kill a cute little lamb named Fluffy. We told John he should buy the lamb, then give it back to her for a pet.

The remarkable thing is that he did just that! I guess that's what he got for having a staff of women![187]

[186] *Jerry Crandall, interview with GW, March 30, 2001.*
[187] *Jill Murphy, interview with GW, August 5, 2002.*

*

John Engler and Coleman Young

The following anecdote gives insight into why Jim Blanchard would not do as well as he needed to in order to win re-election in 1990.

John Engler brought Coleman Young in to speak to Senate Republicans at a time when Jim Blanchard apparently wasn't returning Young's phone calls. John personally escorted Mayor Young in so that he could hear what the Senate was discussing. At the time the Senate was debating whether to renew the utility tax because it funded police protection in Detroit. I thought to myself, "What a brilliant thing to do: a Republican leader reaching out to the city of Detroit."[188]

*

Aspiring to be governor

A revealing exchange

GLEAVES: When did you decide you wanted to be governor?

ENGLER: I don't remember. But when I met Jim Blanchard, I knew I could do it.[189]

Jeff McAlvey

In 1985 everybody assumed John Engler would run for governor in '86. I assumed that, too. But he said, "I'm not running in '86. I'm running in '90. '86 is going to be a terrible year. There is no way we can beat Blanchard in '86. But in '90, it's my turn. I think we can build our team for '90. In the meantime, I've got to make sure this majority stays intact, even if we have a disaster at the top of the ticket."[190]

*

John Truscott would join Engler's gubernatorial campaign and serve as the candidate's spokesman.

John is a natural leader. He is the type of person who wants the top job not for the title, but for the things he can do. That is what really drove him to run for governor: the desire to make changes and improve the state.

In the legislature, John helped make changes. But he saw that you have to be

[188] *Anne Mervenne, interview with GW, February 1, 2001.*
[189] *GW, personal papers, December 1999.*
[190] *Jeff McAlvey, interview with GW, May 29, 2002.*

the governor to make the greatest changes. The governor can do the most to alter the way the state operates and to fundamentally improve the way Michigan is perceived throughout the country.

I think John thought, "I got into the position to run accidentally. I didn't expect this to be a career. But there are things that I know I can do to improve the state and to turn around the economy. These things can only be done from the executive office. So I'm going to take a chance. If it doesn't work out, so be it."[191]

*

Marsha Quebbeman

I think John Engler always wanted to be governor. All you have to do is go back to the early '80s and look at his schedule book when he was in the Senate. He was everywhere—always on the road outside of his district. He wanted to talk to everybody. All that traveling would prepare him for his first campaign, which was truly a grassroots effort.

Staff would joke that our office was the one where people were always working. That's because he was nonstop himself. He was always traveling beyond his district, going above and beyond his duties as a state senator. Driving around in his Oldsmobile, alone, with no one else, he would go from place to place just trying to meet the people and get his message across.

He would always look for the local newspaper or radio station to go on to get his message across. He did tons of radio, every Michigan radio station imaginable. He would call me up and say, "Marsha, I'm going to be in Bad Axe. Find a local radio station for me to go on. " This happened wherever he was. He just didn't like downtime.[192]

*

Gary Wolfram

From 1984 to 1990, when John was the majority leader in the Senate, he began setting the stage for becoming governor. When he became governor he already had developed a whole set of policies so he knew where he was going from day one.

He demonstrated great skills as the majority leader. He controlled his caucus. He united them in blocking bad bills. He selected the right chairmen. He

[191]*John Truscott, interview with GW, October 19, 1999.*
[192]*Marsha Quebbeman, interview with GW, February 23, 2002.*

hired the right staff. He was like a general: he directed the operations but you hardly ever met with him.

John didn't become governor because he wanted people to call him "governor," or because he wanted to have the mansion. Certain people in politics do that, but John is not one of them. The reason John wanted to become governor was that over the years he had developed a policy agenda that he wanted to implement.[193]

John Engler with Annette and Russell Kirk, whom he represented in the Michigan Senate. SOURCE: *Annette Kirk*

[193]*Gary Wolfram, interview with GW, February 13, 2001.*

They should rule who are able to rule best.
ARISTOTLE

★

Chapter Seven
First Gubernatorial Campaign: 1990

Pero

In 1989 Dan and Colleen Pero left their work in Houston so that Dan could direct Engler's gubernatorial campaign. The Peros and Engler had known each other for a decade and a half and were tight. Dan had no doubt that his candidate would continue to live up to his reputation as "John the Giant Killer."

John Engler has bigger *cojones* than anybody I know—they're bowling balls. I knew that he could beat Blanchard and be a great governor.[194]

*

During the summer of 1989, Senate Majority Leader Engler set up an exploratory committee through the Secretary of State—it was pro forma because he already had decided to run against Blanchard. Seven and a half months later, he made his candidacy official by creating the "Engler for Governor Committee." He went on an announcement tour on Lincoln's birthday—February 12, 1990—delivering speeches in bone-chilling cold to crowds in Traverse City, Grand Rapids, Midland, Detroit, and from the Capitol steps in Lansing.[195] Excerpts from his announcement speech follow.

During the last seven and a half months ... I have taken my message of lower taxes, better schools, safer neighborhoods, and a cleaner environment to all 83 counties in our great state. I have toured every courthouse, shared an evening

[194] *Dan Pero, interview with GW, August 2, 2002.*
[195] *Martin et al.,* Journey of John Engler, *p. 32.*

with our farmers at 15 county farm bureau meetings and several Ag conferences, walked Main Streets, stayed overnight in the homes of old friends and new. And the people have responded.

Over 3,500 Michiganians have already contributed more than $850,000 to our campaign for Michigan's future. Hundreds more have volunteered to lick envelopes, staff phone banks, work out of their homes, knock on doors....

For too many struggling communities in our great state, the Blanchard comeback story has been nothing more than a grim fairy tale.

Unemployment is up. Michigan's jobless rate at 8.4 percent is now the highest in America. It is 58 percent above the national average, and there are more people unemployed in Michigan today than at any time since 1986.

New manufacturing jobs are down. Michigan has lost 257,000 such jobs in the 1980s.

Dropout rates are up. Michigan ranks among the worst in the nation, and over half of the students who enter the eighth grade in Detroit's public schools will never get a diploma.

Education test scores are down. Over half of the students in Detroit's public schools flunked their mandated reading test, and 89 percent of the eleventh graders failed a basic science skills test.

Welfare spending is up. One of every ten people in Michigan is on some kind of welfare. The state spends $370 million a month on welfare or $87 a month for every working man and woman.

But the return on the tax dollars we send to Washington is down. Statistics from the U.S. Census Bureau indicate that Michigan ranks last in the return on the tax dollars we send to Washington. In fact, Michigan has ranked near the bottom in federal spending since Blanchard has been in office, placing 47th in 1984, 48th in 1985 and 1986, and 49th in 1987.

Violent crime and drug use are up. Murder is up 9.4 percent since 1983; rape is up 39.9 percent since 1983; aggravated assault is up 24.1 percent since 1983. Since 1985, narcotic arrests have doubled, treatment caseloads have tripled, and felony trafficking and possession convictions have increased five fold.

The number of congressmen Michigan will send to Washington in 1992 after reapportionment is down—from 18 to 16, because more and more Americans are saying "no" to Michigan. Part of the reason is that property taxes are up. Way up to fourth highest in America. Indeed, our entire tax burden is up to fifth highest in the nation. And our working poor and middle class pay more in taxes than in other states.

Pollution is up. Scientists tell us many of our Great Lakes fish are unsafe to eat. Our groundwater is becoming unsafe to drink. Toxic chemicals are filling up our lakes. And the governor has stood by for seven years unable to write rules to begin cleaning up our water, air and land, while allowing Michigan to become a dumpsite for the radioactive waste of six other states.

Infant mortality and hospital closures are up. A black baby born in Detroit has a greater chance of dying before his first birthday than a baby born in many third-world nations and old East European dictatorships. 18 hospitals have closed since 1982, risking the health of many Michiganians.

Access to affordable health care for more and more of our citizens is down.

The number of state employees is up. There are 8,000 more employees on the state payroll since Blanchard took office and thousands more on contracts—including a $32,000 contract to the former executive director of the Michigan Democrats to throw together a 20 year anniversary for Earth Day, and a $15,000 contract to teach state employees how to be more polite on the telephone.

But the efficiency of the state bureaucracy is down....

Incompetence and mismanagement in the administration are up ... and business confidence in Michigan's economy is down. A recent report of Michigan's business leaders says that over half will not be adding jobs in 1990 and that 16 percent will be eliminating jobs.

My friends, it seems to me that after serving for almost eight years in Michigan's most important job, when what's up should be down—and when what's down should be up—it's time for the governor who is in, to be out. I believe it's time the Michigan comeback story had another author, and I'm prepared to write the next chapter....

I can do a better job than Jim Blanchard at creating economic opportunity in every region of Michigan because I know you don't bring jobs here by raising taxes. You keep taxes low. You make education the highest priority. You make business feel welcome here with true reforms in our workers and unemployment compensation systems, and by cutting rules and regulations that strangle economic growth. And you keep government out of the business of picking winners and losers.

I can do a better job than Jim Blanchard at putting quality back in our classrooms, because I'm prepared to fight for some fundamental changes in how we teach our kids. I want parents to have greater choice about which school they send their children to in their local school district.... I'm for giving our teachers the tools to teach and the power to discipline. Because no teacher should have to fear a lawsuit or personal violence if he or she tries to keep order in the classroom. I'm for giving local schools greater flexibility in rewarding excellent teachers and dismissing incompetent ones. At the same time, I'm for "alternative certification" that allows the best and brightest in other professions to teach in our schools. I want every dime of the lottery that was meant for school to go to schools. No more funny money executive budgets that use a lottery dollar to replace a general fund dollar that's being spent on some other program. I want the state to become equal funding partners with local school districts again. Fifty-fifty. We were once. We will be again. And we'll do it by dedicating a fixed percentage of the state budget to education. We'd set that money aside up front, before we try to pay for anything else—just like your family sets aside the home mortgage payment in your personal budget. After that, everything else is open to negotiation.

Government can't pay for everything and shouldn't try.

I can do a better job than Jim Blanchard at holding taxes and spending down because I will be led by my strong belief that the people of Michigan are already taxed enough. We don't need to raise taxes higher, we need to manage what we have better. And we need to do more than merely try and limit assessments on some property. When Michigan's property tax bill is almost $7 billion, the people deserve more than a nickel a week in property tax relief—which is all the governor has proposed. We need to cut property taxes substantially for homeowner and business owner alike. And in the next few days, I will be unveiling a comprehensive property tax plan that does just that.

I can do a better job protecting our environment than Jim Blanchard because, unlike the governor, I know that Iowa and Missouri, indeed, no other state in America, is the environmental equal of Michigan. We are special. We are blessed with natural resources unlike any place in the nation, and we must dedicate ourselves to preserving and protecting our water, air, and land with every ounce of determination we have. This is why I will require the DNR to finally set rules that apply fairly to everyone. I support restructuring the DNR into two divisions—one for the environment, and one for game and wildlife conservation. I'll be tougher on those cities, corporations and on our own state government agencies that continue to dump dangerous pollutants into our air and water. And I'll work vigorously to get Michigan out of the low level radioactive waste compact which the governor never should have gotten us into in the first place. With our water, just one look at the map should tell anyone that Michigan or any Great Lakes state should not be a dumpsite for the radioactive waste of six other states.

I can do a better job than Jim Blanchard at waging the war on crime and drugs because I won't stand quietly by, as the governor has done, and let some liberal committee chairman kill vital anti-crime and anti-drug legislation that can help our police and prosecutors put away the punks and pushers who threaten our neighborhoods. I'll work closely with the Bush administration to make certain that any new federal drug money goes directly into the neighborhoods to fight our war against the drug pushers instead of paying for more paper pushers in Lansing. I want our most violent lawbreakers locked up, and kept locked up. But at the same time for those convicted of lesser, nonviolent crimes we need more creative alternative sentencing approaches. And we need to understand that the long-term solution to our crime problem isn't in more jail cells; it's in better classrooms. Because the lower our dropout rates are today, the lower our crime rates will be tomorrow.

I can do a better job than Jim Blanchard at fighting infant mortality, reforming our welfare system, and rebuilding our cities because I will offer more than the status quo and the pursuit of mediocrity. I'll be more than a cheerleader for Michigan. I'll provide strong, hands-on leadership at every level.

As my campaign progresses ... you won't see Mr. Charisma or hear the best speaker—I know that. But when all is said and done, I believe you'll agree that I can provide stronger leadership for our future than Jim Blanchard has given us in the past....

The framers of our state constitution made the governor the most powerful figure in state government.... And I'm ready to lead the way.[196]

*

"Plan the work; work the plan."

Dan Pero ran a smart, disciplined campaign. Among those at the heart of the team—serving as senior campaign staff or close advisers—were Spencer Abraham, Dave Doyle, Andrea Fischer, John Kost, Jeff McAlvey, Richard McLellan, Colleen Pero, LeAnne Redick, Dennis Schornack, Tom Shields, and John Truscott.[197] *Marsha Quebbeman:*

When the election campaign started, we only had a skeleton crew of six people, but we were all dedicated and well organized. "Plan the work; work the plan." John Engler and Dan Pero would repeat that phrase over and over. "This is our plan and we are going to stick to it. We are not going to be thrown off." This commitment—along with their respect for each other—gave us confidence and put us on the right path. We all believed we could win.[198]

[196] *John Engler, "Announcement Speech," final draft, February 12, 1990.*
[197] *Martin et al.,* Journey of John Engler, *pp. 30-31.*
[198] *Marsha Quebbeman, interview with GW, February 23, 2001.*

Original caption reads: "John Engler, center foreground, is surrounded by his campaign 'brain trust,' from left, John Truscott, Tom Shields, LeAnne Redick, Richard McLellan, Colleen Pero, Dan Pero, Dennis Schornack, and Jeff McAlvey." CREDIT: *Audrey Shehyn*, Detroit News

*

Confidence

David Bertram was staff assistant to Majority Leader Engler during the 1990 campaign. He was with him virtually all his waking hours, serving as his driver. David good-naturedly quips that he did not even have time to cash his paycheck and pay his bills back in Lansing!

During the campaign, John Engler was relentless. He worked every waking moment. He typically got only 5 to 6 hours of sleep a night. We always stayed in people's homes as we traveled around the state.

There were times that he was tired. There were times that he got frustrated—usually by a newspaper column or article. But I never saw him get discouraged. He was never down during the campaign. On the contrary, sometimes after bad polling or bad news, I would get down, and he would always say, "Don't worry about it. We're going to win."

John is naturally shy, but once he gets in a campaign mode, he can suppress his natural temperament and become totally outgoing. At every event during the '90 campaign, he would try to connect with every single person in the room. At the last event of the day, he would stay so late that he'd even talk to the janitors and people cleaning the room. I have seen him go to resorts and take the time to go back into the kitchen and talk to the kitchen help. They were amazed that he was willing to do that. Sometimes very humble people would look at him and ask, "Why are you talking to me?"

"Because I want your vote."

I would call back to headquarters and report to Dan Pero how well an event had gone. I almost always had a great report because Engler was so good at clicking with the crowd. He is so good one-on-one. Really that's when he's best. That skill paid off on Election Day.

Usually at the end of every day, John and I would grade the day and each other. Probably half the time we gave ourselves solid A's and B's: when we

Governor Engler and President George H. W. Bush strategize on Air Force I during the 1990 campaign. CREDIT: *White House*

stayed on time, resonated well with a group, got campaign literature into people's hands, hit all the media, those kinds of things. But he's a perfectionist. It was tough getting an A+ out of him, because he always thought there was room for improvement. But I never thought he was overly critical.

President Bush was flying into Selfridge. We had been told by the White House that we couldn't participate in the motorcade. They didn't want it to turn into a political event. That did not sit well with John. He wouldn't take no for an answer. My assignment as his driver was to find a way into the president's motorcade. So we went to Selfridge, and John gave me directions where to maneuver the Astro van so that we would have the best chance to cut into the motorcade. There was a vehicle off to the side that was intent on keeping us out. I was nervous, but John kept assuring me that it would be all right. We were driving along, and he would say, "Keep trying." After three or four blocks, I was able to squeeze the Astro in. The president's secret service didn't like that. We had a secret service vehicle trailing my bumper more closely than any vehicle has ever been. But we got into that motorcade.

When we would head up north in the Astro, or drive across the state, John liked to pick out back routes we could take. He chose some really bad routes that made it hard to maintain his schedule. Once at dusk we were on our way to Ada, and we got onto a gravel road. I was going pretty fast up a hill. When we crested the hill there were a bunch of deer crossing the road, and we hit one of them.

John said, "Oh, Dave, you got a Bambi!"

During the campaign he was courting Michelle. On several occasions he would give me his credit card to order flowers for her down in Houston. He used to call Michelle every chance he got. I could see in the rearview mirror that there was always a smile on his face when he talked to her; the tone of his voice was so different from his political calls. Sometimes at the end of the evening, he would be so exhausted he'd fall to sleep right in the middle of a sentence. A couple of times I had to take the phone from his hand and tell Michelle that he was totally out.

A couple of weeks before the election—I think it was on a Sunday—Michelle came to Michigan to travel around with John. That day we scheduled a day trip to Macomb County. He didn't want the press to know about their relationship. We would park out of the spotlight and wouldn't make a grand entrance. John hoped people would just assume she was part of the press corps. Michelle kept a low profile, and amazingly no one caught on.

In September, we had a meeting with Governor Milliken at his office in Traverse City. The campaign had made several attempts to set up the meeting, and every time it had fallen through. But this time we succeeded, and John wanted Milliken's endorsement. We got into the meeting, and after the small talk, the conversation turned to the race and how well it was going. Milliken seemed very supportive.

Finally John moved in to close the sale: "I would really like your endorsement. It is important to have all the Republicans on board. Your support would mean a lot to me."

Milliken, though, said that his wife Helen had a different view on abortion, and therefore he couldn't endorse John.

John said, "I am not asking for Helen's endorsement. I am asking for yours."[199]

*

John Truscott

At the beginning of the campaign, I was taking the measure of the man, John Engler, and assessing his weaknesses. I knew there was a great deal of potential, but two things worried me. On the image front, he seemed to lack warmth. I could see it traveling with him day-in and day-out. I knew that he had a great sense of humor, that he was always joking and teasing, and that he was extremely bright, but those qualities didn't always come through the media. John would go immediately into work mode, talking to people about the issues right away in a very serious manner. The pictures of John in the newspapers all looked very serious. His brow would be furrowed. The warmth of the man was not evident to the voters. If he were with a group that he knew, like the Farm Bureau or Republicans at a Lincoln Day speech, he would joke and tell funny stories about the people he knew there. But during interviews and other public forums, he didn't come across as warm.

The other thing that worried me in the campaign—and it carried over into the administration—was the idea that policy comes first and communication second. John is always thinking 10 steps ahead as far as policy is concerned, so we are always trying to catch up on the message front. That is part of what got us in trouble early on. John would say, "Ok, this is our policy. I'll announce it tomorrow, but we'll go ahead and implement it today."

Not that I expect communication always to come first but, hey, give me a chance to catch up! Let's think strategically. Let's think through our way of announcing the policy changes, our timing, and the particular points we should cover before any particular group.

Our strategy has been perfected over the years, but in the campaign, and

[199]*David Bertram, interview with GW, July 11, 2002.*

early in the administration, we just didn't have time. John knew what he was going to do, so he just went ahead and did it, whether we liked it or not.

I don't think John recognized the power of the media and all the methods he could have used to harness that power. His expertise is in policy. He has gotten better on the media front, anticipating where attacks will come from. But his expertise is in policy, and his strength is in legislative strategy. So these are what he relied on to win.

Our day would typically start very early. We would hit the road at six in the morning and we would get back home around ten or eleven at night.

First thing John would do is grab a newspaper to read and work the phone. We always had a full day of meetings and interviews scheduled. We would usually visit three to four courthouses a day. We would also stop in to visit the local radio station and newspaper.

We would meet with the county commissioner or the city treasurer on the courthouse steps and walk through all of the offices and meet everyone. We would get some coverage from the small papers because this kind of thing was a big deal for them. We would always listen to the local radio station when we were driving out of town, to see how they played our story. A lot of people told us, "The last governor I remember coming through here was Soapy Williams." It was fun.

I remember one day in the summer of 1989. We were on our way to Oakland County to meet with Neil Munro; this was the same day the *Detroit News* ran a profile of John. We picked up the newspaper. Then John drove and spread the paper across the steering wheel. He was driving and taking sharp curves while reading this article about himself. John would read faster at the stoplights and continuously glance up at the light to see if it had turned.

This was one of the first trips I took with him and I remember thinking, "Oh, no! I am glad to be wearing a seatbelt." I will never forget tooling around downtown Pontiac while John was reading the paper and driving.[200]

*

Dawson Bell

When John was single, he was living the job. I never saw him when he wasn't doing something related to politics or policy.

[200]*John Truscott, interview with GW, October 19, 1999.*

I remember back in 1989. We had been out on the campaign trail and were driving back from Midland. I was sitting in the back seat interviewing him about different topics. The car radio started to crackle and he heard a little blurb about the Detroit mayoral election results coming in. John made Bertram drive down a different road and park the car at a different angle so the radio would get better reception. He was leaning over the seat, attempting to hear the results. That moment crystallized in my mind just how important politics was in John's life. Just how far John was into politics and how much he loved the competition of politics.[201]

*

Rusty Hills

People working with John Engler on his election campaign always believed that he would win. I remember I was driving Spence Abraham, and during our conversation I said something like, "If John Engler wins...." Spence looked at me and said, "WHEN John Engler wins." From that time on, I always talked about the election in terms of "when" not "if."

We knew winning would be extremely difficult because Blanchard was leading in the polls. But Blanchard was running a terrible campaign in the 1990 election, and we were finding ways to exploit that.

In the fall of 1990, the Detroit Tigers had a player named Cecil Fielder, who was chasing 50 home runs, which today sounds quaint, but at that time it was a big deal. Only a handful of people in Major League Baseball history had hit over 50 home runs in a season. Then on the very last day he hit two home runs, and ended up with 51, and the headline of the paper said, "He Did It!" Jerry Crandall, from the governor's Senate staff, got the paper and he had all the staffers sign it and they gave it to Engler. This was our way of saying, if Cecil could do it, so could we.[202]

*

Marsha Quebbeman

Many people did not believe that John Engler would win the election. The talk around the Capitol was, "You'd better start looking for another job. He's not going to win."

But I never considered sending out my resume. I believed that if anybody

[201]*Dawson Bell, interview with GW, February 27, 2001.*
[202]*Rusty Hills, interview with GW, February 12, 2001.*

had a chance, Engler did. He inspired that belief in me. I saw that he was hungry for it. He worked hard to become the governor; he put his all into that campaign. He wanted it so badly that I felt the same way. I felt that John Engler deserved to win the election.[203]

*

Jim Brandell

I definitely had my doubts that John would win the election for governor in 1990. But I can honestly say that he always projected confidence, always projected the feeling that he was going to win. We never let up. Even in the darkest days of September when we were being pummeled, the attitude in the office was never one of defeat. The camaraderie was excellent. It was one of those experiences that I will always look back on: everyone was working in sync to get the job done. Everyone had a common goal, and everyone knew we were doing the best we could.

John was great to work with; he was always informal. He would call a lot from the road. He wasn't in the campaign office a lot, because we kept him on the road. He was always cordial, professional, and focused. When he called he would always ask how you were doing; he was interested in who you were and what was going on with you. So it was always great when he called. It was a pick-me-up in the office.[204]

*

Selecting a running mate

Connie Binsfeld

John and I had both served in the House and Senate, and he knew I had a background in legislation. I could sit down with him and I knew exactly where he was coming from when he wanted to make changes. He had a strong desire to change things, and he realized he needed to have people on his side so that the dream would become reality. When he would get really upset about things he would tell me, because he knew I was a good listener, and he was a good teacher. He could have easily overlooked me, primarily because of the difference in our ages, but he didn't, and I am still grateful for it.

In the 1970s we had such a small minority, the smallest the Republicans had ever had. The Democrats were passing campaign reform acts, and it was just killing us.

[203] *Marsha Quebbeman, interview with GW, February 23, 2001.*
[204] *Jim Brandell, interview with GW, February 16, 2001.*

We couldn't even get an amendment on a bill. To make matters worse we were having late night sessions because the Democrat-controlled schedule was terrible.

What I really liked about John was that, when we would break for dinner, he would come over to me and say, "We are going out for a hamburger. Why don't you join us?" He took me under his wing when he didn't have to. I was much older than he was, old enough to be his mom! So I benefited greatly from our conversations through the years.

John and I kept in touch throughout his campaign for governor. After he won the primary he began asking my advice. He would call and ask, "What do you think about so and so for state board of education?" or, "What do you think about so and so for attorney general?"

Just before the convention when he would announce who would be on the ballot with him, he called me and said he wanted to talk about who he should choose for lieutenant governor. I told him that he needed someone who was compatible with him. I also said, "You and Blanchard are both young, it wouldn't hurt to have a little gray hair on the ticket."

"It wouldn't hurt to have a woman on the ticket either," he replied, and I agreed. After a silence in the conversation he said, "You have just written your job description."

I took some time to discuss it with my husband and decided to run for lieutenant governor with John.

During the week of the convention John called and asked me to come to Lansing. He told me not to tell anyone that I was coming. I went to Dan and Colleen Pero's house. They had given me directions and instructed me to put my car in the garage. Shortly after I arrived, Dan and Colleen came home with John and other people involved in the campaign. The press had followed them. As it started to get dark, we drew the curtains because some of the media could detect the cars outside, but none of the media had seen me arrive.

The next day the Republicans were informed that John was going to make an announcement at the State Party headquarters followed by a general announcement at the Capitol. After John told the people at headquarters, I went out the back door and arrived at the Capitol ahead of the press. Even my staff didn't know that I was going to run, so I invited them to the press conference. Imagine their surprise when they found out that I was going to be John's running mate![205]

*

[205] *Connie Binsfeld, interview with GW, January 23, 2001.*

Jeff McAlvey

In 1987, Engler worked to get Dick Posthumus into Connie's chair as assistant majority leader. He removed Connie because he wanted Dick to have that spot. This was to prepare the heir apparent. I am not sure he told her ahead of time what he was going to do.

They went into caucus. Dick clearly had the votes lined up. The vote was taken, and Connie went ballistic. She was very angry because she was being removed from this ceremonial spot. But Engler's vision was to move it from being ceremonial to being something real, and he wanted Dick to be the assistant.

There was not a person who was aware of the incident who would have believed in any way, shape, or form that Connie could be his running mate three years later. She was that angry.

I remember the next morning. I saw him coming up the main stairway to go to Connie's office. He was carrying a dozen roses and said in a low voice, "I'm going to see Connie." It took him awhile to build that relationship back up and to rebuild that trust.[206]

*

Dan and Colleen Pero

One of the best things in the campaign was picking Connie Binsfeld—it was a very bold pick. Not only was she a good running mate, but picking her also forced Blanchard to select a woman. So he had to pick someone he didn't really want to pick. He chose Libby Maynard who was not the best possible choice. She just didn't have the qualifications that Connie had. Connie helped moderate John in many circles. She added substance, and brought energy to the ticket.

When we were prepping Connie for the announcement that she would be the lieutenant governor, we conducted the entire event with absolute secrecy, starting at our house. We had her park her car in the garage so that no one could run the license plates and find out who was at the meeting. The next morning, as Connie slept in our guest bedroom, we were walking the dog and noticed a strange car parked just off our driveway, with a small pile of peanut shells and cigarette butts on the ground near the window. It was Roger Martin, the only reporter enterprising enough to do a complete stakeout. He told us

[206]*Jeff McAlvey, interview with GW, May 29, 2002.*

that he actually got out of the car and wandered around the grounds, then ran all of the license plates to see if there was anyone there that was unexpected. He said that he hadn't checked the garage, which was a good thing, because we had left it cracked just a bit.[207]

*

Money

Andrea Fischer Newman

When John told me he was going to run for governor, my advice was, "Don't do it. You can't beat Jim Blanchard. Run against [U.S. Senator] Carl Levin."

He just looked at me and said, "I'm running for governor."

There would be no stopping him. I looked around at the small campaign team and remember thinking, "How are these people going to do it?" I'll admit, I never thought he would win. On the other hand, I'd never met anyone more determined. John made me understand what it means to have fire in the belly.

I agreed to help out on the campaign. I was brought on board in August 1989 because I was the "money person"—I had connections in southeast Michigan with lots of potential donors. I would set up his appointments to meet with donors; sometimes I would go with him; sometimes he would go on his own.

John was a seven-day-a-week workaholic. He would leave his condo in East Lansing at 6:30 in the morning. He would call me to discuss the donors he would be seeing that day. I would give him my insights into the individuals he would be meeting, the issues that concerned them, useful background information, that sort of thing.

Sometimes during these phone calls I used to worry about him because while he was driving he would eat, talk on the phone, and even read the newspapers. And he drove so fast. He got so many tickets that Dan Pero eventually had to get him a driver [David Bertram].

John would rather talk about ideas and policies than money. I remember one time when John and I met with Jim Nicholson at his office in Detroit. We sat down and talked two hours about policy. It was a great conversation, but there was not a word about fundraising. After two hours of this, John excused himself to use the restroom.

[207]*Dan Pero and Colleen Pero, interview with GW, December 2, 2000.*

I said, "Jim, the reason we are here is to ask you for money." Jim was fine with that. He took out his checkbook and wrote out a check. The candidate came back into the room, and they resumed their conversation as if our meeting had nothing to do with fundraising.

John always wanted to connect with people over policy. Sometimes this led to funny incidents. We went to Grand Rapids to meet with the then-CEO of Steelcase. Once we got into his office, John decided to start talking about the importance of higher education. Higher ed was the key to a better economic climate and to business growth. It was higher ed this; higher ed that; here's my agenda for higher ed.

After this went on a while, the CEO looked at John and said, "I didn't go to college."

We're thinking: "Oo-kay, next topic!"[208]

*

Detroit and "that white bitch"

Susy Avery, a friend and political ally of Engler's, offers her unique perspective from Wayne County.

John was a fearless campaigner. Let me tell you why. Since I was the only elected Republican in Wayne County, it was my job to handle GOP events there. Coleman Young, Detroit's mayor, used to call me "that white bitch." We would always have a hard time getting Republicans to come to Detroit. It's so hardcore Democratic, and there was always a fear that you would get shot.

One time Dan Pero called me and said, "You have to set up a dinner with Coleman Young and John Engler."

So I had to call the mansion and say, "Mayor, could you meet with a friend of mine?"

Although we often had problems getting Republicans to go to African-American communities and events, Engler *never* hesitated. He reached out to the community, and they really appreciated it.[209]

*

Diversion: the AG race in 1990

Cliff Taylor, attorney, Court of Appeals judge, Supreme Court justice, and Engler

[208] *Andrea Fischer Newman, interview with GW, August 3, 2002.*
[209] *Susy Avery, interview with GW, December 2, 2000.*

loyalist, tells of a humorous interlude.

John needed somebody to run for attorney general in 1990. We were all sitting around chatting and John said, "I want to make it known that in this room tonight is the candidate for attorney general." Everyone in the room started laughing and diving under chairs to keep from being the Anointed One. It was well known that this was nothing more than a farce. Frank Kelley had held the office for twenty-seven years, and he was an extremely popular incumbent. That's why he was called "the Eternal General."

I said to John, "I guess I'll do it." So I spent $800 on the whole campaign and never took a penny from the state party. I drove around the state going to different newspaper editorial boards and, amusingly enough, five or six newspapers endorsed me.

We had a debate and I kicked it off by saying, "Frank Kelley has held office longer than anybody but the Queen and Fidel Castro, so it's time for him to go." This set the tone and the result was quite a frisky campaign.[210]

*

Taking the measure of the opponent

Lucille Taylor

Engler wanted *to do*. Blanchard wanted *to be*. Engler ran for governor because that was where he could best undertake reform. Blanchard ran for governor because it was where he could best round out his resume.[211]

*

Art Miller

In all the years that Blanchard was governor, I never saw him in the Senate chamber—not one time. By contrast, Engler knew everybody and understood how the legislature works.[212]

*

Anne Mervenne

I would have hated to be Jim Blanchard in the 1980s because John Engler was running rings around him. Blanchard was from Washington and didn't understand Lansing and he didn't care about the mechanics of how to get things

[210]*Cliff Taylor, interview with GW, June 16, 2000.*
[211]*Lucille Taylor, interview with GW, June 28, 2002.*
[212]*Art Miller, interview with GW, September 25, 2002.*

done. John Engler was always outmaneuvering him. He was just smarter.[213]

*

Colleen Pero

We were at a {Republican} Lincoln Day dinner, and we heard that there was a {Democratic} Jefferson-Jackson dinner in the area as well. They had invited Jim Blanchard, but apparently he had not responded. So John told the people at the Lincoln Day dinner, "We're going to leave now because we hear that there is another event tonight that we can hit." So we drove over to the Jeff-Jack event. We walked in and got a standing ovation—from the Democrats! They were just pleased somebody showed.[214]

*

Democratic leaders' perspective as the election drew near

Lew Dodak was Democratic speaker of the Michigan House from 1989 through 1992.

The toughest thing for me as Democratic speaker was to try to keep the Democratic members of the House from beating up on Governor Blanchard. I remember shortly before the election. I was having cocktails here in town, and a couple of Democrats told me they were not going to vote for Blanchard. I was surprised. It was a sign that things would not go well for Blanchard.

On election night, when the race was too close to call, a prominent Democrat came to me and said he hoped Blanchard would lose. I thought, "These guys should be the core supporters, but they are not." They did not think Blanchard had treated the legislature well. They decided to take it out on him in the voting booth.[215]

*

John Truscott recalls Art Miller's words. The prominent Democrat had been the minority leader in the Senate since 1985:

You can't underestimate the impact of our campaign song, "Just Think What John Engler Can Do." The lyrics were great. I remember when Senator Art Miller came and told us that he knew the election was over when he heard his daughter singing, "Just Think What John Engler Can Do."[216]

[213] *Anne Mervenne, interview with GW, February 1, 2001.*
[214] *Colleen Pero, interview with GW, December 2, 2000.*
[215] *Lew Dodak, interview with GW, July 10, 2002.*
[216] *John Truscott, interview with GW, December 2, 2000.*

*

David Hollister

I wrote a letter to Blanchard before he lost the election in 1991 and tried to open his eyes to the dismal situation within the party. We had no anchor. I told him that activists in the party were going to abandon him because he gave them no reason to go out and work the extra hours to do the phoning and knocking on doors. The party had lost its soul.

We hired a pollster for the Democratic Party. He was also polling for Democrats nationally. He told us, "Blanchard's support is a mile wide and an inch thick. Run on your own; don't run with Blanchard." Blanchard couldn't articulate his vision because he didn't have a vision. We were dead meat.[217]

*

The nickel

Effective political campaigning relies on symbols that capture the public's imagination. The Engler campaign found a powerful symbol in the nickel. John Truscott:

We needed to focus our message. We struggled for a while. We knew we were for tax cuts and smaller government, but we never really connected it all until John Kost ran the numbers on the Blanchard tax cut. Kost came up with the fact that it only amounted to a nickel a week. We noted it in a couple of speeches but didn't distill the message into something people could relate to.

Then the idea occurred to me—John thought it was stupid—that we should go out and get $500 in nickels and put them in the trunk of his car and hand them out everywhere we went. All he said was, "That's silly."

Starting in October we carried around ten huge jars of nickels in the campaign van. I remember standing in front of the Oakland County building handing out nickels to everyone who walked by. We told them, "That is what Blanchard has promised to give you—a nickel—but we'll give you more." That kind of campaigning had a great effect. We also put commercials on the air making fun of Blanchard's nickel-a-week promise.

It really caught on and the nickel became our mantra in the campaign.

You can't underestimate the impact the nickel had. People were fed up with property taxes skyrocketing out of control, and Blanchard's tax cut was paltry. In the first debate against Blanchard we all wore lapel pins with nickels on

[217]*David Hollister, interview with GW, March 29, 2001.*

them. It really rattled Blanchard's people and they got angry with us. We knew that we were on to something when they became so upset.

Our campaign was also effective in portraying Blanchard as the Imperial Governor. At that time Blanchard was using the helicopter frequently to fly around the state. We told the voters that we weren't going to fly everywhere; John was going to drive his Oldsmobile. It wasn't even a policy issue; it was an image issue. We used the helicopter to tag Blanchard as the Imperial Governor. We said, "He doesn't understand your problems. He's not driving on these roads. He's not making the sacrifices that you are." I think it drove home the message that Blanchard was not one of us. On the other hand, John was a farm boy from Beal City—one of us.

Blanchard countered our campaign by using negative advertising. He told the voters, "John Engler is going to destroy your schools." The ads painted John as a nasty person. We turned that around by using Agnes Engler, John's mother, in our advertisements. The message was, "If half of what Blanchard said was true, my own mother wouldn't vote for me." In the ad, John was smiling with his mother, and I think that was the first time people had seen him smile. After that ad our numbers really started to turn around. I think that put us over the top.[218]

*

Traverse City debate

Jim Brandell

The one thing during the campaign that demonstrated to me that this man could be governor was at the Grand Traverse Resort during the 1990 Traverse City debate. We had been pummeled all through September, and all of us realized that if we were going to win this election we had to make our move now.

If you ever watch the debate, you'll notice that for the longest time John Engler is just standing there waiting. Jim Blanchard came out late, and when he came out he seemed rushed, while on the opposite end was John Engler, ready, relaxed, composed, and prepared.

Maybe Blanchard looked so bad because Dan Pero had placed nickels all around his dressing area to psych him out. All through the debate he seemed a bit shaken, and we wondered if he was rattled by all those nickels. We like to think he was.[219]

[218]*John Truscott, interview with GW, October 19, 1999, and December 2, 2000.*
[219]*Jim Brandell, interview with GW, February 16, 2001.*

*

October: getting kicked in the teeth

John Truscott

I don't think John ever showed that he had doubts about winning the election. He may have felt it deep down, but he was too smart to show it. I think a lot of people did start having their doubts in October because we weren't on the air and Blanchard was. They were really kicking us in the teeth, but we didn't have the money to counter on the air.

Our internal polling numbers were really bad in October. Dan Pero had to give a pep talk to the staff. He said, "We are going to keep working the plan. We are going to do our best. We are not going to let any stone go unturned."

John just kept working hard. He would not let any person go by without walking up to them, introducing himself, and talking to them. He was the most tireless campaigner I have ever seen.[220]

*

Andrea Fischer Newman

Toward the end of the campaign, there were two ads that had a powerful effect on voters: the ad with his mother and the ad with the nickel. Those ads, I think, helped turn the tide.[221]

*

Ronald Reagan for John Engler

One bright spot in late October occurred when former President Reagan came to Michigan to stump for Engler and other Republicans. Excerpts from Reagan's speech follow:

Coming to Michigan carries with it memories of 1980. Republicans from all across America gathered in Detroit that summer for our national convention. It was ten years ago that you nominated me and George Bush as your ticket. Only a decade ago. My, how things have changed.

Ten years ago interest rates were above 20 percent. Inflation was double-digit, and unemployment was rising. Taxes and spending were out of control. And the government was blaming the people for malaise. Sounds a lot like Michigan today, doesn't it?

Well believe me, I know about governors with initials JB. Or had you forgotten Jerry Brown? They called him Governor Moonbeam.

[220] *John Truscott, interview with GW, October 19, 1999.*
[221] *Andrea Fischer Newman, interview with GW, August 3, 2002.*

Well, you've got one in Jim Blanchard. Under Jim Blanchard's liberal tax and spend policies, Michigan's property taxes have risen 47 percent. State spending has increased too much. A higher percentage of Michigan citizens are on welfare than in any other state. And Michigan's unemployment is the highest of all the industrial states in the nation.

Are you sure Jimmy Carter isn't in charge of this state?

There was a line I used during the 1980 campaign that can be updated here tonight: A recession is when your neighbor loses his job. Depression is when you lose yours. Recovery is when Jim Blanchard loses his....

President Reagan campaigning for candidate Engler, October 1990. SOURCE: *John Engler*

There's another major battleground shaping up in Michigan this year: the Michigan Senate. Republicans control the state Senate by a 20-18 margin.... Under John Engler's leadership, the Republican Senate rolled back Jim Blanchard's 38 percent income tax hike. The Senate cut the state's inheritance tax and reformed the Single Business Tax, so small companies would no longer have to pay taxes when they made no profits. With John Engler's leadership, the Michigan Senate passed a property tax relief bill that will cut your property taxes 20 percent, cap assessments, double the Homestead tax credit, and exempt senior citizens from paying school property taxes.

Gee, maybe I should move to Michigan.

The Senate has also taken the lead in passing polluters' pay legislation, so that those responsible for pollution pick up the tab, instead of the taxpayer. The Republican Senate has provided more money for education, and passed comprehensive quality reform legislation establishing a core curriculum, parental choice and accountability in schools. And the Senate Republican majority has also pushed through a package of tough anti-crime legislation that gives police and prosecutors the tools they need to crack down on criminals....

Michigan is one of our nation's greatest states. Throughout America's history,

Michigan has been an engine of growth, innovation, ideas and development. Michigan put America on wheels at the turn of this century. (I remember it well.) During the terrible crisis of World War II, when the fate of freedom hung in the balance, Michigan was the arsenal of democracy.

Michigan again stands at the brink of a momentous time. Because, ladies and gentlemen, the decisions you make at the polls this November will determine the type of state Michigan is entering the 21st century.[222]

*

1990 Endorsements

Dan Pero

Not many groups endorsed us. We got the Farm Bureau and Right to Life, which made almost half a million phone calls in the last days of the campaign. We also got the endorsement of Martha Griffiths, Tom Washington, and Blanchard's Ag director. Blanchard got everything else.[223]

*

Dennis Cawthorne

Not a lot of Republicans in this town [Lansing] supported John. The Sunday before the election there were full-page ads in the major newspapers: "Businessmen for Blanchard." You knew most of these people were Republicans.

Plus, George Bush had just concluded a terrible budget deal with Congress, agreeing to raise taxes. Many of us thought that would hurt Republican candidates around the country.

1990 was not a good year. John faced an extremely uphill battle.[224]

*

The Detroit Free Press *endorsed Blanchard.*

BLANCHARD AND LEVIN REMAIN THE TOP PICKS

A new *Free Press* poll suggests that the contest for governor of Michigan is tightening up. We'd be happy to see Republican nominee John Engler make a real race of Tuesday's election because incumbent Democrat James Blanchard deserves a serious challenge. At the same time though, we believe that James Blanchard remains overall the better of the two candidates.

[222]*Ronald Reagan, "Campaign Speech to the Michigan GOP," Dearborn, October 23, 1990.*
[223]*Dan Pero, interview with GW, December 2, 2001.*
[224]*Dennis Cawthorne, interview with GW, September 25, 2002.*

Although Mr. Blanchard's record of fiscal management during his second term generally has been sound and innovative, he has refused to provide appropriate leadership on a number of critical state issues....

Yet Sen. Engler's 20-year tenure in the legislature offers little reason to believe he represents a better alternative. We fear an Engler administration would be oriented toward unjustifiably expensive tax cuts and business deregulation at the expense of social and environmental initiatives.[225]

*

The Detroit News *endorsed John Engler.*

THE STAKES FOR MICHIGAN

Gov. James Blanchard has been engaged in a consistent denial of the state's fiscal and economic problems. And he has taken to responding to questions and challenges to his programs as attacks on the state and its people—confusing himself with the state.

Mr. Blanchard vows that he will make the tough choices to keep the state budget balanced, but the last time he was faced with severe economic problems, he raised taxes by $2 billion.

And the fundamental trade-off in state spending, education vs. welfare, remains untouched. Throughout seven years of economic prosperity, the crushing burden of local property taxes went unaddressed and the state's huge welfare complex remained intact. The governor has basically avoided making any real or hard choices at all. Challenger John Engler should be given a chance to make some of those choices. As the economy becomes tighter, the last thing Michigan needs is to become more economically uncompetitive through higher taxes.[226]

*

Inevitable defeat?

Just 48 hours before the polls opened, the following headline appeared in the Detroit News *and* Free Press. *Engler urged his exhausted staff not to pay attention to polls. This front-page article was saved, framed, and hung in Engler's communication office for the next 12 years—a perpetual reminder to staff not to put stock in opinion polls.*

BLANCHARD WELL AHEAD 54% TO 40%

[225]*"Election Day: Blanchard and Levin Remain the Top Choices," editorial,* Detroit Free Press, *November 4, 1990.*

[226]*"The Stakes for Michigan," editorial,* Detroit News, *November 4, 1990.*

Gov. James J. Blanchard's lead over Republican challenger Sen. John Engler has narrowed, but is still a comfortable 14 points two days before Election Day, according to a *Detroit News* poll.

Michigan residents who said they are certain or very likely to vote Tuesday now favor Blanchard over Engler by a margin of 54 to 40, with 6 percent undecided, the poll shows. A month ago, a similar poll had Blanchard ahead by 26 points.

Experts said the survey, conducted Thursday through Saturday, indicates Blanchard is poised to win a third term, barring defections to Engler or a dismal voter turnout in areas of Democratic strength.

"By every historical criterion ... a 14-point lead is very strong for Blanchard at this point in an election," said Tony Casale of the Gannet Corporate Research Department, which designed and analyzed the *News* poll.[227]

*

Final campaign hours

Cliff Taylor

We had a wonderful last day of the campaign. John and his driver [David Bertram] came by at six in the morning and picked me up and we drove to Grand Rapids. When we arrived, there were high school bands out to greet us, and they were going wild. We then drove back to Lansing to my law firm on Seymour Street. Then we went to the campaign headquarters in Mount Pleasant. But because we had press guys in the car, we had to behave and shut up! We spent the day talking about the Detroit Lions and how they could not find a punter. When we were campaigning in Mount Pleasant, we did a drop-by—John loves to do these kinds of things. We stopped at this little restaurant and it was full of blue-collar guys. We went in and I could not believe it: John knew about 90 percent of the people in the restaurant. It was amazing. This was the day that I finally came to the conclusion that he was really going to win. It was a rollicking fun time.[228]

*

John Truscott

It was the night before the election and we were in Mount Pleasant. John had just given his last interview with a local radio station and we were in a back

[227]*Roger Martin, Mark Hornbeck and Yolanda Woodlee, "Blanchard Well Ahead 54% to 40%,"* Detroit News and Free Press, *November 4, 1990.*
[228]*Cliff Taylor, interview with GW, June 16, 2000.*

office of the Isabella County Republican Party, away from everyone, seeking someplace quiet to unwind. We had been through a lot together. Then John did something memorable: he placed his hand on my shoulder and remarked, "Well, this is it. Tomorrow we'll know if I won. It's been a heck of a ride."

John always felt that he would win the election but at that point, the night before, I was pretty emotional. My eyes filled up with tears because there was just nothing more that we could do. We had campaigned our butts off and were at the end of the line. That moment was a very personal one because John is not very demonstrative; he doesn't show a lot of emotion.

I guess that was the most emotional that I had seen him. There were some other times around the debates that were fairly emotional because everyone had been through a lot and was exhausted. John is the type of person that expects a lot from his staff and drives us very, very hard. He hires good people and expects them to perform. John gives his staff a lot of autonomy to do what needs to be done and that policy breeds an extreme amount of loyalty. But there aren't a lot of thanks coming in return. So the gesture that John made was his way of saying how much he appreciated the work. What I felt that night was the most unbelievable roller-coaster of emotion you could ever be on.[229]

[229]*John Truscott, interview with GW, October 19, 1999.*

An election is a bet on the future,
not a popularity contest of the past.
JAMES RESTON

★

Chapter Eight
Election Day: 1990

Everybody associated with the Engler campaign has a vivid story to tell about Election Day 1990. John Truscott:

On the morning of Election Day, John wore a suit and tie, and I drove with him to the small township hall where he was registered to vote. There were a few reporters from the local stations there. He ran in quickly to vote, came back out, and talked briefly with journalists. When he got back in the van he said, "Well, that's it."

At that point there was not a lot he could do. When we got back to Lansing, we were just in time to hit the breakfast crowd at a local restaurant. We had let the media know that John was going to be there. Surprisingly, several of the Lansing media showed up. I had started to notice when we were on our statewide tour a couple days earlier that people's moods were changing about John. You could feel it all around the state. That morning in the diner, people were coming forward, saying, "Hey, I voted for you."

Here in Michigan I think that we were on the leading edge of the anti-incumbency mood that was beginning to sweep the country. People here sensed that it was time for a change. They were tired of the Imperial Governor. We always said that Blanchard's support was a mile wide but only an inch deep. Besides, Blanchard wasn't out there campaigning from morning until night, seven days a week, as we were. We fought like cats and dogs for this election. From our contact with voters, we sensed we could win.[230]

[230]*John Truscott, interview with GW, October 19, 1999.*

*

Jim Brandell

The staff was optimistic, even in those dark days of September when it seemed as if all hope were lost. Although we were never defeatist, we had our doubts. At one point John took his staff aside and said, "We're going to win this thing together, but I need you guys. Don't go out and talk about us not having a chance."

Dan Pero tried to get us psyched up on the big day, Election Day. That afternoon we all gathered in his office—the six or seven of us on John Engler's core staff—and we watched *Rocky I*. Engler had the *Rocky* theme played when he walked into the state convention at Cobo Hall two months earlier. It really set the mood for what was about to happen that day.

Rocky was such a fitting movie for us. We were *Rocky*, the underdog, getting pummeled. Then on Election Day we shocked everyone by winning. We proved to ourselves that with hard work and determination we too could face adversity and come out victorious.[231]

*

Dennis Cawthorne

When I found out the race was close and John had a chance to win, I told people in the campaign, "Whatever you do, secure the ballot boxes in Detroit!" I had visions of the election being stolen.[232]

*

John Kost

The whole Election Day was so emotional for all of the people involved in Engler's campaign. The most memorable moment for me happened at 4:00 in the afternoon. Our group was driving around Saginaw at that time. We called LeAnne Redick to get the lastest news, and she told us that CBS had us ahead in their exit poll. The news made my heart feel—it's indescribable. I was thinking, "Wow! Unbelievable! Just a few days ago we were 14 points behind."

It became even more overwhelming, when in the early morning hours of the next day Spence Abraham burst opened the door of the War Room and said, "We won!" Some people never actually heard him say it, but the announcement traveled in an instant, a nanosecond. It was just an unbelievable emotion for

[231] *Jim Brandell, interview with GW, February 16, 2001.*
[232] *Dennis Cawthorne, interview with GW, September 25, 2002.*

everyone present. I was standing next to Denise Hogan and we grabbed each other and held each other for about five minutes while we cried our eyes out. We were all so exhausted. Our defenses were down. It was a Niagara Falls of emotion.[233]

*

David Bertram

On Election Day we were excited, full of anticipation. We scheduled a light day, just four or five stops at polling places and phone banks. John knew he had done everything that he possibly could have. He was comfortable. He expected to win.

When we pulled up to the Radisson Hotel about 5:30 that evening, he didn't get right out of the car. We talked for a few minutes, reviewing the past 18 months on the campaign trail. He was upbeat. He put his hand on my shoulder and thanked me for all my efforts. I felt a lot of different emotions at that point. I was proud of what we had done, and relieved that the campaign was at an end, and still anxious about the outcome of the election.

No one keeps a secret like John Engler. When he found out he had won, very early Wednesday morning, and was coming down the elevator to rejoin his campaign supporters and field questions from the media, my future wife, Jennifer, happened to get on the elevator with him. But he never said a word to her about the outcome of the election. She didn't know he'd won until they got to the ground floor and she saw the crowd.[234]

*

Rusty Hills

I remember a couple of things about Election Day. I was communications director for State Party, and I had friends in the press corps. I kept calling them to get information, and they were telling us the race was tight.

At some point Dave Doyle called a staff meeting for all of the Michigan Republicans and said, "Listen, this race is tight. We've got to win this thing. I want everyone to get their Christmas card list and Rolodex and start calling people. Call your mom, your dad, your sister, your brother, your relatives—call everybody you know and tell them to get out and vote!"

[233]*John Kost, interview with GW, February 20, 2001.*
[234]*David Bertram, interview with GW, July 11, 2002.*

Everyone ran back to their offices and started to flip through their Rolodexes to call and say, "We can win! Get out and vote!"

It paid off. Later we were holding a lead of a few thousand votes throughout the early morning hours. But at some point, things went south. The numbers flew by and we dropped from a 5,000-vote lead to a 2,500-vote lead.

There were only a few precincts left to be counted, mostly in Wayne County. I was thinking, "Wayne County is going to skew this so much. I can't believe we are so close and we are going to lose this thing now." I just felt that there was no way we would win with precincts in Wayne County still being unaccounted for.

At four in the morning someone walked up to Spence and handed him a slip of paper. Spence looked at it, then looked up at Dave and said, "I think we've won." Richard Czuba overheard that, started screaming, and leapt right into Ronna Romney's arms. At that point everybody started screaming and yelling. It was all pandemonium and euphoria.

I was busy handling the press, although at this point most of them had dispersed. There were a handful of reporters still in the ballroom at the Radisson. The din was so loud that the press down in the ballroom heard the pandemo-

Original caption reads: "Election night [1990], John Engler with Connie Binsfeld are obviously enjoying the moment." CREDIT: *Audrey Shehyn,* Detroit News

nium. They came running down the hallway and flipped on their cameras and stuck their microphones in our faces. We were jumping up and down screaming, "We won, we won, we won!" Tears were pouring down our cheeks. There were only about 20-25 of us in the ballroom.

Where was John? He had gone to bed.

Dave grabbed [Mark] Pischea and me and said, "Listen, I want you to take an adding machine to these numbers. Go in a room, lock yourself in, and add the numbers up again." Spence had been adding the numbers in his head, so we did not have the results down on paper. We still had one or two precincts out, but Spence had figured out that we had enough of a lead that another precinct or two wouldn't take it away. So, Pischea went into the next room and sat there with an adding machine adding up the numbers. He came back and told Dave, "I just did it again and we're behind."

Dave said, "Don't tell anybody. Go add it up again."

While Pischea added the numbers again, Dave and Spence were pacing like nervous housecats. At this point Colleen was on her way up to get John.

We went through the numbers again, and the second time we were back in the lead.

When John came down he did a very joyous press conference in the wee hours of the morning. There were no more than forty people there at the time, twenty or so of us and maybe twelve members of the press. There were a handful of Capitol reporters. Most of the Detroit media outlets had camera crews in attendance and the AP was there. It was an overpowering moment.

After John spoke, Tom Brennan Jr. and I went to 6:30 Mass at St. Mary Cathedral. We ran into a friend and he asked, "What happened?"

And I said, "We won!"

But the public did not yet know. The newspapers would run three different headlines that day. The first *Lansing State Journal* headline said, in effect, "Blanchard on the Way to Win." There were 10,000 or so *Lansing State Journals* that went out with that headline on it. They figured Blanchard would win, and they would set the stride. Other headlines read, "Too close to call." Finally, when the last editions of the day were printed, the headline said, "Engler on top."[235]

*

[235]*Rusty Hills, interview with GW, February 12, 2001.*

Paul Hillegonds

It was about 5:00 Wednesday morning—still dark outside—when I heard the good news. I was in my Capitol office tracking election results. I called home and told Nancy, "I think we are going to win the governor's race!"

Nancy said, "We are in for a great adventure as a state because John Engler is one of the few politicians who doesn't have to be liked."[236]

*

Gary Wolfram

There were many people sitting around in Dick Posthumus's office in the Capitol and monitoring what was going on throughout the whole election night. John Engler and Connie Binsfeld came in early that morning and announced that we won. Everybody was excited. One prominent reporter seemed confused. He kept asking, "What does this mean?" He just couldn't find it in himself to believe the numbers.[237]

*

David Hollister

When I found out Engler won, my sense was that we blew it. Not so much: he won. But: we blew it. And it wasn't just Blanchard who blew it; it was a lot of people. We can't blame anybody else but ourselves.

We didn't stand for anything. Engler stood for something. You might not like him, but he is clear and he is coming to make real change. You'd better not think he is kidding because he is coming straight at you.[238]

*

Betsy DeVos, a prominent Michigan business leader and Republican activist, recalls:

I crossed paths with John a number of times during the 1980s, especially during the 1988 presidential campaign. When John announced that he was running for governor, we became more acquainted with each other. It became clear to me that John had set out a personal course to pursue and had begun to execute it long before any of us understood what his long-term goals were. He is a planner—he's very strategic in the way that he does things. John's persistence, discipline, focus, and acknowledgment that he was an underdog helped him

[236] *Paul Hillegonds, interview with GW, September 27, 2002.*
[237] *Gary Wolfram, interview with GW, February 13, 2001.*
[238] *David Hollister, interview with GW, March 29, 2001.*

win the governor's race. Had John not been as focused or as persevering, he would have missed the window of opportunity that had opened to him. He also had an outstanding staff; the work they did to get him elected was brilliant.

When John was seeking the nomination for governor, a lot of people thought there was no way he could win. Blanchard seemed invulnerable at that point. Most people were saying, "He has got to be nuts to give up being Senate majority leader to seek the governor's office." I must admit, I had serious reservations.

In typical John Engler fashion, however, he disregarded the naysayers. He thought he could win, and his optimism was contagious. During the final days of the campaign, I had this little seed of confidence that started to grow. I, too, became confident that John could win. Even on election night, when the pundits were calling it for Blanchard at two in the morning, I still believed he could pull it out. I was not surprised the next morning when I found out that he had won.[239]

*

1990 election

Tuesday, November 6, 1990, was mostly cloudy around Michigan. A light snowfall fell in parts of the state, especially toward evening. But by Wednesday dawn it was clear that Senate Majority Leader John Engler had upset incumbent James Blanchard. The final count would show Engler winning by 17,595 votes. But it took awhile for the newspapers to sift through incoming numbers. The following headlines from Wednesday, November 7, show the drama of the day. These headlines were framed, and they hung for 12 years in Governor Engler's Communication Division.

ENGLER, BLANCHARD IN DEAD HEAT

ANALYSTS POINT TO LOW TURNOUT IN DETROIT

The race for governor, a nasty contest all along, tumbled into Wednesday like a barroom brawl—a dead heat between Gov. James Blanchard and Republican challenger John Engler....

With 82 percent of all precincts reporting, Blanchard had 1,048,986 votes to Engler's 1,036,989—a margin of about 0.6 percent.

Blanchard apparently was hurt by low voter turnout in heavily Democratic Detroit, where less than 30 percent of the voters had turned out just before the polls closed.

[239]*Betsy DeVos, interview with GW, July 31, 2002.*

Late Tuesday night, Engler acted like a winner as he spoke to cheering supporters at Lansing's Radisson Hotel.

"This is a win for taxpayers and the families of Michigan," he said, and the numbers mean that voters want better schools and "more than a nickel a week in property tax relief."[240]

*

UPSET! ENGLER!
CLIFFHANGER:
GOP CHALLENGER BEATS BLANCHARD BY NARROW MARGIN

Republican challenger John Engler upset incumbent Governor James J. Blanchard by about 13,000 votes—among about 2.5 million votes cast—in Michigan's most exciting statewide race in 40 years.

Original caption reads: "John Engler announcing official acceptance after his stunning upset against incumbent Governor James Blanchard."

CREDIT: *Audrey Shehyn,* Detroit News

With Republicans also maintaining control of the state Senate, Engler's victory Tuesday gives the GOP the upper hand in Lansing for the first time since 1970. Democrats added one seat to their majority in the state House.

[240] *Chris Christoff, "Engler, Blanchard in Dead Heat,"* Detroit Free Press, *November 7, 1990.*

Engler's victory tally was reported by the Associated Press at 9:30 a.m. today. The Associated Press tracks the vote returns from all 83 Michigan counties. Engler earlier had declared victory by about 7,000 votes based on his party's tally of unofficial returns from 99 percent of the precincts.

Blanchard's campaign manager Gary Bachula said the governor was not ready to concede to Engler, but added: "We don't dispute (their) numbers."[241]

*

ENGLER: I WON!
LONG NIGHT:
BOTH CLAIMED VICTORY EARLY BUT THE
TALLY SEESAWED TILL DAWN

Republican candidate for governor John Engler declared victory shortly before 6 a.m. today as nearly complete election results showed him clinging to a narrow lead over Governor James J. Blanchard.

With 99 percent of the vote tallied, Engler held a 1,723-vote lead over Blanchard. Engler said his numbers showed a 7,000-vote victory....

The race for governor pitted two long-time and bitter political enemies in Blanchard and Engler. From the start, the race was expected to be tough, nasty and close—and it was.

Dismal voter turnout estimated at 45 percent to 50 percent of the state's 5.89 million registered voters, and an anti-incumbent mood among the electorate, appeared to turn against Blanchard.[242]

Original caption reads: "John Engler shares an emotional moment with his father, Matt, on election night [1990]." CREDIT: *Audrey Shehyn,* Detroit News

*

[241] *Roger Martin, Mark Hornbeck, and Yolanda Woodlee, "Upset!"* Detroit News, *November 7, 1990.*
[242] *Roger Martin, Mark Hornbeck, and Yolanda Woodlee, "Engler: I Won!"* Detroit News, *November 7, 1990.*

"HOW SWEET IT IS," ENGLER SAYS
A NEW MATE:
ENGLER PULLS OFF ANOTHER SURPRISE: HE'LL MARRY TEXAN

Is John Engler's new fiancée a Democrat?

"I'll let her answer that," laughed Margaret DeMunbrun, mother of Houston attorney Michelle DeMunbrun, 32, who is engaged to Michigan Gov.-elect Engler....

Engler told his staff about the engagement on Wednesday, the day after he captured a stunning upset victory over incumbent James J. Blanchard. But few in the capitol know much about DeMunbrun.[243]

*

TEPID TURNOUT:
BLANCHARD LOST BECAUSE HE FAILED
TO PICK UP ENOUGH VOTES IN DETROIT

Everyone from tax cut advocates to anti-abortion activists to Martha Griffiths were claiming credit Wednesday for Gov. James Blanchard's defeat by Sen. John Engler.

The real reason Blanchard lost was his failure to motivate Detroit voters, a post-election analysis of voting results indicates.

Blanchard tallied about 35,000 fewer votes in the city of Detroit this year than he did in 1986, when he clobbered GOP nominee William Lucas.

The governor also reaped between 4,000 and 8,000 fewer votes than the other Democrats on the top of the statewide ballot—an indication of city voters' lack of enthusiasm for Blanchard.

Detroit turnout was about 35 percent—compared to about 45 percent for the rest of the tri-county area. Considering that about 85 percent of the Detroit vote went to Blanchard, a stronger turnout could have saved the election for him.

Mayor Coleman A. Young gave the governor a tepid endorsement and his machine did not work full tilt for Blanchard.

"We're all in mourning around here," one top mayoral aide said sarcastically Wednesday about Blanchard's defeat.

Blanchard, stunned and humbled by his narrow, 19,000-vote defeat, waited until Wednesday afternoon—19 hours after the polls closed—to concede the race to Republican challenger Engler.[244]

[243]*Roger Martin and George Weeks, "How Sweet It Is,"* Detroit News, *November 8, 1990.*
[244]*Mark Hornbeck and Charlie Cain, "Tepid Turnout,"* Detroit News, *November 8, 1990.*

*

"AN OVERPOWERING MOMENT"
HARD WORK LIES AHEAD, BUT ENGLER SAVORS UPSET

John Engler on Wednesday began planning to take the reigns of state government, after beating Democratic Gov. James Blanchard by fewer than three votes per precinct on average in one of Michigan's biggest political upsets....

It was the closest gubernatorial race since 1952.

"This simply is an overpowering moment," a tearful, shirt-sleeved Engler told supporters, who roused him at 5:50 a.m. Wednesday to tell him he probably would win.

A stunned Blanchard conceded defeat some 19 hours after the polls closed. Final counts showed Engler with ... an edge of 0.75 percent. Less than 45 percent of state voters went to the polls.[245]

*

ENGLER: LET TAXPAYERS KEEP MORE OF EARNINGS

Michigan residents can expect more than a new governor on Jan. 1.

If John Engler delivers on his campaign promises, Michigan will get a streamlined and more accountable state government, a 20-percent property tax cut, a better business climate, lower unemployment and new restrictions on abortion.

"We are going to start at the top and treat every tax dollar that we spend as a dollar that first had to be earned by somebody working," he said. "It has high value and should be accorded that respect."[246]

Percentage-wise, this was the closest race John Engler ever ran in. He won by less than 1 percent of the vote.

1990 Gubernatorial General Election	
John Engler	1,276,134 (49.8%)
James Blanchard	1,258,539 (49.1%)[247]

*

Shock

Veteran Detroit Free Press *columnist Hugh McDiarmid still seemed in shock over Engler's victory several days later.*

[245] *Chris Christoff, "An Overpowering Moment,"* Detroit Free Press, *November 8, 1990.*
[246] *Roger Martin, "Engler: Let Taxpayers Keep More of Their Earnings,"* Detroit News and Free Press, *November 11, 1990.*
[247] Michigan Manual, *1991-1992 ed. (Lansing: The Legislative Service Bureau), p. 878.*

THE UNLIKELY CANDIDATE HAS WON, AND IT'S STILL SHOCKING

There are those in Michigan who know him fairly well and who neither cheer nor gag at the prospect of a John Engler governorship. They are simply flabbergasted by it.

That's because John is ... is...

Well, he's always seemed like such an *unlikely* prospect.

It's just that, well, it was such a shock—such a huge, unexpected SHOCK!—when they woke up Wednesday and discovered that the very same John Engler they'd known and watched over the years (no longer "Johnny" or "Jawn," thank you) would be their next governor.[248]

*

Lucille Taylor

John Engler's victory was stunning. If it was a surprise to us, it was an incredible shock to the opposition. There are stories of people going to see some of Blanchard's appointees who were devastated. They were in tears. They did not expect Engler to win. The staff could not cope with the fact that they had to leave their jobs.[249]

*

Why Engler won. Why Blanchard lost.

Mark Michaelson

In the 1990 election, it was Mr. Integrity, Mr. Substance, Mr. Policy versus Mr. No Ideas, Mr. Form, Mr. Fluff.

In retrospect, it is not surprising that Blanchard lost. His personal life was a disaster. Blanchard had divorced his first wife and married his secretary. Plus he had rocky relations with his lieutenant governor. Going into the election against John Engler, he had a dysfunctional family and a dysfunctional administration.

But the seeds of Blanchard's defeat were really planted some seven years earlier, in 1983. His mistake—pushing for a hike in the income tax—enabled Engler to become Senate majority leader. He was slapped about by the recall and lost all of his political courage. He was never bold again.[250]

[248] *Hugh McDiarmid, "The Unlikely Candidate Has Won, and It's Still Shocking,"* Detroit Free Press, *November 11, 1990.*

[249] *Lucille Taylor, interview with GW, February 3, 2001.*

[250] *Mark Michaelson, interview with GW, February 21, 2001.*

*

Dan Pero

1. Engler's tenacity.

2. Engler had a better message.

3. Blanchard ran a horrible campaign. Doug Ross said that in their internal polling they couldn't come up with a good reason why Blanchard needed a third term. That's why they made the decision to run a totally negative campaign. Blanchard hated Engler, so a negative campaign was convenient. Besides, Blanchard didn't take Engler seriously.

4. Related to the above, the Blanchard people didn't do their homework.

5. Coleman Young sat on his hands.[251]

[251]*Dan Pero, interview with GW, December 2, 2000; for other analyses, see William S. Ballenger, "Sayonara Blanchard,"* Inside Michigan Politics *(vol. 2), December 17, 1990, pp. 1-2; and Thomas J. Bray, "Upset: The Making of a Governor,"* Detroit News, *November 8, 1990.*

To love deeply in one direction makes us more loving in all others.
ANNE-SOPHIE SWETCHINE

★

Chapter Nine
Michelle

In 1990 John Engler was waging another campaign involving a constituency of one. Her name was Michelle.

In July of 1989, I was in Michigan for a friend's wedding. I was in Lansing, hanging out with Colleen Pero for the day. She wanted to stop by her office to pick something up.

That's when I first met John. He was in the office. Colleen introduced us. He seemed very friendly, very down to earth. We stood in his office and talked for a while. Then he reached up to his shelf and grabbed a Detroit Tigers cap and handed it to me. When he gave me the cap I said, "Oh, that's really nice, really sweet." I left the office and never thought about it again.

(However—when John and I were packing my things for my move to Michigan in 1990, he was looking for the cap. I had no clue where it was and I told him, "You couldn't care less about that cap." The cap has become a running joke between the two of us. Now, in his revisionist telling of the story, he claims that he was so struck by our first meeting that he gave me his most prized possession. All the while I just thought he was being a typical politician trying to win me over by giving me something.)

Not quite a year later Colleen, her husband Dan, and I planned a vacation to Florida for the Easter holiday. This would have been in April of 1990. Colleen called me and said, "John Engler really needs a break from the campaign. He is going to come to Florida with us." I had mixed feelings. Colleen and Dan had no intention of setting us up that weekend—they really didn't—but I just

John Engler and Michelle DeMunbrun along the romantic Riverwalk in San Antonio, prior to their wedding. CREDIT: *Audrey Shehyn,* Detroit News

wanted to be with close friends. We were just trying to get away and relax.

Colleen, Dan, and I arrived in Miami Beach on Holy Thursday [April 12]. John flew in the next day, Good Friday. Dan drove to the airport to pick him up. They came back when Colleen and I were having a great time talking and just lying on the beach. Imagine: the sound of the waves, the warm sun, a soft breeze, a beautiful beach. All of a sudden I hear this man's voice. It's John, and he's complaining about his flight arriving early and about having to wait for Dan. He was also unhappy about the staffers at campaign headquarters calling him from Michigan. He's saying, "Can't I get away for just a couple of days?"

I remember thinking to myself, "Great. He's in a lovely mood. Please, just don't ruin the weekend!"

Then John got settled on the beach, and we started to talk. And we really hit it off. We found ourselves talking the remainder of the day. I knew literally nothing about politics, but we didn't talk about politics or his campaign. We talked about all kinds of interesting things. We stayed up till 2:00 or 3:00 in the morning talking.

We decided to attend Mass together on Easter Sunday [April 15]. By this time I was hooked. After we went to Mass, John gave me his Senate majority leader business card, and he wrote his home number on the card. I still have that card and carry it with me to this day. Then Dan and John flew back to Michigan.

After they left, I told Colleen, "I really like him. I really do like him."

When I got back to my office in Houston Monday morning, John sent me flowers. I called my friend Kathy Watkins to tell her about the weekend and she said to me, "Michelle, I have never heard you talk about any person the way you are talking about him."

John called me later that day—that was the beginning of our daily phone calls. Every day he would call me in the morning before he left to campaign, and again at night when he returned home. In those conversations we rarely talked about the campaign. We would talk about everyday things. We shared so much, and these phone calls helped make us close friends.

Sometimes when he would call me late at night, after a long day of campaigning, he would be exhausted. He would fall asleep while we were on the phone. I found that so endearing.

Back then John was always attending county fairs. Without fail I received a gift in the mail when he made an appearance at a fair. I would get a stuffed bunny one day and a ceramic dish the next. The fact that he always took time to think of me was impressive. John was traveling all over the state and yet he still took time out of his day to buy little gifts and send them to me.

My next visit to Michigan was over Memorial Day weekend in 1990, and I was staying at Dan and Colleen's house. John came over around 1:00 in the morning and we all sat around and talked for a while.

My second night in town I felt very nervous. I was going to go to dinner and meet, for the first time, some of John's close friends. I had gone shopping in Texas for a new outfit for the big event. It was a beautiful blue and yellow silk suit. Yes, I was dressed in "maize and blue," and John—bless his heart—never said a word to me about it. We all met at the Lansing Country Club for dinner.

After we had been at dinner for a while, John's friend Linda Gobler, whom I had just met for the first time, told me, "I want to get to know you, and I want you to be involved in this group." She then turned to John and said, "I think you should marry this woman." She just blurted it out for everyone at the table to hear.

She elaborated, "John is going to be governor and you are going to be first lady and we're going to Mackinac." I was laughing and thinking, "What's a Mackinac?" (Only later did I realize what this mysterious place called Mackinac Island was.) They all talked about sitting on the porch of the Mackinac Island residence, drinking champagne, and watching the sunset. It was all very overwhelming for me. Marriage had not occurred to me at this point.

The next day, Linda came back to the topic. She told John—in front of me—"Well, it took you long enough, but you finally found The One. Don't let this woman get away. I want you to marry her." This was all very flattering to me. I also had strong feelings. I had never felt about anyone the way I felt about John.

The last part of the campaign was a difficult time for us. Our relationship was kept private for my sake. John was extremely protective and told me, "You don't want to get involved in this race, and you don't want to be associated with a gubernatorial candidate." Here I was in Texas, getting no news about the election, and John was in Michigan. All I knew was what the papers were saying. In essence it was: "John Engler is going to lose and he is going to lose big." During that time I subscribed to the *Detroit Free Press*, and all the information I was getting was from that paper. They lacked objectivity when it came to John.

In July of 1990, we started discussing marriage—seriously discussing it. I knew that I was attracted to him. I knew that he was brilliant. I thought that he was a Renaissance Man because he knew something interesting about everything, and I loved that about him. I was reluctant to commit, but John said to me, "You know we are going to get married, so why not now?" He is extremely persuasive, and on Saturday, July 28, I accepted his proposal of marriage.

John and I decided to keep our decision to marry a secret. We kept it just between us for quite a while and didn't tell anyone. If you asked our friends now, they would all tell you that they knew early on that we were going to get married. They could just tell. Linda [Gobler] says she knew by the Fourth of July that her proclamation of marriage was going to come true. That was the evening we went to a party on top of Cobo Hall in Detroit and had a lovely time.

The 1990 Republican Convention in early September was a wonderful time for me. As incredible as it sounds, that was when it struck me. That is when I fully realized the scope and significance of John's undertaking. I had fallen in love with the man, not the powerful politician. I was so focused on the two of us as a couple that I didn't think much about his work in state government. But when I saw more than 3,000 people cheering in Cobo Hall, it really struck me how important John's position was in the Republican Party and Michigan government. From that point forward I understood a lot more about John's role in state politics and about the interconnectedness of our lives with politics.

My experiences with the press while we were planning the wedding were not great. John never asked me to sell my blue BMW convertible. But while I was finalizing plans to move to Michigan, I decided to sell the car out of respect for Michigan workers. My mom told me that she knew I was in love when I decided to sell my BMW; I had so much fun with it.

A reporter, unaware of my decision to sell the car, saw me get into the BMW while I was still in Houston. A very negative story appeared shortly afterward. The article made it seem that I was deliberately insulting Michiganians and the Motor City. I was dismayed by the misrepresentation.

Another example of the relentless media coverage of our relationship was the way we had to break the news of our engagement to the public. John and I had told Dan and Colleen of our decision to get married. But otherwise it was a closely guarded secret. We decided that it would be best to announce our engagement well after the election; we wanted to give the campaign workers the opportunity to celebrate the victory. But our plans abruptly changed when Dawson Bell called John early Wednesday afternoon and said, "I know you are getting married, I am going to write the story, and you should talk."

John told him, "You have to give me a chance to tell my staff first." So the day after the election, John took his staff into a room in the Capitol. I left because I felt that this should be his time with his staff. Linda later told me that John started to tear up the moment he walked into the room. From what I have been told, it was an emotional gathering.

Thursday after the election, Dan, Colleen, John, and I went to breakfast. The three of them decided, right there, "We are going to have a press conference with you this morning."

"What are you talking about? What am I going to say? I've never talked to the press before."

They said, "You'll do fine."

The only advice that John would give me was, "Always tell the truth. Whatever they ask you, always tell the truth."

Later that day we walked into a room and it looked like a sea of reporters and photographers. It was terribly frightening. I was shaking, afraid that I would embarrass John in some way. We sat together and he held my hand as I fielded questions. I thought it went all right.

But the story the next day was, "Engler is marrying a pro-choice, BMW-driving Democrat."

From the point of view of the press, it was probably a compliment. But I was in tears after seeing the headline, anticipating how I might have adversely affected John. I thought, "I'm not going to be good for his career."[252]

*

[252] *Michelle Engler, interview with GW, January 26, 2001; Linda Gobler also contributed.*

Here is how the Detroit Free Press *introduced Michelle Engler to Michigan citizens.*

ENGLER, FIANCE PROVE OPPOSITES ATTRACT
MR. AFFABLE LANDS PRO-CHOICE EX-DEMOCRAT

John Engler's bride-to-be is a BMW-driving Houston lawyer with one marriage behind her, a pro-choice stand on abortion and a past political allegiance to—surprise—the Democratic Party.

She is also a former prom queen and devout Catholic who says her first priority right now is being Engler's wife and who isn't sure she'll continue her career in Michigan.[253]

*

John Truscott

I think back to the night of the Republican Convention in September of '90. We had not really gotten to know Michelle yet. She had visited and we knew that she and John were dating. But it was my suspicion that that was the weekend they became engaged—they were so lovey-dovey. John ordered up champagne, fruit trays, and crackers and cheese for those of us who were there—Dan and Colleen, LeAnne Redick, Dave Bertram, and myself. John and Michelle were arm-in-arm, giggling. I had never seen John so in love.[254]

*

Richard McLellan

After the polls had closed, I went to bed at 3:00 in the morning, thinking to myself, "We put up a good fight, but we still lost. I was shocked to hear on the radio in the morning that we had won. I could hardly believe it.

So I called John on Wednesday and asked if he had any plans for dinner. He said no, so I asked if he would like to go to Dusty's English Inn. John and Michelle, Dan and Colleen, Spence and Jane, and I all met there. And John was late, of course, because he was giving interviews.

When he walked in, we were having champagne and he said, "We're not only going to have an inauguration, but we're also going to have a wedding!" And that was the first I had ever heard of their engagement. Although I do have to say, John had asked me in the fall if I knew anybody who wanted to hire a good bankruptcy lawyer from Texas![255]

[253]*Dawson Bell and Amy Wilson,* Detroit Free Press, *Friday, November 9, 1990.*
[254]*John Truscott, interview with GW, October 19, 1999.*
[255]*Richard McLellan, interview with GW, December 2, 2000.*

*

Dick Posthumus

I think Michelle came along at the right time in John's life. She really humanized him. After fighting the battles that he fought, 1990 was a great turning point in his life. The dream he had since 1970 was now a reality—he had become the governor—and then came the best of all, Michelle. If you ask me, 1990 was really the start of his blossoming as a person, and also of his blossoming as a great leader.

Michelle gave him that roundedness that is needed to be an effective leader. She made him realize that there was more to life than just politics and rational thinking, that there were love and emotion, too. A true leader cannot lead with just his head. There must be a balance between the head and the heart. You need to be in love and to love to achieve that balance.[256]

*

Marsha Quebbeman

I believe John deep down always wanted a family. I think that piece was missing in his life before he met Michelle. It was hidden inside. Before Michelle, John didn't have a soul mate to come home to at night. He didn't have that special person to share things with.

When John announced after the election that he and Michelle were engaged, it was a tearful moment. We had all crowded into his office. I felt as though he were finally getting what had been missing in his life. It doesn't matter if you have everything else; if you don't have a home, and someone to love, you are missing the best in life.[257]

*

John Truscott

John tells a great story about Michelle talking with her father over the phone. Her father was concerned because in Texas the news was that John wouldn't win. He wanted to know what they were going to do if he lost. They would be married and he would be unemployed and her father really wondered what was she getting herself into. Were they going to move to Texas and Michelle support the two of them as a bankruptcy attorney? Michelle

[256]*Dick Posthumus, interview with GW, February 7, 2001.*
[257]*Marsha Quebbeman, interview with GW, February 23, 2001.*

gave it some thought and spoke to John about her father's worries. John told her not to worry about that—he was going to win.[258]

*

Wedding—December 8, 1990

John Truscott

For John and Michelle's wedding, we went down to San Antonio. It was a private ceremony for close family and friends. It was a beautiful warm day and people lined up outside the church. I met Michelle and John at the door and walked them out. They were all grins and holding hands.

Original caption reads: "Longtime friend Colleen Pero hugs Michelle after her wedding to John Engler in San Antonio." CREDIT: *Audrey Shehyn,* Detroit News

Everybody was in a great mood. Even the reporters were friendly and appreciative. Although they followed the newlyweds to the car and wanted the photos, they didn't hound Michelle and John. Everybody understood that it was not a political event.

But the newlyweds didn't have a lot of time to relax. Right after the wedding, they went to the NGA School for New Governors in North Carolina. They

[258] *John Truscott, interview with GW, October 27, 1999.*

ended up taking their real honeymoon much later, because there just wasn't any time for it during the transition.[259]

*

John: on Michelle

DAWSON BELL: There are people who have been watching you for a long time and they would say before you were married to Michelle, you were too consumed with politics. You were focused too much on the whole government game, but that changed when you married Michelle and even more with the birth of your children. Do you disagree with that theory?

GOVERNOR ENGLER: I wouldn't disagree with that at all. I think being married to Michelle is the greatest thing that has ever happened to me. I love her very much and we have a tremendous relationship. She makes me proud every day. There is no question that my marriage to Michelle has enriched my life and it has been further enhanced by the birth of our children. It is a wonderful thing that has happened to me.

I come from a big family; I have lots of nieces and nephews. But there is nothing like seeing the birth of your own children. In terms of watching a miracle take place, nothing can compare. The emotions that it unleashes are quite remarkable.

I would say that the time I have spent with Michelle has been the best time of my life. There is no question about that.[260]

[259] *John Truscott, interview with GW, October 27, 1999.*
[260] *JE, interview (taped) with Dawson Bell, February 1995.*

There is nothing more difficult...or more uncertain in its success, than to take the lead in the introduction of a new order of things.
MACHIAVELLI

★

Chapter Ten
Transition: November - December 1990

Hail to the victor!

Jeff McAlvey

John and I were walking over to Richard McLellan's office to talk about the transition, and there were some construction workers up on the scaffold, working on the Capitol restoration. As we were walking by, they said, "Yeah! Go Engler!" They were screaming and cheering, and all of this is new to us because we had been so used to walking in relative obscurity. Now, all of a sudden, people are cheering and screaming from the street.[261]

*

Martha Griffiths was the first Michigan woman to be elected lieutenant governor. A Democrat, she served in the Blanchard administration from 1983-1991. In one of the surprise moves of the 1990 campaign, Blanchard threw her off the ticket. He thought she was too old. Blanchard lost Griffiths's allegiance—and her vote.

This is one of the great moments of the transition. After Engler was elected, he got a standing ovation when he appeared before the Senate. Apparently Martha Griffiths approached the rostrum and said to the governor-elect, "I'm glad my vote wasn't wasted!"[262]

*

[261] *Jeff McAlvey, interview with GW, May 29, 2002.*
[262] *John McConnell, interview with GW, June 17, 2002.*

Two cheers for the victor

Lew Dodak

Right after the results were known, I came back to Lansing. I called on the governor-elect to congratulate him. Normally he would come to my office, but since he had just won the election, I went to his. I congratulated him, and immediately John went to work. He wanted to get right down to business.

When we concluded Engler said, "I'm looking forward to working with you."

I told him, "You have to understand that I am now the leader of the loyal opposition. I didn't run for it and I didn't ask for it, but...."

"Yeah, but we'll still be able to work together," Engler said.

"But you have to understand, I learned from a master—you."

He laughed. He understood what I had to do as speaker and with the Democratic caucus.[263]

*

Joanne Emmons

Not everyone in his home district was thrilled when John Engler won. There is always envy toward people who achieve, and some people back home felt envy because this little farm kid from Beal City had made good.[264]

*

Prepared to lead

Dan Pero

This is a man who had been preparing to lead for 20 years. He'd seen government work, he'd seen plans proposed, he'd seen alternatives, and he'd developed his own vision for where he wanted to take Michigan. So when he actually had the opportunity to do something (the day after the election), he was ready to do it.[265]

*

John Engler explains his approach to governance.

Each branch of government should vigorously exercise the powers the constitution gives it. When I was in the Senate, I exercised to the fullest the powers the Michigan constitution grants to the legislative branch of government.

[263] *Lew Dodak, interview with GW, July 10, 2002.*
[264] *Joanne Emmons, interview with GW, September 25, 2002.*
[265] *Dan Pero, interview with GW, February 3, 2001.*

Now that I am governor, I will exercise to the fullest the powers the constitution grants to the executive branch.[266]

After the election I went to the New Governors School in North Carolina. Pete DuPont gave us some advice I will never forget. He said, "Being governor is the greatest job in the world. You can do anything you want—but you can't do everything."[267]

Original caption reads: "Governor and Mrs. Engler with John's mom Agnes greet supporters at a reception in Mount Pleasant." CREDIT: *Audrey Shehyn,* Detroit News

*

No entourages!

Michelle Engler

John and I had a meeting with the head of our security detail, Lieutenant Gary Calder, and he asked, "How would you like for us to interface and interact with you?"

John said, "I would like for you to dress the way we're dressed. If it's a formal event, dress formally. If it's a casual event, be casual. Blend in with the crowd and please don't hang around me. I don't like entourages."

This was so in contrast with the instructions Lieutenant Calder had received

[266]*JE, said numerous times to staff during his 12 years as governor.*
[267]*JE to GW, March 6, 2000.*

from a previous governor, which were: always wear a suit, no matter what, so that you stick out. And stay close.

John likes to look like everyone else in the crowd and not have our security people right next to us.[268]

*

The hard work of the transition

John Truscott

When the transition first started, we had the euphoria of winning and making a major change in the state. It was the feeling of a complete power shift in Lansing. But pretty soon we realized how overwhelming that task was.

The transition is hard enough when you go from one administration to another one in the same party with similar philosophies. In our case, we were coming at it from a much different philosophical approach. It was basically a new start.

That whole time is such a blur. It was endless hours of hard work. We had two months to go through everything, to make decisions on many policy issues. We soon realized that we would have to institute some very difficult policy and budgetary changes. It weighed pretty heavily on our shoulders. The pressure of the work was just overwhelming.

John didn't spend too much time in the transition office because he was still busy running the Senate.

I remember being on the phone from early morning until late at night—about ten hours a day. That is

Governor-elect Engler meets with colleagues — from left, Democratic Senators Art Miller and John Cherry, and senior aide Lucille Taylor—in his waning hours in the Senate. CREDIT: *Audrey Shehyn,* Detroit News

[268] *Michelle Engler, interview with GW, January 26, 2001.*

when I realized that I could no longer sleep on my right side because the cartilage in my ear was bruised from spending so many hours on the phone. I averaged fifty calls a day.

During the transition, we found out that we had been sold a bill of goods by the Blanchard administration. We soon learned about the extent of the deficit. The economy was on the decline, but we had no idea how bad things really were or how slow revenues were coming in. We were in for a rough ride.[269]

*

Richard McLellan

There was an attempt to cover up the state's fiscal problems. When we had our first meeting with Blanchard to discuss the budget, he said, "We don't know that it is out of balance because we haven't completed the books."

I thought that was a brilliant ploy on his part. During an election he could say with a straight face that we don't know that the budget is out of balance.

Clearly it was. We were totally justified when we hammered him on that issue throughout the campaign. We knew that we were going to have a deficit, but no one believed us. There was Blanchard, like an ostrich with his head in the sand, plausibly able to deny the deficit. "Budget deficit? What budget deficit?"[270]

*

RICHARD McLELLAN: Frank Kelley called several times during the transition and, of course, I was blowing him off because he was a Democrat. Since we had won, I was feeling real full of myself. Then I made the connection: "Wait a second. This guy is our lawyer: the attorney general of Michigan: Frank J. Kelley. We need to have him over here." But John said, "No. Don't have him come here, Richard. We'll go see him on his turf."

I think that the decision to see him in his office paid great dividends in the years to follow. I remember Kelley commenting, "I am your lawyer. We may have different politics, but you are my client."

LUCILLE TAYLOR: That's true. He assured us that he would be there for us. Frank either communicated verbally or gave other indications that he did share views with John on issues like welfare reform and life issues. On many issues, he parted ways with his constituency to go right down the line with us;

[269] *John Truscott, interview with GW, October 19 and 27, 1999.*
[270] *Richard McLellan, interview with GW, December 2, 2000.*

he never undercut us in terms of public comments or due diligence.

We learned early on that the attorney general had a different bully pulpit in Michigan politics. It is extremely important that your attorney general not be out making public statements about how the governor is trying to do something unauthorized, illegal, or unconstitutional. We had to constantly keep this base covered to make sure that the relationship did not break down.

BILL WHITBECK: And here would be a good place to add that a very important reason the relationship didn't break down was because of Lucille's efforts. But it's also a credit to Frank and the people he had working for him. Many of them are really professional lawyers. Think of all the lawsuits we had to defend in those years. We never lost a single one—not one. That is great lawyering."[271]

*

Frank Kelley

The governor-elect made a courtesy call to my office with Dan Pero, Lucille Taylor [and Richard McLellan]. I had worked with four previous governors. So over a cup of coffee, I gave him my perspective. I was prepared to get along with him. We would work cooperatively. Since I would be representing him, we would have a confidential relationship. There would be no cheap shots from my office, no political grandstanding. I would keep my political agenda separate from my legal duties as attorney general and as his lawyer. I was not closed minded or politically motivated. If I had a political difference with him over a matter of considerable importance, I would tell him in advance of going public.

Then we talked specifics. The first thing he brought up was the Accident Fund, which he wanted to sell. I told him that it was a matter of policy. He would be working with the legislature. "If they go along with you, I will make sure the sale is done properly."

It was a good first meeting.[272]

*

Inaugural eve

Jim Brandell

The transition time was very intense, but also very exciting. There were

[271] *Richard McLellan, Lucille Taylor, and Bill Whitbeck, interview with GW, December 2, 2000.*
[272] *Frank Kelley, interview with GW, October 1, 2002.*

some funny moments. I remember when inaugural programs got me out of trouble with the State Police.

John Engler didn't have state police protection until he was sworn in as governor, so I was still doing some of the driving. I was working the night before the Inaugural, on New Year's Eve. I drove John and Michelle back to their condo.

After I dropped them off, I returned the car to the back of the Capitol. I pulled up around 1:15 a.m., and suddenly the Capitol police were all over me. You can imagine: people were getting ready for the Inaugural the next day and a mysterious car pulls up.

When the police asked me what I was doing there, I said, "This is the car for Governor-elect Engler. I'm just dropping it off." My ID didn't show whom I worked for, so I could not prove it.

The Capitol police looked skeptical. But then I thought, "I have tons of inaugural programs in the back." So I opened up the trunk and showed the policemen.

They laughed and asked, "Can we have one?"[273]

[273] *Jim Brandell, interview with GW, February 16, 2001.*

PART II

Governor:
1991-2002

The foremost art of kings is the power to endure hatred.
SENECA

In crises the most daring course is often safest.
HENRY KISSINGER

★

Chapter Eleven
First Term from January 1991 - July 1993

Preparing Engler's first speech as governor

During the transition, Spencer Abraham began working on Engler's First Inaugural Address. Abraham was at the time Vice President Dan Quayle's deputy chief of staff. Reporting to Abraham was John McConnell, the vice president's speechwriter. McConnell recalls:

One morning while driving to work, Spence dictated Engler's Inaugural Address into a tape recorder. He came into the office, handed me the tape, and asked me to write it up. As I listened to Spence's words, I realized that it was an amazing performance, and much of that dictation made the final cut.

Additional ideas and language for the speech came from Dan Pero and other staff members. Some of the really nice touches were provided by Russell Kirk.[274]

*

Engler—moments before the Inauguration

John Truscott

The Inaugural was an emotional time for staff. We were back in his office before the speech—Dan Pero, Spence and I—talking about how far we had come and how this was the day to begin changing the direction of Michigan. John was extremely laid back and matter of fact. Given what he was about to embark upon, he seemed unbelievably calm as he stood and chatted among

[274] *John McConnell, interview with GW, June 17, 2002.*

friends. We talked about how glad we were that the election had solidified the Republican majority in the Senate. And about what it was going to be like to move out of the Senate office. And about the great changes that would occur in Michigan with John Engler as governor. Then we all shook hands and left so that John could gather his thoughts.

Dan, Spence, and I walked down to the front of the Capitol. All of the military personnel, office holders, and public were already lining up to listen to the Inauguration. I went to the press platform, and the first person I ran into

Michelle at his side, John Engler reaches out to his father Matt at the Inaugural Mass, St. Mary Cathedral, Lansing, January 1, 1991. CREDIT: *David Coates,* Detroit News

happened to be Blanchard. This had to be an awkward day for him, but he was pleasant.

We saw John walk out confidently, Michelle next to him. It seemed as if it were the coldest day in years, but John wasn't wearing gloves or a hat. He was so proud that I don't think he even felt the cold.

For the ceremony, he knew where to go and what to do. Everything went as planned. But when it came time to take the oath of office, he put his hand on the Bible and then choked up. My eyes teared up too.[275]

[275] *John Truscott, interview with GW, October 19, 1999.*

Chief Justice Dorothy Comstock Riley swearing in the new governor, with Michelle at his side. CREDIT: *Audrey Shebyn,* Detroit News

*

First Inaugural Address

Spencer Abraham served as master of ceremonies of the inauguration. Chief Justice Dorothy Comstock Riley administered the oath of office:

"I do solemnly swear that I will support the Constitution of the United States and the constitution of this state, and that I will faithfully discharge the duties of the office of governor according to the best of my ability."[276]

*

John Engler's first speech as Michigan's 46th governor:

As we gather today for the Inauguration of a new governor, we once again do so in the shadow of the building which, more than any other, symbolizes our state government. But today, things are a little different. Our old beloved Capitol is undergoing much needed repairs. Indeed, our Capitol restoration project will truly breathe new life into this grand structure.

Fellow citizens, just as we are restoring and renewing this great building, it is now our opportunity and our responsibility to restore and renew this great state. For as we enter this new decade, and as we look ahead to the new century

[276] *Michigan Constitution, art. XI, sec. 1.*

beyond, it is abundantly clear that Michigan's future greatness is directly linked to our ability to restore and renew the important and fundamental values, institutions, and resources that led to Michigan's greatness in the past.

"It is now our opportunity and our responsibility to restore and renew this great state." Engler delivering his First Inaugural Address.

SOURCE: *Engler administration*

To begin, we must restore the spirit of enterprise in Michigan. At the turn of this century, the spark of entrepreneurial genius that caused America to lead the Industrial Revolution was ignited right here in our state. It was in the garages and workshops of people like Henry Ford, R. E. Olds, the Dodge Brothers, and the Fishers that the ideas for a whole industry and indeed a whole system of manufacturing were born.

Fellow citizens, those were not produced by state government. Our industrial might was not forged in the planning divisions of state agencies. It was molded by the hard work and the creative spirit of our people. And we must not forget that.

We still have the same creative spirit. But sadly, because of government, it has been impaired. And, as a result, the capacity of citizens in Michigan today to achieve their dreams has been diminished. My friends, it is our job, it is our duty, to allow that spirit fully to flourish again. We must restore the values and principles that ignited the genius of the Michigan that was the arsenal of democracy and the manufacturing leader of the world. As we enter this century, we must allow the inventors and entrepreneurs of today the same opportunities enjoyed by their predecessors when this century began.

To start we will restore the most fundamental principle of economic growth: a commitment to a true market-based economy. No bureaucratic decision as to who should be an economic winner or loser will ever substitute for the decisions made in the marketplace. Therefore, it is time to renew our commitment to free enterprise. We must free our economy from government planning, and reduce the intervention and cost of government in the operation of that economy. Today, the grip of state government on individual initiative has become a stranglehold on individual initiative.

And the tightest grip of all is taxes. Revitalizing our economy means reducing our tax burden. On election day the people demanded a significant tax cut. We will answer their call without compromise and without delay. We will cut taxes.

But just as we must in many ways reduce the role of government if the spirit of enterprise is to thrive, we must also recognize that there is an important role for government to play if we are to foster the spirit of which I speak. Our task is to establish new priorities for government and make sure government performs more effectively. The reality of our age is that Michigan is in fierce competition with 49 other states and most foreign countries for economic survival. Future jobs will be created where employers find workers who meet the ever-higher standards made necessary by global competition. The skills needed to fill the jobs of tomorrow are no longer ones that can be learned in the family workshop. Nor can they be learned by those who attend inferior schools—or by those who do not graduate at all.

For the children of Michigan to compete, we must revitalize our state's education system. The jobs of tomorrow demand it. And our commitment to provide real opportunity for every one of our children demands it as well. We must assure that our schools and teachers are committed to excellence at all levels. And we must guarantee that a fixed percentage of all state revenues will forever be dedicated to the education and training of our youth.

Just as we must restore the spirit of enterprise in Michigan, it is also critical that we restore our citizens' full confidence in our government. In an age of declining voter turnout and declining respect for public officials, it is imperative that we address the root causes of this decay. We will build public trust in Lansing by providing the citizens of Michigan with the most direct possible opportunity to know their leaders and let their leaders know them. To do this, we shall rely on a time-tested method: We will let them meet each other.

Beginning next week, and for every week of the administration, this governor's door will be open to all citizens as we institute regular public office hours. And the same will be the case for each department director who serves in this administration. In the same spirit, this governor's office will reach out to people in every corner of our great state. I will visit every one of our 83 counties every year of my administration. We pledge to talk to people and let them talk to us. And, most importantly, we promise to listen.

It is time to restore a strong bond between the governor and the legislature. And I will seek cooperation with our legislative leaders in matters of state.

Finally, if we are to restore the confidence of people in government then we must directly address the ethical and moral issues which confront public officials. My administration will work to reform our ethics and election laws. And we will insist upon the highest standards for our appointed officials, so that our citizens will have full confidence in the integrity of our government.

I know this state; I know its people; I understand their spiritual strength and their determined presence of mind. Of all our extraordinary resources, the most valuable are our people—all of our fellow citizens who pay taxes, raise the children, farm the land, and build the future. Every one of us has a stake in our success—and in each other.

Therefore, in each and every one of our endeavors, this administration will be guided by an undeviating principle: we will trust the people of Michigan. We will restore the power of individuals and families to shape their lives. As a step in that direction, we will pursue the promising agenda of choice in education. The decision to select one school or another for a child is best made by the child's parents—not by government officials. Choice is fair; and I am convinced that it will restore a great Michigan legacy: the finest schools in the nation.

For the too large number of us who are disadvantaged, we will build an era of renewed hope and opportunity—through welfare reform, enterprise zones, and private control and ownership of public housing. Our message will be: We will not consign you or anyone else to hopeless oblivion. You, too, are stakeholders in the future of Michigan. Your future is our future. And you, too, will help us restore the greatness of our state.

Today I have spoken of our need to renew many things. The spirit of enterprise, confidence in public officials, the proper role of government, and the fuller empowerment of people. But all of these objectives, even when met, will not restore Michigan's full promise unless we also restore the most central of all characteristics of human achievement: the need for individuals to commit themselves to improving their communities and their own lives as well.

One hundred sixty years ago, two perceptive Frenchmen, Alexis de Tocqueville and Gustave de Beaumont, made their difficult way through the Michigan wilderness from Detroit to Saginaw. Detroit then was a little town of two or three thousand people. Troy consisted of a few log houses. Pontiac had twenty buildings. Saginaw, a far-flung outpost of civilization, had a population of thirty. There was then no Lansing.

Tocqueville, who was yet to write his great book about democracy, was mightily impressed by the high degree of personal responsibility he saw among Michigan's pioneers. Though lacking capital, governmental assistance, roads, and most machines, within a few decades those pioneer men and women would make out of Michigan Territory a great state of the Union.

What made the Michigan experience—the American experience—so successful? Tocqueville concluded that the Americans' success was the result of their moral habits and beliefs—founded most often upon religious convictions. They knew that human beings all have duties to perform as well as rights to enjoy. This unique American belief in personal responsibility turned the howling wilderness of Michigan into a strong, orderly, wonderfully productive modern state.

Ladies and gentlemen, here at our old Capitol today I appeal to our Michigan heritage of moral and personal responsibility. We have built healthy communities in America because our men and women have been ever mindful of their responsibilities to family, to neighbors, to local community, to our state, and to our nation. And where we have failed, it has inevitably been because too many have refused or been unable to accept the responsibilities demanded of them as individuals in a free society.

Fellow citizens, I ask you today to join with me in taking up our common burden of duties, in high hopes of renewal. Let future generations think of the 1990s as the decade when the people of Michigan accepted the challenges of difficult times and, employing the same convictions, hard work, and personal responsibility as their forefathers, overcame them....

My friends, it is my great honor to serve as your governor, and I thank you for giving me this opportunity. Now, I hope you will join me as we build Michigan—together. God bless you, and God bless our great state.[277]

*

Several long-serving aides and allies who listened to John Engler's First Inaugural Address admitted to surprise at how conservative the speech sounded. Cliff Taylor:

When I heard John's First Inaugural Address, I realized he had the makings of a great leader. It was the most conservative statement made by a Michigan governor in the post-war era, or perhaps in the 20th century. It was rock-solid philosophical conservatism. I always knew John to be a good solid Republican, but I didn't know how good of a Republican until that Inaugural Address.[278]

*

[277]*John Engler, First Inaugural Address, Lansing, January 1, 1991.*
[278]*Cliff Taylor, interview with GW, June 16, 2000.*

Lucille Taylor

Before the inaugural address in 1991, we were not quite sure how conservative John was. But in that speech he made it clear that we were actually going to try to do what a new wave of conservative economists and social scientists were suggesting. I must admit, I was somewhat surprised by how conservative it sounded. He had been elected by some 17,000 votes—enough to avoid a recount, but not enough to be a mandate. We all came into this office with the general public thinking: We are an accident; John Engler is the accidental governor; this is the accidental administration.

Newly inaugurated governor and first lady share a happy moment, January 1, 1991.

SOURCE: *Engler administration*

You can be dogmatic with your ideas when you don't know much about a problem or when you are not the one in a position to solve it. "The Solution" then seems quite simple and apparent. But once you become governor in a state of 9 million people, and a government of 60,000 employees, you become more aware of the problems, and it is not so easy to make them black and white.[279]

*

The reporters covering the Inaugural were also struck by the conservative tone of the speech. Detroit Free Press *reporter Chris Christoff:*

The First Inaugural was one of John Engler's best speeches because it laid out a blueprint of what was to come. As a legislator he had been known for his pragmatism. But in that speech he set a tone of conservatism. It was a hard turn to the right. That was the direction on the map: go right. I think that he remained pretty true to that vision over the next twelve years.[280]

*

[279] *Lucille Taylor, interview with GW, October 20, 1999.*
[280] *Chris Christoff, interview with GW, July 11, 2002.*

Lansing State Journal *reporter Chris Andrews:*

"RESTORE AND RENEW"

DOWNSCALED ENGLER INAUGURAL IS UPBEAT

The big chill wasn't about to spoil John Engler's Big Day.

Not by a long shot.

From morning to night, Engler savored the day he spent two decades building toward—his inauguration as governor of Michigan.

The Republican from Mount Pleasant beamed as a crowd estimated by state police at 1,500 gave him a standing ovation. The applause, muffled by gloves, sounded like a buffalo stampede as a mostly partisan group cheered enthusiastically.

Later Tuesday evening at the Grass Roots Gala at the Lansing Center, some 3,500 in-the-trenches Engler supporters gathered to get a little piece of inaugural magic.

"I came here to people-watch," said Kathy Brooks of Delta Township.

The people-watching was of the decidedly mild variety. Tuesday's event was not one of the $ 150-a-plate balls for the movers and shakers. Rather, it was a business suit and sweater set affair for the Republicans next door.

No sequins, no skin, no glitz, no daring necklines. Few furs, plastic plates and country music.

It was, well, downscaled—a buzzword of the new governor....

Engler and his new wife, Michelle, laughed and nuzzled as they sat on the edge of an empty dance floor listening to Lee Greenwood's music. She wore a sleek cream-colored dress studded with large faux pearls, he—a dark business suit.

For the inaugural festivities, some came from as far as the Upper Peninsula to witness a piece of history.

Spectators sipped hot cider, coffee and cocoa to cope with icy temperatures while the wind chill hit zero right around the start of the inauguration.

Four jets from the Michigan National Guard roared over the Capitol at precisely 11:30 a.m. to launch the ceremony. Four others soon followed.

Minutes later, Supreme Court Chief Justice Dorothy Comstock Riley administered the oath of office, and Michigan had a new governor.

As an Army band played, cannons roared as the 119th Field Artillery honored Engler with a 13-gun salute that sent pigeons flying....

The vast majority of those attending were Engler loyalists....

Still, supporters were impressed by Engler's 20-minute speech, which included promises of tax cuts, education choices and an open-door policy for Engler and department heads.

"Be bold!" Governor George Romney congratulates Michigan's new governor. SOURCE: *Engler administration*

"I was surprised when he said parents would be able to choose the school for their children," said Tom Darlington of Northville. "My daughter goes to a private school right now, but I like the idea of being able to send her anywhere I like."

After the swearing-in ceremony, hundreds of people lined up inside the Michigan Library and Historical Center for a chance to meet and shake hands with John and Michelle Engler....

Inauguration activities began with mass at St. Mary Cathedral. Engler carried a Bible in his left hand and wrapped his right arm around his wife's waist as they walked up the aisle.

The Rt. Rev. Kenneth Povish, bishop of the Catholic Diocese of Lansing, presided at the service attended by about 900 people.

"Beginnings are usually exciting. They are usually challenging. Beginnings are always significant."

After the service, the masses huddled outside in the brisk January cold waiting to get into the cathedral hall for coffee and doughnuts. But before most got in, the Englers were on their way to the Capitol for a brunch for legislators and supporters....

Former Republican Gov. George Romney posed for pictures with Engler and offered him two sentences of advice.

"I said, 'Take bold actions, not weak actions. Restore the state's soul.'"[281]

[281]*Chris Andrews, "Restore and Renew: Downscaled Engler Inaugural Is Upbeat,"* Lansing State Journal, *January 2, 1991, p. A1.*

*

Okay. Fun's over. Time to work.

Jeff McAlvey

At the end of the Inaugural Ball, John Engler went up to the microphone and said, "This has been great fun, but I have to get home, and all my senior staff does too, because they'd better be in the office at 7:00 tomorrow morning ready to work!"

Sure enough, we met on January 2nd for our first senior staff meeting. This administration has been hard at work since day one.[282]

*

One measure of success

Jeff McAlvey

We had just finished our first senior staff meeting in Dan Pero's office. Dan stepped out and it was just the governor and I. He was sitting on the corner of Dan's desk, looking out the window at the Capitol. I said, "I know how your supporters will judge your success as governor—cutting property taxes, reforming welfare, lowering the cost of doing business in Michigan—but what about you? How will you judge if you are a success as governor?"

John didn't pause long. He said, "This may surprise you. It certainly would surprise most of my supporters. But I'm a kid from Beal City. Every time I go to Detroit, I can sense the despair. So I think: Can I make a difference in Detroit? Can I change state policies and make Detroit a city where people will want to raise their families? A city where it's safe to walk on the streets? Where kids can go to good schools? Where city government actually functions well? That's what I'd like to have happen."[283]

*

The context

From day one, the overarching problem the new governor faced was the budget deficit. Michigan's constitution required a balanced budget. Engler, looking back, recalls:

Do you know what the first line of the 1991 budget was? The preceding year's deficit: $310 million. Do you know what the first line of the 1992 budget was? The preceding year's deficit: $169 million. That was our starting point. That was the Christmas present my predecessor left to the people of Michigan.

[282] *Jeff McAlvey, interview with GW, May 29, 2002.*
[283] *Jeff McAlvey, interview with GW, May 29, 2002 and October 1, 2002.*

At the start of my first term, we had to make across-the-board cuts of 9.2 percent. Over the next nine months we had to redo the '91 budget and resolve a $1.8 billion shortfall that grew to $2 billion by year's end. We had to put everything on the table.[284]

*

First State of the State Address

Urgently needed budget cuts would set the tone for Engler's first State of the State Address. Spence Abraham had Vice President Quayle's speechwriter work up a first draft. The speechwriter was John McConnell, a shirt-tail relative of Engler's. McConnell records one moment in particular.

Speech practice was in John Engler's room in the J. W. Marriott near the White House: Spence Abraham and I met with the governor. Spence read the speech to Engler to show him how it should be delivered. There was a tough line in the speech. Was it too tough, too harsh, advisors wondered?

I said, "Reagan would have said it."

"Yeah, Reagan would have said it!" That settled the matter. The line stayed in. That speech worked. It still resonates.[285]

*

Engler delivered his first State of the State Address on the eve of Lincoln's birthday. In the address the new governor laid out the case for the 20 percent property tax cut he had campaigned on. Given the budget crisis in Lansing, he also declared his intention of using executive orders to tighten state government's belt. An excerpt:

Year after year, even though our population has not grown at all, government spending in Michigan

Governor delivering his first State of the State Address, on the eve of Lincoln's birthday (February 11, 1991)

CREDIT: *Greg Domagalski, Michigan Senate*

[284] *JE, press conference on the FY 2003 budget, Lansing, July 25, 2002.*
[285] *John McConnell, interview with GW, June 17, 2002.*

has grown relentlessly. And, in spite of greater and greater amounts of taxes paid by the working citizens of our state, government has persistently failed to live within its means.

I pledge to the people of Michigan: the 1990s will mark the end of this disastrous cycle.[286]

*

What manner of conservative?

Once Engler delivered his Inaugural Address and First State of the State Address, setting his priorities in motion, the question arose: Just how conservative is he? For answers, Donovan Reynolds, executive director of Michigan Public Radio, interviewed one of the founders of modern American conservative thought, Russell Kirk, who lived in Engler's senate district. Kirk had been consulted when the Inaugural Address was being drafted. He maintained that Engler had a great grasp of practical politics, and affinities with the Burkean tradition of historical conservatism.

I always expected John Engler to go far because he has tenacity. He's quiet, thoughtful, patient, doesn't give up, realizes things take time, and understands that politics is the art of the possible, not the art of the perfect. By patience and tenacity he has gone to the top.

He's certainly not an ideologue because the word "ideology" means political fanaticism, a belief that one can achieve earthy paradise through politics. And there's nothing of that in John Engler. "Pragmatist" is not quite the right word either, although it is closer. A pragmatist believes in what seems to work, what seems practical or successful at the moment. To describe the philosophy of John Engler, you might call him an "empiricist," one who looks to history and long-term experience, what is functional of the past, what has worked well over long periods of time, lessons of history, lessons of philosophers, sages of the past. That's the kind of mind he has. Here in central Michigan he is attached to what has been working successfully in rural society: local self-government, functioning systems of agriculture, the feeling of community. This is his background. The spirit of Michigan and its politics is to defend and extend this body of experience which is Michigan's traditional past.

Like myself he is staggered by what to do about Detroit. There are still certain principles which can be applied. He understands what many people don't. What keeps Detroit functioning at all now is its churches. Within city limits there are about 2,500 functioning churches, some with rather strange doc-

[286] *JE, "Taxpayers' Agenda," first State of the State Address, February 11, 1991.*

trines, but all anchors of community. Our word "culture" comes from the Latin *cultus*, a gathering of people to worship a divine wisdom and love. It is these churches that do keep people as neighbors, working together, and having some moral principles. As most politicians in the region know, religion is the basis for civil social order. That's one of the reasons John Engler is interested in voting for variety and choice in education.

It's true that all men's motives are mixed, and when one engages in politics he must have some instinct of power. By employment of power he can do some good and advance himself. John Engler is not primarily in it for glory. He seems to have no vanity. He's humble and has easy manners. By and large he is in politics by example of his father who didn't get very far but aspired to represent central Michigan in politics and desired to preserve prescriptive politics in Michigan—things that are long customary here....

He sees things in a prescriptive sort of way, what has worked here for a long time. He's not a man of theory. Edmund Burke, a founder of [modern] conservative thought, said we are fortunate to have escaped from abstract doctrine and theoretic dogma. Don't be governed by pedantic theories. Be governed by your historical experience as a people, by what has functioned well for a long time. That's political prudence. While John Engler wouldn't put it in those words, that is the general principle by which he has governed.

If anyone can resist the lobbyists and special interests John Engler can. I'm painfully aware of the pressure from entrenched lobbyists and special interest groups, which practically all legislators are terrified of nowadays. And a gubernatorial race is often determined by a few thousand votes. Engler won, surprisingly to many, by a small margin. So it requires his kind of courage and tenacity to resist pressures which come from all corners. They all have some kind of power or money. Most legislatures and governors are content to give them what they want to placate them. His inclination is otherwise. I think he has the resolution and tenacity to resist these pressures.

My advice to John Engler is to persevere. In the arguments Burke made contesting the election of Bristol in the 1770s, he pointed out that the duty of a representative is to represent the people's interest, their interest in the long run and not just today. What the people of Michigan want in the long run is what John Engler has to bear in mind. That's why we elected him, to look after the long run, not the temporary interests of a few pressure groups. I think he has the mind to do it.[287]

[287]*Russell Kirk, interviewed by Donovan Reynolds (video taped), c. February 1991.*

*

Team Engler

Jim Brandell

I remember one of our first senior staff meetings. I remember being awestruck by the sight of the Capitol right outside the window. It was just a gorgeous picture. It never ceased to amaze me.

Each staff member brought a lot to the table. Dan Pero, Lucille Taylor, John Truscott, Rusty Hills, Jeff McAlvey, Carol Viventi, Anne Mervenne, Mark Michaelson, Bill Whitbeck, David Bertram, LeAnne Redick [Wilson], Colleen Pero—it was a great team.

Dan Pero was the rock. He never flinched. He never let the staff see him with his guard down.[288]

*

Budget battle

John Truscott

Most people didn't really realize how bad things were. We needed to visually demonstrate that the state treasury was broke. That was when Rusty Hills came up with the idea of an empty wallet. He said, "Look! I'm always broke. I don't have any money in my wallet." We all laughed and thought that it was a great idea. So at the press conference, the governor actually used Rusty's wallet. He held it out, opened it up, and said,

"This is the state treasury." Dramatic moment from the "empty wallet" press conference, June 4, 1991. DMB director Patti Woodworth is in background. Communications director Rusty Hills provided the wallet.

SOURCE: *Engler administration*

[288] *Jim Brandell, interview with GW, February 16, 2001.*

"This is the state treasury." Only after that did people realize how bad the budget crisis was.

The further we got into the budget process, the more it felt like David and Goliath. We played the role of David, the lone defender against an army of special interests that were trying to impose their will and to keep their ox from being gored. It was emotionally draining day after day, because the opposition was attacking us on every policy issue. Sometimes it was pretty disheartening, but I stuck it out because we were fighting for a greater good in implementing the governor's agenda.[289]

*

Mark Michaelson

Traditionally, budgets are the source of negotiation. The Senate puts in their priorities, and the House puts in their priorities, and then they negotiate in conference committees. Some kind of compromise emerges, and then the budget goes to the governor for his signature or veto.

John Engler and Dick Posthumus cooked up what I think was the single most brilliant tactic during that first budget year. Engler began by issuing an executive order to cut spending by 9.2 percent. The Democrat-controlled House presented their budget priorities, figuring they'd ask for a full loaf and only get half a loaf. They sent their priorities over to the Republican-controlled Senate, expecting the Senate to present a very different budget. There would be drawn-out negotiations and gridlock. But instead of gridlock, the Senate concurred with the House and pretty much sent their budget straight to Engler to exercise his line-item veto.

House Democrats were totally snookered. The House Appropriations members were being held up to public ridicule because they said, "That's not fair. We put more in that budget than we expected to get." Given the huge budget deficit, their excuses just didn't resonate. Engler got the line-item veto going and whacked out big lines.[290]

*

Dawson Bell

Looking back on the 1991 budget, I don't think the cuts were a miscalculation on Engler's part. The state was in a budget crisis and something had to be

[289] *John Truscott, interview with GW, October 27, 1999.*
[290] *Mark Michaelson, interview with GW, February 28, 2001.*

done immediately. The longer the governor waited to make a decision, the more draconian the cuts would have to be. So instead of cutting programs by 9.2 percent, he would have had to cut them by 20 percent. If he had waited till the end of the fiscal year to act, he would have been cutting programs by 80 percent. Engler didn't have time to wait and see what everybody thought; he needed to act. Any other way of explaining that first year is revisionist history.[291]

*

Mark Murray was a top aide in the Department of Management and Budget (DMB) at this time.

The more liberal House Democrats were sometimes frustrated by Blanchard because he was more of a centrist. They couldn't attack him in the open. But when John Engler became governor, they were liberated. Having a Republican in the governor's office allowed them to go on the offensive—openly attacking.[292]

*

An exchange among staffers who went through the 1991 budget crisis. (Patti Woodworth was director of DMB and Gerry Miller was director of the Department of Social Services.)

PATTI WOODWORTH: Engler's thorough preparation was one of his great strengths that first year. We would sit down with budget analysts from DMB. John would arrive at the meeting having read every single line in every single appropriations bill, and he would grill the DMB analysts with questions. These people were just blown away. We're talking 18 or 19 appropriations bills, each one with hundreds of lines. All together, the material that we had to go through was about six to eight inches of paper. He went through them the night before.

LUCILLE TAYLOR: You have to remember he'd been doing budgets for 20 years. He'd debated them, amended them, watched others debate and amend them. He'd seen them added to, subtracted from, adjusted, and readjusted more than anyone else at the table. He knew all the tricks.

Essentially there were two ways we could reduce the amount of spending from the executive branch. One way was executive order reductions, which required the approval of both appropriations committees; of course, we could never get [House Appropriations Chair Dominic] Jacobetti's agreement.

[291]*Dawson Bell, interview with GW, February 27, 2001.*
[292]*Mark Murray, interview with GW, December 2, 2000.*

The other was through State Administrative Board transfers. In the 1920s when the legislature met less often, they created the State Administrative Board. The Ad Board essentially made the statewide elected officials the state's board of directors. It allowed the Ad Board to make administrative transfers and effectively administer the state's finances in the absence of the legislature. Well, as the legislature exercised more of its perogative, the Ad Board was relegated to more business matters.

But the 1928 statute was still good and the governor decided that it was time to be brought back to the forefront. Now, reviving the use of the Ad Board lessened the control of the legislature. When we set up 28 administrative transfers, the legislature took notice of what we were doing. We eventually negotiated 27 of them. We preserved one for purposes of litigation (*Dodak v. Engler*, which the courts decided in our favor). But that was the turning point.

GERRY MILLER: This is the same Ad Board that Governor Milliken called a waste of time. He once told me, "If you ever sit in on an Ad Board meeting, I'll fire you." So John Engler's use of the Ad Board was certainly innovative.

MARK MURRAY: I wouldn't call it so much innovative as meticulously careful. John knew about it and took the time to learn the rules.[293]

*

Tough love: General Assistance (GA) cuts

David Hollister

When Engler started closing down General Assistance, I protested the cuts by helping set up a tent city on the Capitol lawn. During that time there was a coalition of human service advocates that was composed of people who ran homeless shelters, people who ran human service agencies, and some clergy including radical priests in Detroit. They all helped with the tent city. Engler argued that the people cut from General Assistance were employable men, but many of them were disabled because they were either high-school dropouts, substance abusers, or hadn't been employed in three years or more.

You walk by homeless people every day and you don't see them. It's a phenomenon that goes on in every city in the country. We don't want to see homeless people, so we don't. In 1991 we decided to make it real with our tent city.

When Engler was cutting GA, we didn't have an advocate who could articu-

[293] *Patti Woodworth, Lucille Taylor, Gerald Miller, Mark Murray, interview with GW, February 3, 2001.*

late the liberal human services vision. The last leader to have the vision and hold the line was Republican Bill Milliken. I got along better with him than I did with Blanchard. In fact, I got along better with both Milliken and Engler than with Blanchard. I continue to do so to this day. I disagree with Engler, but I respect him and I can negotiate with him.[294]

*

Jim Haveman was director of the Department of Community Health.

In those early days, we would walk through the tent city, and the welfare mothers were screaming, "Give us our money! It's our money. We deserve it!" I can honestly say that we never saw John Engler blink. And that was a good model for all of us.[295]

*

Bill Whitbeck

The reason no one connects the public John Engler with the private John Engler is that he often gives the appearance of being glib and uncaring. We were walking through the tent city and a protester demanded that he be given a job. John turned to me and said, "Find this man a job." So I found him a job at $7 an hour, and the guy wouldn't take it. So John announced, "This man isn't jobless; he's on strike."[296]

*

Lew Dodak

Our main task was to work on the budget. We were in a recession and the numbers were down. The governor from the start had made it clear he wanted a smaller state government. We would go through every line item of the budget. I'll give John Engler credit. He had very capable people who were tough on me and the Democrats. Patti Woodworth was tough but fair. I admire and respect her. She is exactly what you want in a DMB director.

That first year GA was part of the budget problem. It was a fight I could not win: the media were not on our side but on the governor's side. He won the argument politically. Taxpayers don't want to pay people for doing nothing. However, to this day I don't think we saved a dime because those people were

[294] *David Hollister, interview with GW, March 29, 2001.*
[295] *Jim Haveman, interview with GW, December 2, 2000.*
[296] *Gerry Miller, interview with GW, February 3, 2001.*

either back in community placement or incarcerated, which costs a lot more than GA ever did.

I remember going to the governor's residence for breakfast in April or May of '91. I think he and Jeff McAlvey thought they could get me one-on-one to make more concessions, but there was no way. The budget had been too polarized. Breakfast came in. "Do I need a tester?" I asked. I was trying to break the ice, but the governor didn't like that comment too much. I didn't think we could accomplish much because of the politics.

He asked if I wanted to ride back to the Capitol with him. But I thought of all the people camped out on the Lawn, in the tent city called "Englerville."

"No thanks."

"You sure? Come on, ride with me," he persisted.

I didn't want to. I told him, "There are enough people after your ass. I think I'll ride in my truck."[297]

*

A discussion among staff about welfare and GA:

DAN PERO: One thing that really hurt was when people called John uncaring. He was very caring—in fact, he cared so much he wanted the poor to break the cycle of dependency. It was tough love.

COLLEEN PERO: They also accused him of being unable to relate. That is not true. He could relate better than most. He grew up in a hard-working family, lived in a rural community, and never mixed with the rich until he became governor.

LUCILLE TAYLOR: This is John Engler's philosophy on welfare: "If I have given you an education, if I have given you job training, I have given you something significant. On the other hand, if I have given you a welfare check or some entitlement, I have bought you off so that you won't bother me until the next check comes."

GERRY MILLER: That's absolutely right. Although there were some people in my department who wanted this to be purely about budget concerns, for John Engler it was never just that. For him it was a debate about true compassion, the size and scope of government, and conservative philosophy. And that hasn't changed to this day. He was on the leading edge.

PATTI WOODWORTH: But John was so smart to realize that a tight budget was a vehicle for getting some of his policy passed.

[297]*Lew Dodak, interview with GW, July 10, 2002.*

GERRY MILLER: The budget was the tool to get it passed. We used the budget crisis to change the philosophical debate. People have asked me if we would have cut GA if there had not been a budget crisis. The answer is yes—absolutely yes! It was the right thing to do. If we had had a surplus, it still would have been the right thing to do. This was a policy debate.[298]

*

Pain

Dawson Bell wrote in the Detroit Free Press:

TIME'S UP FOR SACRED COWS

It was a restless night for state government's sacred cows.

Today is the day Gov. John Engler has set aside to unsheath his veto pen (or meat ax, as many would have it) to trim about $200 million from the state budget.

The victims are expected to include longtime pet projects of powerful lawmakers, and some areas of education, Engler's own pet project....

"It's going to be deep, very deep ... and painful," said House Minority Leader Paul Hillegonds, R-Holland, after a meeting with Engler Thursday.[299]

*

Rusty Hills served as director of the governor's Communication Division.

Governing is about choices. As we went through budget choices, we opted not to hurt education, because we thought that the long-term effects would be horrible for the state. We were not going to shortchange kids. But that meant we had to cut elsewhere. And that meant we had to let people go. That was painful on a personal level.

I remember a conversation with Jeff McAlvey. He went to church with other state employees. Some of them were affected by the budget cuts. Jeff knew that and it hurt him deeply to talk to these people. Jeff believed that John Engler was doing the right thing for the right reasons. He was doing it for the state of Michigan. He was trying to put the commonweal first.

But that's cold comfort when you are face-to-face with someone who has lost a job. I felt sorry for Jeff, who knew some of those people personally. It was hard for him.[300]

[298]*Dan Pero, Patti Woodworth, Lucille Taylor, Colleen Pero, Gerry Miller, interview with GW, February 3, 2001.*

[299]*Dawson Bell, "Time's up for Sacred Cows,"* Detroit Free Press, *October 11, 1991.*

[300]*Rusty Hills, interview with GW, February 12, 2001.*

*

John Truscott

John has always been protective of his family. During the budget cuts, his brothers and sisters had to deal with people who hassled them. At the store people would approach them and protest the cuts. John wanted to tell people that his family didn't ask for this life, so leave them out of it. He wanted to say, "If you have a problem with my decision, come and talk to me."

During the first year or two, the staff was also under a terrible strain, but we pulled together as a family. The camaraderie was incredible, and it was because all we had were each other. We didn't have anything if we didn't back each other.

There were so many times that three or four of us would go to lunch and vent our problems, air our concerns, and talk about how we were getting hit with criticism. The bonds that we developed were probably much stronger than in many other administrations. The intensity of the attacks and the difficulty of the decisions we needed to make is part of what brought us close together. And this camaraderie was developing up and down the staff, not just at the director level. Constituent Services alone was getting hundreds of calls a day and thousands of letters a week, all negative, all attacking the staff. So everyone just pulled together. They were very, very tough times. The only alternatives were to pull together or quit. And for me quitting was not an option. I wanted to tough the whole thing out and, if we didn't get re-elected, so be it.[301]

*

Lew Dodak

Gov. John Engler's first 100 days in office have been a major disappointment. He is leading a mean-spirited administration, dedicated to an extreme and radical policy of dismantling vital state services and programs with little regard for the human impact. His reckless approach to downsizing state government has created chaos in state-provided human services, causing needless suffering for our most vulnerable residents. And his obstructionist approach to the legislature has led to a stalemate on budget negotiations for the current and upcoming fiscal years, causing uncertainty, fear and anger in many families and communities....

John Engler still has time to re-chart his course, for his administration and

[301] *John Truscott, interview with GW, October 27, 1999.*

for the people of Michigan. If he fails to do so, he will become, as others have begun to suggest, a one-term governor.[302]

*

I can't take it anymore!

Rusty Hills

During one meeting Lucille came in and said, "Today is our sixth month anniversary. Only seven more periods of time like this." And I thought to myself, "I can't take seven more periods like the six months we had just been through."[303]

*

John Truscott

At the time of the '90 election, we were in a pretty severe economic downturn. In John Engler, the people elected a governor that was not going to take the situation lying down. He was determined to make sure that during the next downturn we would be much better prepared. That meant that we needed to fundamentally change the way state government operated by changing the tax structure, workers' compensation, unemployment compensation—all the things that influenced whether new businesses would locate here or existing businesses would expand here. That kind of fundamental change is hard.

When I would talk with other colleagues in other administrations around the nation, there was a sense that our staff had the toughest job in the country. No other gubernatorial administration was going through what we were going through at that time.

There were only 17 Republican governors in the whole country in 1991. Most of those states were pretty comfortably Republican—like Utah, where Republican leadership is the status quo. There had been only a couple of surprise elections where Republicans won where they weren't predicted to win. We were one of them.

In Michigan, the Engler administration had to make fundamental changes. We had the worst budget and had terrible tax and regulatory burdens. I think John's attitude was, "Let's take it all on. Let's do it all at once. Here's our opportunity."

[302]*Lewis N. Dodak, "Chaos and Divisiveness Mark Engler's Start,"* Detroit Free Press, *April 10, 1991.*
[303]*Rusty Hills, interview with GW, February 12, 2001.*

I was travelling a lot with the governor in the early days. We would go out to try to talk about the agenda and what we were doing in this new era of government.

Once we released our budget, we were met with protestors everywhere we went. The Democratic Party had done a very good job organizing the opposition.

We were driving up to a Lincoln Day dinner in Jackson County and we saw protestors in front of the building. There were a significant number of them. When I saw the protestors, I said, "Oh no."

When John saw the protestors, he asked the driver to stop. The Oldsmobile wasn't even in park yet and he hopped out of the car. His security detail wasn't even out of the car yet and John was walking right into the crowd. Everyone went dead silent. John spent 10 to 15 minutes talking to the protestors, trying to convince them that he was right and they were wrong. The protestors respected that.

Security detail wasn't used to this kind of behavior from a governor. The previous governor liked to enter events through the back door.[304]

*

Lucille Taylor

The governor was committed to change. What that meant was this: every Friday, at 4:30 p.m., I would get a call from some court somewhere notifying us that we had been sued—every Friday, for months.[305]

*

David Bertram

After the GA cuts, we were out on a county visit. We went to Baldwin, in Lake County, the poorest county in the nation east of the Mississippi. We had made a few stops and were concluding the day in a main-street diner. The event was a "meet-and-greet." The Michigan State Police were extremely nervous about our going there. They recommended that we not do the final stop because of the size and attitude of the crowd. We were getting word ahead of time that they were very hostile.

"We are going through with this event," John told the MSP.

So we got to the diner. The place was packed. They had moved the tables and it was wall-to-wall people. They had been directly affected by GA cuts and they

[304]*John Truscott, interviews with GW, October 19 and October 27, 1999.*
[305]*Lucille Taylor, interview with GW, February 3, 2001*

were mad. I had been to literally hundreds of events with John. Never before had I felt unsafe. But when we got to that diner, I felt unsafe. We were confronting not just another crowd, but a mob. John did not show any fear, did not even show any hesitation. He stood the whole time, addressed the crowd, and did an amazing job explaining the rationale for the cuts. He confronted the issue head on and fielded every hostile question. His manner toned the crowd down. I was just amazed.

This is typical John Engler. He is not just another politician making decisions in Lansing. Once he makes a decision, he goes out and explains it to the people who are most affected. This shows his tremendous political courage and leadership.[306]

*

Media criticism

Detroit Free Press *editorial page*

Gov. John Engler's budget vetoes continue the dismantling of state government's social contract with all of its constituents, not merely a favored segment. But before Lansing Democrats wail loudly about the "mean-spirited" GOP governor, they might re-examine their own roles in the process.

The $7.5-billion general fund budget Mr. Engler signed last week not only ends general-assistance grants for nearly 90,000 Michiganians whose "able-bodied" status has been more asserted than shown, it also denies most of them any health care. The new budget makes large cuts in aid to many of the state's premier arts institutions, local governments, civil rights enforcement efforts and youth and public health programs.

That slash-and-burn budget could not have passed without Democratic votes in the state House...

Gov. Engler hardly pretends any more that massive cuts in state spending, often afflicting Michigan's most vulnerable citizens, will not be an inevitable element of his regressive property tax cut plan. But it will be difficult for Democrats to claim the high ground now or in future election years, given their complicity in the dismal process that created this year's budget.

Mr. Engler is doing just what he said he would do. It's time—and it already may be too late—for Democratic lawmakers to match their rhetoric with effective action.[307]

[306]*David Bertram, interview with GW, July 11, 2002.*

[307]*"Democrats Shouldn't Whine after Giving in So Easily," editorial,* Detroit Free Press, *October 17, 1991.*

*

John Truscott

The honeymoon between John Engler and the media was over after the first State of the State. After that he had to deal with many nasty things told about him. The Democrats took advantage of the biased reporting and tried to solidify this image of John Engler as a hard-nosed, uncaring, political animal.

During the first couple of years, when special interests groups were attacking Engler, we felt so alone. We were such a small army trying to do what was right. From the governor's perspective, he knew what was wrong with government: the special interests groups were trying to completely control the appropriations process. John really took on these special interests groups; he wanted to change the status quo. Any time you challenge the status quo you are going to upset people and you're going to make the opposition come out in full force. When you are defending the status quo it is much easier because they have the stories, they have the people; they have the sympathy on their side.[308]

*

Frank Garrison was head of the AFL-CIO, Michigan.

When you look up "mean-spirited" in the dictionary, there should be a picture of John Engler next to the definition....

If anyone previously doubted the cold-heartedness of John Engler, one need only take a close look at his state budget....

It's going to be a long, hard winter for the poor, unemployed, sick and elderly.[309]

*

Dawson Bell

The main problem Engler faced during his first year in office was that he didn't seem to care about people. Even some of his allies questioned his decisions. People knew that it was necessary to cut back on the extravagance of the Blanchard administration. But even a close adviser like Richard McLellan thought that the reduction in executive office staff hurt Engler's ability to carry out some of his agenda. Other Engler allies were frustrated because the reductions made it appear that the governor didn't care about state workers.

[308] *John Truscott, interview with GW, October 27, 1999.*
[309] *Frank Garrison, "Ill Will Permeates Engler Budget." From photocopy of column in Engler administration files. Source and date unknown.*

This criticism flared up when the Englers did a public service announcement for the Humane Society. I remember thinking that Engler has a terrible problem with public relations when he is criticized for being nice to puppies. A PSA like this should have been a no-brainer for a new governor. But it got turned around. The press presented Engler as a guy who paid more attention to dogs than to people.[310]

*

Following are editorials and articles that appeared during Engler's first year in office.

HOW HAS GOV. ENGLER MANAGED IT?

The common assumption is that Gov. John Engler's popularity with the voters must be taking a terrible beating. Headlines scream of pain inflicted by budget cutbacks. He has played no favorites either. Both social services for the needy and arts for the wealthy have felt the ax.

Yet a poll conducted for Bill Ballenger's *Inside Michigan Politics* newsletter has discovered a real shocker.

When asked who is to blame for the current budget problems, former Gov. James Blanchard properly is named the chief culprit by a wide margin among respondents from all walks of life.

Much to the surprise of most "experts," fewer than one in 10 points the finger at his successor.

But the poll also found that about half of us don't like the budget-cutting while roughly 40 percent do.

One pollster commented, "It's as though voters are saying, 'We know we've got the disease; we're just not sure we like the medicine.'"

But the point is that voters aren't as uninformed as was supposed. They didn't fall for the Democrats' tactic of blaming the mess on Engler.

There's hope for democracy yet.[311]

*

ENGLER'S KEEPING PROMISES

John M. Engler's strong steps as governor were bound to provoke criticism and perhaps even the recall campaign being mounted now.

But none of the major moves taken by Engler should prompt surprise. The governor is doing precisely what, as a candidate last fall, he said he would do

[310] *Dawson Bell, interview with GW, February 27, 2001.*
[311] *"How Has Gov. Engler Managed It?" editorial,* Oakland Press, *June 1, 1991.*

and what a majority of voters now have a right to expect. In addition, he predicted—as it turns out quite accurately—that something dramatic would have to be done, regardless of who was elected governor, because that person would inherit a huge, hanging deficit.

The particulars are simple. Engler in his campaign promised a smaller state government, less taxation and more emphasis on education. Everything he has done since Jan. 1 has been in that vein. He has eliminated one whole department of government and scaled back most others, reduced appointive jobs and shrunk the state work force. He failed to get a property tax cut from the legislature, but did get a freeze on assessments. And he has increased the share of state spending going for schools, reversing what had been a longstanding pattern in the Blanchard administration.

Why would anyone expect anything different? In John Engler, Michigan last fall had a clear alternative to the incumbent. Anyone who gave even passing attention to the issues and to Engler's words knew what was ahead. Those who voted for him and are muttering now are suggesting that they spent the autumn in a coma or on another planet.

What makes the case for Engler's program much more compelling is the absence of alternatives. This state simply cannot continue spending and taxing as though Americans had not yet bought their first Toyota. Times have changed...

Former Gov. James Blanchard never confronted this new reality. As recently as this month, he was flimflamming that he left office with a $420 million surplus in the Treasury—never mind that the legislature and Engler have been absorbed for months in trying to pare down a deficit which remains at $664 million despite a half-billion dollars in cuts made by the legislature last December.

...There is no question that Michigan cannot afford to spend and tax as it once did. That is the truth which will survive the protests and the recall petitions, and which Engler's critics, sooner or later, will have to admit.[312]

*

CUTS PUT STATE IN SPOTLIGHT

Gov. John Engler's grand plan to slash spending, cut welfare and balance the budget without a general tax increase has made Michigan a media darling.

[312] *"Engler's Keeping Promises," editorial,* Flint Journal, *June 9, 1991.*

In the past eight weeks, Michigan has been highlighted in the *Wall Street Journal*, the *New York Times*, *USA Today*, *Newsweek*, on National Public Radio and by CBS News....

"The national media have recognized the leadership of Governor Engler in making the tough decisions that other governors haven't had the courage to make," Truscott said.

Tom Shields of Marketing Resource Group in Lansing said the national media take a broader approach than the state media. "The articles nationally seem to focus more on the methodology, the fact that Michigan is one of only a handful of states trying to get through this recession without a tax increase," he said.[313]

*

THE MAN OF THE YEAR

Gov. John Engler is taking a beating as the year turns. He is caricatured by left-liberal groups as a kind of political grim reaper, personally responsible for the death of any homeless person who succumbs to the harshness of life on the streets. When Michiganians look back on 1991, however, we think he'll come to be seen as this state's man of the year.

This time two years ago, only John Engler and his closest associates thought he could be elected governor. Gov. James Blanchard had survived a very rocky first term to cruise into what seemed a fairly uneventful second term. He was not obviously beatable and was even talked of by some as a potential vice-presidential candidate or cabinet member in any new Democratic administration.

Those hopes died on election night 1990, when Mr. Engler, then state Senate majority leader, squeaked past Mr. Blanchard by barely 18,000 votes. It soon transpired that Mr. Blanchard, who had claimed throughout the campaign that the state budget was balanced, had in fact been hiding a $1 billion deficit. Mr. Engler had not only pledged not to raise taxes, he had promised to cut them, and boost education spending to boot.

It seemed an impossible task, especially for someone like John Engler, with a reputation as a moderate and a conciliator. It seemed only a matter of time before he, like fellow Republican Pete Wilson in California and George Bush in Washington, was forced to break his pledge and ask for new taxes.

Much to his credit, Gov. Engler has refused to cave in. He merged or eliminated dozens of state boards and commissions, fired a few thousand state work-

[313] *Kathy Barks Hoffman, "Cuts Put State in Spotlight,"* Lansing State Journal, *December 9, 1991.*

ers and, in the most controversial move of all, eliminated General Assistance welfare benefits for able-bodied single adults. Yet this was not the action of a green-eyeshades accountant. It was the action of a governor trying to work a revolution in state priorities, including an increase in the share of education funding that comes from the state.

The governor thus acted to halt a process that was apparent to sharp-eyed observers for a long time: A critical margin of productive people were leaving Michigan. The state will lose two congressional seats following the 1990 census, costing the state voices and votes in Washington. To turn that around, Michigan will have to stop talking about being more competitive and actually do something about it.

Michigan is a highly taxed state by almost any definition, but the outflow of productive people means a bloated state bureaucracy is being supported by fewer and fewer taxpaying citizens. A tax increase, as so many urged on the governor, would simply have accelerated the process of decay. History bears this out: Both William Milliken and James Blanchard hiked taxes substantially, and both left office with deficits.

The cuts have and will cause some short-term pain, which liberal interest groups are using to make political hay. The governor himself looks a bit worn after the battles of the past year. He is displaying some of the tell-tale signs of an embattled politico, such as blaming the press for a poor image.

No doubt the press can always do a better job, but any governor who makes painful decisions, especially in the midst of a recession, is going to catch flak because those losing their benefits are easily identifiable and eager to talk. Those who gain, such as the folks who don't see ever higher percentages of their paychecks going to taxes, are less visible.

But by holding the line, the governor has sent a valuable message to those who are thinking of investing and creating jobs in Michigan. The message is this: We are not going to tax the productive sector more and more in order to support the nonproductive sector.

In essence, George Bush sought to send the same message in 1988 when he asked voters to "read my lips." He reversed himself on that, and the recession is the price he is paying. Gov. Engler need look no further if he has any ideas of making a U-turn in the new year.[314]

*

[314]*"The Man of the Year," editorial,* Detroit News, *January 1, 1992, p. 10A.*

How did he do it?

Jeff McAlvey

When Engler wanted a bill, he was good at finessing and charming. He could also be threatening and tough. He could pull out every trick. It was all role playing.

When we met with legislators, we usually were in the parlor [adjacent to his desk in the Capitol]. He would sit at one end of the table, and I would sit at the other end. I did that to maintain eye contact with him. We had a wonderful relationship, and I really believe that I could almost read his mind. I knew where he was going. I knew what he'd say next. And I could help him control his temper. He has that very sharp wit, which with some people does not play well. I knew the members better than he did because I was out on the floor with them all the time. Sometimes, when we were at that table, I would put my hand up to give him the sign that he was going too far and needed to back off. He normally respected that. I knew when he could be cutting and when he could not.

There were some interesting times in the parlor. One of the most famous was when he was trying to move the corrections bill. He had some of the House appropriations committee in, including Representative Clyde LaTarte from Jackson, a good man. Engler couldn't get the votes. He was talking to them and finessing them. When I left to go back onto the floor, it was a very nice discussion. There was give and take. But after a while, Don Gilmer, who was chairman of the appropriations committee, came out, grabbed me, and said, "You better get back in there. He's going to kill them!"

"What?"

"You won't believe it!" Gilmer said.

I went back in, and Engler was sitting at the table, on the edge of his seat, and he was looking at LaTarte.

And LaTarte was saying, "Well, governor, I just think it's bad policy. I just don't think you've thought it out well enough."

Engler said, "You know, Clyde, the problem is, it's time for you to start doing some work of your own. You're right that the bill needs some more work. You're right that it needs some committee meetings. So stop whining. You're chair of a committee. Get to work!"

I was at the other end of the table, motioning him to stop. He looked back at me as if to say, "I know exactly what I'm doing." And he kept going and he got hotter and even used the "f" word, which I've heard him use only two or three times in all the years I've known him.

I held my hand up again, and again he shook me off. "I know what I'm doing," he was signaling me.

Unfortunately, news of this encounter spread on the House floor like wildfire. That kind of treatment by Engler soon became a verb: "I do not want to be LaTartized!" For weeks after that, I could say to a difficult legislator, "You could say yes to me now, or I could take you in to talk to the governor." And the legislator would say, "I don't want to be LaTartized! That's all right. I'll vote yes."

Engler did not do that very often with legislators—he was hot maybe only five percent of the time. Sometimes he'd use that sharp wit to slice somebody. Sometimes he'd be funny in a good-natured way. Most often he was very charming. He would approach negotiation as problem solving. "What's your issue? Let me explain to you why this is such important policy."

Still, legislators knew Engler was very good at getting what he wanted. Situations would frequently arise where I would need one more vote for a bill. I'd be at the legislator's desk on the floor, down on one knee, talking about how we had to have this vote; the governor really needed this vote. I'll never forget the time I was working on Carl Gnodke. He was my only hope. The voting board had been open 45 minutes, which was unheard of in House history. Mick Middaugh was sitting next to Gnodke and piped up, loud enough for everybody to hear: "Okay, Lard Ass, you know what's going to happen. You're going to tell McAlvey no. He's going to take you to the back and talk to Engler, and then you're going to say yes, and then you're going to come out here and vote. That's all going to take another 45 minutes. We're all tired. We all want to go home. Just face the fact that if he takes you in to see Engler, you're going to vote yes. Just do it, would you?" Gnodke thought about it for two minutes—and voted yes [on the real estate transfer tax, which was part of Proposal A, in late December 1993].

I remember another time in the House Republican caucus when Gary Randall got up and said: "You all talk tough. You all beat your chest here. You all know that John Engler is going to come in here in ten minutes, and we're all going to melt like butter. So why don't we just get it over with and decide that we are going to support him on this."

Usually Engler did not have a very direct way unless he was very close to you. With most members he would "go around the barnyard." That's what we called it. He would go all the way around before he would get to the topic. He's trying to work a Republican and get him to the right spot.

Or it's like fencing. He's parrying. He's looking for an opening. He tries and tries and tries till he finds what works. This technique almost always brought them around.[315]

*

Dennis Schornack

When it comes to getting his way with the legislature, John is the absolute master.

Sometimes he uses "the hairy arm." It's the diversion. You put in the big ugly thing that everybody hates and wants to beat up on. Everybody focuses on that. Meanwhile what you really want the legislature to pass escapes notice. Behind the scenes, you carefully work out the details and get your legislation passed.

Other times John "kills 'em with kindness." This is a stealth technique he uses to kill a bill that has something we don't want in it. To kill the bill, you out-Democrat the Democrats. In other words, Democrats usually want to give away the store, so you pile on even more give-aways. You heap on so much that the bill dies and collapses of its own weight.

Still other times John will deploy the "irresistible amendment"—usually something having to do with kids that legislators wouldn't dare vote against. This is a good technique to use when there is resistance to something you want passed. Adding a child-friendly amendment changes the equation altogether.[316]

*

Paul Hillegonds

There would be a lot of give and take at the beginning of a legislative session. John always had strong ideas, but he was good about negotiating when someone would point out why a particular policy issue might not work the next two years. Still, he would push us. And once we signed on the dotted line, he was *ruthless* in holding us to our commitment.

Once our agenda was decided on, we would have weekly leadership meetings in the governor's Capitol office conference room. House and Senate Republicans would sit around a big table, and the governor would be at the head of the table. At these weekly leadership meetings, there were times when one chamber or the other would be holding up our mutually agreed upon agenda. There would be times when we would have internal dissent in our caucuses.

When that happened, John showed no hesitation—no matter who the person

[315] *Jeff McAlvey, interview with GW, May 29, 2002.*
[316] *Dennis Schornack, interview with GW, June 7, 2002.*

was or how close to him—to stare at the person with a firm jaw. "I understand you have a problem with what we had all agreed to do. Do you want to tell me why?"

Suffice it to say, usually by the end of the meeting John would get his way![317]

*

Lew Dodak

John Engler, like Gary Owen, loved the partisan politics. When he negotiated with me, he was hard-nosed. He would always push. Even after you thought you'd reached a deal, he was always pushing you a little bit further. He was good at pushing.[318]

*

Engler and Jesse Jackson

Dawson Bell

Engler has seldom played defense.... Amid the siege early in 1992, about the time Engler reached the nadir of his personal popularity, the Rev. Jesse Jackson came to town [January 14, 1992]. Jackson apparently thought the turmoil in Michigan would make a good backdrop for a national story about the Reagan-Bush era's tattered safety net. Engler didn't wait in his office for Jackson to show up, however. He issued a press release saying that he looked forward to meeting Jackson so that they could discuss making Michigan a standard to which Democratic candidates for president could aspire. Even after cutting its budget, Engler pointed out, Michigan provided more welfare benefits than the home states of that year's Democratic presidential hopefuls, including then-Arkansas Gov. Bill Clinton. The Democrats weren't amused. But they got used to it. Subtle, mocking sarcasm, delivered with the barest hint of irony, was an Engler trademark.[319]

*

Bill Whitbeck

I remember the meeting with Jesse Jackson in connection with our GA cuts. John came out and the media asked him, "How did the meeting go?" John answered, "It put me a half an hour behind schedule."[320]

[317]*Paul Hillegonds, interview with GW, September 27, 2002.*
[318]*Lew Dodak, interview with GW, July 10, 2002.*
[319]*Dawson Bell, "Engler's Michigan: A Reign of Change,"* Detroit Free Press, *January 14, 2002.*
[320]*Bill Whitbeck, interview with GW, February 3, 2001.*

*

Lafayette Clinic

No sooner had the furor over budget cuts and General Assistance died down than a major new crisis reared up. Community Health director James Haveman tells of one of the most dramatic moments the administration faced.

Lafayette Clinic came to symbolize very bold, gutsy action by the governor early in his administration. Here's what happened.

In 1992 the Michigan Department of Mental Health was engaged in a months-long trial in Judge Hathaway's courtroom in Wayne County. Those filing the suit wanted to keep Lafayette Clinic open. The Engler administration believed that the Clinic was no longer serving a therapeutic purpose: 240 persons were employed to provide treatment to 30 persons, many of them no longer needing hospitalization. The annual cost of providing these services for each patient was over $500,000, and we felt these funds could be better used to provide community based services.

The week of March 21, 1992, was very contentious. I was on the stand and the plaintiffs' attorneys were very aggressive with the support of the judge, who obviously was siding with the UAW's position and that of Michigan Legal Services. Judge Hathaway on Friday, March 26, was admonishing me in court for not keeping the clinic open and was threatening to order me to keep it open. If I didn't, he said that he would hold me in contempt of court. If I were held in contempt of court, he would have me arrested. I remember that day well because the plaintiffs cheered in the courtroom when they heard the threat to have me held in contempt.

The judge adjourned for lunch and ordered me back at 2:00 p.m. to sign a consent order he was supporting to keep the clinic open. By signing the consent order, I would have been showing my agreement with the order. But the order was contrary to my position, which was to close the clinic and not spend the funds to keep it operating.

The attorneys for Attorney General Frank Kelley had been doing a stellar job in the courtroom representing our position. I went out to lunch with attorneys Mark Meadows and Al Hoffman, plus Diane Censoni (director of the Bureau of Hospital and Facilities for the Department of Mental Health). We were at Fishbones in Greektown when my phone rang. I was asked to call a number on a secure phone. I called and was put through to Governor Engler, who said that he didn't want me to sign the consent.

"Get back to Lansing," the governor said. "We need you back here immediately."

I looked at Mark, "I'm leaving," I told him.

Mark was very uncomfortable and suggested that I appear in court as ordered. "You can't leave," he said. "I'm your attorney. You have to stay." Clearly he was wondering, if I didn't stay, what would happen to *him*. This is when I realized that the attorney general's staff assigned to our case were more interested in their office than in my predicament.

I knew that I had to get out of Wayne County quickly, so I hastened back to Lansing (leaving the others to pay the bill). On the way back, I was told to come back to the Olds Plaza where the governor's office was located. I was secreted to Jeff McAlvey's office.

When the court reconvened at 2:00 p.m. that day, our attorneys appeared in front of Judge Hathaway and the Wayne County media. They said that they had advised me to appear for the consent order, but that I had chosen not to appear—against their wishes! I was held in contempt of court. An order was entered on the lien system requiring that law enforcement authorities pick me up and place me under arrest. So back in Lansing that afternoon, I was dodging the governor's security detail since they were Michigan State Police; they would have had to place me in custody on behalf of Wayne County authorities.

The governor's office went to work immediately with the attorney general's office to appeal the contempt order. Governor Engler indicated to me that afternoon that, if the appeal was not heard immediately, my wife Barb and I could stay at the governor's residence on Mackinac Island for the weekend. "Just make sure you have a good time," he said. What a great gesture at a time like this. I will always be appreciative of that offer. Later that day, in the early evening, the Court of Appeals overturned Judge Hathaway's order of contempt.

Give Governor Engler all the credit. He was willing to stare down a judge in Wayne County because a judge was making policy, not enforcing policy or the law or the rights of the administration. The governor's bold action eventually led to the closure of Lafayette Clinic seven months later. He was gutsy.[321]

*

RICHARD McLELLAN: The worst and most unfair criticism was the Lafayette Clinic hullabaloo. That was the worst, the ugliest sort of thing. But I don't think it could have been done any other way. If we could have had a cordon of 200 policemen, that would have been better, but the Detroit police pulled out of there.

[321]*James Haveman, interviews with GW, December 2, 2000 and August 4, 2002.*

PATTI WOODWORTH: They refused to help us! They refused to provide protection for the patients. On top of that, you had the employees of the clinic chaining the doors and blocking the fire escapes.

LUCILLE TAYLOR: It was theater staged by John Engler's opponents.

MARK MURRAY: But what was so unfortunate about it was that there were vulnerable people being hurt—they were really terrified.

PATTI WOODWORTH: And the people who were hurting them were the people running the clinic—the union organizers.[322]

*

John Engler: revolutionary

Doug Rothwell was brought on board the Engler administration to head up the governor's economic development initiatives. He recalls:

When I joined the administration, I was taken around and being introduced to the staff. Jeff McAlvey greeted me with, "Welcome to the Engler revolution. We are turning government upside-down and inside-out."[323]

*

William D. Eggers and John O'Leary are the authors of the 1995 book, Revolution at the Roots.

THE REVOLUTIONARIES

Governors such as John Engler of Michigan, William Weld of Massachusetts, Tommy Thompson of Wisconsin, and New Jersey's Christine Todd Whitman, have been streamlining state government. These and other leaders have started the process of doing more with less by lowering taxes, shrinking the bureaucracy, and making state government competitive. They have also stood up to entrenched interest groups to push through historic reforms in education and welfare.

In the future, America's governors will take on greater importance. In part because of technology, we are witnessing a worldwide trend toward decentralized decision-making, in business as well as in politics. In the new Era of Radical Devolution, power will shift from Washington, D.C., to state capi-tals. No longer will the federal government issue mandates controlling everything from water quality to classroom standards to speed limits. Increasingly, states will call the shots on welfare, transportation, environmental issues, property rights, and a host of other issues.

[322] *Richard McLellan, Patti Woodworth, Lucille Taylor, and Mark Murray, interview with GW, February 3, 2001.*
[323] *Doug Rothwell, interview with GW, March 16, 2001.*

JOHN ENGLER'S BOLD USE OF THE EXECUTIVE ORDER

Michigan Governor John Engler's first year in office in 1991 marked the beginning of a new era in Michigan politics. After squeaking out a win (17,595 votes) over Democratic incumbent James Blanchard, Engler immediately started downsizing Michigan's bloated government. Within months of taking office, Governor Engler had cut back the Michigan Council for the Arts (savings: $11 million); closed down the Department of Licensing and Regulation (savings: $25 million); cut the budget for the Department of Commerce in half (eliminated four gubernatorial councils); and ended welfare for able-bodied adults (savings: $150 million).

Even with a Democrat-controlled house, Engler was able to achieve these politically volatile reforms through the executive order. In Michigan, overturning an executive order requires a majority vote of *both* houses of the legislature. With Republicans controlling the Senate, all 13 orders signed by Engler in his first three-and-a-half months were sustained. "It's a remarkable tool for consolidating functions and eliminating superfluous commissions, of which Michigan has hundreds," said Bill Whitbeck, Engler's legal advisor.

The governor's reductions at the Michigan Council for the Arts were immensely controversial. The media attacked Engler, a middle-class guy who grew up on a farm, as a philistine. The *Detroit News* called Engler an "arts ogre ... whose idea of high culture is a weekend with [his wife] at Boblo." (Boblo was a honky-tonk amusement park.) The governor's gutsy termination of the general relief program and closure of five under-utilized state mental hospitals (one hospital housed six patients and had a staff of 120) were also widely decried. Still the governor held firm. After the media storm blew over, voters liked the results, and in 1994 Engler cruised to re-election with 61 percent of the vote.

Several lessons emerge from Engler's success. First, downsizing requires bold, decisive action. The governor did not spend years studying whether the Department of Licensing and Regulation was truly providing value for the taxpayer. After 20 years in the state legislature, Engler knew very well that it wasn't. So he simply pulled the plug.

Secondly, unlike more timid politicians, Engler made the tough decisions knowing they would be unpopular in the near term, especially with the media. Engler did what he thought was right, hoping that Michigan's electorate would respect him for it. He gambled right. John Engler has demonstrated that downsizing can be good government *and* good politics. "I think there's a huge constituency out there for shrinking government," says Engler. "I think we've shown you can take risks beyond what was thought politically possible."

ENCOURAGING PRIVATE CHARITY

When the government pulls back on aid, the private sector often steps in. In 1991, Governor John Engler of Michigan discontinued general assistance (GA) for childless able-bodied adults, saving the state $250 million in benefits. This move spawned dramatic protests, including a "Tent City" at a park near the capitol in Lansing. When the shouting was over and the deed was done, however, the dire predictions failed to come true; and the move proved overwhelmingly popular with the voting public (one poll showed 81 percent support).

When he announced the end of the GA program, Governor Engler called for churches, civic groups, charities, private businesses, and families to fill the gap left by the state: "Taxpayers had neither the obligation nor the limitless resources to subsidize perpetually single adults."

Dozens of private programs have sprung up—and existing programs have been expanded—to meet the increased demand. For example, a group of volunteers from Harrison, Michigan, opened up the Hard Times Café, a privately-funded center that offers companionship and job counseling to former GA Recipients. Faith, Inc., a locally initiated program out of Grand Rapids, was formed to help the homeless get jobs and get clean. The key to the group's success is developing important skills such as hard work, self reliance, and responsibility. The best way to inculcate these skills is through work. "At Faith, we don't send them to 'assessment school' for six months to decide what career they would like," says a Faith volunteer. "We help them start work immediately. It's essential to enhancing their self-worth."

Despite the protests and uproar it caused, Engler doesn't regret cutting off GA. "I think we did the right thing," he says, "and the evidence is quite compelling that we did." In 1991, 82 percent of Michigan's GA recipients had never held a job. By April 1993, 34 percent of all terminated GA clients had been employed at some point during the year, at least part time. (The disabled continue to be served by other state programs.)

An interesting byproduct of Engler's elimination of General Assistance was that the state contracted with the Salvation Army to lodge any former GA recipients in shelters. "Because of this partnership, no one in Michigan need spend the night without shelter," says Engler.[324]

*

[324] *William D. Eggers and John O'Leary,* Revolution at the Roots: Making Our Government Smaller, Better, and Closer to Home *(New York: Free Press, 1995), pp. 10, 55-56, 245-246.*

Detroit

Anne Mervenne

John Engler has had to deal with a lot of criticism, but it's been particularly hard regarding Detroit. We met resistance on many policy issues, but worse was when the governor was accused of not caring about Detroit and of being a racist.

That was absolutely wrong. He has always cared about Detroit—it's the biggest city in the state with ten percent of the state's school-age population. He's taken enormous political risks, sticking his neck out when it came to policy issues regarding Detroit. Many politicians wouldn't have done that, because they wouldn't have wanted to deal with the opposition. John Engler has done more for Detroit than the previous governor ever did.

Some people did recognize this fact and it was always so refreshing to feel their support. At one event in Detroit, he came into a room of 300 African-Americans and received a standing ovation. It was a party for sending Betty Applebee off to South Africa, and he addressed the people and said, "I don't regret anything I've done. I only regret I had to do it the way I did." He was referring to cuts in General Assistance and the fact that he had no choice because of the budget deficit. That remark was totally impromptu, and the people there respected him for saying that. Everyone wanted to talk to him afterwards, shake his hand, and get his autograph. It was an amazing night. It was refreshing after all the criticism that we heard.[325]

*

Election Day 1992

Michigan was a battleground state in the 1992 presidential contest between George H. W. Bush and William Jefferson Clinton. John Engler campaigned hard for his friend Bush, but on November 3 Clinton prevailed in the Great Lakes State as well as nationally. As the New York Times *put it, "The Democrats came out of the wilderness on Tuesday. The Republicans entered it." Nationally, that is. For in Michigan, the GOP made a strong showing in state House races. Republicans picked up six seats, making for a 55-55 tie in the lower chamber. John Engler was jubilant—it was the first time in his career that Republicans were not a minority in the House. Part of the reason for GOP gains was the strong anti-incumbency mood of voters. In a related campaign, a constitutional amendment—Proposal B, calling for term limits on federal and state officeholders in the executive and legislative branches—passed overwhelmingly with 59 percent of the vote. Engler supported the measure in 1992, but in later years he thought it*

[325] *Anne Mervenne, interview with GW, February 1, 2001.*

too restrictive. In the 2002 elections, for instance, state government lost, in one fell swoop, more than 500 years of experience in the Michigan Senate alone.

Michigan Jobs Commission

During his first term, Engler embarked on an economic development program that to some of his staff bore resemblance to the old Strategic Fund he had criticized. In 1992 he created the Michigan Jobs Commission and put Doug Rothwell in charge. Just two years earlier, in a white paper prepared for the 1990 campaign, candidate Engler had come up with a ten-point job development plan that included (1) a tax structure that promoted economic growth, (2) the elimination of bureaucratic costs of regulation, (3) privatization, and (4) better job training, among other things. There was no proposal in the white paper for the creation of the Jobs Commission. In fact, Engler roundly attacked Blanchard's initiative:

The Michigan Strategic Fund [was] created by the Blanchard administration in the mid-1980s. From a job development standpoint, it has been an unqualified disaster. In providing preferential subsidies to a favored few, it has built an alarming portfolio of questionable multimillion dollar loans....[326]

*

Once he became governor, Engler was the first to admit that he did not want to create the Jobs Commission. But he felt his hand was forced because other states had such programs and thus were positioning themselves to rob Michigan of jobs. He could not sit on the sidelines. He was doing all he could to improve the economic structure of the state—lowering taxes, cutting red tape, reducing the size of government—but in the competitive atmosphere of the 1990s, it was not enough. So he launched the Michigan Jobs Commission. As the following exchange shows, many senior staff and friends groused.

BILL WHITBECK: The question, "Is this an appropriate function of government?" was often asked during the campaign and first term. Look at the Accident Fund. John felt strongly that the government ought not to be in the workers' compensation business. And so he got the state out of it, and at a considerable profit.

RICHARD McLELLAN: The Strategic Fund—which is economic development, picking winners and losers—is one area where John has done a complete 180 degree turn as governor. He had the position when he started that it was

[326] *Draft of "New Priorities for a New Decade in Economic Development," white paper for the John Engler for Governor campaign, c. 1990, p. 10.*

inappropriate, and then he changed his mind. Now he's outdoing Blanchard and Milliken in economic development. It is stunning for those of us who usually find him ideologically consistent.

PATTI WOODWORTH: I hated it when he started thinking that way. It pissed me off. I was driving today on I-69, and I saw a Jobs Commission sign and thought, "Yuck!"

LUCILLE TAYLOR: There has been some backsliding, Patti.

RICHARD McLELLAN: I think it all started when John was running for re-election and Dan Pero was thinking, "What can we give them?" I think it was a political switch for the first re-election. Then he got Doug Rothwell, and Doug somehow captured the governor on this.

LUCILLE TAYLOR: My justification for this is that every state has a Jobs Commission. You can't be the only one out there that is ideologically pure and still compete for these companies.

DAN PERO: The toughest challenge to John's original principles was when we lost Willow Run and GM chose to go to Texas. That was devastating to him. He watched [Texas Governor] Ann Richards dancing and coaxing them to come down there. Although he was doing much behind the scenes, and constantly in touch with GM's leadership, it looked as though he didn't lift a finger to keep them from moving to Texas.

Then he had to go down and face the workers the day his father died. It was one of the most incredible exhibitions of courage that I ever saw. He went down to talk to them face-to-face and explain to them why GM decided on Texas and why they lost their jobs. He had to put up with the accusation that he didn't fight to save the plant. The truth is, he did everything he could but just didn't have the tools.

What he didn't say, which he could have said, was that we lost Willow Run because we have more strident unions than Texas has.

RICHARD McLELLAN: He didn't have MEGA (Michigan Economic Growth Authority); he couldn't give away the store.

LUCILLE TAYLOR: There was a study that had a whole list of measurements that were used by companies to gauge competitiveness and whether to locate there. There were several areas that we could not do much about: we're among the most heavily unionized states in the nation; we will never be a sunbelt state; we are not going to be a no-income-tax state.

Regarding economic development, we were at a competitive disadvantage and the governor addressed the problems systematically and effectively.

MARK MURRAY: The list of economic tools Michigan now has is considerable. We have enterprise zones, renaissance zones, different kinds of MEGA credits, smart zones, research parks, and the list goes on.

COLLEEN PERO: It has become a very slippery slope!

RICHARD McLELLAN: The surprising thing is not that we have so many tools but that we have adopted the faith that the government can pick winners and losers—that certain technologies are where it's at. It's industrial planning from a Republican point of view.

In fact, every governor since Romney has had these programs. They have a lot of sizzle. I'm not sure that you can actually study their effect because every governor changes their names several times. But there's a lot of anecdotal evidence that "this plant would not have been built if it hadn't been for program X."[327]

*

Lawrence (Larry) Reed is president of the Mackinac Center for Public Policy, a free-market think tank in Midland that John Engler helped establish in the late 1980s.

The Michigan Economic Growth Authority was simply a poor policy. To Governor Engler's credit, I don't think that he started the business incentive schemes because he had become a true believer in them. Rather, I think he would probably tell you that if the other states would stop doing it, he would too. He continued to do it because other states did it.[328]

*

Matt Engler, RIP

On Monday, March 2, 1992, Mathias Engler passed away. The next day, the governor was scheduled to appear in Ypsilanti to give one of the most difficult speeches of his first term. It concerned General Motors' decision to close its historic Willow Run plant in Ypsilanti, Michigan, and jobs were at stake. All would have understood had the governor cancelled. John Truscott recalls:

The end was coming for John's father. He had been in a nursing home in Mount Pleasant. Sometime early in the evening of March 2nd, John got the call that his dad had passed away. I was at the office when I heard the news. No one in the press knew.

[327]*Bill Whitbeck, Richard McLellan, Patti Woodworth, Lucille Taylor, Dan Pero, Colleen Pero, Mark Murray, interview with GW, February 3, 2001.*
[328]*Larry Reed, interview with GW, July 6, 2000.*

Early the next morning, I met the governor at the residence. He looked tired. I told him I was sorry to hear about his dad.

"He was a great man," the governor said.

I wanted to be supportive, so I offered him a way out. "You don't have to do this. You don't need to go to Ypsilanti to give that speech—they'd understand."

"No," the governor said firmly, "I gave them my word."

We drove down to Ypsilanti. It was a quiet ride down. The governor was solemn. Mostly we read the papers.

When we arrived at Washtenaw Community College, there were probably a hundred union protestors with nasty signs. I thought, "Of all times to have to deal with this."

But when he got out of the car, he took time to talk to a few of the protesters. He always talked to protesters. Then he went inside, gave his speech, and took a few questions. It was a courageous performance, considering all he'd been through.

When he walked off the stage, *Detroit Free Press* columnist Hugh McDiarmid was waiting and took him aside. I heard Hugh say, "I'm very sorry to hear about your father...."

The governor couldn't hold his grief back any longer. He broke down. They talked several minutes, just the two of them.[329]

*

Columnist Hugh McDiarmid wrote:

GOVERNOR FINDS STRENGTH DURING
A MOST DIFFICULT TIME:
HIS MOST DIFFICULT SPEECH

Let's hand it to Engler.

He performed, not perfectly, but with remarkable grace and candor Tuesday morning in what may have been the most difficult public speaking engagement of his life.

The most difficult?

Oh, it wasn't just the subject matter—Willow Run—or the overflow breakfast audience, made up mostly of still-shocked members of the Ypsilanti Area Chamber of Commerce. And it wasn't the table down front, filled with glaring, v-e-r-y hostile representatives of UAW Local 1776. And it wasn't the pickets

[329] *John Truscott, interview with GW, July 29, 2002.*

with their nasty signs (e.g., "Breakfast with Engler? Why Bite the Hand that Bites Us?") outside the hall at the Washtenaw Community College.

It was his father.

Matt Engler had died Monday evening at the Isabella County Medical Care Facility in Mt. Pleasant, near Beal City and the Engler cattle farm where John grew up.

And though it was not obvious to everyone (the governor is not a very demonstrative person), John, 44, and Matt, 68, were very, very close.

They had touched insiders who had witnessed them hugging warmly and at surprising length in Cobo Hall in September 1990 right after John was nominated for governor. And those that paid attention were touched again four months later when they saw John grasp Matt's hand, then his arm, then his shoulder as they sat side by side during the inaugural mass at Lansing's St. Mary's Cathedral.

Anyway, John found out about 8 p.m. Monday that Matt had died. It wasn't a complete shock because he'd been in declining health. But it was an awkward surprise.

At such times, most of us—even governors—would clear the decks and head home. After all, John's mother, Agnes, survives and, with six other children ... well the clan would be gathering.

So, yes, the staff did scrub Tuesday's midday trip to Washington, D.C. And the whole rest of this week was cleared.

But not the breakfast.

"It was a tough call," acknowledged one Engler aide. But with all the finger-pointing, scape-goating and genuine anger accompanying the Willow Run plant-closing ... well, there would no doubt be some who would figure the governor had cut and run.

So he didn't.

Instead he got up at dawn in Lansing and headed to Ypsilanti, passing word that he didn't want the death mentioned to the crowd.

The introductions and preliminary remarks lasted f-o-r-e-v-e-r.

Then there was a long introduction of the governor before he spoke.

It was a workman-like address—the "bitter disappointment" of the Willow Run announcement, the helpful but not-yet-complete explanation from GM, the warning that more plant-closings would come unless ... and, finally, the cure, including specifics of the Engler program for tax cuts, for "a healthier entrepreneurial climate," etc.

It lasted exactly 25 minutes.

And it was followed by questions from the audience, a news conference in a nearby auditorium and, finally, a very private meeting with UAW leaders.

Through it all, John was very, very ... well, gubernatorial.

With one exception.

Backstage before the press conference, a reporter who'd heard about Matt mumbled to the governor that he knew how close they were and was sorry.

At that point—unseen by anyone else—John cried some hot, genuine tears, said thanks for the kind words and talked briefly about Matt's poor health and how his death was a mixed blessing.

But it was only for a moment. Then, dry-eyed, he went back to being governor.[330]

[330]*Hugh McDiarmid, "Governor Finds Strength During a Most Difficult Time: His Most Difficult Speech,"* Detroit Free Press, *March 4, 1992.*

Religion, morality and knowledge, being necessary to good government and the happiness of mankind, schools and the means of education shall forever be encouraged.
NORTHWEST ORDINANCE OF 1787
MICHIGAN CONSTITUTION OF 1963

★

Chapter Twelve

First Term from July 1993 - December 1994

Ask observers of the Engler administration: What was John Engler's best moment? His greatest triumph? The turning point in that tumultuous first term? The answer is unanimous: passage of Proposal A—by a landslide—on March 15, 1994. It was a policy and political masterstroke that garnered national attention. Engler himself later remarked that the evening of March 15 was the most fulfilling in his 12 years as governor.[331]

The dramatic story of Proposal A began eight months earlier, on a warm July evening in 1993. Engler was well past the midpoint of his first term. He had campaigned for governor on the promise of a 20 percent cut in property taxes, but had not been able to deliver. Two ballot proposals had gone down in defeat, the latter as recently as June 1993. Engler frankly needed some stroke of luck, some major policy success, some major mistake on the part of Democrats to put him on a smooth glide path to re-election in November of 1994. To his incredible good fortune, the Democrats obliged.

But it took Engler's courage, experience, and intelligence to turn the Democrats' misstep into a victory, not just for himself politically but also for Michigan property owners and school children. The result, as then-Senate Minority Leader Art Miller put it, was "one of the best pieces of legislation this state has ever seen."[332]

Dennis Schornack

If any single incident captures John's gifts and abilities as a person, this has

[331] *GW, personal papers, September 2002.*
[332] *Art Miller, interview with GW, September 25, 2002.*

got to be it: Proposal A. You have a Democratic bluff, a phone call, a split-second decision calculating the risk, the gamesmanship, the ability to look forward, and the courage to carry it all out.[333]

*

Patti Woodworth

When I think of John Engler as a leader, what immediately comes to mind is all that happened to get from Senate Bill 1 to Proposal A. That took extraordinary leadership. It best shows John Engler as governor. It best shows how he is a master of strategic and political thinking. It shows that he thoroughly prepares and knows his options when the time comes to make decisions. It shows that he can roll up his sleeves and do the hard work. It shows that he's got the guts to play the games you have to play to get anything important done.[334]

*

Background to the drama

Doug Roberts

Look at what happened during John Engler's career. Between 1970 and 1993, there were at least eleven proposed constitutional amendments over seven different elections that tried to address the problem of property taxes and/or school funding. Voters rejected all eleven proposals. But the problem didn't go away. Michigan property taxes remained among the highest in the nation, and the gap between rich and poor school districts was growing. We faced a terrible and intractable problem. If some solution didn't materialize, we were headed for a court-imposed settlement, as had happened in so many other states.[335]

*

Bill Browne

A comment reflecting despair after house Democrats had failed to support Governor Blanchard's 1988 plan to reform public school finance illustrates the significance and failure of Michigan interest groups in deal making. A handful of legislators walked dejectedly down the capitol corridor, irritated that this issue kept coming back to them. All nodded in agreement as one legislator sug-

[333] *Dennis Schornack, interview with GW, February 3, 2001.*
[334] *Patti Woodworth, interview with GW, February 3, 2001.*
[335] *Doug Roberts, interview with GW, October 14, 2002; the ballot proposals are summarized in the* Michigan Manual, *1997-1998 ed. (Lansing: Legislative Service Bureau), pp. 114-19.*

gested that tax reform would neither pass nor disappear as an issue until the Michigan Education Association and the State Chamber of Commerce jointly drafted a bill. The two groups, of course, did not—at least, until Governor John Engler almost successfully linked educational equity and a shift in tax policies in {June} 1993. At that point, he insisted that everyone participate or exit the arena. It was not until 1994 that school finance and property tax reform were linked....[336]

*

Art Miller

Property taxes were a runaway train in this state. Every time local governments had a budget problem, they'd send the assessor out to increase property taxes. Every election the problem hung around our necks like an albatross.[337]

*

Al Short

Property taxes in Michigan were just a thorn in every politician's side. It didn't matter if you were Democrat, Republican, liberal, or conservative: property taxes were way too high. We were out there every year having to run millage elections. Due to the tremendous appreciation of property in this state, we had local property taxes funding close to 70 percent of the cost of K-12 schools, along with funding the community colleges. Cities, townships, and counties had to have the property tax to fund their government as well. As a result, we had all of these anti-tax groups in the state roaming around and protesting.

There were committees put together to study the problem and try to come up with a plan. It all came to a head in June of 1993. There was a ballot provision called the "Star Plan." It was a bipartisan plan to increase the income tax, lower property tax, and deal with school finance. Engler supported it, both parties in the House and Senate supported it, and we {MEA} supported it. But that proposal lost 51-49. We had all met at the Radisson Hotel, and it looked as if we were going to win, but when the results came in from the three big counties in southeast Michigan, our proposal went down. Looking back, I think one of the problems was that the voter was confronted with this choice: "If I vote no, I won't have a tax increase, but if I vote yes, I will." The plan was seen not as an education issue but a pocketbook issue and it lost.

[336] *William Browne, Kenneth VerBurg, et al., "Influencing Michigan Politics," in* Michigan Politics, *p. 219.*
[337] *Art Miller, interview with GW, September 25, 2002.*

So in June everybody was really down. That set the stage for an extremely frustrated legislature and an extremely frustrated executive branch. This state was at its wits' end about what to do with property taxes.[338]

*

Since voters had recently rejected a ballot proposal to fix the school finance/property tax quagmire (June 1993), there were few public hints of the drama to come barely six weeks later. On Monday of the historic week in which Democrats bluffed Engler and Republican lawmakers, the Detroit Free Press *ran a prescient editorial.*

TAX CUT:

WHERE WILL STATE FIND MONEY FOR SCHOOLS?

As a legislative committee works on an agreement to reduce local property taxes, the focus has been primarily on whether such a tax cut can be achieved without offsetting tax increases to pay for public schools....

Michigan has a property tax problem and a school finance problem. The legislature and Gov. John Engler must respond to that reality in all its dimensions.

Doing so is complex. Surely, though, the governor and lawmakers can start to move us toward correcting what is in many ways a debilitating problem for Michigan, one that creates unconscionable inequities and holds back the state's chance to rebuild its economy and assure hope for all our children.[339]

*

The Lansing State Journal *ran a front-page article reporting on what happened during the day of Tuesday, July 20, 1993.*

Earlier Tuesday, a House-Senate conference committee quit work on a property tax cut plan as lawmakers differed over raising other taxes to replace the money.

The conference committee began meeting last week in a bid to reach agreement on property tax relief. Although it considered a number of plans, it foundered when Democratic leaders insisted on tax increases to fund the tax cut and Republican leaders pressed for a property tax cut with no other tax raises.

The Republican-run Senate called a rare evening session to discuss a GOP plan to cut school operating property taxes by 20 percent over three years.[340]

[338] *Al Short, interview with GW, February 26, 2001.*

[339] *"Tax Cut: Where Will State Find Money for Schools?"* Detroit Free Press, *editorial, July 19, 1993.*

[340] *Malcolm Johnson, "Senate Bill Cuts Taxes, and School Funding,"* Lansing State Journal, *July 21, 1993, p. 1A.*

*

Gambit

The breakthrough would occur in the Michigan legislature on the evening of Tuesday, July 20, 1993. During the day the Democratic caucus in the Senate met and agreed to have Debbie Stabenow sponsor an amendment to Senate Bill 1. Stabenow was given the go-ahead because she was running for governor.[341] *The amendment called for breathtakingly bold action: eliminating the property taxes that paid for public schools.*

Engler conferred with Democratic Minority Leader Art Miller and immediately sensed that the Democrats were bluffing. Given the Michigan Education Association's influence with Democrats, there was no way Stabenow was serious. Democrats just wanted to embarrass Republicans going into the 1994 elections. It was a crucial electoral year because the governor, 38 senators, and 110 representatives were up for re-election. By having Republican lawmakers vote against SB 1, Democrats could truthfully say that Republicans were not really serious about cutting property taxes. This would keep the GOP on the defensive.

Engler decided to call the Democrats' bluff. He quickly brought Senate Majority Leader Dick Posthumus on board. The governor and majority leader also called Co-Speaker Paul Hillegonds and urged him to start working the Republican caucus in the House. Everyone involved on both sides of the aisle has vivid—if diverging—memories of what took place.

Art Miller

It turned out to be quite a poker game that night—and the winner was the public.

It started when Stabenow had this wild idea: get rid of property taxes to pay for schools. Initially in my [Democratic] caucus there was a lot of doubt whether either caucus—Republican or Democrat—would accept the idea. Would the governor buy it? All my members needed to check with the MEA: "I've got to stick with the MEA. What does the MEA want?" Well, the MEA was sitting on the sidelines because they liked the fact that property taxes were generating a lot of income. The status quo helped teachers get a bigger paycheck. Their attitude was: Why are we playing this game of Russian roulette? Besides, you know the governor isn't going to buy it. Were they in for a surprise.[342]

*

[341] *JE, interview with GW, September 11, 2002; see also "Senate Eliminates Taxes for Schools,"* Detroit News, *July 21, 1993, p. 3B.*

[342] *Art Miller, interview with GW, September 25, 2002.*

Patti Woodworth

I was with the governor in the Capitol when Debbie Stabenow introduced the amendment to eliminate property taxes as a funding source for education. She introduced it as a bluff or joke. Somebody came running in to tell us, and we all gathered because we needed to discuss it. There were arguments among the staff, some saying, "You need to take it. Here's why." Or, "You shouldn't take it. Here's the danger."

John Engler just listened. After everyone had spoken, he said, "Tell them to pass it. Tell them I'll sign it."

My stomach just fell. I was afraid that if we eliminated property taxes, we wouldn't get other reforms and, in the meantime, the schools would be without funding. I felt it was walking to the brink of political suicide.[343]

*

Joanne Emmons

I will never forget that night in the Senate. I was the new chair of the finance committee. We had recently brought forward several property-tax proposals, and I had another one that evening, but frankly it wasn't very good.

Then we heard a rumor that Debbie Stabenow was going to propose abolishing property taxes for school operating expenses. Republicans went into caucus and agreed to go for it. This might be the way out of a decades-long logjam. So we went back to work, and I was arguing for the previous proposal, when Debbie did indeed put the tax repeal amendment up.

About 7:30 or so, Dick Posthumus said to me, "Just talk. Just buy some time. Argue against Debbie's amendment. I want to talk to the governor one last time to make sure this is really what he wants us to do."

So Dick talked to the governor, and the governor said, "Go for it!" And Debbie had her amendment voted on, and we voted overwhelmingly for it.

As the votes went up on the board, Debbie was nervously pacing. When the amendment passed, the look on her face was, "What have I done?" She looked as if she could barely breathe. She looked as if somebody had hit her in the gut and knocked the wind out of her. She had no idea that this was going to happen. And the MEA that set her up had no idea that this was going to happen. Heads were going to roll.[344]

*

[343]*Patti Woodworth, interview with GW, February 3, 2001.*

[344]*Joanne Emmons, interview with GW, September 25, 2002.*

Senators Debbie Stabenow and John Schwarz later told a reporter what they recalled happening in the Senate chamber:

[Debbie Stabenow] "We'd already seen the Kalkaska schools close. The Lansing schools were saying they were out of money. But property taxes were too high and we had to replace the revenue.... But we just weren't getting anywhere. So I put this out there thinking it might set a deadline."

Both Stabenow and [Sen. John] Schwarz recalled Posthumus immediately standing up to label the idea "irresponsible"—and then his phone rang. It was Engler, who'd been closely following the action, telling him to take the Stabenow plan.

"Then my phone rang," said Schwarz, who was presiding in the Senate at the time. "It was the governor. He said we were going to take it because it was going to force the writing of some real tax reform. That set the stage."[345]

*

John Engler

There was a reason Dick stood up and called the amendment "irresponsible." It was a ruse to lure the Democrats into committing themselves before we closed the trap. It worked.[346]

*

Paul Hillegonds was in an historically unusual position. In 1993 the House was evenly split between Republicans and Democrats. Republican Hillegonds and Democrat Curtis Hertel served as co-speakers in a power-sharing arrangement that enabled each speaker to preside in alternating months. As luck would have it for the Republicans, Hillegonds was the presiding speaker of the House in July. He recalls:

I'll never forget that evening. I was at home making hamburgers with my wife, and I got a call from the governor and Dick.

"Guess what we've just done?" the governor began. "Would you be prepared to move on the elimination of property taxes in the House tomorrow?"

Cautious person that I am, I thought, "This is a huge risk. This could destroy us. If the Democrats allow us to go over a cliff...." The governor could see I was reluctant.

"No one is going to allow that to happen," he responded. "But, Paul, if you don't move quickly, nothing is going to happen. If you sit on this, all the cau-

[345]*Debbie Stabenow and John Schwarz, quoted by Ron Dzwonkowski, "The 'A' Team,"* Detroit Free Press, *September 29, 2002.*

[346]*JE, interview with GW, October 23, 2002.*

tious lawmakers and interest groups and editorial writers and public opinion will make this a lost opportunity."

By the end of the conversation he and Dick had convinced me.

He had made the promise on property taxes and was willing to take the risk to fulfill that promise. My wife Nancy was as astounded as I was.[347]

*

Newspapers chronicled the unfolding drama:

STATE SENATE VOTES TO END PROPERTY TAX FOR SCHOOLS

The Senate, in a stunning move Tuesday evening, voted overwhelmingly to repeal the use of property taxes for school operations. That would mean a massive tax cut for Michigan property owners and businesses.

But Senators did not identify another way to fund schools.

The bill passed 33-4, and backers vowed to press for quick agreement in the House.

If enacted, the bill would cut property taxes by about $5.6 billion, or roughly two-thirds of all property taxes levied annually. Lawmakers said it would force officials to rebuild Michigan's school finance system.

"With the start we have tonight, we're off and running," a jubilant Gov. John Engler said Tuesday night....

The tax-repeal amendment would take effect Dec. 31, affecting 1994 taxes.

It was sponsored by Sen. Debbie Stabenow, D-Lansing, who is running for governor, and embraced by minority Democrats. But majority Republicans shocked them when they agreed to it and dropped their own tax rollback plan.[348]

*

DEMS DEALT, ENGLER WON
POOR PEOPLE, STATE EMPLOYEES AND
STABENOW COULD BE LOSERS

"They won't do it," Gov. John Engler said to State Sen. Dan DeGrow, R-Port Huron, at midday Tuesday.

Democratic Senate Minority Leader Art Miller had just left a meeting with the two men, saying his party wanted more property tax relief than the Republicans had on the table.

[347] *Paul Hillegonds, interview with GW, September 27, 2002.*
[348] *Malcolm Johnson, "State Senate Votes to End Property Tax for Schools,"* Detroit Free Press, *July 21, 1993, p. 1B.*

The GOP proposal—a 20 percent cut—was "just peanuts," Miller had said.

At a Senate session later that day, the Democrats intended to up the ante, wiping out local school property taxes altogether, Miller said.

"They won't do it," Engler said again.

"But what if they do?" DeGrow asked Engler.

'They won't ... but if they do ... we take it," Engler responded, effectively setting the stage for what a few hours later became the largest tax cut in Michigan history.

And a reaffirmation of the lesson most Lansing political observers thought Democrats had learned by now—don't play poker with John Engler....

State Sen. Debbie Stabenow, D-Lansing, the purported leading Democratic candidate to challenge Engler in 1994, led the charge. Engler cheered them on throughout....

But the one question on the minds of many in Lansing on Thursday was: What were Miller, Stabenow and the Democrats thinking about when they dared the Republicans to give it a try?

In the campaign biography she released just two months ago, Stabenow said she "has taken the lead against unfunded property tax proposals jeopardizing our schools."

On Thursday, Stabenow said: "If we hadn't done what we did, we would be limping along with continued hemorrhaging in our schools."

Other Democrats, however, described Stabenow's bold step as a "catastrophe" that touched off "mass psychosis" in the legislature, threatens all of their core constituencies and plays directly to Engler's advantage.

State Rep. Mary Schroer, D-Ann Arbor, an early supporter of Stabenow's gubernatorial bid, called the legislation "nonsensical."

"I will find it very difficult to continue that support" for Stabenow, Schroer said. "... this is nuts."

Nor will Democrats get much credit for delivering property tax relief. That's a Republican issue....

Certainly, the huge education lobby at the Capitol was rolled over in the rapid pace of events this week.

As the Senate first took up the Stabenow amendment, Michigan Education Association Lobbyist Al Short told DeGrow and other lawmakers to "go for it."

By Wednesday, the union was having second thoughts when it became clear that the finished product would contain no guaranteed reimbursement.

As the House debated the measure, an array of education lobbyists sat high above the chamber in the gallery, head in hands. The MEA put out a news release late Wednesday that said the governor and legislature were "about to railroad through one of the most destructive pieces of legislation affecting children in recent history."

And for that, Stabenow, a longtime darling of the MEA, will have to take some considerable credit.[349]

*

Al Short

I'll never forget that night in July when the Senate was in session. They had come back from a break and Debbie Stabenow, out of the blue, offered the proposal to call the bluff of the Republicans.

For the record: that proposal did *not* originate with me or the MEA. It originated with her and a few members of her caucus. I got tagged with it because somebody asked me afterwards if I were going to approve the plan and I said, "We have tried everything else. Maybe this will work to bring the problem to a head." The next morning, I was quoted in the papers as supporting it. I *should* have said, "Look, we can't support anything that doesn't have replacement dollars."

The next day the proposal went over to the House. They debated, and the morning after that, they passed the thing, because the Democrats said they could not win back the House in the coming elections if they didn't do something about property taxes.

Now, we were in a state of shock. We had wiped out billions of dollars. For the next school year there wasn't a dime.

To best understand why this happened, you have to go back to that day in June when the previous plan was rejected by voters. Just the month before, everybody seemed to support school finance reform—yet it failed, by a very narrow margin. So the governor gave Posthumus the responsibility of trying to put something together. During the weeks that followed, legislative committees were meeting constantly, trying to work something out. But there were so many interests to balance, so many problems to solve. We were not making progress. The frustration just kept building and building.

What happened that night in July reflected the frustration of the legislature, especially the leadership and the people on the taxation committees. I think when this opportunity suddenly popped up the thinking was, By God, let's grab this thing, wipe out the system we have, and maybe it will force a com-

[349]*Dawson Bell, "Dems Dealt, Engler Won: Poor People, State Employees And Stabenow Could Be Losers,"* Detroit Free Press, *July 23, 1993, p. 1A.*

promise. Everybody was thinking: this will force the other guy to come my way. Democrats knew that Engler could not keep from funding schools. They figured this was a way they could beat him.

Now, the legislature is a reactive, not a proactive, body. If you accept that concept of the legislature, you realize that you can have the grandest ideas, but if there is not a readiness, if there is not some external force pushing you to react, you can't line up the votes. I don't care what reform it involves—telecommunications, electricity deregulation, school finance, the health industry. You will go months and only pass bills in the last 24 hours, because it is the force of the deadline, the force of the next election, that brings about results.

That's what happened on that July night. It was the exact point in time when something had to be done. Debbie Stabenow threw this thing out thinking, "We'll show the Republicans—we'll show John Engler and Dick Posthumus and the whole crew." Of course, Engler called her bluff. Boom!—it passed.

When the House passed it, too, the MEA panicked. Our policy was to support wiping out the property tax only if we had the replacement dollars, and I didn't have the two pieces together. I appeared to be soft on wiping out the property tax. I was director of government affairs at the time. Because I was quoted as supporting the Stabenow amendment, a lot of people wanted me fired. They thought I should have just stomped it down then and there.

What some people were not able to see was the bigger picture. If we had kept the status quo, we would have had an open revolt in this state on property taxes. We would have school districts going bankrupt because voters would just refuse to pay. You get a house and it keeps going up 10 percent and 20 percent and you're paying $12-, $14-, $15,000 on a $150,000 house. No way. It's just beyond people's means. And remember, local governments wanted their property tax, too.

I thought that we could go through the legislative process and (1) come out of the crisis with more money, (2) get rid of millage elections, and (3) narrow the disparity between rich and poor districts.[350]

*

Joanne Emmons

Stop and think about what we did. There was no funding for schools. *No funding*. Billions of education dollars had been taken off the table. Think how

[350] *Al Short, interview with GW, February 26, 2001.*

dicey that was. John Engler could not afford to fail. Without a solution by the new year, there would be total chaos. John would be recalled and finished as a politician right then and there.[351]

*

The "A" Team

Gleaves Whitney

Doug Roberts telephoned in late July and asked that I serve on the task force that would overhaul school finance and revolutionize public education in Michigan. Our first meeting was at 8:30 sharp on August 6, 1993. Gathered in the director's conference room at Treasury were Doug—the state treasurer and director of Engler's working group—plus Mike Addonizio, Madhu Anderson, Mark Haas, Howard Heideman, Mark Hilpert, Robbie Jameson, Nick Khouri, Bobbie McKennon, Georgia Van Adestine, and I.

For all of us, I think, the next eight weeks would be the most intense and exhilarating of our careers. Doug, standing at the head of the table, opened our first meeting with why it would be the high point of his career.

"Our governor is going to change Michigan," he began, "and we have been chosen to help him do it. Over the next weeks we are going to eat, sleep, and I hope dream school finance reform and education reform. Our specific mission is to help the governor come up with a plan—a plan that breaks Michigan out of the decades-old logjam over school finance; a plan that revolutionizes public education; and a plan that improves the relationship between state and local governments. The governor will be involved and directing our work. When our work is finished, when the governor has his plan, he will make a special address to the legislature. Then the bills will be passed, and probably a constitutional amendment will be passed, and the reforms will take effect, and we will look back on these days as the best of our career. The best because"—Doug paused for dramatic effect—"because we will have made a real difference in the lives of Michigan taxpayers and Michigan children. That's what this is all about: improving the lives of people."[352]

My job on the "A" Team was (1) to apprise leading education thinkers around the nation of the situation in Michigan and gather their ideas, (2) to handle some of the national media covering our progress, (3) to write the education

[351] *Joanne Emmons, interview with GW, September 25, 2002.*
[352] *GW, personal papers, July 1993-March 1994.*

address that the governor would give in a special session of the legislature, and (4) to help sell our plan to the public.

Within days, I was communicating with the nation's leading education thinkers and writers, gathering ideas: Grover Norquist (Americans for Tax Reform), Checker Finn and Diane Ravitch (Educational Excellence Network), John Fund (*Wall Street Journal*), Stephen Moore and David Boaz (Cato Institute), Peter Brimelow and Leslie Spencer (*Forbes* magazine). All were excited by what was happening in Michigan. They saw in John Engler the governor, and in Michigan the opportunity, to blaze a new trail in education reform. Within six weeks I would bring many of these stars into the state to meet with the governor.

The calls coming in from the national news media were also heartening. Reporters were hungry for details, and privately many of them said that they were excited by our reform ideas.

Within the state, I kept a number of our allies in the education-reform and think-tank community apprised. I drew on the expertise of Russell Kirk, Annette Kirk, Larry Reed, Paul DeWeese, Bob Whitman, Marilyn Lundy, and many others. All of them grasped the significance of the moment and recognized that far-reaching reforms were finally possible.

One afternoon I got a call from the governor. "Bill Bennett is in Michigan, on his way to Grand Rapids, and I'd like you to drive over and brief him."

So I drove to Grand Rapids and briefed Bennett in the Amway Grand Plaza. The former U.S. education secretary asked good questions and was cautiously optimistic. He closed our meeting with, "When you get back to Lansing, tell John I'm pulling for him. If any governor can take on the education establishment and fix a broken system, it's John Engler."[353]

*

Mark Haas is the director of the Treasury Department's Office of Revenue and Tax Analysis.

The remarkable thing about Proposal A is how Engler managed to pull together so much. It started out as a bill to replace school funding. But Engler seized the opportunity to make it so much more—an opportunity to improve public education, increase accountability, help teachers develop professionally, start charter schools, and much else. That's leadership.

[353]*GW, personal papers, September 1993.*

This governor is different from the two previous governors I worked for. He has a more complete understanding, a more in-depth knowledge, of the issues he cares about. When we were working on the legislative language for Proposal A, we would meet with him on Sunday afternoons. We all had big, thick 4-inch notebooks crammed with details about all the various bills that were being drafted up. Someone would be discussing some minute aspect of some particular bill, and the governor would say, "What you are suggesting contradicts what is said on page 117 of this other notebook. We have to reconcile the two." We would turn to page 117 and, sure enough, the governor would be right. We were amazed.[354]

*

Tim Skubick, the dean of Lansing reporters, wrote:

GOV. ENGLER ADORES THE STABENOW STUMBLE

The "wisdom" portends that [Sen. Debbie Stabenow]:

- Put the state's entire educational system at risk.
- Handed the incumbent John Engler the 1994 election.
- Allowed the religious right and GOP anti-union zealots to tear the Michigan Education Association to shreds.
- Risked her own impressive campaign momentum, or Big Mo is no mo.... John Engler just loves what she did.[355]

*

Some of the national press were already speculating how education reform in Michigan could boost John Engler's prospects in the next presidential election.

MR. ENGLER'S EDUCATION

One of the more creatively conservative governors has been John Engler of Michigan....

The cause of education reform requires that the governor not flinch and that he insist on genuine school choice.... Leadership today may be nationally noticed in 1996.[356]

*

[354] *Mark Haas, interview with GW, August 7, 2002.*
[355] *Tim Skubick, "Gov. Engler Just Adores the Stabenow Stumble,"* Lansing State Journal, *August 20, 1993.*
[356] *No author, "Mr. Engler's Education,"* National Review, *August 23, 1993.*

The birth of a revolution—and a baby

Many people have observed that John Engler's most important and most impassioned speech was "Our Kids Deserve Better," delivered to a special session of the Michigan legislature on October 5, 1993. The speech was covered by the national media and appeared in Vital Speeches of the Day.[357] *Gleaves Whitney recalls:*

On Wednesday, September 22, the governor and I met in the Detroit office to discuss the specifics of his upcoming speech. I was concerned because he was scheduled to deliver the address within two weeks. Given the revolutionary content, given the length of the speech, given the expectations in every quarter and what was at stake, we had to get it right: we had to set the stage for successful reform.

By the end of the first meeting, I knew we *would* get it right. I had submitted a 12-page draft with the major ideas blocked out and some suggested language. The governor immediately began shaping the whole text. He had the vision, focus, grasp of detail, and passion to make this the speech of a lifetime. Over the next 13 days, amazingly, we went through only six drafts. (For inaugural addresses and state of the state addresses, it is not unusual to go through 12 or 15 drafts.)

When the big day came, the governor and I met one last time to refine the text. We were in his parlor in the Capitol. His adrenaline was pumping, yet I was astounded by the calm manner in which he thought through the final changes he wanted to make.

After this final speech practice, I walked over to the gallery above the House floor and sat next to Larry Reed, president of the Mackinac Center. The governor walked in to thunderous ovation. He proceeded to deliver the speech brilliantly and with frequent interruptions by applause. At one point, when the governor was criticizing the MEA and its allies for putting up a Berlin Wall around our children, Larry grabbed my arm. Tears were in his eyes. "This is the greatest education speech I have ever heard."

The governor hit a grand slam and everybody on our side knew it. Our Democratic opponents knew it, too, but didn't want to admit it. Moments after the speech, I made my way back to the governor's parlor. He was talking to Michelle and to Doug Roberts and was just beaming. As I approached him, I felt powerful emotions—pride in him, gratitude to be a part of the administration, honored to be a part of history, relief that all had gone well, triumph for all who sought reform, and anticipation at what would come.

[357] *JE, "Our Kids Deserve Better,"* Vital Speeches of the Day, *November 15, 1993, pp. 71 ff.*

"I am honored to be a part of this moment. I am so proud of you...."

He put his hand on my shoulder and thanked me warmly. It was a richly memorable experience.

The next morning, my wife Louise was scheduled to have a c-section; we had joked how the birthday of our third child Andrew would be determined by the October 5 education address.

John Engler fully appreciated that fact and did not let Andrew's birth pass unnoticed. Whereas most people would have been preoccupied with the revolution they had started 24 hours before, John Engler showed a remarkable trait—one that friends consistently comment on. Amid all the education reform hubbub, the governor was the first person to call Louise after our baby was born. She was in recovery and feeling dopey, but able to take the call. The conversation coincided with the delivery of a beautiful spray of flowers and a teddy bear—from John and Michelle. Louise concluded the conversation with, "It was so kind of you to call."

After Louise hung up, the nurse asked, "Already getting congratulatory calls?"

"Yes," said Louise blearily. "From the governor."

The nurse spied her patient skeptically, "From the who?"

"The governor."

Louise noticed the doubtful expression on the nurse's face. "But it was the governor," she protested.

Alas, the more Louise asserted the fact, the worse it sounded. Patting her patient's hand and tucking the blanket in tighter, the nurse said, "*Of course* it was the governor. Now, dear, you get some rest and the anesthesia will wear off soon."[358]

*

After the speech, this article appeared in the newspaper.

ENGLER: SCHOOLS DESERVE BETTER

Gov. John Engler declared Michigan public schools a "monopoly of mediocrity" Tuesday and proposed a reform plan laced with free-market ideals to produce a "world-class education."...

Engler, speaking to a joint session of the legislature, was animated and even ad-libbed joking remarks during his hour-long speech.... He called on lawmakers to put aside politics and take a chance to boldly reform the state's schools.

[358]*GW, personal papers, September-October 1993.*

"This is a once-in-a-lifetime opportunity that transcends my political career and yours," he said.

Engler portrayed school choice as the centerpiece of his reform plan.

In his hour-long speech, Engler referred to schools as an "educational gulag" and a "Berlin Wall of separation" that denies students their right to choose which schools they attend.

"It's a strange system that says to families, 'You can choose where to buy your children's clothes, but not the school where they'll be worn,'" Engler said....

He chided opponents of school choice, adding, "I would sooner trust parents who love their children than bureaucrats who love their paycheck."

Engler used dramatics, humorous flourishes and compelling stories in one of his best major speeches.[359]

The governor fielding questions from school children during the first term

SOURCE: *Engler administration*

*

Al Short

Engler's October 5th speech set the stage for the most intense legislative session in the history of this state.[360]

*

Christmas Eve (legislative) package

All through the autumn, Engler, his staff, and allies worked hard to fashion more than two dozen reform bills and to craft a constitutional amendment that would put school funding on a stable foundation.

[359] *Chris Christoff, Dawson Bell, et al., "Engler: Schools Deserve Better,"* Detroit Free Press, *October 6, 1993.*
[360] *Al Short, interview with GW, February 26, 2001.*

Jeff McAlvey

Even within the Republican caucus, the negotiations over Proposal A became very heated and tense. Dick Posthumus's office was across the way from mine, and I could look right into one of his windows. I spied on his office during a caucus with the senators. They were talking about how they wanted Proposal A to look. To have a little fun, I called his office and said, "I see that you're all in there scheming against us again."

Dick looked out of the window and saw me waving to him. Immediately they closed the shutters, and those shutters were never opened again while I worked in the Capitol.

On December 21, the legislature decided they were going to pass one of their tax plans. It was an evening session, emotions were running high, and Engler told me, "I want you to go home. If they're going to do this, we're not going to be part of it. It's wrong. It'll destroy the plan. We're going home."

So I went to tell Dick Posthumus that we were going home. Then the governor and I walked out of the Capitol. It was the only time that I ever wasn't in the building, or didn't have somebody in the building, while they were in session.

The next day, December 22, we came back at 9:00 a.m. We were all exhausted. We'd been up until 3:00 a.m. the night before. We were all on the end of our emotional tether because we thought we had gotten a deal a couple of times and it kept falling through. Manny Lentine and I were putting the negotiations on a white board, our proposal on one side and their proposal on the other side. Everybody had shaken hands. We all thought it was going to work. We thought the deal was done. But on December 22 the legislature balked again. We were trying to get them to agree to allow us to put something in their plan in exchange for them putting something in our plan. There was a lot of finesse in these negotiations to bring it together. But, in the end, we couldn't get Senator John Cherry to make a decision.

We came back from the caucus that afternoon, exhausted. We had been trying to push them on the final pieces, the transfer tax and some other things. The governor threw himself in his chair in the Capitol, tears welled up in his eyes, and he said, "I lost it. I can't do it anymore. That was my caucus. In the past I could always get them to go where I needed them to. I can't do it anymore. I just can't get them to go where I need them to."

He was speaking specifically of this fight, yet we all knew this was our whole career—and whether he would be re-elected in 1994. You get this right, and you're re-elected. But it was also the first time he'd ever failed. Before then, anything that we'd ever tried to pass, we passed.

I knew him well enough to know that a lot of it was just exhaustion. All I could say was, "You know, we all need to go home and get some rest. I think the Senate is tired and we're tired."

The next day, December 23, I showed up in khakis and a cashmere shirt. I'd always worn a suit and tie before. Engler looked at me and said, "What are you doing?" In contrast to the previous night, it was clear that he was in the mood to roll up his sleeves and get back to work.

I said, "John, we can't do this. We have played every possible angle. The Dems don't want to do this. And I'm not gonna sit here in a suit and tie and go through this game if we can't get this done. I'm just exhausted."

But I could tell he thought we could do it. We worked through the night and on into the morning of Christmas Eve. Sure enough, we had successfully worked through the issues, and we were exhausted. It was a very emotional scene, with lots of hugs. The governor and Dick Posthumus both had tears in their eyes. We had been in session since 9:00 the morning before and we all made it to 1:00 p.m. the next day without ever stopping.[361]

*

A perspective on the final negotiations from Lana Pollack, a Democrat in the Senate:

Very early on December 23, 1993, we'd been working on what became Proposal A, and had had a "call of the house" on for nearly 24 hours. After a sleepless night, I'd been catching a nap on the floor of the Senate. (I'd realized that if I tucked my head under my desk and positioned my chair just right to block the view, I could lay down without being seen from the gallery—or so I hoped.) The phone rang on my desk, and in a near stupor I sat up and pulled it down so I could talk.

"Lana, this is John. What do you need?" an unfamiliar voice asked.

"John who?" I asked. "I need sleep."

"John Engler," the governor responded, "and I need to know what you need in the bill to vote yes."

Awake more or less by then, and inclined to vote for the bill at any rate, I

[361] *Jeff McAlvey, interview with GW, May 29, 2002.*

offered two provisions as "must haves" and John said he'd send Jeff McAlvey over to talk to me about them. I figured that as usual, Jeff would agree, or quasi agree, saying he'd have to talk to John. We'd subsequently agree, and in the end they'd deliver about half of what they promised to deliver. That pretty much turned out to be the case on Proposal A legislation....

The story is prophetic in that, while I with normal human capacities needed a nap in a marathon session, John Engler was wide awake and dealing on all possible fronts—and some impossible fronts, too.[362]

*

Al Short

It came out that John Engler said he was going to put the MEA out of business. Whether John ever said that or not is beside the point. We felt that he had, so we played that against him. In fact, the perception that he would enabled us to raise dues and bring people together. We even brought in a whole special lobbying team.

In August of '93, we brought in field people and we assigned them very specific territories in the state, under my direction here [at MEA headquarters in East Lansing]. We assigned them specific House and Senate members. They worked these people. I had a meeting in this building with those people every day, Monday through Friday, at 8:00 in the morning, every day from September through the infamous Christmas Eve finale. We went over the day's assignments; we went over the bills; we had people assigned to specific committees; we had analysis; and we'd push information out to our membership all across this state.

This was by far the MEA's most critical time, its most important battle, with the legislature and with the governor, that we ever faced or probably ever will face.[363]

*

Dawson Bell

For many of the participants, the legislature's frantic, all-consuming December rush to retool Michigan's public schools was the work of a lifetime.

Gov. John Engler called it the most important challenge he has faced in his 23 years in Lansing.[364]

[362] *Lana Pollack, interview with GW, July 30, 2002.*
[363] *Al Short, interview with GW, February 26, 2001.*
[364] *Dawson Bell, "Some Legislators Skipped Votes on School Plan,"* Detroit Free Press, *December 30, 1993.*

*

Tim Skubick

Whether you are pro- or anti-Engler, this guy deserves a heap of credit for his leadership performance on this education funding agreement.

John Engler demonstrated flexibility, toughness, perseverance, and a willingness to take some big-time political hits....

And when the dust finally settled, moments before Santa Claus climbed down the chimney, Engler had agreed to an income tax as a fall back plan to fund schools. He dropped all the union-bashing lingo and, at least for now, gave in on schools of choice....

This was truly a triumph of policy over politics. They—eventually including some Senate Republicans— did what was right even though that meant taking a huge political gamble....

Engler...remember... is the guy who likes to say, "promise made, promise kept."[365]

*

Ides of March

During the winter months of 1994, Engler and a large and unusually broad coalition that included many Democrats campaigned hard for Proposal A and against the alternative proposal. The historic measure passed in a landslide. Following are excerpts from newspapers. The first is from the Miami Herald.

"We made history in Michigan," said Gov. John Engler.[366]

*

From the Lansing State Journal

'A' LANDSLIDE

VOTERS OK SALES TAX HIKE TO PAY FOR SCHOOLS;

IT KICKS IN MAY 1

Michigan residents will pay higher taxes on money they spend—not the money they earn—after voters' overwhelming approval of Proposal A Tuesday. The sales tax boost from 4 cents to 6 cents—and most of the other tax changes that Proposal A triggers—take effect May 1.

"It's a victory for school children, it's a victory for taxpayers and for homeowners; and most of all, it's a victory for Michigan," a buoyant Gov. Engler told supporters at the Sheraton Inn.

[365]*Tim Skubick, "Governor Exhibited Leadership in Tax Fight,"* Lansing State Journal, *December 31, 1993.*
[366]*Associated Press, "Michigan Chooses to Finance Schools with Higher Sales Tax,"* Miami Herald, *March 17, 1994.*

With 94 percent of the precincts reporting, Proposal A was winning with 70 percent of the vote....

Tuesday's vote culminates an eight-month debate over school reform that began when the legislature voted last July to eliminate property taxes for schools....

The plan also reduces the gap between rich and poor districts by moving the lower spending districts toward a $5,000-per-student grant beginning this fall.

Stabenow, whose amendment in July led to the elimination of school property taxes, opposed Proposal A but argued that either it or the backup plan was better than the old system.

A distorted ad campaign by Proposal A's foes and the tobacco industry's role in funding [opposition to Proposal A] also contributed to the landslide, said Craig Ruff, president of Public Sector Consultants Inc.

The plan even won approval in the Detroit area, where voters had overwhelmingly rejected a similar plan last June.

The Proposal A gathering at the Sheraton had all the trappings of an Engler re-election rally, as supporters chanted "Four more years, four more years."

"It's a great way to start out," said Republican consultant Tom Shields. "This is the biggest promise he's kept as governor."...

"This is the outcome of Stabenow launching the effort and Engler taking the controls," said Larry Owen. "I'm concerned about the crash landing I see coming."[367]

*

From the Detroit News

VOTERS OVERWHELMINGLY BACK SALES TAX HIKE TO FUND SCHOOLS IN WHAT GOVERNOR CALLS "A GREAT VICTORY"

Michigan's tax system looks profoundly different today, following overwhelming voter approval Tuesday of the state's first sales tax hike since 1960.

In a stunningly lopsided special election, voters approved Proposal A by 70 percent to 30 percent, with 94 percent of precincts counted. The proposal claimed a majority in virtually every county in the state....

The governor, who stumped tirelessly on behalf of Proposal A, overcame a $4 million opposition campaign that experts say was ineffective because of

[367] *Chris Andrews, "'A' Landslide, Voters OK Sales Tax Hike to Pay for Schools,"* Lansing State Journal, *March 16, 1994, p. A1.*

grossly misleading TV ads that insulted voters. The opposition's effort was funded chiefly by tobacco interests trying to beat back the cigarette tax increase linked to the ballot plan....

Instead of having the nation's third highest levy on property, the state will fall back to the middle of the pack.

Even with the sales tax hike, the state will be at the national average and slightly below the 6.4 percent average for the Great Lake region. Engler repeatedly reminded voters that part of the tax will be paid by tourists from out of state....

The new tax scheme will provide about $10.2 billion for education.... The $10.2 billion represents a 5-percent funding increase for schools....

Tuesday's passage of Proposal A marked the second time in 13 tries since 1972 that a tax proposal on the ballot was successful. The only other success was the Headlee Tax Limitation Amendment passed in 1978.

For the first time ever with Proposal A, according to state elections officials, voters were faced with an either-or proposition that critics describe as "blackmail." Had voters rejected Proposal A, they would have been hit with a series of other tax increases, including a 30-percent state income tax hike....

The campaign for Proposal A created some eyebrow-raising political bedmates. Engler was joined by Democratic Detroit Mayor Dennis Archer, and the Detroit Board of Education, as well as leading Democrats in the state Senate.

Political observers say the passage of Proposal A bolsters Engler's chances to win a second term.[368]

*

There were some nay-sayers.

Even though the plan passed overwhelmingly, voters and polls indicated many voted for it only because they felt they had no other choice or didn't understand the issue....

"A lot of people voted out of the threat that one was bad and the other was worse," said David Littman, chief economist for Detroit-based Comerica Bank. "We'll have to wait and see what people really thought [next] November," he said, when Mr. Engler stands for re-election.[369]

[368] *Mark Hornbeck, "Voters Overwhelmingly Back Sales Tax Hike to Fund Schools in What Governor Calls a 'Great Victory,'"* Detroit News, *March 16, 1994, p. A1.*

[369] *Jacqueline Mitchell, "Michigan Voters Approve Shift in Taxes for Schools Away from Property Levy,"* Wall Street Journal, *March 17, 1994.*

*

From the Washington Post

MICHIGAN'S SHIFT ON SCHOOL TAXES
HERALDS A NATIONAL CHANGE

The decision Tuesday by Michigan voters to increase the sales tax to pay for their schools is leading a national movement to alter the financing of public education fundamentally....

"Everybody is looking at this," said Mary F. Fulton, policy analyst for the Education Commission of the States, a Denver group monitoring national education trends. "A number of other states are considering something this bold." The current property tax system "is a means of guaranteeing a superior education for the rich," said Jonathan Kozol, author of the best selling book on school funding, "Savage Inequalities."...

Jerome T. Murphy, dean of Harvard University's graduate school of education, said he believes many states will be examining what Michigan did.[370]

*

From the New York Times

FAIRER SCHOOLING FOR MICHIGAN

This week citizens of Michigan voted courageously to toss out decades of tradition in public school financing. It is the first statewide, voluntary shift from property taxes, as a rising national chorus of disgruntled homeowners and civil rights activists seek more equitable ways to provide one of society's most basic services....

The public schools have given generations of Americans a chance to fight their way up from poverty. If America is to live up to its promise of equal opportunity, this glaring inequity in education must be addressed. The fact that Michigan voters have voluntarily, and so overwhelmingly, tried to make school financing fairer should make other states sit up and take notice.[371]

*

Proposal A continued to draw praise from the national press corps eight years after it passed. Washington Post *columnist David S. Broder wrote a retrospective in 2002, excerpts of which follow.*

Michigan faced the [school finance] problem—and a taxpayer revolt against

[370] *Mary Jordan, "Michigan's Shift on School Taxes Heralds a National Change,"* Washington Post, *March 17, 1994.*
[371] *Editorial, "Fairer Schooling for Michigan," editorial,* New York Times, *March 18, 1994.*

rapidly rising property taxes—when Engler, then state Senate majority leader, ran for governor in 1990 against incumbent James J. Blanchard, now one of three Democrats trying for the nomination to succeed Engler.

As Douglas B. Roberts, a veteran of almost 30 years in senior state government positions under governors of both parties and now the appointed state treasurer, recalled recently, efforts to resolve the issue had been rejected by voters in 1972, 1980 and 1981, through a combination of anti-tax sentiment and the fear of rich districts losing funds. When Engler tried in 1992 and 1993, he too was rebuffed by the voters.

After the second failure, Republicans in the state Senate tried to put through a simple 20 percent cut in the property tax. Deborah Ann Stabenow, now U.S. senator but then a Democratic state senator aspiring to challenge Engler's re-election in 1994, saw a chance to trump him, and proposed eliminating school property taxes entirely.

Engler huddled with his legislative leaders and, to his opponents' surprise, announced that if the Democrats in the state House would support Stabenow's radical proposal, he would sign it. Their bluff having been called, Democrats had no choice but to follow through.

With public education now penniless, at least on paper, a tense negotiation followed, culminating in a 26-hour marathon session that ended midday on Christmas Eve 1993. The deal hammered out was approved in a referendum by more than a 2-1 ratio. The scope of the victory was increased by the Democrats' insistence that Engler's plan to increase the sales tax to provide property tax relief be tested against their preference, a higher income tax. With no way to vote for the status quo, the voters chose to boost the sales tax from 4 percent to 6 percent in return for a cut in property taxes averaging almost 50 percent.

As a direct result of Proposal A, as the 1994 referendum was called, the state share of Michigan's elementary and secondary school spending has jumped from less than 29 percent to more than 77 percent, with a commensurate decline in local burdens. Where all but 42 of Michigan's 554 districts had less than $6,700 per pupil to spend in 1994, now all of them are above that figure. And the gap between the 10 richest districts and the 10 poorest has been reduced from almost a 3-1 ratio to barely more than 3-2.

Grumbling is now heard in some wealthy districts that the property tax limits imposed by Proposal A are preventing them from spending as much on their schools as some would like. But Lu Battaglieri, president of the Michigan Education Association, which has battled Engler on many teachers' union issues, said, "Proposal A may need some tweaking, but it has fundamentally changed the way we fund education. It has raised the base and narrowed the gap, and a lot of good has come out of it."[372]

*

Lucille Taylor

I will tell you where John Engler was really masterful: school finance reform. He knows an opening when he sees it. For the governor, Proposal A was a turning point for everything that followed.[373]

*

Chris Christoff later summarized the achievement of Proposal A in the Detroit Free Press.

Shortly after noon on Christmas Eve 1993, exhausted state lawmakers ended 26 straight hours of toil with a historic agreement on how to fundamentally change the way Michigan would pay for schools.

Gov. John Engler had been in the thick of negotiations. Unshaven and physically and mentally drained, he turned to those assembled in his Capitol office and said, "Now I know why no one's ever done this before."

In 70 days, they had accomplished what no one thought was possible. Three months later in March 1994, Michigan voters approved the ballot issue, called Proposal A, in a special election that deeply cut school property taxes—a feat Engler had sought unsuccessfully since his election four years earlier....

Today, Proposal A stands as Engler's greatest policy achievement in the breadth of issues it addressed and the political crosscurrents it overcame. It was the envy of other states....[374]

*

A closer look at the governor and first lady

March of 1994: re-election was looming in eight months. After a stormy start in the executive office, the weather was clearing and the tide was turning for John Engler. Proposal A would pass in a landslide in a few days. Michelle Engler would continue to humanize the public's perception of her husband. This feature story from the Detroit Free Press Magazine *illustrates.*

[372] *David S. Broder, "Conservative Leaves Progressive Legacy: Michigan Governor Led School Finance Reform Seen as Model of Equity, Innovation,"* Washington Post, *July 28, 2002, p. A4.*

[373] *Lucille Taylor, interview with GW, October 20, 1999.*

[374] *Chris Christoff, "Engler's Michigan: Gamble on Proposal A Pays Off for Governor,"* Detroit Free Press, *January 15, 2002.*

TEAM ENGLER

It is the evening of the State of the State speech, and one of the coldest nights of the century.

The governor and his spouse have only a short block's drive from his administrative office to the more majestic one under the beige dome, but 25 below zero, courtesy of a brutal Arctic front, is enough to chill the bones of the Texas-born first lady of Michigan.

At the Capitol, Michelle Engler pulls off her gloves and says her hands are freezing. She says it to herself, really. There is bustle all around her—aides checking that advance copies of the governor's address are being distributed, state troopers conferring about security checkpoints, robed justices of the Supreme Court queuing up in the corridor for their ceremonial entrance into the House chamber where the speech will be delivered.

Amidst the hubbub, John Engler walks to the office teapot, pours some piping hot water into a Styrofoam cup and goes to his wife. As her face erupts in a smile, he takes her hands and cradles them around the cup, inside his.

Cold, stiff and remote. Flinty-hearted. King John the Imperious. And—still the slur of choice among the Republican governor's Democratic adversaries—mean-spirited.

When he ascended to the governor's office in 1991—having surprised just about everybody with his hairbreadth win—the former Senate majority leader who had begun his political career at 22 already had a reputation as a heavy. Then he proceeded to implement tough, government-shrinking policies with all the subtlety of Bill Laimbeer setting a pick. When he cut welfare, he cut with a hatchet, more drastically than any governor, anywhere. When he restructured mental health programs, he came down hammer-hard, closing the doors to Detroit's Lafayette Clinic with brutal abruptness and leaving the mentally ill patients weeping in the street.

With the State of the State speech, the governor would begin making his case for re-election. Michigan was in dire straits when he came into office, he'd say, and he had no time to waste. He had to push, push, push to eliminate waste, to get the economy rolling, to find a sensible way to fund education. Who could be concerned with appearing warm and fuzzy when there was so much to be done?

And yet there is a problem. This is exactly how Democratic Gov. Jim Blanchard went down in 1990: Good approval ratings of about 50 percent (right where Engler's are now), but something wrong with his appeal to voters whose party loyalties are mushy. Simply put, not enough people liked the guy.

The likability factor could be significant this time around, too, re-election strategists worry. Especially since the opponent in November could very well be a female, Sen. Debbie Stabenow (D-Lansing), no low scorer on the niceness meter.

The governor's top aides agree that what they have to work with is essentially a policy wonk, a driven detail man with a 10-pound brain. But that's not the whole man, they say. For the government junkie and politics nerd is also the man who is attentive and caring toward Michelle, who loves and is loved by Michelle, who wants children with Michelle. That John Engler can be—even some Democrats have glimpsed it—soft as a summer night on Grand Traverse Bay.

Displaying emotion is not his forte, however. He chafes at having his personal life watched. When he married Michelle, 23 days before his inauguration, it took a ton of cajoling and considerable time before he accepted that the hot glare of the media would overlay the glow of his nuptials.

How to bring out their man's inner warmth in the campaign? The political handlers' instincts have fastened unerringly at one locus: Michelle Engler.

Pretty, vivacious and smart, she's a natural at dealing with people. And in her presence—even before the cameras—he can seem ... well, the opposite of mean-spirited.

Will the stratagem work? Stabenow has her doubts. "She can't undo his record, or his personality. People are not voting for her. I can't imagine overall it will work. Michelle came into the state not knowing him in the context in which we all know him, the way he treated people. He seems very gracious around her. But we who worked with him when he was in the Senate know he can be ruthless, that his word doesn't mean anything."

In any case, in January, months before the governor will formally announce his re-election bid, his people calculate it's none too soon to throw open the door to the Englers' private life. Accordingly, a reporter and photographer for the *Free Press Magazine* are granted unprecedented access for two weeks to everything from breakfast at the Lansing mansion to a gathering of the Engler clan in Mt. Pleasant to speech practice for the State of the State address.

Clearly, the governor has his misgivings about the project. "I have this job as governor, and then I have my life with Michelle," he says in an interview. "I think what I'm trying to do, what I'd like to do, I guess, is keep some separation. I don't want to be so swallowed up that you're unable to distinguish between the two and you don't any longer know who you are."

The governor may be wary, but he does let us in, and the first lady holds open the door. Everybody ought to know the "real John," she says, or at least know about him.

"He is warm," she says of her man. "He's warm with me."

It is 8:30 a.m. at the little breakfast bar in the cheery red-and-white kitchen of the first couple's official home. The fare is homemade oatmeal (for her), spoon-sized shredded wheat with bananas (for him) and coffee. The Englers watch on color TV a weary-looking Pete Wilson, governor of California, cope with the latest disaster in his state, a powerful earthquake that hit near Los Angeles the day before.

"Wow, what he's been through!" the Michigan governor says. There is an interesting article about the California economy somewhere in a pile beside his bed, he adds.

"No one can compete with his piles of books and magazines, about this high," says Michelle, laughing. She holds her hand at chest level, pronouncing "high" like "hah" and endowing it with two syllables, the way Texans do.

"Yeah, that's because I don't have any room," he counters.

She sucks in her breath. "John! And when I say, 'John, which of these can I take back to the library?'" She affects a gruff voice, pretending to be him, "'I'm reading all of them.'"

"I belong to three book clubs, too," he says affably. "I like history, mysteries, biography. I have a book on Daniel Boone I'm reading. I do have several others...." He breaks into a sheepish grin. "They can go back," he adds.

He says he has a bookcase stored at the residence, modest as governors' mansions go with only three bedrooms downstairs and a ranch-style facade, a place far outclassed by several other houses in the neighborhood. He would like to bring his bookcase upstairs, but it won't fit. And his wife has taken all the closet space.

"I'm allowed one closet," the governor says.

"Aw. Such a pitiful story." Michelle giggles.

"I have room for my suit and a couple of shirts," he continues. "The all-time power shopper," he says, holding out a hand to his wife.

She chortles. "When I came to Michigan, I didn't have enough clothes, and ... these clothes are thick!"

Engler affects a hangdog look. "Mine are thin, and there are so few."

They laugh, something they do a lot, their friends say. Usually Michelle leads the way—propping a sombrero on John's head at a birthday party, teasing him about his claims to have helped raise his six siblings although he was a toddler himself when several were born, kissing him on the lips at a staff meeting to provoke "oohs" and "aahs."

They argue, too. Colleen House, Engler's first wife (they were married for 12 years), once told a reporter she and John never argued. "We do!" Michelle says fervently. "But mostly about silly stuff."

In the beginning, when she came up from Houston, leaving behind her family, her job and her name, they quarreled about scheduling, as she puts it. When and how much politics, government and public life would take from their new life together.

Engler met Michelle DeMunbrun, whose heritage is part Polish, part Mexican and part French, on a Miami Beach vacation four years ago. They were introduced by Engler's campaign manager, Dan Pero, and Pero's wife, Colleen [who had practiced law with Michelle in Houston]. The governor-elect was 41 then, a career politician on the brink of his most demanding job. Michelle was 31, an attorney who liked her work but knew it wasn't at the top of her list. After a brief mismatch of a marriage to another attorney at age 28, her first priority was making a good marriage and building a family.

From the start, the new governor set a pattern of not letting his work invade their home life. But his days are long—sometimes, as with the tortured struggle to get a school finance plan at Christmastime, absurdly long. And the competition for his attention is enormous. There are dozens of invitations to appear for every night of the week.

So it took some negotiating to work out the schedule of their married life and finding, as with the furniture in the governor's mansion, where things fit. Michelle found she fit just fine by his side in the social arena. He's never been a small-talk artist, and his jowly, hefty, hesitant presence doesn't exactly lend glamour to the events he must attend. She, on the other hand, is a born schmoozer, sincere and interested, or at least able to look like she is. Her former-prom-queen looks draw people to her, too.

She entered easily into the traditional first lady's domain of volunteerism, working on breast cancer awareness, child abuse prevention, whatever committees needed chairing or events hosted or meetings attended. When children didn't materialize as fast as she hoped, she went back to work part-time, doing bankruptcies and other business-related legal tasks in a law firm down the street from the big beige dome. It feels good, she says, to go there and work on briefs, and just be Michelle.

So the balance is improving. It's still not perfect, though.

While visiting a school in Clawson recently, she was asked by a child what the worst part of her job as first lady was. She replied, "I wish I had more time with my husband."

She was a Democrat before the marriage, although that was in Texas where that party label can stretch as far as the open range, well into conservative terrain. And she was—is—pro-choice on abortion, whereas her husband is solidly pro-life.

So what, exactly, is there about John Engler the political leader that connects with her?

"He's courageous," she says. "These three years, he has always done what he considers to be right in the face of enormous and vocal opposition."

He went to address a meeting of workers from the General Motors Willow Run assembly plant the morning after his father died, she notes, even though that was one of the hardest times in his life. He went because the workers' jobs were on the line, she says, and he believed he needed to be there.

In fact, the governor wept at Willow Run when *Free Press* politics columnist Hugh McDiarmid approached him and murmured condolences about his father. McDiarmid was so struck that he wrote about Engler's tears in his front-page column about the meeting.

"No one works harder than he does," Michelle insists. "He's so hands-on. He was out there night after night on school finance. He was so tired, he was getting sort of dazed. He puts his neck on the line for every issue he believes in. I said to him one time, 'Do we have to go out on a limb on every single issue? Can't we just sit one out?' And he said, 'No. We can't.' And I admire him for that."

But he's older than she, heavier, stiffer. People who don't like him—and there are plenty, after all these years in the fray—say he's impatient, overbearing, even kind of a dork.

So what does she see in him as a man? What connects them romantically?

Her voice goes soft. "He's so appealing," she says in her musical drawl. "He doesn't spread it all around everywhere, but maybe part of it is I know I bring that really good part out in him, 'cause I see it in his eyes."

When Michelle met John, she knew nothing of his public reputation, even though he was in the midst of a gubernatorial bid. "I don't know what sort of man it takes to appeal to every woman, but he's attentive and considerate, in a way that impressed me from the first time we met. He's someone who—if we're at a flea market, he picks up a shirt depicting cows, and he'll say, 'You know, Penny (one of his schedulers) likes cows. This would be a great thing for Penny.'"

She thinks it's significant that her husband's friends are as likely to be female as male, perhaps more likely. "From the first, he struck me as someone who is so unintimidated by a successful woman. It didn't faze him one whit. He was married to a successful woman before. He has an excellent record for promoting women to executive positions. Not all men are like that. I was a lawyer for eight or nine years before we met. I know."

Because of how she sees him, Michelle is careful—and sensitive—about John's public image. Insulting comments from opponents and commentators—he is boring, he is cruel—rankle her in a way they do not rankle her thick-skinned spouse. So she does what she can to help groom the gubernatorial persona.

One day, she breezes into a conference room in the governor's administrative offices, carrying an orange and some mineral water. The governor is practicing his State of the State message, and the first lady assumes the seat of re-election campaign director Pero, who's on his way out to a Birmingham fund-raiser where the Englers will appear later. Pero has just gotten a little lecture from his boss about leaving early from the last fund-raiser. "It's going to snow tonight," the governor says, "and I don't want to be all alone on that road coming back to Lansing."

Attacking the draft of his speech, the governor is typically focused. On every line. Every word. "Does African-American have a hyphen?" he asks. "Better check. And how about here in the crime section ... does the subject agree with the verb in that first sentence?"

Communications director Rusty Hills keeps trying to interject that it's time to start making some cuts—a big, bloated address is going to bomb. But the governor continues laboring over each passage, wanting to say it all, lay out each accomplishment and goal.

"How much of it are they going to remember at the end of an hour-long speech?" Hills finally pleads.

"Is it an hour?" Michelle asks with eyebrows up.

"So many good things..." the governor says, palms up in a gesture of helplessness.

"Oh, I'm crossing my legs!" says the first lady, miming the severe rest-room deprivation that could result from sitting through a recitation of the whole list.

"We'll take an intermission, that's all," says the governor.

Michelle takes the fat draft in her hand. "Look, just holding it makes me fall asleep." She looks at the speechwriter. "Write a book. It'd be shorter." She turns to the governor. "I'm the only one who can tell you this." She starts slashing at her neck with her hand. "Cut! Cut! Cut!"

The room resounds with laughter, but the speechwriter picks up his red pencil.

A bit later, John and Michelle zip back to the mansion, change clothes and drive through a snowstorm to the fund-raiser, a cocktail party at a private home where $100,000 will be taken in for the re-election campaign.

The first lady wears a smart black suit and pumps and holds court in the living room while her husband talks policy in the dining room. First, a guy wants to install a new phone system in the governor's mansion. Next, a coffee importer wants to tell her about the old days when her husband was a wheeler-dealer in the Senate. Then, a young woman wants to speak to her about females and lawyering.

The first lady chats, listens and dispenses hugs until it's time for her husband to speak. She moves to his side. Their bodies touch, and he reaches behind her to rub her back while the room quiets down. She leans into him, rests her head on his shoulder for a second, then, as he begins to talk, clasps her hands together, tilts her chin, fixes her eyes respectfully on the candidate.

It is almost a week later, and John and Michelle are wrapped in warm conversation and sharing pasta with close friends and key staff members at a favorite Lansing hangout, Emil's Restaurant, just after the big speech.

Over their heads, a television mounted on the wall throws out snatches of instant, unsparing analysis of the address: "Well, he's never been a great orator"... "comprehensive, if not inspiring"..."got his only standing ovation when he introduced Mayor Archer."

The first lady tries to tune the barbs out, showing only her pride in him with a big, beaming smile.

There are times when she is grateful her husband can be stronger than she. The things she hears on TV and sees in print—rubbishy, personal attacks on her man—do unhinge her sometimes because they seem so unfair.

But the governor, the old pro, tells her it's not worth it to feel so hurt. He's been through it, he's survived every time, and he knows by now how much easier one moves on without the dead weight of a grudge.

"He tells me, 'This is not important,'" she says. "He says, 'We know what is happening,' and 'Our families know the truth.' That always makes me feel better."

Family is crucial to both Englers. They say that and their shared Catholic faith are the true rudders in a life on the high seas of public opinion. This is the Year of the Family, and in the State of the State address the governor named his wife to the state commission to celebrate it. But that's ceremony. Family, as he would be the first to point out, is really about more personal things: who makes you laugh, whom you relax with, who's there when you need them.

Michelle Engler has been transplanted away from her people, so she nurtures those connections on visits and, almost every day, over the phone. She holds all of them close—her sibs in Texas, her mom and dad (now divorced) and the Mexican-American grandma who helped raise her (and who still guards the many mementos of her childhood, including one humiliating grade-school picture of Michelle in cat-eye glasses recently smuggled to John).

His family, however, is close at hand in the Mt. Pleasant area, where the Engler brood grew up on a farm and the next generation of kids and dogs run in the fields.... The governor's mother, Agnes, and four of his siblings live within a few miles of the original homestead. Two sisters have moved a bit farther afield, to Grand Rapids and Lake Orion. Yet the circle remains tight.

On a visit to the old hometown, when the governor ducks out for a meeting with the town fathers, Michelle settles in for a family chat. She sits in her mother-in-law's little living room, among the handmade teddy bears, and drinks from a mug emblazoned with the Michigan state seal.

"We all knew he was gonna marry her," says youngest Engler sister Jean Bigard, "from the first time he brought her to the Green Spot (a local bar)."

She cackles with his sisters about John's meticulous ways in the kitchen, how he rushes the dishes into the dishwasher the moment diners finish with them, how he frets over guests at the official residence grinding food droppings into the white dining room carpet with their heels....

Children are rocketing around the room while the adults talk, and two more run in from outside, squealing about the cold.

"Y'all sound like you're having a great time!" Michelle calls out, grinning her gap-toothed grin. And, in a flash, she has two pairs of small, snowsuited arms clasped around her waist.

The first couple is at Children's Hospital of Michigan for a press conference on state health policies. The Englers are shown a new brain scanner, and they view its amazing color pictures of brain tissue.

The governor asks sharp, focused questions of the hospital brass, prompting exclamations of "Yes! That's precisely the problem!" and "You're right up-to-date there, governor!"

Engler introduces to the assembled media a boy with brain cancer who is benefiting from a program that helps those without medical insurance. He is gracious toward the child and his family, noting how tough it is to appear in public like this. He handles the questions about state health policy in front of the cameras in his typical style: businesslike, if not smooth.

Then, as he prepares to go, he stands in the corner with the hospital chief. "She has a tumor...," the governor is confiding.

He is not easily overheard as cameras are packed up and children in wheelchairs are rolled by. "Right here." He holds his hand to his brow.

He is talking about his niece, the daughter of one of his sisters. She is 14 years old.

It was brain cancer that took his dad—slowly, cruelly, reducing his capacity to savor the full meaning of the day his son, a cattle feeder's boy, took over as boss of the state.

John Engler wept at Willow Run, but today he tries to hold it all in. He speaks with the doctor and then—subdued but polite—answers a few last questions for a reporter about health care.

Across the room, Michelle is holding in her emotions, too. Until someone asks about the girl. Then her eyes grow moist. They've just heard the news, she says. "We're still ... we're still ... we're ... it's scary."

John's niece, whose name is Laura, has a sarcoma behind one of her eyes. It's inoperable. Radiation and chemotherapy must begin right away.

"She's only 14," says Michelle. "Just a girl."

The next morning, the Englers are in Mt. Pleasant, at Stan's coffeehouse, which John's father visited every day in his retirement years. The governor is off chatting up some of the patrons, and Michelle is thinking again about his niece.

"Laura's handling it OK," she says, blinking back tears. "I'm not sure I'm that OK. What she's really worried about is losing her hair. Well, she's a kid."

The first lady looks down, looks back up with wet eyes. She's had a couple of miscarriages since she's been married to John, she says. "We want kids so much."

"Oh God." It hits her later. "I just can't take it if this is somehow seen as a ploy." She's back in Lansing now, sitting alone in her law office, not ensconced with family at Stan's. She's thinking about the political sniping that goes on—even about something like this—the way adversaries whisper that macho John Engler needs a bouncing baby to gain a few points in the polls.

"People could say, 'Why are they talking about it now—in an election year?'" she frets. "But there's no calculation involved. All this stuff about me being warm and everything, I think it's overdone. Probably I just don't have the skills most politicians possess. I open my mouth, and what I feel comes out."

The doctors Michelle has been seeing for a couple of years—enduring the fertility regimen of needle pokes, ultrasounds, shots and drugs—now believe they can prevent another pregnancy loss. "I'd like to have twins," she says, eyes alight. But she wants three kids. "We can adopt, too," she says. "It'll be great." In fact, she adds, they initiated the adoption process after her second miscarriage, last June.

Her longing, stoked by the years of waiting, is fierce. But she knows she's not on this journey alone. "You know, John was crushed, too," she says. "People just don't give men as much support...."

The governor has spoken about their loss only rarely, and in private, to several people he knows who've had miscarriages, Michelle says. On the last day he was available for this story, he says only, "You know, we've had a couple...." That's as far as he gets.

Michelle wants her husband to count on her for this campaign. Unless, of course, another fragile pregnancy should ensue. Then, priority No. 1 kicks in, and it doesn't have anything to do with politics. In some ways, that would be a relief, for both the governor and his wife sense the coming battle will be nasty and wonder how she will hold up.

Michelle made a little statement about civility in politics last December, calling for the common courtesy of old. That provoked a letter to the editor in the *Free Press* about how mean her own husband is, and no discernible letup in the intensity of invective from other candidates. One TV interviewer presented a quip from Lansing Mayor David Hollister that the only good thing the governor had done in the past three years was marry Michelle.

"I'm supposed to be flattered?" Michelle bridled after that. "That's really a punch in the gut for my husband."

The governor hopes she doesn't fret too much. He can take it, and besides, his wife has really done her part already. The things people say about him? Being misunderstood? "In the end," he says, "I don't worry too much about that—because I've got Michelle. She loves me, and I love her, and that's the aid and comfort I need."[375]

*

Russell Kirk, RIP

The last occasion on which John Engler was with Russell Kirk was Saturday, October 2, 1993, at the Philadelphia Society regional meeting in Dearborn. Conservatives from

[375] *Antoinette Martin, "Team Engler,"* Detroit Free Press Magazine, *March 6, 1994.*

around the nation gathered at the Dearborn Inn to celebrate the 40th anniversary of Kirk's famous work, The Conservative Mind. *Engler gave the keynote luncheon address in which he praised Kirk's commitment to "the Permanent Things."*

Some seven months later—on Friday, April 29th—a splendidly sunny day in mid-Michigan—there were finally signs of spring. About 2:00 in the afternoon, Gleaves Whitney received a call from Russell Kirk's son-in-law, Jeff Nelson, with the sad news that "the American Cicero" had died that morning. Gleaves tracked down the governor, who was on the road. In their phone conversation they talked through the language of a press release that was to be sent out before the news bureaus closed.

FOR IMMEDIATE RELEASE CONTACT: John Truscott
Friday, April 29, 1994 (517) 335-NEWS

Statement by Governor John Engler on the Passing of Dr. Russell Kirk

It was with the deepest sadness that I learned of the passing of my close friend, Dr. Russell Kirk, earlier today. Dr. Kirk was a cherished friend, a wise mentor, and a great American.

I grew up near the Kirk's ancestral home at Piety Hill, in Mecosta. When I was a state senator, I had the privilege of representing Dr. Kirk and his family. Their home was always open. Their conversation was always cheerful and enlightening. Their advice was always welcome. I sought his counsel and would stop by and visit with him, his lovely wife, Annette, and their four beautiful daughters.

Over the past four decades, Dr. Kirk has been a towering figure in humane letters. He is revered around the world, and his books have been translated into many languages.

But it is the power and the truth of his ideas for which he will be remembered for generations to come. Dr. Russell Kirk had great insight into the human condition. He had a profound grasp of history. His vision of the American republic and his ideas for its renewal made him one of our nation's wisest men.

Dr. Russell Kirk's generous spirit touched the lives of many people and greatly influenced many students. His impact on conservative thought and policy in America has been decisive. It was his writings, and in particular his seminal work, *The Conservative Mind*, that laid the foundation for many of the ideas that continue to shape public discourse and debate to this day.

I will miss my dear friend, Dr. Russell Kirk. With his passing, Michigan has lost its pre-eminent man of letters. And America has lost one of the men who understood her best.

The next day, Saturday, was overcast and dreary. The governor drove up to Mecosta to have a long, consoling visit with Annette. They talked in the parlor of the Kirk's Italianate home. She told him that the last book Russell Kirk had signed (fittingly, The Politics of Prudence*) was to Engler.*[376]

*

Teachers

Just about everybody in the Engler administration has teacher stories to tell. Brian Swift headed Engler's northern Michigan office.

The governor was in the U.P. for the state fair, and I was telling him about these two former teachers of mine that would ride me relentlessly about the governor's policies regarding teachers, the MEA, school funding, etc. These guys were friends, but when it came to that subject, they were hardcore anti-Engler. The golf store that these guys owned was not far from the fairgrounds, so I asked the governor if he wanted to pay a visit to them in person. Never one to back away from a good debate, the governor decided to go and see them unannounced.

As luck would have it, they were both in the back of the shop when we arrived. I poked my head in to say "hi," and they did not notice that the governor was with me. On cue they started in on me again—about my "boy" (the governor) and, "What is Engler gonna do to mess with teachers again?"

With a huge smile on my face, I said, "Why don't you ask him yourself?"

With that, the governor poked his head in, and the two teachers almost lost their lunch. Suddenly they were as nice as pie and started talking about the weather and other small talk. I told them I didn't bring him here to talk about the weather, and they ended up having a civil conversation about education.

Whenever I go back to their store, they talk about the day the governor stopped by to see them. They have never forgotten how he listened to their issues. I'm not sure they ever voted for him, but they gained a new respect for the governor that day.[377]

*

Engler's family also has stories. Sue (Engler) Gonzales:

A person I met found out that I was John's sister. She said, "Your brother hates me."

[376] *GW, conversation with Annette Kirk, April 29, 1993.*
[377] *Brian Swift, interview with GW, August 5, 2002.*

"Why do you say that?" I asked.

"Because I am a teacher."

"Then you must be a *bad* teacher. My brother likes *good* teachers."[378]

*

MEA vs. the devil

Al Short

Going into the'94 election, I knew there would be no rapport between the MEA and John Engler. He and I wouldn't even speak to each other in public. It was even more confrontational between MEA director Julius Maddox and John Engler. Julius couldn't even sit down and have a congenial conversation with John. One time he attacked John on affirmative action, though there was no purpose in doing that.

The MEA painted John Engler as the devil. There was open warfare against him. We did things like putting out bumper stickers that read, "Anybody But Engler." We kept saying to the media that he was anti-education and anti-public employee; that he wanted to take your bargaining rights and your tenure rights; that he wanted to have tax reforms and pay you less and provide less money to schools. The villain—always—was John Engler. The devil.

This had practical consequences. For example, the MEA couldn't offer compromises in the legislature because we were so set on our goal to defeat Engler in '94. There was only one vision, and that became a problem—*our* problem. We oversold our people on how bad John Engler was, and we couldn't retract it. I couldn't go over to the Capitol and sit down and negotiate a settlement on a bill because any compromise would have been considered a sign of weakness. We adopted one vision and one strategy. We had to beat John Engler.[379]

*

Campaigning for the second term

With the resounding victory of Proposal A the previous March, John Engler and Connie Binsfeld were able to launch a confident, upbeat campaign that kept the Democratic opponent, Howard Wolpe, on the defensive. As in 1990, Dan Pero engineered a highly disciplined, focused campaign in which he and the candidates "planned the work and worked the plan."

[378] *Sue (Engler) Gonzales, interview with GW, August 5, 2002.*

[379] *Al Short, interview with GW, February 26, 2001.*

Dan Pero

The day those summer tax bills came out in 1994 and showed zero property taxes, it didn't matter who the opposition was. We knew it was over. The tax bill showed zero due, and the people had tangible evidence of promises made and promises kept. John Engler would be re-elected governor.[380]

*

Rusty Hills

You know what is interesting about this election? Despite all that was written and said against John back in 1991 when we cut General Assistance, not one Democratic candidate for governor is calling for bringing GA back. Not one.

John knows the politics in this state better than anybody else. He has the populist touch.[381]

*

John Nevin was Engler's first chief speechwriter.

People always asked, "Will John Engler be a one term governor?" But I don't think anyone on staff really thought that. Even in the darkest days of the first term, when everyone was against us, John Engler would always keep pushing on. He never gave up. He might be making just one move at a time, but he already had the end game in mind. He always knew where he was, and where he was going, and that is what made him the master strategist. Even when we were losing a battle, he still kept the larger war plan in mind. He was always looking at the big picture. As a result, his staff was always confident. No matter what the poll numbers, we thought, "He'll just pull another rabbit out of his hat." He was always planning in advance what the next move would be, and he would march forward until what he wanted done was done.[382]

*

Connie Binsfeld

It is hard for me when people say that John is a cold person, because he is really a very warm individual. You see it on the campaign trail with him. He has to stop and talk to everybody. In 1994, I remember when we were at a Muskegon football game. We were shaking hands as people were coming into

[380] *Dan Pero, interview with GW, February 3, 2001.*
[381] *Rusty Hills to GW, on the eve of the Democratic primary, August 1994.*
[382] *John Nevin, interview with GW, February 12, 2001.*

the stadium, and then we were shaking hands as they were coming out of the stadium. I got so worn out I had to go sit in the car.

I said to John Truscott, "Watch, he's going to talk to those people, and I'll bet he'll walk all the way out to the parking lot with them."

Sure enough, that's just what he did. He walked all the way out to the parking lot with them, opened their door, and put them in their car.[383]

*

Major newspapers on the eve of the election

From the Detroit Free Press

GOV. ENGLER: IF RE-ELECTED,
HE'LL HAVE TO BE LESS DIVISIVE

As John Engler awaits the big re-election victory he is supposed to win, he might do well to remember the experience of his predecessor. Jim Blanchard, in 1986, won re-election by the third largest margin in Michigan history. You might have thought that election would have been the prelude to a time of progress and change. In fact, Gov. Blanchard frittered away that big mandate and opened the way for his defeat in 1990 by John Engler.

In his term as governor, John Engler has drastically reshaped state government. The centerpiece of the revolution—the re-structuring of the state's tax and school finance system—is still bitterly contested by a minority of Michigan's citizens.

But Gov. Engler is likely to be re-elected precisely because a strong majority of the populace believes the state is better off for those changes and that they outweigh many other, more dubious Engler policies. The school finance changes will be a long-term gain—and a big one—for the state.

Michigan, though, is now deeply divided, to some extent over education policy, to a larger extent because the governor's policies regarding mental health care, welfare, the arts, the environment and social values were so divisive. Teachers feel under siege. Many who support compassionate human services and many of the state's black citizens are very much alienated from a governor they see as hostile. Many of them are angry at us too.

This election is likely to hand Gov. Engler a different kind of opportunity than he had in the first term. He has the chance to reach out to pull the state together. Some of us have taken a chance on him. He needs to take some

[383]*Connie Binsfeld, interview with GW, January 23, 2001.*

chances, too. He needs to realize that he must be the governor of all the people. Being decisive doesn't always have to involve being divisive.

We would hope the governor, if he does win the expected victory on Tuesday, will pursue a clear, but inclusive agenda. It is past time for him to be a healer.[384]

*

From the Detroit News

ENGLERNOMICS VS. CLINTONOMICS

President Clinton is making a swing back to Michigan one more time tomorrow in a bid to strengthen the candidacies of Bob Carr and other Democratic nominees for Congress. But what does the president have to sell compared with Gov. John Engler's success in Michigan?

Late last week, the most recent unemployment figures were released. Michigan's unemployment rate of 5.1 percent hit a 22-year low—and was significantly lower than the national rate of 5.8 percent. Michigan has added some 508,000 jobs since August of 1991, including 25,000 since August of this year. And in Michigan, Gov. John Engler has managed to cut taxes and reform school finance.

Mr. Clinton has taken credit for Michigan's economic turnaround. Certainly, a rebound by the auto industry has a lot to do with Michigan's good economic performance. But that rebound in turn has had a lot more to do with the auto industry and its workers than with Washington—and, frankly, we think it's an insult for Mr. Clinton to claim otherwise. Washington could benefit from some of the leaning down and productivity improvement that Michiganians have had to endure.

The Engler approach goes at economic growth from the bottom up. Cut taxes and reduce regulations. The result has been the lowest unemployment rate since 1972 and personal income growth rates that outpaced the national rate in 1993. Taxes as a share of personal income in Michigan fell from 15th to 24th highest.

What is the national record? In 1993, national median family income fell by 1.9 percent. Meanwhile, the share of total national income earned by the top 20 percent of earners jumped to 48.2 percent, higher than at any point since the Carter administration. No doubt the president tomorrow will also try to scare voters with phony threats about what Republican control of Congress

[384]*"Gov. Engler: If Re-elected, He'll Need to Be Less Divisive," editorial,* Detroit Free Press, *November 6, 1990.*

would mean—an end to Social Security, poor people thrown into the street, the evil Newt Gingrich in charge of the House of Representatives, etc. He will also thunder that Rep. Gingrich's "Contract with America," with its tax-cut proposals, would add $1 trillion to the deficit.

But what has a half-century of Democratic control of Congress given the country? And what about the tax increase being suggested by Mr. Clinton's own budget director as a means of dealing with the expected increase in the deficits beginning in a few years? On top of last year's $245-billion tax hike, that would be a sure economy-killer. The Contract with America is nothing for which Republicans need apologize. It stakes out the same basic approach that is working so well to balance the budget and produce healthy government surpluses here in Michigan—tax cuts and spending restraints. There is nothing extreme or unusual about it—unless you believe, as many in Washington seem to believe, that Americans are still undertaxed.

At least the GOP has dared to spell out a program and ask for a mandate. In his desperate tour around the country in the last week, President Clinton has offered little but fear. We suspect voters hereabouts are not going to be very impressed—and that on Tuesday Englernomics will come out ahead of Clintonomics.[385]

*

Annus Mirabilis: Election Day 1994

Conventional wisdom holds that during mid-term elections the party not occupying the White House does well. On November 8, 1994, with Democratic President Bill Clinton in office, the GOP did well. No—that's an understatement. The very stars were aligned to usher in a new era. In a stunning repudiation of the president, Americans favored Republican candidates in races in Michigan and throughout the nation. Newt Gingrich and GOP candidates who had signed the "Contract with America" were swept into Congress, giving Republicans control over the House for the first time in 40 years. Enjoying a 230 to 205 majority,[386] congressional Republicans would pursue an ambitious agenda during their first 100 days. As Governor Engler and Speaker Gingrich worked well together, the 104th Congress would also make a priority of cooperating with the states, a majority of whose statehouses and governors were now Republican.

The U.S. Senate also swung dramatically to the Republicans as a result of the elections. Before November 8 Democrats had enjoyed a 57 to 43 majority in the upper house. After Election Day, the GOP controlled the chamber by a 52 to 48 margin. Among the

[385]*Editorial, "Englernomics vs. Clintonomics," editorial,* Detroit News, *November 6, 1996*
[386]*The 104th Congress had 230 Republicans, 204 Democrats, and 1 Independent.*

newcomers was Michigan's own Spencer Abraham, a longtime ally and friend of Engler's.

Gubernatorial elections around the nation went to Republicans. In fact, there were 14 more Republican governors-elect in 1994 than in 1992. That translated into 74 percent of Americans living in a state with a Republican governor.[387] *Most dramatic was the New York governor's race, which saw liberal icon Mario Cuomo toppled by Republican George Pataki. Most significant for the future of the nation was the Texas governor's race, which saw George W. Bush beat out incumbent Ann Richards. In Michigan, Engler easily won a second term as governor over Howard Wolpe, a former U.S. representative. With almost 62 percent of the vote, Engler enjoyed the second largest victory margin by which he had ever beaten a Democrat. What a turnaround from three years earlier, when the governor's re-elect numbers dropped to an all-time low of 18 percent. The landslide re-election would set the stage for Engler to lead his 31 peers in the Republican Governors Association (1996).*

Also on November 8, Michigan voters elected Candice Miller to be the first Republican secretary of state in 40 years. A conservative, Clark Durant, now headed the State Board of Education, which was also dominated by Republicans. To top off Republican successes, voters ratified GOP control of the Michigan Senate, where Republicans continued to hold a 22 to 16 advantage.

Clinton, stung by Republican successes in Washington and in swing states like Michigan, said the day after the election, "They [the voters] sent us a clear message—I got it."[388]

From the Detroit News

WIN GIVES ENGLER MANDATE
TO PUSH CONSERVATIVE AGENDA

Gov. John Engler won a resounding mandate from voters Tuesday to continue his conservative revolution in Michigan, for four more years.

The 46-year-old incumbent, riding his twin themes of lower taxes and less government, was on his way to a lopsided victory Tuesday over Democratic challenger Howard Wolpe by nearly a 3-2 margin.

"This is a vote of confidence from the people of Michigan," said Engler campaign manager Dan Pero.[389]

*

[387] *For a complete summary of election results and what they meant to Republican governors, see John Engler, "The Liberal Rout: Why Conservatives Are Winning in the 1990s,"* Policy Review, *January-February, 1997, pp. 44 ff.*
[388] *Bill Clinton quoted in "Republicans Take the Hill in Elections," in* America's Century, *ed. Clifton Daniel (London: Dorling-Kindersley, 2000), p. 407.*
[389] *Mark Hornbeck, "Win Gives Engler Mandate to Push Conservative Agenda,"* Detroit News, *November 9, 1994.*

From the Detroit Free Press

GOP'S BIG DAY

Gov. John Engler rolled to a re-election landslide Tuesday and completed his first term transformation from public ogre to taxpayers' pal.

Engler's huge margin ... also helped Republican Spencer Abraham defeat Democrat Bob Carr, 52 percent to 42 percent, in their U.S. Senate race for the seat of retiring Democrat Donald Riegle Jr.[390]

*

Engler's landslide re-election marked only the fourth time since the Second World War that a gubernatorial candidate in a general election won with more than 60 percent of the vote.[391]

John Engler	1,899,101 votes (61.5%)
Howard Wolpe	1,188,438 votes (38.5%)[392]

*

Finding a new chief of staff

Jeff McAlvey

Engler was always more comfortable having a female as the top staff person. Back in the Senate days, it was Gail Torreano. I talked to him about that once. After Carol Viventi left at the end of the first term, he called me into his office.

"Would you like to be considered for chief of staff?" he asked.

I said, "I would be delighted to be considered. But I have to be honest, John. I've watched you for 10 years, and you would be better off with a female as your chief of staff. Everything would run better. You'd have a higher comfort level with the communication. I'm not saying that's a negative. It's just a fact."

The next day, the governor talked to Carol Viventi. "Jeff tells me that I work better with a female chief of staff. Is that true?"

"Yes," Carol said, "that's true."

And that is what led to Sharon Rothwell being selected as chief of staff. He eliminated the men from his list. It is easier for him to communicate at that high level with somebody who can call him up short when he needs to be called up short. Engler is comfortable with a woman doing that.[393]

[390] *Chris Christoff and Dawson Bell, "GOP's Big Day,"* Detroit Free Press, *November 9, 1994, p. 1A.*
[391] *Ibid.*
[392] Michigan Manual, *1991-1992 ed. (Lansing Legislative Service Bureau), p. 831.*
[393] *Jeff McAlvey, interview with GW, May 29, 2002.*

Children sweeten labours.
FRANCIS BACON

★

Chapter Thirteen
Hannah, Madeleine, Maggie

John and Michelle Engler's three daughters were born on Sunday, November 13, 1994, just five days after the election. John Truscott recalls:

We had been kidding Michelle and John during the campaign. "Couldn't you just give birth *before* the election? It would be a perfect way to cap the campaign."

Dan Pero would joke, "Can't we just drive Michelle down a bumpy dirt road so that the triplets will come early?"

Election night was Michelle's first public appearance in months. She could hardly move. She couldn't even sit straight because she was so uncomfortable. She would half lie back in a chair to try to get in a manageable position. Toward the end of the evening, it took all of her strength just to walk through the crowd and get to the stage.

Dan, Rusty, and I had guaranteed the media that they would have a heads up when it was time for Michelle to give birth. We knew that none of them wanted to get scooped, so we tried to help them as much as possible. But we didn't know precisely when the c-section was scheduled. You know John Engler: information only on an as-needed basis!

In fact, I didn't find out from the governor that the time had arrived. I found out later that one of the medical team at the U of M Hospital had a mother working at Channel 4. She was excited and told her mom on November 12th that the Englers would be in the next day to give birth to the triplets. Once Channel 4 knew that, I started getting calls. And getting more calls. "We hear that the triplets are about to be born," they'd say. "The surgery has been scheduled. Do you have any more information?"

At that point, I really didn't. Finally the governor called me about 6:00 the next morning. "Get ready to go to Ann Arbor," he said.

"I know."

"How do *you* know?" he asked.

"Because reporters have been calling me all night. By the way, there's a Channel 4 camera waiting for you to come out."

"How do *they* know?"

"I don't know, but I've been up all night talking to reporters. They all know."

The Englers got to Ann Arbor and entered the U of M Hospital by a private entry. We put out a press release, got the press room set up, and waited where we could meet the governor after the surgery.

The surgery seemed to go fast. Afterwards they wheeled Michelle to recovery and the governor walked at her side, holding her hand. They had big smiles and waved to Rusty and me. The governor took a minute to talk to us. Everything had gone fine. He was unbelievably ecstatic. We told him that the press were waiting, but that he shouldn't feel rushed.

He was enthusiastic to share the great news: "I want to go down and talk to them as soon as possible."

He still hadn't told us whether he was a dad to all boys or all girls or some combination of boys and girls. But we knew that he had packed two shirts—a light blue shirt in case Michelle had given birth to all boys, and a pink shirt in case it was all girls.

He spent about 10 minutes with Michelle in the recovery room, then came out wearing a pink shirt. So—it was three girls and we congratulated him. He was beaming.

"I'm ready," he said.

"Give me just five minutes to notify the press that you're coming," I said.

I went to the press room. It was packed with photographers and member of the press. Doctors and nurses lined the walls. All the reporters were yelling, "How many girls? How many boys?"

I held them off, and the governor came in just two minutes behind me. He walked into the room with Dr. Johnson, and they proceeded to the podium. He had a great big smile on his face.

He stood at the podium and at first didn't speak. He just seemed to be

taking it all in and maybe keeping himself from getting too emotional. Everybody was dying to know the details.

"I am proud," he began, "to announce the birth of Margaret Rose, Hannah Michelle, and Madeleine Jenny."

There was cheering and applause.

"Michelle is healthy," he continued, "and all are doing fine."

Then he described what it was like to be present at the births. The feeling, he said, was indescribable, unlike anything he had ever experienced. It was a miracle. You just have to go through it to know what it's like.... And then he got choked up. He couldn't go on. The *Free Press* photographer got a wonderful shot of him wiping away the tears. It got to everybody—there wasn't a dry eye in the place. Here were the media—all these reporters who had been so tough on him for all these years—and even they were crying. They finally looked beyond the politician, and saw into the man, this new father.

"Indescribably beautiful" is how John Engler characterized the birth of his and Michelle's three girls, on Sunday, November 13, 1994.
CREDIT: *Richard Lee,* Detroit Free Press

It was a moving moment. I think this was the first time the media and the public had ever seen the governor become very emotional.

The next day [November 14th], the governor and I went to have lunch in the cafeteria. Dozens of people walked up to him and said, "Congratulations, Dad." Many had the newspaper with them and they asked him to autograph it. There was an outpouring of warmth from the public that I'd never seen before. That was the turning point in our relations with the media.[394]

*

Chris Christoff

We were at the University of Michigan Hospital. All the reporters were waiting for Engler to come out for the press conference after the triplets were born.

[394] *John Truscott, interview with GW, July 29, 2002.*

I remember asking, "Governor, how do you feel?" Then he broke down—really choked up. That was the first time I or anybody there had ever seen him cry. The birth of the girls changed him. He seemed to mellow.[395]

*

From the Detroit News

TRIPLETS DOING WELL
BIRTHS BRING EMOTIONAL GOVERNOR TO TEARS:
"THIS IS JUST TERRIFIC"

Michelle and John Engler were triply blessed with a set of healthy girls Sunday morning in what their father, re-elected governor of Michigan five days earlier, described as "just the most beautiful thing ... anyone can go through."

Margaret Rose (5 pounds, 3-1/2 ounces), Hannah Michelle (4 pounds, 11-1/2 ounces) and Madeleine Jenny (4 pounds, 15-1/2 ounces) were delivered by Caesarean section at 11 a.m. at the University of Michigan Women's Hospital in Ann Arbor. There were no complications....

"This is the happiest day of my life," Michelle Engler said through a spokesperson. "We feel so fortunate that God has given us this precious miracle of life."

The babies' arrival was announced by their father, who wiped tears from red-rimmed eyes as he said in a breaking voice: "Dad's just hanging in there, but very happy."

Asked if this experience surpassed his political victories, Engler said, "No question. This is just terrific."[396]

*

From the Detroit Free Press

TRIPLETS IMPROVE, MOM'S FINE—
AND DAD'S OUT OF THIS WORLD

Watching him [the governor] said everything. More than once, he struggled to say what filled his heart.

He failed. Instead, he settled for thanking the U-M staff profusely for their help, answering inane questions about sleep, enumerating the many kindnesses of well-wishing strangers—and, of course, talking about his daughters.

[395] *Chris Christoff, interview with GW, July 11, 2002.*
[396] *James R. Tobin, "Triplets Doing Well,"* Detroit News, *November 14, 1994, p. 1A.*

Unprompted by reporters, the governor mimicked his children at birth, stretching out his hands as they did in reaching for life outside the womb.[397]

Governor Engler with President and Mrs. Bush, at the University of Michigan, Ann Arbor, May 1991. CREDIT: *White House*

*

President Bush

Shortly after the birth of the Englers' three daughters, former President Bush wrote the following note to the governor and first lady, and sent photos with a handwritten message to each of the girls.

November 16, 1994

Dear John and Michelle,

I can't begin to tell you of the joy I feel in my heart over the birth of your three daughters. Bar has stopped her tears of joy, too, but just barely.

Here are three shots to tuck into the back of the girls' scrapbooks.

When I am 91, and they are 21, I plan to dance at their weddings—well, maybe not dance, but I plan to be around to watch them grow and watch their parents love them.

All Bushes send love to Les Girls!

—George

[397] *Amy Wilson, "Triplets Improve, Mom's Fine—and Dad's Out of This World,"* Detroit Free Press, *November 16, 2002, p. 1A.*

Michelle, John, and their three daughters—from left, Madeleine, Maggie, and Hannah—at the governor's residence, Lansing, summer 1996. SOURCE: *John Engler*

Hannah, Hooray—you are here in this great big world of ours. At one time I was president. Your dad helped me to get to be president. He and your mom are our dear friends. Now I am in this grandchild business. I am going to pretend that you are one of our very own. Love, George Bush.

Madeleine, welcome to this exciting world! When you get older, will you go fishing with me? I love your mom and dad. They helped me get to be president a long time ago. I love you already. George Bush

Margaret, welcome to this world of ours. You have wonderful parents who we Bushes love. We love you, too—I used to be president. Now, I just count blessings. You are one of my blessings. George Bush.[398]

[398] *JE and ME, personal papers, November 16, 1994.*

Denial of the right to experiment may be fraught with serious consequences to the nation. It is one of the happy incidents of the federal system that a single courageous state may, if its citizens choose, serve as a laboratory of democracy; and try novel social and economic experiments without risk to the rest of the country.

LOUIS BRANDEIS

★

Chapter Fourteen

Second Term: 1995 - 1998

Second Inaugural Address

Change was in the air. The Congress was in GOP hands for the first time in four decades. Speaker Newt Gingrich was eager to work with John Engler and other Republican governors to revive federalism, reform welfare, cut taxes, and bring about tort reform. A portion of Engler's Second Inaugural Address, delivered January 1, 1995, was directed at the new 104th Congress, encouraging the new Republican majority to work with governors and reform boldly.

Four years ago, as I prepared to take the oath of office, Governor George Romney looked at me with those steel gray eyes and said: "Be bold." The promises we made that day were bold. And my friends, together, we kept those promises. We cut taxes. We restored the spirit of enterprise and personal responsibility. We renewed the values and principles that have made Michigan great. I pledge today to the people of Michigan that we will continue to be bold, courageous, decisive....

Two days from now, a new Congress will be sworn in. We pray they will have the courage to be bold, to follow Michigan's course, to make history just as we have made history. Their mandate is for nothing less than the most sweeping changes in our government since the Great Depression. This is a defining moment in American history. Overwhelmingly, the American people voted for change in Washington.

Change to cut taxes and help families. Change to limit government and balance the budget. Change to restore the American dream and put you—the people—in charge.

This incredible chance for change will come only once in our lifetime. It will not be easy, for with major change comes risk and uncertainty. But as our Michigan experience has taught us, by being bold, by staying the course, by holding fast to our principles, the people will take up the challenge and accomplish great things.

Leadership in the 21st century will be defined by taking risks, not by clinging to the failed policies and ideas of the past. It is imperative to the people of Michigan that this new Congress succeed. Michigan has already accomplished much, but there is much more to do. In a second term, we seek to build upon our legacy as Michigan continues its quest to lead and innovate.

We will seek to free the power and money that for too long have been held captive in Washington. Not to hoard them in Lansing, but to put your money back in your pocket and to put you back in charge.

*

Heart attack

Connie Binsfeld

I had my heart attack in January of 1995. I had just checked into the Radisson Hotel and was sitting on the bed watching television. I felt tightness in my throat and I was having trouble breathing. I remembered what my son's cardiologist at the University of Michigan Hospital had told me about silent heart attacks. He said, "Silent heart attacks cause you to have a tightening sensation in your throat and trouble breathing." I began to think I was having a silent heart attack.

I did not want to call 911 and get publicity for being rushed to the hospital if there was no cause for alarm. So I decided to call the governor and ask him what to do. When I called Michelle answered the phone.

"Is John there?"

The first lady asked, "Is everything all right?"

"Well, I don't know," I answered. "But I would really like to talk with John."

John picked up the phone and I told him what was happening. He said, "Stay right where you are—I'll be right there."

John didn't even call security. He jumped in the car right outside the back door and came to the Radisson himself. Meanwhile, he called Rachel Blake, the state trooper on duty at the Capitol that night. She ran from the Capitol to the Radisson. They came up to my room in the elevator together.

When John arrived he asked, "Do you think you can walk to the car?"

I said, "Yes, I can." He grabbed my coat and helped me put it on and we left for the hospital.

When we stepped out of the elevator in the lobby, I saw paramedics coming into the hotel, and I wondered what they were there for. Apparently, John had called 911 in case I needed medical attention immediately. But John was so focused on getting me to the hospital that he didn't take the time to stop them.

We got in the car and John said, "We are going to Ingham Medical. I just read an article about a heart specialist who performed his 1,000th heart surgery. He is highly praised. So I think Ingham is the place to go." Security at the [governor's] residence talked us all the way to the hospital, because we weren't sure what the fastest route was.

When we arrived at Ingham Medical, John went banging through the doors of the emergency room. Of course everyone was turning around and saying, "Isn't that the governor?" It was midnight by the time I got to an examination table.

The governor wanted to call my husband John, and I asked him not to because he was sick.

The governor said, "I am going to call John because they are going to do an angiogram and a heart catheterization at 6:00 tomorrow morning and he has to know that."

I said, "OK, but tell him not to worry." I then told John to go home and get some rest.

He said, "Not yet." He did not want to leave until I talked to my husband. He stayed with me until I was placed in a room where I could receive phone calls.

John Engler then got John Binsfeld on the line. He arranged to have the state police pick him up. The governor told him, "Don't you drive to Lansing. I am sending a state police car to pick you up and you'll be here before she goes under the anaesthetic." It would be the fastest ride my husband ever had to Lansing.

The doctors found that surgery was necessary. I wanted to postpone it until after the State of the State Address, when it would be more convenient.

John wouldn't hear of it. "Connie, first things first," was his reply. It was a good thing I did not wait; the doctors found four blockages.

The first flowers I received while I was in the hospital were beautiful yellow roses from John and Michelle.[399]

*

[399] *Connie Binsfeld, interview with GW, January 23, 2001.*

1995 State of the State Address

Engler has never been comfortable bearing his soul in public, but citizens saw a different side of their governor in his 1995 State of the State Address, delivered Tuesday, January 17. In one of the last speech practice sessions, the governor was inspired to say the following:

Tonight, I've presented my administration's blueprint for Michigan's future. My goal is to build on our accomplishments of the first four years. And make no mistake: These are *our* accomplishments. We did it together. And we must continue to build together if we are to make Michigan's renaissance real for more of our workers, families, and communities.

We must recognize that the stakes in this quest are extraordinarily high. The literal costs of failure—in dollars and cents—are dramatically reflected in our corrections budget. But no budget can reckon the human costs of failure. Broken homes, violent streets, a corrupting welfare system, government barriers to liberty and opportunity—these exact a toll on our society that is infinitely greater than any dollar amount can measure.

Of all the things I've addressed tonight, the most significant is the need for moral leadership. So much of what is failing, so much of what puts us at risk, so much of what afflicts us, reflects what is broken deep inside our souls. As a legislature, as a governor, we are unable to heal that brokenness. It is rather in our families, among our friends, and through our faith that we must seek true healing.

For our part, the direction we chart must be consistent with the core values that have made Michigan great. At the very least, what you and I can do is insist that government do no harm to our families, neighborhoods, and communities. At our very best, we can come together—regardless of party or region—and do great good.

I call out to all Michigan citizens to do their duty by caring for themselves and those around them. If each of us takes up the challenge close to home, then Michigan's renaissance is assured.

*

Engler the moralist?

The 1995 State of the State was a remarkable speech for Engler to give. It revealed the inner man in a way that friends and advisors had been calling for. The ending in particular inspired Detroit Free Press *reporter Dawson Bell to interview and write about the moral and spiritual qualities that John Engler seemed more willing to show.*

Like so many of his speeches, the chief virtue of the one Gov. John Engler delivered to the legislature on Jan. 17 was its relative brevity.

A straightforward, if uninspiring, report on the State of the State. Good, getting better, Engler said. Taxes lower, employment higher. More and better coming.

Then something happened.

John Engler, the stolid, phlegmatic, intensely private career politician, closed with a somber plea for an examination of souls.

The "most significant" need we have now is for "moral leadership," he said. "So much of what is failing...so much of what afflicts us, reflects what is broken deep inside our souls," and it can't be fixed by government.

Suddenly, the governor—whose first term had been a bulldozer push for pragmatic policy (cut taxes and spending, reform education)—was saying what we really need is to be better people.

Senate Majority Leader Dick Posthumus, one of Engler's oldest friends, said the comments reflected a change that began in 1990 when Engler remarried and intensified in November when his three children were born.

Engler aides said the "broken souls" passages were the only ones in the speech he wrote entirely on his own. He wanted to broach this subject before but didn't because advisers convinced him a campaign was no time to be talking morality.

With his mandate from voters in November, Michigan's chief elected leader was free to speak about moral leadership.

In an interview last week, Engler said that while his marriage and children have reshaped his thinking, so has "unfortunately, the experience of being governor for four years."

"No matter how much good we do or think we do, that doesn't prevent somebody from going berserk and battering their wife, or killing their baby...committing unspeakable acts of violence."

"There is loose in our society a degree of violence that is abhorrent. And it comes from people who don't have a respect for law or respect for life or a set of values that give them any kind of moral compass."

Engler is characteristically circumspect about whether he, as governor, should be setting that compass. He avoids statements that would place him in a Dan Quayle-like position of arguing about unwed motherhood with TV's Murphy Brown.

At the same time, Engler says that Quayle's message—that there is conclusive evidence that kids have a better chance in life when they grow up with two parents—is essentially correct.

Similarly, the sexual promiscuity and drug use that arose out of the cultural revolution of the 1960s (Engler, 46, said he was only an observer) has resulted in rotten consequences, he said.

"We went through a period where personal responsibility went out the window," Engler said.

It may have seemed like a good idea at the time, but he maintains the pleasure was short-lived.

"In the final analysis, we really didn't want to be liberated because we didn't want to live with the consequences of our deeds."

In that, Engler is on what is for him the relatively comfortable ground of defining the role of government in the lives of citizens. The cultural revolution and expansion in government programs didn't work, he has argued in Michigan and, lately, in Washington.

But he also suggests that a reconfiguration of government programs, even along conservative lines, won't work either if they're not accompanied by moral regeneration.

People need to understand that there is right and wrong conduct, Engler said. Wrong conduct leads, as he wrote last year in response to a questionnaire from a traditional values organization, to illegitimacy, sexually transmitted diseases, declining schools, teen suicide, violence and moral drift—a "foundering on the shoals of nihilism."

That message has to come from religious, societal and even political leaders, he said.

"The pendulum has swung back on this. What started as a tiny sound out in the distance now is steadily increasing in volume. It's becoming more clear," he said.

Not so clear is what role Engler sees for himself in delivering the message. Nor is it clear what public policy implications stem from his notion of the message.

He said he wants to be "a moral leader"—one who acts morally—not "everybody's moral leader. A secular governor cannot and should not attempt to become a religious leader."

But despite what he called the swing of the pendulum, Engler is seldom at the forefront, even in Michigan, on many of the politically divisive social issues that propel religious conservatives.

Although a lifelong Catholic, Engler's opposition to abortion has been more a matter of fact than part of his political agenda since he arrived in the governor's office. He has scrupulously avoided taking sides in the sometimes volatile debate over gay rights.

In last week's interview, he dismissed abortion and gay rights as "part of the national debate." He said the success of the new Republican majority in Congress will be measured by whether they "strengthen families and reduce the tax burden" rather than on whether they can reinstate prayer in schools.

James Muffett, president of the Lansing-based Foundation for Traditional Values, said Engler's positioning is politically astute.

"He's a political pragmatist," Muffett said.

Engler can't afford to be defined as a right-wing religious fanatic who wants to impose rigid values on all of society. The caricature may be unfair, Muffett said, but the perception is real enough to be politically damaging.

Muffett said he believes the negative view of the so-called religious right is changing. People are beginning to understand that "every time an elected official votes on anything, they're telling us what they think is right and wrong."

By talking about morality, Engler is pushing public consciousness in the right direction, Muffett said.

Of course, some Michiganders recoil at the prospect of getting moral leadership from John Engler.

Those who tried to block his re-election may have been ineffectual. But many of his opponents had been moved to a visceral distrust and dislike of someone they regarded as mean, deceitful and even immoral.

For two years before the [1994] election, hundreds of Engler's enemies gleefully displayed "Engler Hates Me" campaign buttons. In rallies at the Capitol in 1992, and on the campaign trail in 1994, he was vilified as a latter-day Hitler by opponents of his welfare and public education policies.

In an ad broadcast early in the campaign, Engler was all but accused of murder in the death of a patient forced to leave the Lafayette Clinic, a state psychiatric center he closed in Detroit.

Some Engler aides who spoke on condition they not be named suggested his recent attempts to stake out a moral high ground are, in part, a reaction to that vitriol—he wants to take the discussion to a higher plane.

The governor's problem, said one, is like that faced by Hillary Rodham Clinton in 1993 when she attempted in a speech following her father's death to define her antidote for sick souls. She fretted about the "alienation, hopelessness, despair...a crisis of meaning" that she sensed in America.

But nobody was really sure what she was talking about.

In that vein, those listening might have wondered what Engler's public policy imperative was when—in the State of the State—he spoke of a duty to care for ourselves and those around us.

In some ways, "It's about everything and it's about nothing," the aide said.

Engler seems to be aware that moral authority is less precise than the authority conferred on the winner of an election.

It is sometimes accorded to those who don't deserve it and sometimes denied to those who do.

He realizes that, having declared that broken souls can't be healed by government, he limits his own options. Engler has a day job. And he gets paid for practical problem solving, not societal introspection or prayer.

In fact, Engler seems most at ease when the discussion of moral uncertainties drifts back to practical reality.

Says Muffett: "He goes as far as he can."[400]

*

Governor Engler meeting with Pope John Paul II, the Vatican, May 1997. SOURCE: *John Engler*

Connie Binsfeld

John and Michelle are both more deeply religious than you might think they are. You know, we don't wear our religion on our sleeves. When John went over to Rome, he bought me a rosary that was blessed by the Pope, which I still carry with me to this day.

[400] *Dawson Bell, "The Hesitant Moralist,"* Detroit Free Press, *February 19, 1995, p. 1F.*

We both looked upon our public service as having a strong moral and ethical root in the Church.[401]

*

Defined contributions battle

Many of Engler's staff have reflected on the governor's skill at shepherding difficult bills through the legislature. One particularly thorny issue was "defined contributions," which involved changing the retirement funding of state workers. Jeff McAlvey reflected on the governor's strategic skills and "personal touch" in getting defined contributions through the legislature.

It was Election Day, 1996. Dick Posthumus, Paul Hillegonds, and I were having a strategy meeting in Engler's office, thinking about the fall session agenda. One thing Engler wanted to pass was defined contributions. It was Engler's idea. He was a strategic genius and he came up with the strategy to get the votes.

"I want defined contributions," he said, "*and* I will offer early retirement in one bill that is linked to defined contributions. Early retirement will be the horse that pulls the defined contributions cart along. I will not only offer defined contributions for state employees, but I will also propose it for teachers. I know I will never get it for teachers. I can never beat the MEA on this one, but I'll draw all the fire there. I'll get all the guns blazing at the teachers' pension system and have it get through the state employees' system."

I said, "For the record, I don't think that horse is strong enough to pull the cart."

John just laughed and said, "Jeff, you are always the pessimist."

As the battle developed, we were a couple of votes short. In the House we were trying to pick up votes for defined contributions. Again, we were pushing the teachers' proposal, but never with any belief that we could actually pass that. The MEA was just going nuts. We had a good core of state employees who wanted early retirement. That was dividing the state employees' union, which had come out against defined contributions.

We were trying to get one rep's vote in particular. Engler had this rep in his office. I came in and saw the rep sitting there. Engler was shaking his finger in the rep's face, saying, "Get yourself out of here. The next time I want to talk to you, I'll just talk to an empty chair, because I'll get more response out of an empty chair than I'll get out of you! And I think there's more IQ in an empty chair than there is in you!"

[401]*Connie Binsfeld, interview with GW, January 23, 2001.*

Beet red, the rep left the office and returned to the floor of the House. Moments after this encounter, however, that rep cast the winning vote for the legislation Engler wanted."[402]

*

Engler criticizes Clinton for blocking welfare reform

Presidential election years focused and energized John Engler even more than usual, and 1996 was no exception. The governor knew that President Clinton would be vulnerable in the November election if he did not sign far-reaching welfare reform legislation. So Engler began the year by challenging the president in the national press. He criticized Clinton for reneging on his promise to the American people "to end welfare as we know it." The president had vetoed previous welfare reform legislation sent to his desk because it would have alienated him from his liberal constituency. Engler took advantage of the double-talking Man from Hope, arguing that Clinton could hardly claim to be a New Democrat when he was protecting the centerpiece of the Great Society, a failed welfare system that trapped "people in a life of dependency with little hope for the future."[403]

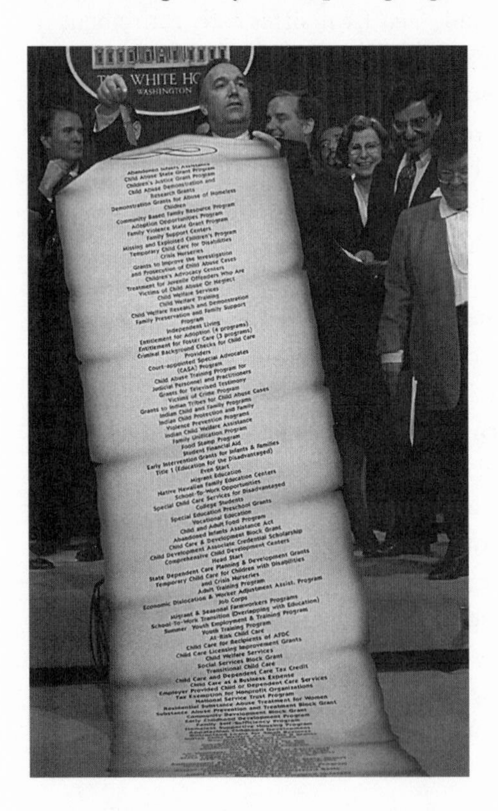

At a White House press conference, John Engler unfurls a scroll listing hundreds of welfare programs, January 28, 1995. This image was broadcast nationwide. CREDIT: *Gannett News Service*

*

Michigan in national spotlight: welfare reform

From the Washington Post

In the absence of national legislation, the nation's governors who are gathering here today for their semiannual convention may well shape the future of welfare in this country.

[402] *Jeff McAlvey, interview with GW, May 29, 2002.*
[403] *JE, "Michigan's Welfare Lessons,"* Washington Times, *January 19, 1996, p. A19.*

Many of them already are moving to require welfare recipients to find jobs. But their new plans also extend health- and child-care benefits once recipients are working to keep them from falling back onto the rolls....

Michigan Gov. John Engler (R), who played a major role in shaping GOP budget and welfare proposals in Washington, recently unveiled a plan significantly more generous to welfare recipients than the federal legislation he has tirelessly promoted for the past year.

Michigan's plan, unlike the federal measure, would provide community service work for welfare recipients who could not find private employment. But if they refused to look for work, recipients would lose their benefits.

Unlike many in Congress, Engler did not call for the "family cap" that would ban additional benefits for babies born to welfare mothers.

"The compassionate, caring approach is the one we're saying," said Gerald Miller, director of social services in Michigan. "We're willing to help people remove the barriers to work."...

Many of these experiments got started under a system of federal "waivers," which allow states to deviate from federal rules. Since he took office, Clinton has approved experiments in 35 states, beginning what his administration has called a "move toward a new welfare system."

Several governors, including Engler, Whitman and Thompson, have complained that the waiver process is cumbersome and does not allow them sufficient freedom to institute real change. Engler has complained that governors shouldn't have to go to Washington "on bended knee" asking for permission to improve their welfare systems. And New Hampshire Gov. Steve Merrill (R) recently vowed to carry out his reforms with or without federal permission.

Those kinds of complaints helped produce the Republican welfare bill, which would have ended the federal system and turned major programs over to the states.[404]

*

Lucille Taylor

John Engler started to think about welfare system reform back in 1971. It was really hard not to become skeptical about what we were doing to keep the welfare system. We were spending more money on welfare than on schools. The more money we were putting into welfare, the more the welfare rolls grew, and

[404] *Barbara Vobejda and Judith Havemann, "Most States Are Shaping Their Own Welfare Reform,"* Washington Post, *February 3, 1996, p. A1.*

the more illegitimacy and dropouts we had.

Many people were skeptical about the system and there had been a lot of criticism expressed in opinion journals and newspaper editorial pages. So, when John Engler decided to become an innovator and introduce far-reaching welfare reforms, he was not doing something that was out of step with American public opinion.

But no one else anywhere in the country was so committed to implementing the new thinking about welfare. John Engler had the courage to make changes rather than merely talk about them. Arguably he was the first in the nation to take that risk.[405]

*

From the Washington Times

CAN WELFARE REFORM SURVIVE FRIENDLY FIRE?

Potentially breaking a welfare reform deadlock, a plan embracing goals sought by conservatives for 25 years has won bipartisan endorsement by all 50 of the nation's governors.

Govs. Tommy Thompson, John Engler and Mike Leavitt brilliantly orchestrated the unanimity that brought support for a program that would achieve 90 percent or more of the block grant goals sought by the Reagan administration in its attempts at welfare reform.

No one would have thought a year ago that the person to stop welfare reform in this Congress would not be President Clinton, but Robert Rector of the Heritage Foundation. But that is how it may turn out....

Throughout all these years, what Mr. Reagan and the rest of the conservative movement wanted was to end the entitlement status of Aid to Families with Dependent Children (AFDC) and other federal welfare programs and turn them into block grants to the states. These block grants would allow states to completely redesign their own welfare programs. The block grants would remove the entire federal bureaucracy from welfare policy and allow voters to hold their own state's government directly responsible for welfare.

The most conservative states would then be free to experiment with the most conservative welfare reforms. Once their success was demonstrated, political and economic competition among the states would force the rest to adopt these reforms as well. The liberal establishment recognizes this for the

[405]*Lucille Taylor, interview with GW, October 20, 1999.*

deadly threat to them that it is. They call it a "race to the bottom," which from their perspective, standing on their heads, it is.

Remarkably, at the start of this Congress, a consensus in favor of this long-standing conservative position had arrived. This formerly impossible Reaganite position was now embraced by the House and Senate leadership, and the Republican governors who now controlled most of the states.

But Robert Rector had other ideas. He was sure he had the right solutions for welfare policy and wanted the federal government to impose them on every state, rather than restoring state control through block grants....

Mr. Rector is willing to scrap the whole reform effort. He denounces the governors' plan, saying they refuse "to acknowledge or mention the collapse of marriage and the rise of illegitimacy." He says, "The rise in illegitimacy and collapse of marriage do not merit even a token comment ... from the governors." He says, "The governors' plan blithely ignores ... the catastrophic rise in illegitimacy."

These are outright falsehoods. The governors' plan endorses the findings of the Republican reform plan passed by Congress, which included three single-spaced pages raising the central problem of illegitimacy and marital breakdown. Those findings state "marriage is the foundation of a successful society," recite the problems caused by soaring illegitimacy, and conclude, "It is the view of the Congress that prevention of out-of-wedlock pregnancy and reduction in out-of-wedlock births are very important government interests, and the policy contained in {this bill} is intended to address the crisis."...

Congress should enact the governors' plan without change to maximize pressure on Mr. Clinton and avoid any excuse for a veto. And conservative groups need to examine more closely what they are fed by various policy experts.[406]

*

Engler for VP?

By mid 1995, articles were appearing that explored the prospects of Engler being the GOP vice presidential pick. The following two articles appeared in the Lansing State Journal *in 1995.*

SAVVY POL, PROUD POP:
GOP ANALYSTS THINK GOV. ENGLER COULD CATCH NATIONAL AUDIENCE

[406]*Robert Carleson, "Can Welfare Reform Survive Friendly Fire?"* Washington Times, *February 29, 1996, p. A21.*

To Bill Clinton's image-makers, he was the man from Hope, the man of hope.

For Republicans framing the story of John Engler for a national audience, his life might look like this:

The young man from Beal City who outgrew the cattle farm but never shed his small-town, Midwestern, conservative roots.

The ambitious candidate who went on to slay political giants, never losing an election. Not one.

The determined governor who dared to shrink bloated bureaucracies, slash taxes—16 times—and force welfare recipients to work.

The proud pappa who pads around the kitchen and cares for the triplets Margaret, Madeleine, and Hannah with his telegenic wife Michelle.

Republican analysts think that Engler could catch on with a national public that now knows little about him. In a March-April poll, 72 percent of U.S. voters didn't recognize his name.

"John Engler has a great welfare, education and tax reform story to tell," said Mike Murphy, Engler's Virginia-based media consultant.

Engler and his handlers readily admit that neither his looks nor eloquence have swept him into office. Still, his 9-0 record in elections dating back to 1970 speaks for itself.

"He's always been criticized for the charisma factor, but I'm not sure people are looking for that blow-dried, slick politician," said Republican strategist Tom Shields of Marketing Resource Group.

What counts are the results, and Engler's "done" list includes many problems Washington is only beginning to tackle, said U.S. Sen. Spencer Abraham, R-Michigan.

"The voters in Illinois and the voters in Ohio, for example, care as much about reforming welfare and cutting taxes as voters in Michigan," said Abraham, who is promoting Engler as the vice-presidential pick in Washington.

While Engler's critics may claim Engler has been mean-spirited in cutting government programs, that strategy could back-fire, Republicans say.

"Given the current political winds, that story will make him a very popular candidate," Shields said. "It'll make him a hero among most voters."[407]

*

[407] *Chris Andrews, "Savvy Pol, Proud Pop: GOP Analysts Think Gov. Engler Could Catch National Audience,"* Lansing State Journal, *August 14, 1995, p. 5A.*

JUST THE TICKET: ENGLER IN '96

Gov. John Engler, it seems, is everywhere these days.

In Washington, lecturing Congress about welfare reform. In Atlanta, toasting the Contract with America with Newt Gingrich. In Japan, just last week, talking trade with the prime minister.

On television: "Meet the Press," "Nightline," "MacNeil/Lehrer."

In print: *Washington Post*, *New York Times*, *National Review*.

Where is John Engler headed?

Maybe nowhere.

Maybe the vice presidency.

One year before the Republican National Convention, the persistent talk of Engler as vice president nominee has moved from idle speculation to a real possibility.

Analysts and party insiders say a strong case can be made for Engler as a running mate, no matter who wins the nomination next year. What's more, many of the other potential picks have drawbacks that could give a further edge to Engler.

"Everyone has slightly different short lists," said strategist Mike Murphy, who has worked for Engler and now is part of the Lamar Alexander presidential campaign. "John Engler is the only one on everybody's list."

Historically, vice presidential picks involve as much chance as logic, with factors ranging from balancing the ticket to the gut-level feeling of the presidential nominee.

Here's what Engler has going for him:

- Michigan. With 18 electoral votes, Michigan will play a key role in determining who wins the White House. Engler, who cruised to re-election last year, could help Republicans pick up a state that went to Democrats in 1992.
- A get-it-done record. From reforming welfare to cutting taxes to shrinking government, Engler's actions in Michigan match the issues Republicans hope to win on in 1996.
- Family. As a new father—of triplets, no less—Engler, 46, could project a youthful but solid image. It could be a useful balance if 72-year-old Bob Dole, the current front-runner, gets the party's nod.

As his national profile continues to rise, Engler repeatedly downplays any ambitions of being vice-president. All he wants, Engler says, over and over, is to be governor of Michigan.

So that's it, right?

Wrong.

"Go Green!" Homecoming parade at John Engler's alma mater, Michigan State University, October 6, 1995. The children from left are Madeleine, Hannah, and Maggie. CREDIT: *David Olds,* Lansing State Journal

Such protestations don't mean much when a running mate offer is on the table. And some of Engler's closest friends and advisers say there's little question he would say yes if asked.

"I have no doubt," said U.S. Sen. Spencer Abraham, a longtime confidant and former state party chairman.

"Obviously there are some issues he'd have to confront, but I think if his party called on him to help win the presidency and help change the direction of the country, I think he would want to do it."

It's as simple as this, said Virginia-based analyst Larry Sabato: You don't say yes until you're asked.

"It's something that is traditionally viewed as a burden to be accepted on behalf of the country," said Sabato a political science professor at the University of Virginia. "Of course they all want to be vice president. They're all lean and hungry for it."

The best scenario for Engler: A member of Congress—say Dole, Phil Gramm or even Newt Gingrich—wins the nomination. As Washington insiders they would be most likely to turn to a governor to balance the ticket....

No matter who wins the Republican nomination, the general election theme is likely to be the same: Smaller government. Lower taxes. More power to the states, where today's problems are already being solved.

Enter Engler.

Since January, he has emerged as a darling of conservatives and a frequent guest on television talk shows. One day he's chatting it up with Rush Limbaugh, the next day columnist Robert Novak is touting Engler as VP timber.[408]

At a White House conference on welfare reform, Engler stole a news conference packed with governors when he unrolled a scroll listing about 300 programs he said should be consolidated into eight block grants to the states. It made the evening news, drew the notice of President Clinton and became a blueprint for the plan now being considered by the U.S. Senate.

Why is Engler's star rising now?

First, with Republicans now controlling Congress, the ideas and programs Engler pushed in Michigan are simply more in vogue. They are pointed to as examples of successful programs Republicans want to implement nationally.

Second, Engler's staff works hard to tell the Michigan story—low unemployment, 16 tax cuts, and a drop in those on the welfare rolls.

His trips to Washington—there have been 13 since January—are packed minute-by-minute with appointments and meetings. What's more, national columnists like Novak and David Broder have a long history with Engler aides.

After his election is 1990, when the governor was being hammered in the state media for things like ending General Assistance welfare and closing the Lafayette mental health clinic in Detroit, there was a deliberate effort to go national where the aides figured they'd get a better shake.

It's paying off now with frequent mentions by figures such as Paul Harvey and G. Gordon Liddy, whose radio shows reach millions of voters nationwide.

"No one runs for vice president, but you can put yourself in a position to be chosen," said Tom Shields, a Republican strategist and longtime Engler ally. "I don't know if that was the intent, but it may be the end result."

Former Engler chief of staff Dan Pero, who is now managing the Alexander campaign, said he has not discussed the vice-presidential talk with the governor—as a friend or as a campaign representative.

"I've come to know that with this governor, you don't try to guess what he thinks and you take him at his word," said Pero.

Plenty of pundits will be watching those words next year, especially once the Republican nominee is determined and attention turns to the vice-presidential pick.

[408]*Robert Novak, "My Favorite Career Pol,"* American Spectator, *July 1995, pp.18-21.*

Analysts say to keep one thing in mind: There is a difference between saying you're content to be governor and saying you don't want to be vice-president.

And John Engler hasn't said that.[409]

*

By the winter of 1996, Engler was receiving even more intense national (and international) press—and not just for leading the charge on welfare reform. As the presidential primaries were heating up, observers were also wondering if Engler might be dubbed Bob Dole's running mate. Donald Lambro wrote in the Washington Times*:*

Sen. Bob Dole's advance toward the Republican presidential nomination has triggered new debate over who would be his strongest running mate, with Michigan Gov. John Engler appearing on virtually every GOP list.

Mr. Engler is the popular two-term governor of a key Midwestern, industrial swing state whose 18 electoral votes could help determine who wins the presidential election in November. He is conservative, Catholic and pro-life, and has turned his state's economy around with an agenda of tax cuts and welfare reform.

"It has to be someone who is relatively conservative and who is broadly acceptable to the core of the party. And Engler fits the criteria. He is my first choice," said GOP strategist David Keene.

Of all the possible choices being talked about for vice president, Mr. Engler, who is close to Mr. Dole, seems to draw support across the party's spectrum.[410]

*

The Economist *(London) coined a new noun: Englerization.*

THE NEXT-BUT-ONE PRESIDENT

Hardly a week passes without his popping up in Washington for some top Republican strategy session on budget-balancing. The other day he was to be seen riding through Michigan in Newt Gingrich's car and wallowing in praise from the speaker, who called him "the leading revolutionary in America." Then he showed up briefly in San Diego, where he told the winter meeting of the Republican National Committee that the core of the party's 1996 presidential campaign "must be to tell the success stories of America's Republican governors."

Stories such as his own, perhaps. Our pop-up politician is John Engler, governor of Michigan since 1991 and current chairman of the Republican

[409] *Chris Andrews and Tim Makinen, "Just the Ticket: Engler in '96,"* Lansing State Journal, *August 14, 1995, p. 5A.*
[410] *Donald Lambro, "Engler Tops Wish List for Dole Running Mate,"* Washington Times, *March 7, 1996, p. A10.*

Governors' Association. The chances are he will pop up a lot between now and when the Republicans next gather in San Diego, for their convention in August. For Mr. Engler is not only ubiquitous; he is also the very embodiment of the Republican plan for beating Bill Clinton. Mr. Clinton has "triangulation"; Republicans have Englerization.

First, Mr. Engler comes from a decisive battleground of the 1996 election, the industrial midwest. An urbanized, unflamboyant son of a cattle farmer, he oozes midwesternness. In Michigan, he has a 63 percent approval rating. He even has solid support in the blue-collar areas around Detroit, where David Bonior, a local congressman who is Democratic whip in the House of Representatives and a persistent scourge of Mr. Gingrich, is now thought to be vulnerable.

Next, Mr. Engler is a Roman Catholic—albeit a divorced, remarried one. Republicans are aiming at the Catholic vote. Catholics used to be a solid part of the Democratic coalition, but in 1994, for the first time, a majority voted Republican. As luck would have it, Mr. Engler now has three perfect props for a platform of family values: his one-year-old triplet daughters, Margaret, Hannah and Madeleine.

Then there is the hope of emulating the Engler story. In his early days as governor, when Mr. Engler was cutting spending, heading for a showdown with teachers and being attacked as "mean-spirited," the polls at one point showed that only 19 percent of voters would re-elect him. But he bounced back, much as the Republicans hope to bounce back nationally from their "mean-spirited" budget fight. "We have a very similar style," Mr. Gingrich said in Detroit this month. "We just charge straight ahead and hope that you'll figure out later why we were right."

Mr. Engler won his battles—notably a daring reform of school financing—and kept his promises. In 1994 he coasted to re-election. His reforms continue apace....

As for the economy, boosters talk of a "Michigan miracle." The rustbelt is dead, says the governor, replaced by the "high-performance heartland." Unemployment, now 4.6 percent, dipped below the national average in 1994 and has stayed below, a sustained success the like of which Michigan has not seen for a quarter of a century....

But the most powerful aspect of Englerization is welfare reform. Republicans see a delicious opportunity to attack a president who pledged to "end welfare as we know it" and yet vetoed Congress's attempt to do it. Back in Michigan, Mr. Engler has been Mr. Welfare Reform, cutting so-called general assistance for able-bodied people with no children, improving incentives to work, and threatening to cut off benefits after 12 months for shirkers. Nearly one out of every three welfare recipients in Michigan now has a job, a higher proportion than in any other state. For 21 straight months, Michigan's welfare rolls have shrunk. More than 70,000 families have left the system over the past two years, saving taxpayers over $100 million.

Mr. Engler raised eyebrows by revealing in his State of the State address last week "Project Zero," a plan for research, in six pilot areas, into the barriers between welfare and work, with the aim of getting everyone into jobs....

"Of all the governors," says Ron Kaufman, who was in George Bush's White House, "tactically, he's the best."

Now he may have his sights set on the White House. He is mentioned as a possible vice-presidential nominee for 1996. He is perhaps not the ideal person for the ticket—since, in the words of one of Bob Dole's people, he is white and urinates standing up—but he is clearly in the running. Don't be surprised if one day John Engler pops up as president.[411]

*

With Margaret Thatcher

Not only was John Engler receiving press in a British publication, but he was also receiving praise from a former prime minister. In fact, during the mid 1990s Engler was sometimes referred to as the "Margaret Thatcher of the Midwest." Michelle Engler recalls:

We went to England in 1996 and we met with Margaret Thatcher. She invited us to have coffee with her and Sir Denis. She was quite worried about Bob Dole's chances of winning the election. We talked about the campaign quite a bit and she also talked about Ronald Reagan and his legacy.

It was fascinating to see how much Lady Thatcher knew about John. It's one thing for us to know so much about her. She is a world leader. But she is such a fan of John's. She invited us to a fundraising event in London where she was the honored guest. And the people at that event were Tories and thrilled to have John on hand. Lady Thatcher got up on stage and brought John up and talked about him for three or four minutes.

Later, John sort of pinched himself. "Wow. She knew I cut taxes!"

It's one of the cool things about John that he always feels that kind of humility with people he admires.[412]

[411]*"The Next-But-One-President,"* Economist, *January 27, 1996.*
[412]*Michelle Engler, interview with GW, January 26, 2001.*

Governor Engler with Lady Margaret Thatcher and Sir Denis, in London, 1996. SOURCE: *John Engler*

*

Engler featured: on the front page of the *Washington Times*

Gov. John Engler of Michigan does not deny he is a politically ambitious and tenacious politician who believes he has what it takes to be vice president of the United States.

"Yes, I've had to be very tenacious because I'm not a guy who wins it on the basis of my good looks or charming personality," the portly, balding and bankerish-looking Mr. Engler said in an interview during a recent day of strategy meetings here with Republican leaders.

His schedule last Thursday on Capitol Hill, one of two dozen trips here in the past year, illustrates just how ambitious he is to be a major player in national politics and why he is considered a strong contender to be Sen. Bob Dole's running mate.

Mr. Engler and four other Republican governors met Thursday with House and Senate GOP leaders to finalize the welfare and Medicaid reforms that he helped to negotiate at the National Governors' Association February meeting and that are scheduled to be voted on by Congress next month.

He then led a news conference with House Speaker Newt Gingrich to announce the legislative initiatives that he said would spell "the end of individual entitlements to cash welfare."

Next he addressed the National Federation of Republican Women, where he was introduced as someone "who may very well be the next vice president of the United States."

Then he sped over to the House Rayburn Building for a meeting with GOP lawmakers on future legislative strategy. He ended the hectic day with a speech in New York.

The two-term governor and vice chairman of the Republican Governors' Association has been a frequent visitor to Capitol Hill since Republicans won control in 1994.

"Engler has been to a lot of our strategy meetings, and he's not shy about speaking up," said a House leadership official. "He is one of the few governors who has clearly moved into the center of national policy-making."

And he does not hide his ambition to be on the GOP ticket. When asked by *Time* magazine about whether he thought he was qualified to take on the responsibilities of vice president, Mr. Engler shot back, "If Al Gore can do this job, then I can do this job."

But some Republican governors find Mr. Engler's ambition a bit hard to stomach.

"There's a consensus view that he's very aggressive and driven by ambition," says a chief aide to a Midwestern Republican governor.

"He is seen as too pushy, too self-promotional, a little too eager to grab the spotlight. That has rubbed some of his fellow governors the wrong way at times," said the aide.

A sign of this coolness occurred during a National Governors' Association meeting in February when a vote was to take place on picking the next vice chairman.

Mr. Engler and Ohio Gov. George V. Voinovich were running for the post, and several Republican governors requested a meeting to vote on the new vice chairman. According to those familiar with the situation, Mr. Engler refused to hold the meeting after learning he had the support of only eight of 31 Republican governors and would not prevail over Mr. Voinovich.

Of his political ambitions for higher office, Mr. Engler has said, "I know you don't always get what you want the first time out, but you have to be prepared, you have to be ready, and you have to stay with it."

Mr. Dole says he has made no decision about a running mate, though he has spoken warmly of retired Army Gen. Colin Powell. But Mr. Powell insists he is not interested in elective office, and senior Dole campaign aides say Mr. Engler is getting a serious look.

"Engler would bring a lot to the ticket," said a senior Dole strategist. "He's Catholic, conservative, a successful governor of a key Midwestern, industrial state. He appeals to virtually all sectors of the party, the economic conservatives and the social conservatives, and that would help unite us."

In a close election, Michigan's 18 electoral votes could provide the winning margin. The state is thought to be leaning toward Mr. Clinton in the upcoming presidential campaign. But the GOP has carried Michigan in five out of the last seven presidential elections, and party strategists believe Mr. Engler could put it in the GOP column in November.

"Engler brings an awful lot with him to the table. Roman Catholics will be the swing votes in 1996, and he would be strong in the industrial Midwest, which will decide the outcome in the electoral college," said Ralph Reed, executive director of the Christian Coalition.

"He is strongly pro-life and has a deep reservoir of support from the religious conservative movement," Mr. Reed said.

Mr. Engler delivered a major address this month to the Focus on the Family organization headed by Dr. James Dobson that has won him strong support among GOP social conservatives.

"It's not just the budget, or economy, or campaign laws that are crying out for reform. The most urgent problems we face today are cultural and spiritual," Mr. Engler said.

Mr. Engler's political career began in 1970, when, at age 22, he was elected to the state House of Representatives while still a student at Michigan State University. Eight years later, he was elected to the state Senate, where he served as majority leader from 1983 until he ran for governor in 1990.

He challenged Democratic incumbent James Blanchard, a national party leader who was mentioned as a presidential contender. He defeated him by less than 1 percent.

Mr. Engler inherited a $1.8 billion deficit and a state stuck in a recession. The governor's job-approval ratings sank the following year as unemployment rose and the economy worsened. By the end of 1991, Mr. Engler's approval ratings had plummeted to 18 percent. Pundits were writing his political obituary.

In response, Mr. Engler pushed a "taxpayers' agenda" that called for cutting taxes and downsizing government. He also led the passage of welfare reforms that ended the general assistance program for 83,000 childless, able-bodied poor adults and eliminated 5,000 state jobs and nearly two dozen state boards and commissions.

Yet the economy remained weak, and criticism of his administration mounted. The low point in his governorship came in the fall of 1991, after he ended the welfare program, when two homeless men whose benefits had been cut died of smoke inhalation in an abandoned house where they had lit a fire for warmth.

Protesters erected an "Englerville" shantytown at the state Capitol, and he was bitterly attacked as mean-spirited and lacking compassion for the poor.

But Mr. Engler stuck with his budget-cutting programs, and the economy began to recover, along with the state's automotive industry. The budget deficit turned into a $300 million surplus, and he claimed that his welfare-to-work program had found jobs for 30 percent of welfare recipients, saving taxpayers $100 million.

Then on March 15, 1994, Michigan voters approved Mr. Engler's plan to cut property taxes and raise the sales tax in a dramatic shift of public-school financing. His approval ratings soared.

Declaring that "the image of the Midwest rustbelt is history," he swept to an easy re-election victory in 1994 with 61 percent of the vote.

The Engler comeback from the brink of political failure soon became the inspiration for House GOP leaders in their ill-fated attempt to get their "Contract With America" agenda passed in 1995.

Mr. Gingrich often met with Mr. Engler and referred to "the Engler model" in his pep talks to his House colleagues.

"I am by nature an optimistic person. I'm a positive person," Mr. Engler said. "In part my role during those days was to keep everybody else up, keep everybody focused on the goal. We felt that if we had deviated from our plan, said that our assumptions were wrong, that that was the path to doom, that would lead nowhere."

No matter how bad things looked, he said he continued to believe "that our decisions were consistent, logical and made sense. You need repetition of your goals, a constancy of purpose, a persistence and tenacity as you hang in there and move forward."

Some of Mr. Engler's early successes, however, have shown signs of fatigue.

Total state spending, which now exceeds $28 billion, is 35 percent higher than it was when Mr. Engler was elected. And the state bureaucracy, reduced in the early Engler years, is now virtually the same size it was in 1991.

Though Mr. Engler remains popular in Michigan—his approval ratings stand at 62 percent—Democrats say his policies have harmed the poor and gutted environmental protection.

"He's been a very bad governor. While he's been posing and preening in the national limelight over the past year, he's been ignoring critical Michigan needs," said Steve Gools, chief spokesman for the state Democratic Party.

"The welfare cuts were very abrupt and hurt a lot of people. Those images of the shantytown at the statehouse are going to come back to hurt him if he is Dole's running mate," Mr. Gools said. "His reorganization of the Department of Natural Resources gutted the state's ability to safeguard the environment. He made a series of promises to reduce toxic substances in Lake Michigan that have not been kept."

The issue that Leo Lalonde, chairman of the Macomb County Democratic Committee, thinks will hurt Mr. Engler more than any other deals with Vietnam—a subject that dogs President Clinton.

It was recently disclosed that Mr. Engler failed his Army physical during the Vietnam War, while a college student in 1969, because he was over the maximum weight limit by 2 pounds. He failed the exam a second time because of his weight and was classified 1-Y. He never served in the military.

"How is this going to play with Bob Dole, who was a war hero," asks Mr. Lalonde, a Vietnam War veteran. "This guy can't lose 2 pounds to serve his country? Bill Clinton may be a draft-dodger, but Engler is a draft-evader."

Michigan has also encountered trouble in its handling of Medicare and Medicaid. And some of the difficulties coincide with Mr. Engler's reign as governor.

In 1993, according to a General Accounting Office report, Michigan used loopholes in Medicaid rules to recapture all but $6 million of $458 million in payments to 53 state hospitals. This allowed Michigan to collect more than the original $256 million federal Medicaid reimbursement.

The following year, Michigan exploited other loopholes in Medicaid rules and funneled $489 million in Medicaid payments to the state-owned University of Michigan. The hospital returned the entire payment to the state the same day, allowing the state to increase its federal share of Medicaid payments from the legal limit of 56 percent to 68 percent.

The GAO report said Michigan used "illusory financing mechanisms" to collect Medicaid reimbursements it was not legally entitled to.

Medicaid is a federal-state program that provides health care to the poor and disabled. Overall, states cover about 43 percent of the costs. The amount paid by each state depends on its wealth.

Blue Cross and Blue Shield of Michigan also paid the federal government nearly $52 million in 1995 to settle two unrelated lawsuits dealing with its administration of Medicare.

The first settlement, involving some $24 million, ends a controversy that pre-dates Mr. Engler's governorship over how to enforce Medicare Secondary Payer rules.

The other settlement was with the Health Care Financing Administration, which oversees federal Medicare payments. The health care administration accused Blue Cross and Blue Shield of Michigan of improper billing and submission of false documentation.

The Justice Department filed suit in 1992 alleging that Michigan and other states received Medicare payments to hospitals for procedures that should not have qualified for coverage.

Blue Cross and Blue Shield of Michigan acknowledged the cost-reporting problem and agreed to pay the health care administration $27.6 million as compensation.

SIDEBAR: LEGISLATIVE RECORD

Taxes

Gov. John Engler's administration has enacted 21 tax cuts, nine of them last year [1995]. Among them:

- The largest tax cut in Michigan history, which reduced property taxes by $3.4 billion and limited assessment increases to the inflation rate. The revenue loss was offset with an increase in the sales tax approved in a referendum.
- A reduction in the personal income tax rate from 4.6 percent to 4.4 percent.
- The elimination of the state inheritance tax.
- A cut in the state's principal business tax from 2.35 percent to 2.3 percent.

The Economy

More than 400,000 jobs, including 65,000 in manufacturing, have been created in Michigan since 1991. The state unemployment rate fell to 4.4 percent by the end of 1995, the lowest ever. Mr. Engler inherited a $1.8 billion budget deficit and produced a $1.2 billion surplus in his fifth year as governor.

Welfare Reform

A law enacted last year requires able-bodied welfare recipients to work or lose their benefits. The welfare caseload fell by more than 186,000 cases by October to the lowest level since 1974.

Education Reform

Sweeping legislation set up more than 30 charter schools in 1995. The legislation gives teachers and administrators wider freedom to create the core curriculum and compete with other public schools. It lengthened the school year by 10 days.

SIDEBAR: THE GOVERNOR'S VIEWS

On President Clinton: "Clinton doesn't want to deal with the problem. He wants to feel your pain rather than deal with it."

On Tax Reform: "I think Bob Dole has already embraced tax reform. The specific flat tax that Steve Forbes is an advocate of is one that meets the tests generally laid down by the Kemp commission, which Dole appointed. Tax reform is going to be a major issue in the campaign."

On Welfare Reform: "We have 70,000 fewer families in Michigan today on public assistance who are now in charge of their own lives because of our welfare reforms. We are going to give Clinton a third chance to sign a welfare-reform bill this year, and if he doesn't, then it's three strikes and he's out."

On Trade: "Our future is linked directly to our ability to compete in the world, and 250 million Americans have to be able to access a market that is over 4 billion people. I would like to see us move toward freer trade, removing barriers. But I think Pat Buchanan is right when he says we don't have free access to, and fair trade with, some countries. We have to be rigorous about the rules of the game, but I don't think that we can withdraw from the game.

On the Vice Presidential Nomination: "That's really a question for Bob Dole. He's going to pick someone who is qualified, someone he is comfortable with. It's his decision. I have no disappointment about being in the job I'm in and no expectation about being in any other job."

On Social and Cultural Issues: "It's not just the budget or economy or campaign laws that are crying out for reform. The most urgent problems we face today are cultural and spiritual."[413]

*

[413]*Donald Lambro, "Engler Runs Hard for No. 2 Spot on Ticket but 'Abrasive' Personality Bothers Some Politicians,"* Washington Times, *March 18, 1996, p. A1.*

False Rumors

Sharon Rothwell

My heart just ached for John back in 1996 when we were working on the Dole campaign. John was being considered as a vice presidential candidate, and the newspapers were running stories about him. Some of the stories were just awful.

I started a policy with the staff. I told everyone, "I am rumor central. If you hear something, you don't tell anyone else. You come to me and tell me what you have heard. Anything, no matter how outrageous or how nasty, you come to me and tell me."

Then I would go tell him about the rumors. At one point, I spent four hours with him and he basically told me his whole personal history. He told me everything so that I could distinguish between fact and fiction. I hugged him afterward and told him, "Look, everyone is human. I would hate for everything I had done when I was young to be laid out on the front page of the newspaper, and so would everybody else."

All the stories that were out there, all the rumors—they were just awful. They were false. It was just so vicious. He was concerned about his wife and his girls. You know his girls could some day read these newspaper stories. That was what hurt.

The story about him being two pounds overweight got to him. It hurt him. It was bad enough that he has had a weight problem all of his life. But even as a young man he had to deal with that during the time of the draft. Now people were accusing him of manipulating his weight to avoid the draft. It was so demeaning.[414]

*

From Newsweek

THE SEXIEST GOVERNOR

The sexiest governor alive (though you wouldn't know it looking at him) is John Engler of Michigan, short-listed by the press for the vice presidential nomination after Colin Powell seemed to demur....

In any event, the political wise guys are in heat over Engler, which means, of course, that Dole will probably pick someone else. The early money is rarely right. But whatever happens, Engler represents state-of-the-art GOP governance. In terms of getting what he wants, he is phenomenally successful.[415]

[414] *Sharon Rothwell, interview with GW, March 16, 2001.*
[415] *Jonathan Alter, "The Sexiest Governor,"* Newsweek, *April 1, 1996.*

*

Michelle Engler

Throughout the vice-presidential selection process, John was convinced that he was not going to be picked as Dole's running mate. "It's not going to be me," he said.

A few weeks before the convention Dole's people called and asked John, "Will you get a physical?"

"I don't think so. Call me when you whittle the list down. If I'm still on it, call me back and I'll do it," John answered. "I don't think it's going to happen. I hate physicals," he joked with me.

They called again a week before the convention and said, "Go get a physical." John finally agreed and got the physical.

It wasn't until just before the start of the Republican National Convention that we learned that Kemp was chosen as Dole's running mate. Nobody ever called to tell us. We just saw it on TV.

John had been right all along. He never believed Dole would pick him, because he thought Dole would go with someone he knew better, someone with whom he felt more comfortable.

Frankly, it was a relief to me that John wasn't picked.[416]

*

Anne Mervenne

John and Michelle were flying to San Diego on a private plane, but there were a lot of Republicans and Engler staff on a commercial flight at the same time. When Kemp was announced as Dole's running mate, the Republicans' beepers all started going off. I felt terrible for the governor and first lady.[417]

*

Election Day 1996

November 5, 1996, was a bad day for most Michigan Republicans and for John Engler. President Clinton easily won re-election over Senator Robert Dole and Reform Party candidate Ross Perot. Clinton received 49.2 percent of the vote; Dole 40.7 percent; Perot 8.4 percent. In their post-election analyses, GOP party leadership concluded, "Attacks on the Education Department cost Republican candidates crucial support among female voters." As a result, "Republican National Committee Chairman Haley

[416]*Michelle Engler, interview with GW, January 26, 2001.*
[417]*Anne Mervenne, interview with GW, February 1, 2002.*

Barbour today urged GOP governors to recast the party's position on education issues."[418]

In Michigan, Republicans lost control of the House, where they had not been in the minority since 1992. Going into the 1996 election they had a 56-54 majority; coming out they lost four seats and were in the minority. As there were no state Senate elections in 1996, the status quo continued with Republicans dominating that chamber 22 to 16.[419]

The highly controversial Proposal E, which gave Engler much grief and would allow non-Indian casino gaming in Michigan, passed by 109,000 votes.

*

Gambling

One of the most difficult social, political, and economic issues Engler faced as governor was casino gaming. Sharon Rothwell recalls:

First a little history. In 1994, when we were debating Indian gaming, John took his time to decide. He went back and forth. It was a difficult issue because, on the one hand, Detroit had a local ballot initiative and they wanted casinos. The governor truly wanted to help Detroit, but he struggled. We had sat through months of meetings, talking to people on both sides of the issue. We had meetings with the mayor and all of the people putting in casino proposals. Also—the gaming commission the governor had set up recommended approving the casinos.

The governor really struggled, but not because it was a moral absolute or puritanical issue for him. It was more a concern over some of the things that we are hearing about now: the gambling addicts, the suicides, the desperation of people going into debt. It was a concern for the citizens of Detroit.

Lucille and I talked on the phone one night. We thought the governor should just say no to casinos. I told her that I was going to call the governor with our advice, and assure him that we would be there to support and defend him. Mayor Archer would be upset and certain people on the gaming commission would think that he let them down, but Indian gaming was not the best thing for Detroit.

In our phone conversation, John said that he had come to the same conclusion and agreed with Lucille and me. The next morning he still felt that way. So we brought in Dick Posthumus, the Senate majority leader, and Dan

[418] *Dan Balz, "Stands on Education Cost GOP among Women, Governors Told,"* Washington Post, *November 27, 1996, p. A6.*

[419] Michigan Manual, *1997-1998 ed. (Lansing: Legislative Service Bureau), p. 338.*

Pero, and we briefed them on what we were doing and why we were doing it. When we went to the press conference, the governor said, "No casinos in Detroit."

I am sure everyone thought this had been his decision all along. Nobody knew how he had wrestled with it.

In 1996, the ballot initiative Proposal E changed things. It wasn't like the 1994 Indian gaming proposals where the decision rested solely on his shoulders. The governor did not think it would pass. We were just as surprised that it passed as anyone else. It was frustrating how he took the blame from the conservatives. They were very unforgiving and mean spirited in their response to him. They thought he hadn't worked hard enough to defeat casinos. But it really wasn't his responsibility at that point. He had said no to casinos when it was his decision in 1994. 1996 was an election year and he was working to get people elected.

We tried to get Dick Posthumus to step up to the plate on Proposal E. The governor said, "Somebody needs to be out there leading the charge. I shouldn't always be the one doing that." But nobody else stepped up to the plate and, lo and behold, he caught all the crap.[420]

*

A discussion among friends about Engler and gambling: most agreed that the governor was willing to wager small amounts in private card games, but that he did not like the idea of commercial gaming in Michigan for a host of social and political reasons.

RICHARD McLELLAN: You know, we've talked about how it is not wise to bluff John Engler. Debbie Stabenow found that out with Proposal A. But on the issue of casino gambling, the gambling forces called his bluff. He called a press conference and said that the only way he would allow gambling in Michigan was if the voters approved it in a statewide referendum.

The gaming proponents took him up on it. They circulated the petitions and got it on the ballot. By August, though, they were broke. They had spent everything to get it on the ballot. But then there was no money for a campaign.

Then some folks came forward and offered to fund the campaign. The governor, as he always does, said, "Don't worry. It's not going to pass." And he was right—up until October 1. Then $6 million came into the opposition's hands, and they organized a campaign, and it passed.

[420]*Sharon Rothwell, interview with GW, March 16, 2001.*

And all of a sudden the governor, who's against gambling and had vetoed gambling in Detroit, now has a statewide referendum approving casinos in Detroit.

BILL WHITBECK: Not only was it Engler's biggest tactical mistake, but it was also probably the worst day in the Engler administration when gambling came legally to this state. Not necessarily for him personally, but the worst day for Michigan on his watch.

RICHARD McLELLAN: John Engler's position is that he's a Republican governor and opposed to the expansion of gambling. That's been his position and he's been consistent. But every time the Indians act under federal law, he's forced to negotiate compacts. And when the people of Michigan pass a law, he has to acquiesce.[421]

*

Midpoint interview

This conversation with political analyst Gerald Faverman occurred at slightly past the midpoint in John Engler's 12 years as governor. As always, education was his number one concern.

A CONVERSATION WITH JOHN M. ENGLER:
MICHIGAN'S CONSERVATIVE REVOLUTIONARY

GERALD A. FAVERMAN, Ph.D.: Governor, you have less than two years left in your second term. What is your vision about the important issues that remain?

GOVERNOR JOHN M. ENGLER: Education has been a priority from day one. It will remain my top priority, because the future of the 1.7 million children in Michigan's public schools is of paramount importance to our state's success in the 21st century. We can't have the kind of state that we want Michigan to be with incomes rising and job opportunities multiplying without a highly skilled, trained populace. That means young people can go to college and succeed or that young people can go into the world of work with the skills and the training necessary to succeed and to help their employers succeed....

GAF: In most states there does not appear to be a strong partisan disagreement about education. Democrats and Republicans do certain kinds of things together. In this state, education seems to be a matter of warfare. For instance,

[421]*Richard McLellan and Bill Whitbeck, interview with GW, February 3, 2001.*

the National Education Association has voiced enthusiasm for charter schools, which are viewed by the Michigan Education Association (MEA) with apprehension and suspicion.

GOVERNOR ENGLER: I believe some years ago the MEA made a tactical blunder and decided to become an appendage of the Democratic Party. The consequence of that for Michigan's professional teachers has been devastating because their own union, which they support through very expensive dues, now puts everything through the prism of Democratic politics. While there is now unrest, it has not yet become an organization for professional educators who want to improve public education in Michigan.

If you were to go back over the last decade and ask what the education reform agenda of an organization purporting to represent teachers and professional educators was, you would find there is none. There's a social agenda. There's a collective bargaining agenda. But there's no agenda that talks about helping children. I think that we saw them grow so strong and so powerful that they intimidated the administrators. Organizations like the Michigan Association of School Administrators and Michigan Association of School Boards simply were impotent when faced with the challenge of the MEA. What Michigan has needed and America has benefited by is the strong leadership of a leader like the late Al Shanker. His recent passing was a terrific blow to public education. (The late Albert Shanker was the president of the American Federation of Teachers, the AFL-CIO affiliated rival to the MEA.)

GAF: Indeed. I was overwhelmed by the breadth of his vision and his surprisingly innovative ideas and style, which indicated a person concerned about educating people.

GOVERNOR ENGLER: That's right. He cared deeply and passionately about quality education. He wanted educated children to emerge from the schools and he was willing to be quite innovative in the pursuit of that objective. It's important to realize that the press coverage of education has been a contributing factor to the problem because so much has been devoted to the contest of winning and losing, who's ahead, who's falling back, who's coming up. The result doesn't give a good sense of what the fundamental issues and questions are. This is a state, unlike many, where there hasn't been a debate over phonics versus whole English. This has been a major debate in other states. I could go through issue after issue where the education debate over the education topic never publicly surfaced. Instead, what it became was "right-wing" critics over this and "liberal" critics of that.

GAF: There has been no discussion in our public policy debates about what it is we want schools to do. You've had a significant victory in dealing with the K-12 finance side and not on the curriculum side.

GOVERNOR ENGLER: Michigan's had a tradition, which I have supported, of local control. We allow the curriculum to be determined locally. If people want to know what state government thinks about things they ought to be able to look at the department of education and see a model curriculum there. They ought not to feel they are obliged to adopt it in toto. What they do need to have though, I think, is the recognition that every child who goes to a Michigan school represents on average an investment of $75,000 during their K-12 schooling. For a $75,000 investment, we would expect that they would have a minimum knowledge of mathematics.

GAF: In your State of the State Address you spoke of your disappointment and distress about MEAP scores. In fact, our mathematics education in this state is so poor because most of the school districts do not offer an adequate mathematics curriculum.

GOVERNOR ENGLER: We also have a challenge as a nation. Our scores do not compare favorably enough with other nations. One of the recent initiatives of President Clinton was to make available to every student in the eighth grade the Third International Mathematics and Science (TIMS) test. Professor William Schmidt at MSU is the key academician connected to that test, and I have offered Michigan as the first state to give that test. Every parent in Michigan will be able to look and assess where their eighth-grader is in relation to every other student in America or in the world. That's a very important bit of knowledge. While there is controversy over testing, the state's obligation is to continue to develop rigorous tests that measure what every child should know and then challenge those who are writing curricula, choosing the mathematics textbooks, and educating the teachers to get the job done. Some schools are succeeding brilliantly. Our math and science centers are in markedly better than many of our traditional public schools.

GAF: People talk about local control as if it were one of the Ten Commandments of western civilization. Yet every time one deals with the issue of local control, you find that all of the problems that come from local control are state problems. Unemployment, lack of competitiveness in being able to recruit jobs—

GOVERNOR ENGLER: Unacceptable failure rates of minority students. I don't think that local control should be stretched to justify the proposition that it would be okay for the community to decide that failure is acceptable. I think that there are limits. When, as I cited in my State of the State speech, the Benton Harbor Public Schools give a science proficiency test to 205 high school eleventh graders and 203 students fail the test, then that tells me there is a need for intervention.

I think of the social consequences of that failure in terms of the lives that are being damaged because of their inability to compete when they leave school. It also needs to be pointed out that the number taking the test is significantly reduced from the potential test-takers because there has already been a significant dropout rate by the time we have reached the eleventh grade. So, the failure rate is actually significantly higher. As bad as those numbers are, they understate the problem we face....

GAF: I think that we have spent a lot more money than any other country in the world on almost every social program from education to health. The solutions don't exist, for me, purely in terms of spending more money. I am interested in effective operation. And yet that seems to be a major barrier, because the answer for everybody seems to be, "let's have more money."

GOVERNOR ENGLER: We have upset people by suggesting that the appropriate measure is the outcome. By shifting that focus you suddenly say, "Well, for $11 billion, which is the state's annual investment in our K-12 system, we should be doing better. We should have more to show for that investment." In fact, as we got into it, we found there were precious few ways that you could even measure what was happening with that investment.

Now all the test scores for the last four years, broken down school building by building, are available on the Internet.... We have tried to develop a consumer's guide to schools. Michigan has been very innovative. Nontraditional public education today includes the charter schools network, with about 12,000 students attending some 75 schools.... I think the number of children moving to charter schools will grow significantly.[422]

*

President Clinton comes to Lansing

Gleaves Whitney recalls:

The president's visit to the Michigan Capitol on Thursday, March 6th was to be an august occasion. Lots of pomp and circumstance. Political leaders from both parties. Everyone would behave.

Speech practice was arranged for 3:30 p.m. on Friday, February 28th—six days before Clinton's visit. When the governor came in, I put a speech outline

[422]The FG Report, *FG Consulting Publications, Lansing, 1996.*

in front of him that talked about Michigan's great gains [read: Republican leadership] during the 1990s. The governor looked summarily at the outline. I could tell he wasn't interested. A smile slowly crept across his face and he got a mischievous look we had seen many times before.

Rusty said, "Uh-oh."

Uh-oh was right. The governor announced that he would speak on education reform but—chuckle, chuckle—with a devilish twist. He pointed out the obvious: Clinton's education policies were starting to look like a lot of Republican policies. After all, Clinton was a former governor, and New Democrats and the GOP actually championed some of the same reforms. Not the education establishment in Michigan, however. Particularly the MEA, which was way to the left of Clinton.

Ergo, the president's visit the following week would give the governor the opportunity to embarrass the MEA and its Democratic allies in the legislature. An irresistible opportunity to lavish praise on Clinton's education policies and make Michigan Democrats look totally retro.

A rhetorical coup, totally orchestrated by the canny Engler. He would deliver a political punch with the stroke of a velvet glove. The general public would listen to the speech and think, "Oh, how nice that Republicans and Democrats are all getting along." But to the legislators in the chamber, John Engler's dispensation of praise and blame would hit their targets.[423]

*

Third term?

In politics there is always more than meets the eye. So much happens behind the scenes. Throughout the early months of 1997, John Engler was weighing the pros and cons of running for a third term. The decision was not coming easily for him and Michelle. Their announcement was pushed up by an unfortunate incident involving news reporters and editors. The incident infuriated Engler; it also revealed his strategic mind and his determination not to be bested. John Truscott recalls:

For six months the rumor mill had been running rampant: the Englers' marriage was breaking up, and Michelle had packed up and taken the girls to Texas. We were sick of hearing it. I used to tell all the journalists who'd ask about an impending divorce: show up at the next event the governor was scheduled to appear at, and ask him about it. Or go to the next event where the governor and Michelle would appear jointly, and ask them directly. Only one

[423] *GW, personal papers, March 1997.*

reporter, Lisa Zagaroli, dared to ask him about it to his face. The press didn't really think it was true, but because of the competition they didn't want to be scooped either.

In June of 1997 the *Detroit News* decided to write a story. It was to be called, "The Anatomy of a Rumor." Their goal was to raise the marriage issue but without necessarily confirming it. They started to write the story and wanted the governor's viewpoint. When we knew what they were up to, we started researching how journalists should handle rumors; we looked at the ethical standards taught at places like the Columbia journalism school and were confident that it was unethical for the *News* to run a story based on rumors, especially one ginned up by political opponents. So we met with people from the *News* in the governor's conference room. Our viewpoint was: if you can prove the rumor's true, go for it. But if we can prove that it is not true, then there's no story. You shouldn't run it.

We met at noon for an hour. Michelle, who was up on Mackinac Island, was on the speaker-phone. It was a tense meeting. The governor answered all the questions forthrightly. At the end, everybody stood up, and Charlie Cain said the *News* was going to run the story because they had the governor's quotations. I know Charlie. I am sure that he did not want to do this story, but there was pressure on him to do it.

The governor was not happy. He knew that we had lost the battle, but that we could still win the war. We went back into the room and the governor started strategizing with Michelle on the speaker-phone. It was obvious that the two of them had had a private conversation about his running again. This was just accelerating their timetable.

Michelle said, "Maybe I should make the announcement and let people know that I support you running for re-election."

The governor quickly agreed, saying, "That will really make news."

So we developed our strategy between about 1:00 and 1:15. We decided that Michelle would make the announcement, and that she would come back down from the Island to do it in person.

About 1:15 I called the *Detroit Free Press*, the rival of the *News*. I asked their political reporter, Dawson Bell, "Are you ready for one of the biggest scoops of the year?"

"Heck yes I'm interested. What is it?"

"Meet us at the Lansing Residence at 5:00."[424]

[424]*John Truscott, interview with GW, July 29, 2002.*

*

Dawson Bell

When JT called me, his voice had that "campaign mode" sound to it. I knew right away that something was up. He said he had a big story. Could I meet the first lady out at the governor's residence? He added, "You'll definitely want to bring a photographer along."

I said, "Not if I don't have more information. The photographers are busy."

JT gave me just enough information that I was 99 percent sure the interview would be about the governor's re-election decision. Based on that premise, I started writing the story before I went to the residence. I knew that I was being used. But in this instance I didn't mind. It was an important story.[425]

*

John Truscott

Michelle came in, hot from the ride back from the Island. She was so nervous her hands were shaking. She asked if she had time for a shower. I told her, "Whatever you need to do to feel ready for the interview." She took a shower, composed herself, and gave the interview of her life.[426]

*

Dawson Bell

Michelle is always a great interview. But this time she seemed nervous at the start. I could tell that there were strong emotions. She was really angry at the Democrats who were spreading the rumors.[427]

*

Following is Dawson Bell's article that appeared in the Detroit Free Press.

ENGLER WILL RUN AGAIN
FIRST LADY PUTS RUMORS TO REST,
SAYS THE GOVERNOR WILL SEEK 3RD TERM

Gov. John Engler intends to run for a third term, his wife, Michelle, said Thursday.

She said she was making the announcement to quell rumors that Michigan's first marriage is on the rocks and to end speculation about her husband's polit-

[425]*Dawson Bell, interview with GW, July 31, 2002.*
[426]*John Truscott, interview with GW, July 29, 2002.*
[427]*Dawson Bell, interview with GW, July 31, 2002.*

ical future. She said questions about both were disrupting the family.

"I think it is very important for him to run," Engler said in an exclusive interview with the *Free Press* at the governor's residence.

John Engler was in Lansing and planned to attend the interview but did not. His spokesman, John Truscott, who was there, said Michelle Engler "speaks for the family."

It was an extraordinary setting to announce that John Engler—who has risen to national prominence as a conservative leader slashing taxes and welfare—would seek re-election. The first lady said she and her husband had "discussions, soul-searching and a lot of prayer" over his decision to run again.

"I believe strongly the people of Michigan don't want this campaign to start now," she said.

But she said the timetable was moved up because of speculation about his plans and what she characterized as wild rumor-mongering about their marriage.

"Neither of us can go anywhere without him being asked five to 10 times a day whether he's going to run again," she said. "It is impeding his work; it's impeding our lives."

But she said the rumors convinced her that "it's all that much more important that good people run for office."

No formal campaign announcement is planned for some time, she said.

Engler said she had spoken to her husband by telephone Thursday about making an announcement and said he told her, "If you feel comfortable doing that, go ahead. I'm proud of you."

He enters the race as a presumptive favorite based on high ratings over the last three years.

Lansing pollster Ed Sarpolus of EPIC/MRA said John Engler enjoys a strong core of support among Republicans, and that he has shown an ability to energize those voters.

But even with the advantages of incumbency, an Engler victory in 1998 is far from assured. The Englers have been torn about another run almost since the beginning of the second term. And he pledged in 1990 to run only twice.

The governor's aspirations for national office remain in question. Thursday, when asked whether a third term would be a prelude to a run for the presidency in 2000, Michelle Engler said, "We have not discussed" that issue, and it was "not a factor in this decision."

A decision not to run would have cooled speculation that the governor was interested in national office. It is almost certain to become a super-heated topic during the campaign as he is asked whether he plans to serve a full term.

Michelle Engler had long been regarded as more opposed to a third term than her husband. She said repeatedly during the 1994 campaign that she hoped it would be her husband's last. Rumors circulated that friction over the decision was putting a severe strain on the marriage.

But Thursday she gave no indication that she was equivocal about the decision to seek a third term.

She said their 3-year-old triplets made the decision more complicated. But, she added, "I've come to the conclusion that it is important to have someone in that office who has a firm, steady hand on the wheels of government."

The first lady also responded vigorously to questions about increasingly frequent rumors in Lansing and elsewhere about her husband's marital fidelity.

"This is silly. We are defending ourselves against something we've never done," she said. "It is so out of left field.

"I feel very confident about our relationship. It bothers me that I have to dignify any of this with a response."

She and Truscott said the speculation about the marriage had reached a point at which the first couple had to consider how her absence in the governor's public appearances would affect the rumors. Truscott said he has been asked recently about reports that Michelle Engler was seen packing her bags and leaving the governor's Lansing residence with the three children.

Others close to the Englers suggested that the timetable for the announcement on running again had been hastened by the rumors, which some administration officials have said they suspect were fanned by Democrats who don't want the governor to run.

One Democrat, who asked not to be identified, agreed that the Engler marriage rumor mill is "definitely out of control."

"But I think the Engler spin machine is out of control, too," if Republicans are trying to attribute the phenomena to a coordinated plan by Democrats, the source said. "We couldn't pull that off if we tried."

John Engler's decision to run perhaps makes it clearer that he has his eye on a national office—many observers say the presidency.[428]

*

John Truscott

During the afternoon we assumed that the *Detroit News* story was going to

[428] *Dawson Bell, "Engler Will Run Again: First Lady Puts Rumors to Rest,"* Detroit Free Press, *June 27, 1997, p. 1A.*

run. So timing was of the essence, and here we had good luck. Dawson must have called in much of the article by phone before he ever got back to the office. It was filed early that evening and went into print around 10:00 or 10:30. All the TV stations picked up the story and reported it.

About 7:30 or 8:00 p.m., the *News* had said they wouldn't run their "Anatomy" piece in the print edition. But when they found out the *Free Press* had something, they ran it on their Web site. Still, it was a victory for us. Not only did we get the counterbalancing story in the *Free Press*, but we also beat their "Anatomy of a Rumor." It was a stroke of luck.[429]

*

The Detroit News *ran this article.*

ENGLER TO RUN FOR THIRD TERM AS GOVERNOR

Gov. John Engler will run for a third term, an aide said in a Thursday announcement aimed at deflecting rumors that the governor's marriage is on the rocks.

A whisper campaign, suggesting the governor has marital problems, has stretched from Lansing to Washington in recent weeks.

John Truscott, Engler's spokesman, said the Englers decided to make the announcement in part to quell rumors about their marriage.

Both Englers told the *Detroit News* on Thursday that there's absolutely no truth to rumors that their marriage is in trouble.

In fact, the governor, who rarely swears in public, called the rumors "bullshit."

The content of the rumors ranges wildly—kind of like the children's game of "telephone," in which each player elaborates a little before whispering it on to the next.

Reporters in Washington as well as Lansing have been besieged in recent weeks by phone calls—some anonymous—asking if they had heard the rumor and when are they going to write about it. Public officials, bureaucrats, lobbyists and even citizens not associated with government have heard the pervasive whispers.

Truscott accused Democrat Faylene Owen of starting the rumor. Her husband, Democrat Larry Owen, is also running for governor next year.

Said Faylene Owen: "Of course I have had nothing to do with this. I am deeply offended that the governor's press secretary would attempt to politicize such a personal matter."

[429]*John Truscott, interview with GW, July 29, 2002.*

Kathy Wilbur, director of the Michigan Department of Consumer and Industry Services, disputes that. Wilbur, a longtime Engler friend, said Faylene Owen told her late last month that the Engler marriage was in trouble.

Both women were attending the Greater Detroit Chamber of Commerce annual legislative conference at the Grand Hotel on Mackinac Island.

"I was standing near the registration desk with someone and Faylene came up and said, 'Well, have you heard why Michelle didn't go [on the governor's late May trip to the Mideast and Italy]?' I said no. And Faylene said, 'Well, he's having an affair.' I just laughed and said, 'C'mon, Faylene.'"

"I didn't assume I was the only receiver."

Wilbur said Larry Owen was with his wife at the time; the woman who was with Wilbur when the comment was made, Gail Torreano of Mt. Pleasant, confirmed the story....

In an interview with *Detroit News* editors Thursday, Engler said the rumors were baseless.

"Both Michelle and I want to make it very clear for the record there are no problems in our marriage," he said.

"We think these are damn lies. Understand that they (Democrats) do this all the time," Engler said. "The question is why are you doing this now?"

The first lady participated by speaker phone in the meeting, which occurred before the surprise announcement of a bid for a third term.

"I would suggest that it's sort of a desperation move on the part of Democrats, clearly," she said. "If John were to run for re-election, he would be far and away the strongest candidate. And I just think it's, you know, desperate times call for desperate moves. And that's what they're trying to do. They're just trying to discredit John and me and our marriage and our families.

"And it's not going to work. In fact it's going to backfire because John and I are both fighters and I'm not going to back down. And I'm not going to teach my children to back down from a fight.

"But we don't engage in the same kinds of tactics," she said. "We'll just continue to tell the truth and have a great deal of confidence in each other and our marriage and our family. And we're very strong together."

The governor said he has no doubt Democrats are behind the whisper campaign: "Yes, I believe it can only come from there because there is no truth to the story. And none of our friends are responsible for spreading gossip which is designed to be hurtful to both Michelle and to me and to our families."[430]

[430] *Charlie Cain, "Engler to Run for Third Term as Governor,"* Detroit News, *June 27, 1997, p. A1.*

*

Lieutenant governor?

Connie Binsfeld

I remember when I told John that I was not going to run again. "I want to quit while I'm ahead."

He kidded me: "Yeah, that's what I should've done!"

I wanted to leave him the opportunity to select someone else to fill the position, someone that he could groom to be the next governor. Plus I didn't want people to make a big fuss over my age. So I decided that I would not be his lieutenant governor for the next term.

Every time I'd bring it up, John would put it off. I remember bringing it up three or four times, and each time he'd say, "Let's wait until after this happens"—"Let's wait until after that happens."

Even the announcement itself took a while. We kept putting it off and putting it off until John finally decided now was a good time, if we were going to do it. I remember it because it happened to be the weekend that Lenore Romney died. It was a tearful weekend, very emotional. John was misty eyed. I was crying. But it was something that I knew I had to do. I had run a good race. I had fought a good fight.[431]

*

In July 1998, after Connie Binsfeld decided to retire, Engler selected Dick Posthumus to be his running mate. Following in Engler's footsteps, Posthumus was senate majority leader. He discusses the long relationship and complementary leadership qualities that he and Engler possess.

One of the reasons I believe we are such a good team is that he is the ideas guy, and I am the organization guy. His strength is in coming up with all of the great ideas. My strength is in organizing them and managing them. This is the main reason why I think we have made such a great team through the years.

We've always been a good team, starting with the 1970 campaign, when John was running for the House of Representatives in Mount Pleasant. He wanted to change the direction of both the Republican leadership and the legislature, and therefore change the direction of the state. He had a vision of where he wanted to go, and where the state needed to go.

[431] *Connie Binsfeld, interview with GW, January 23, 2001.*

It is John Engler's style to get out in front, set a goal, and push people there. We are different in this respect. My style is more to convince people that this is where we have to go, and then move forward. Our political philosophies have always been similar, but our approaches to leading have been very different.

The difference comes, in part, from our different farming background. John grew up on a cattle-feeding farm. Cattle feeders are considered the gamblers of agriculture. It is make-it-or-break-it. I grew up on a dairy farm, where you work hard, you make progress, and you keep moving forward to have a steady income. It's the difference between the team that wins games by throwing long passes and the team that wins games by grinding the ball out.

This background in cattle shaped John Engler as a leader, to a significant extent I believe. He is a remarkable strategist. He always looked at what had to be done and then asked, how do we get there? Years of being a minority member in the House of Representatives taught him that to be successful in achieving your goal, one needed to be a good negotiator. He learned by hard knocks, by observing weaknesses in Republicans when conducting negotiations. John Engler learned from their mistakes and this made him a skilled negotiator.

There are two distinct characteristics of his career. First, he studied the issues and knew them. He was one of the few people I ever knew who read almost every bill word for word. He knew more than the other guy, no matter who that guy was. Second, he had the courage to stick it out even when they kept pushing him and pushing him. But at the same time, he understood when it was time to compromise. He knew how to close the deal.

When Engler was Senate minority leader, he realized that Republicans ought to take a proactive role in directing Michigan rather than just let the Democrats, as a majority, lead and relegate us [the GOP] to merely being the naysayer. This is a guy who, during his first term in the Senate, was trying to push his fellow Republicans to share his proactive position so that they could make a difference. To bring in the changes, he encouraged a whole lot of new folks to run for the Senate in 1982.

During his first term, Engler was not always supported in his proactive position; in fact, he met with a fair amount of resistance, not only from the Democrats but also from the Republican leadership. However, he could see beyond a short-term loss.

John Engler was called the "Phoenix" by some. After his own party attacked and demoted him, he rose from the ashes to become the minority leader after the 1982 election, and in a short time became the majority leader. I believe he had a vision of where he wanted the state to go and had the courage to just head there, even when it meant running into stone walls from time to time.[432]

*

Setback at the convention

In 1998, Attorney General Frank Kelley, a Democrat, announced that he would not seek re-election; his 37 years as Michigan's "Eternal General" were coming to an end. Engler saw immediately that the Republican Party had an unparalleled opportunity to take back the AG's office—if the GOP fielded the right candidate.

Engler wanted Scott Romney to run on the Republican ticket. Romney, the son of the former Michigan governor, was a strong candidate: he had name ID, had raised money, and could run a smart campaign. The only problem was that John Smietanka also wanted to run for AG. Smietanka had campaigned for the office four years earlier—at Engler's invitation—but in that election had been crushed by Kelley in an otherwise great year for Republicans.

Smietanka had a powerful ally in Chuck Yob, the Republican national committeeman from Michigan. Yob had supported Smietanka in 1994 and would do so in 1998. With that endorsement, and Tom Monaghan's promise to raise at least $1.0 million for the campaign, Smietanka declared his intention to run again. On Saturday, August 29, 1998, at the Republican State Convention, there would be a showdown between Romney and Smietanka—and by extention between Engler and Yob. On the eve of the showdown the Detroit Free Press *reported:*

The race between Scott Romney and John Smietanka came down Friday night to breathless, mad dashes from delegation to delegation at the Republican State Convention....

Party insiders, while giving Smietanka a slight edge going into the convention, said the race was too close to call.[433]

*

[432]*Dick Posthumus, interview with GW, February 7, 2001.*
[433]*Joe Swickard and Dawson Bell, "On Eve of Decision, Two Candidates Hustle,"* Detroit Free Press, *August 29, 1998, p. 3A.*

George Weeks observed:

Smietanka ... had a rose placed on each delegate's bed at the Amway Grand Plaza.[434]

*

The next day, after Smietanka won the nomination, the Detroit News *ran the headline:*

ENGER SUFFERS STUNNING SETBACK
AS GOP REJECTS SCOTT ROMNEY[435]

*

Andrea Fischer Newman

For John Engler, the 1998 convention in Grand Rapids should have been a moment of triumph. It was probably one of the low points in his career.

Engler just didn't want Smietanka to run in the convention against Scott Romney. Engler didn't think Smietanka would be as strong a candidate as Romney when he faced a Democrat in the general election. So Engler offered Smietanka the sun and the moon and the stars—a judgeship, the court of appeals, anything to keep him from running. Smietanka wouldn't budge. And Yob said he would remain loyal to Smietanka, despite the governor's view that Romney would be a superior candidate in the general election.

Yob also made it an issue of who controlled the GOP: John Engler or the grassroots? Yob kept saying that the governor should not be in control of the party. The grassroots should be. Furthermore, Yob said, there were grassroots Republicans who couldn't stand Engler. Clearly Yob was using Smietanka as a rallying point for his own vision of the party.

Yob's actions made Engler angry. At the convention the governor probably would have exploded if he had confronted Yob face to face.

The vote was very close. Smietanka won; Romney lost. The vote was a referendum not just on Romney, but on John Engler. And John Engler lost. He was bitterly disappointed. Michelle was so upset after the vote she was in the bathroom crying.

One of the reasons the governor lost was that the state party was different

[434] *George Weeks, "Engler Suffers Stunning Setback as GOP Rejects Scott Romney,"* Detroit News, *August 30, 1998, p. B1.*
[435] *Ibid.*

now under Betsy DeVos. Before 1998, when Spence Abraham and then Dave Doyle chaired the party, the governor could have counted on their direct help. But Betsy didn't think it was appropriate for the state party chair to intervene in a fight on the convention floor. Because Engler couldn't count on Betsy's help, he didn't have the organization in place to deal with Smietanka's candidacy. So Engler was down on the floor, doing everything on his own.

That had to be one of John's lowest points. He understood the stakes. He saw the future. He knew the consequences of this defeat. Jennifer Granholm would win and present a major problem for the GOP.[436]

*

Peter Secchia

John Engler is a strategic genius—absolutely brilliant. He knew Scott Romney should run for attorney general. Some people from the west side of the state didn't listen to him. At the convention they insisted on nominating John Smietanka instead.

Two years later, Romney went on to win a statewide race for MSU trustee. He did better in Wayne County than in any other. It was then obvious that the convention had made a mistake. This may have been the biggest political blunder I've seen in my 30 years of political activism. Because now we have Jennifer Granholm.[437]

*

Cliff Taylor

I have not known John Engler to hold grudges. But I've seen him feel righteous indignation. Some issues are big, like the support of John Smietanka for attorney general by a certain faction of the Republican Party. That offended John, and with good reason: the attorney general is the governor's lawyer, and governors have always chosen their own attorney. So it's logical that the governor should be able to pick his own lawyer, rather than go with a person the party wants. John had plenty of reason to be incensed about that, regardless of the worth or lack thereof of the candidate.[438]

*

[436] *Andrea Fischer Newman, interview with GW, August 3, 2002.*
[437] *Peter Secchia, interview with GW, July 12, 2002.*
[438] *Cliff Taylor, interview with GW, June 16, 2000.*

Fieger

Geoffrey Fieger would win the Democratic primary and run for governor. Since he is so quotable, in this section we shall let him speak for himself. From various newspapers:

Jack Kevorkian's lawyer Geoffry Fieger put his theatrical training to good use Thursday as he announced his candidacy for governor on the steps of the state Capitol....

Characterizing himself as an "anti-politician," Fieger hurled a string of insults at Gov. John Engler [and] elected officials of every stripe....

"I have utter contempt for career politicians and their mealy mouthed equivocations. I have contempt for the men who occupy this building."...

Fieger, 47, of West Bloomfield Township, has never run for public office. But he has been a longtime nemesis of Engler, whom he referred to again in a Thursday morning radio appearance as the product of "miscegenation between barnyard animals and humans."[439]

*

"I am the Democratic Party."[440]

"I don't believe [the triplets are] his.... Unless they have cork-screw tails, those are not his kids."[441]

"...[Engler] literally sounds to me like he is semi-retarded."[442]

"I'm going to kick the man's a-- .... I'm going to make it so much fun."[443]

"He [Engler] is about as conservative as Adolph Hitler and Joseph Stalin, and we let him get away with it."[444]

"Isn't qualified to bring coffee."[445] *Fieger referring to Lieutenant Governor Connie Binsfield.*

"How can somebody say I don't have a grasp of the issues? That's nonsense, especially when I see who's in politics. I haven't met my match yet."[446]

"And since I'm among friends, I'm going to kick his [Engler's] a-- all over this election. Enough of this God-d--- political correctness!"[447]

[439] *Dawson Bell, "It's Official: Feiger Running for Governor,"* Detroit Free Press, *April 17, 1998, p. 3B.*
[440] *Geoffrey Fieger, quoted in the* Kalamazoo Gazette, *August 22, 1998.*
[441] *Geoffrey Fieger, quoted on "Mike and the Beagle Morning Show," radio station 92.1, Detroit.*
[442] *Geoffrey Fieger, quoted in the* Oakland Press, *May 19, 1998.*
[443] *Geoffrey Fieger, quoted in the* Chicago Tribune, *June 14, 1998.*
[444] *Geoffrey Fieger, quoted in the* Jackson Citizen Patriot, *May 12, 1998.*
[445] *Geoffrey Fieger, quoted in the* Detroit Free Press, *July 4, 1998.*
[446] *Geoffrey Fieger, quoted in the* Detroit Free Press, *July 9, 1998.*
[447] *Geoffrey Fieger, quoted in the* Petoskey News Review, *September 21, 1998.*

Engler on the campaign trail in 1998. SOURCE: *Engler administration*

"I should get an Emmy for the best sound bites."[448]
"A lot of it is coming back to roost for me."[449] *Fieger on his past quotations.*

*

In October of 1997, Tim Ward became manager of Engler's third campaign for governor. Previously Tim was the Engler administration's deputy director of public affairs, then director of internal affairs.

Our campaign strategy? Once we knew who would be running in the general, our strategy was to ignore Fieger. It was a strategy of disengagement.[450]

In the 13 months leading up to the '98 election, I never once saw John Engler sweat or fret about the campaign. Not once. It's not that he was cocky. Every day there were issues that needed to be addressed. It's just that he was so able, experienced, and purposeful. He had a glacial steadiness.

*

[448] *Geoffrey Fieger, quoted in the* Detroit Legal News, *September 18, 1998.*
[449] *Ibid.*
[450] *Tim Ward, interview with GW, July 12, 2002*

1998 gubernatorial general election

Continuing his victory streak, John Engler won a third term as governor in a landslide over Democratic candidate Geoffrey Fieger. From the Lansing State Journal:

GOVERNOR'S RACE ENDS AS EXPECTED

Republican Gov. John Engler won a landslide victory over Geoffrey Fieger Tuesday, burying the Democrat under the weight of his own words.

For Engler, his second landslide re-election win ensures his place as one of the state's most successful politicians. Since first winning a state House seat as a Michigan State University student in 1970, he has never lost a race.[451]

CREDIT: *Booth Newspapers*

*

From the Detroit Free Press

ENGLER CRUSHES FIREBRAND FIEGER

Gov. John Engler cruised toward a third term unto the 21st century on Tuesday, apparently crushing a caustic Democratic opponent he avoided and virtually ignored.

[451] *Chris Andrews, "Governor's race ends as expected,"* Lansing State Journal, *November 4, 1998.*

Tuesday's vote concluded a gubernatorial campaign that was one of Michigan's oddest. Engler is poised to become only the second governor in state history elected to a third four-year-term.[452]

*

1998 general election results

John Engler	1,883,005 votes (62.2%)
Geoffrey Fieger	1,143,574 votes (37.8%)
Jennifer Granholm	1,557,310 votes (52.1%)
John Smietanka	1,432,604 votes (47.9%)[453]

*

Craig Ruff's assessment:

A POSTMORTEM ON THE 1998 ELECTION
MICHIGAN'S GOP IS LESS IN SHAMBLES
THAN THE DEMOCRATIC PARTY

In 1948, Kim Singler was governor, Eugene Keyes was lieutenant governor, Fred Alger Jr. was secretary of state, and Republicans controlled the state senate 28-4 and the state house of representatives 95-5. That is the last time, prior to the 1998 elections, that Republicans held all those posts and control of both legislative houses.

Republicans can grouse about not winning the attorney general post, not sweeping all the statewide educational posts, and failing to knock off any Democratic congresspersons. But their primary aims are met. They pick up control of the state House of Representatives (the single biggest consequence of Tuesday), pad their margin in the senate, and put Maura Corrigan and retain Cliff Taylor on the Supreme Court (producing an edge of four Republican-nominated justices to three Democratic-nominated ones).[454]

[452] *Chris Christoff and Dawson Bell, "Engler Crushes Firebrand Fieger,"* Detroit Free Press, *November 4, 1998.*
[453] Michigan Manual, *1999-2000 ed. (Lansing: Legislative Service Bureau), pp. 873, 879.*
[454] *Craig Ruff, "A Postmortem on the 1998 Election" (Lansing: Public Sector Consultants, November 6, 1998).*

This is not the end.
It is not even the beginning of the end.
But it is, perhaps, the end of the beginning.
WINSTON CHURCHILL

★

Chapter Fifteen
Third Term: 1999 - 2002

Michigan at the end of the millennium

As John Engler entered his ninth year as governor, Michigan was in great shape. Unemployment remained consistently below the national average. Record numbers of jobs were being created. Welfare caseloads were down dramatically. Crime was substantially lower. Abortions were rarer; adoptions higher. Spending on K-12 and higher education reached record levels. New tax cuts were being rolled out. State spending was kept in check. The state had enormous reserves in its rainy day fund. Michigan's credit rating on Wall Street was once again excellent. No scandals plagued the administration.

John Engler, having easily won re-election, was regarded as a hero in the Republican establishment, one of the brightest political stars of the '90s. Not only had he vanquished the perception of Michigan being a rustbelt state; he had also led Republicans to impressive gains in every branch of government. In addition to retaining the governor's office, the GOP enjoyed majorities in the Michigan House and Senate, and conservatives were beginning to dominate the judiciary. This bode well for reapportionment after the 2000 census. Moreover, Engler was frequently in Washington meeting with Republican leaders on Capitol Hill. There was little doubt that he would be a kingmaker in the 2000 presidential contest, and on the nominee's VP shortlist.

As the 21st century approached, as the U.S. was able to enforce a Pax Americana *abroad, as the dot-com economy swelled the portfolios of the middle class at home, it must have seemed as if happy days were here to stay.*

Third Inaugural Address

John Engler, infectiously optimistic by nature, nevertheless remained clear headed about the challenges facing Michigan. There were clouds casting shadows on the sunny tableau of the dot-com economy. Among the worrisome issues in the governor's office were burgeoning Medicaid costs, low student test scores in the cities, needed telecommunications reform, a hodgepodge of issues in Detroit, the effect of term limits on state government, the election of Jennifer Granholm, and public cynicism generated by President Clinton's scandal-ridden administration. While there was more optimism than pessimism in the executive office, Engler did not succumb to "irrational exuberance" in his third and final Inaugural Address. The times called for cautious optimism. Excerpts from the address, delivered January 1, 1999, follow:

To meet the challenges of our future, we are well served to learn from our past. To my left is the granite cornerstone of this magnificent Capitol. Back in 1873, when the Capitol was under construction, 48 items were placed into the cornerstone, representing the "Permanent Things" in our heritage. Each item symbolizes a value that has made Michigan great: a Bible, the U.S. Constitution and Declaration of Independence, the 1837 Ordinance of Congress admitting Michigan into the Union, even coins dating from the 1700s.

Ladies and gentlemen, the Permanent Things in that cornerstone remind us of who we are as a people, and of the Michigan we want for our children. The Declaration and Constitution remind us to guard our liberties jealously. The Bible reminds us to nurture our faiths. And the coins? They remind us to do our utmost to provide opportunity for all our citizens.

The history in that cornerstone shows how much Michigan has contributed to the miracle that is America. From the beginning, Michigan, like America, has defended and promoted a legacy of liberty. You see it in the 18th century, in our Founders' commitment to keeping the Northwest Territory a land of "free soil" and free schools. You see it in the 19th century, when Michigan was a destination of the Underground Railroad as well as a beacon for immigrants. You see it in the 20th century, as Michigan put America on wheels and became the free world's Arsenal of Democracy.

We are rightfully proud of our state's legacy of liberty, and we have a solemn duty to hand our freedoms on to future generations. We hand those freedoms on by reaffirming our historic commitment to education—education of the mind and character. The Founders, with their hopes and dreams for Michigan, knew that we would be great only if our citizens possessed the knowledge to be self-reliant, and the character to be free. As Thomas Jefferson put it: "If a nation expects to be ignorant and free ... it expects what never was and never will be."

Mr. Jefferson's insight was true then; it is even truer now. That is why education has been, is now, and will remain, a cornerstone of my administration.

A second cornerstone of my administration—another way to preserve and protect our legacy of liberty—is to keep expanding opportunity. We reaffirm our commitment today to help even more Michigan citizens achieve their dreams. Michigan is home to many of the hardest-working, most creative people in the world. I am confident that Michigan workers will be setting the pace in the global marketplace of the 21st century. To unleash the energies and genius of our citizens, we will continue to observe my first principle of governance: to uphold the rule of law, while limiting government, reducing regulations, and cutting taxes. And this you can count on: We will cut taxes—again.

A third cornerstone is family. Families, after all, give our individual lives meaning and frame our pursuit of happiness. We reaffirm our commitment today to help even more families take charge of their lives and achieve independence. We will continue to help, consistent with a principle that Lincoln famously expressed in these words: "The legitimate object of government is to do for a community of people whatever they need to have done, but cannot do at all, or cannot so well do for themselves in their separate and individual capacities. In all that the people can individually do as well for themselves, government ought not to interfere."

In the coming years, our families will be confronted by change, the scale and pace of which no previous generation has encountered. In the face of this change, my goal as governor is that no child, no family, be left behind as we cross the threshold of the 21st century.

The fourth cornerstone of my administration is community—community built on the principle of service to others. We reaffirm our commitment today to build a better community of Michigan. Our communities are a wonderful reminder of the diversity that has strengthened us, and the unity that has sustained us.

Civil society is premised on an ethos of service. It's the spirit of the Good Samaritan helping one less fortunate. It's the love of people giving generously of themselves—our teachers, clergy, volunteers—who are the true builders of community. Without that spirit and love, Michigan can be neither good nor great. So I urge each citizen to put the principle of service into action: give back to your community. Rediscover the truth St. Francis taught: "it is in giving that we receive."

Education, opportunity, family, community—these are the cornerstones that have made Michigan great. These are the cornerstones that have built our legacy of liberty. And these are the cornerstones on which we will continue to build to make Michigan an even greater state for us and for our children.

My friends, we have learned much and accomplished more than was ever thought possible over the past eight years. For all our successes, you, the citizens of our great state, deserve the credit. After all, what is Michigan but you? Your hopes are Michigan's hopes. Your achievements are Michigan's achievements.

So today, by all means, let us celebrate the great state we are. At this time of new beginnings, let us rededicate ourselves to becoming an even greater state. I ask that we work together to arm the rising generation with knowledge; to help more of our citizens achieve their dreams in freedom and opportunity; to make more of our families self-reliant; and to strengthen the community of Michigan. When we do these things, we are true to our legacy of liberty, and will bequeath to our children an even greater state than the one we have known.[455]

*

Term limits

By 1999 it was dawning on people that Engler's last four years would mark not just the end of an administration, but the end of an era. Term limits would change the relations between elected officials, the bureaucracy, and lobbyists. Engler, encountering the inexperience in the 90th Legislature (1999-2000), realized that he had been mistaken to support the highly restrictive term limits law passed by Michigan voters in 1992. For many people who knew the inner workings of state government, Engler's very career was the best argument against highly restrictive term limits.

Lucille Taylor

John Engler spent 20 years in the legislature, and that developed him into the skilled leader he is today. Had the present term limits been in effect then, he could have only spent 14 years in the legislature. Spending two decades in the legislature helped groom him for higher office. The biggest example of this, year in and year out, is how he could handle the budget.

The budget of the State of Michigan is a complex document, and John Engler knows every program that goes into that budget. He doesn't know that because he walked off the street last year. He knows because he has been working with it for many years. He knows the programs; he has seen them come and

[455] *JE, Third Inaugural Address, January 1, 1999.*

go; he knows how they perform; he knew all the tricks that departments engage in—he knows all this before he even hits the budget office. With term limits, he wouldn't have had that invaluable experience.[456]

*

Carol Weissert, a political science professor at Michigan State University, observes:

Engler, in his third and final term in office, is an extremely important political and policy presence in the state. In his tenth year in office, he continues to reshape the face of Michigan's bureaucracy and the way that services are carried out. He has not only led the state on policies such as welfare reform and education funding, but has initiated major changes in civil service, legislative review of administrative rules, state control over local governments, and bureaucratic responsibility over issues ranging from environmental policy to job training.

One knowledgeable observer told me that in the past 10 years, Michigan has become "less like Minnesota and more like Indiana," meaning that the state has moved away from a strong governmental presence to one where privatization and an emphasis on the market are paramount.[457]

*

1999 State of the State address

Many people who listened to Engler's 1999 State of the State address commented that he seemed to escape the third-term doldrums that overtake many long-serving politicians. Michigan's last three-term governor showed no signs of running out of ideas. Among other things, the January 28 speech proposed the popular Michigan Merit Award for high school seniors headed for college; the awards were to be funded from the recently concluded tobacco settlement.[458] *He also proposed across-the-board cuts in Michigan's income tax, from 4.4 to 3.9 percent.*

*

Praising President Ford (blaming President Clinton)

Engler was invited to speak at a Capitol Hill ceremony in which President Gerald R. Ford would receive the Congressional Gold Medal. The event was scheduled to take

[456] *Lucille Taylor, interview with GW, October 20, 1999.*

[457] *Carol Weissert, "The Engler Factor," PBS Online Newshour, November 1999.*

[458] *In 1998, the attorneys general of 46 states signed an agreement with the four largest tobacco companies in the U.S. to settle state suits to recover costs associated with treating smoking-related illnesses. According to the agreement, the tobacco industry is projected to pay the settling states in excess of $200 billion over the next 25 years. Four states—Florida, Minnesota, Texas, and Mississippi—settled their tobacco cases separately from the other 46.*

Governor Engler enjoying a light-hearted moment with President Ford in Grand Rapids, 1997. The governor called the president "a chief executive who selflessly served the American people." SOURCE: *John Engler*

place in the Capitol rotunda on October 27, 1999. Our office knew in advance that President Clinton would attend. Following are (1) Engler's initial response to the speech prospectus, (2) an excerpt from the speech, (3) what happened when he delivered the remarks in the presence of Bill Clinton, and (4) Engler's comment about the event two weeks later. Gleaves Whitney recalls:

The governor would only have five minutes. His remarks would have to be tightly scripted. What to do with President Clinton? He probably didn't feel at home on Capitol Hill where he had so recently been chastised. The previous December, the House had voted to impeach the president on two articles—lying under oath to a federal grand jury and obstructing justice. On February 12, 1999—Lincoln's birthday—with Chief Justice William Rehnquist presiding over the Senate trial, Clinton was acquitted of both impeachment charges. That was the charged backdrop to the ceremony honoring President Ford.

I worked up a prospectus for Engler's speech. His remarks would subtly contrast Ford's honorable conduct while in the Oval Office with Clinton's dishonorable conduct while in the Oval Office. On this occasion I thought it would be rhetorically and historically interesting for Engler to offer "a simple test for assessing an American president."

At speech practice on October 12—Engler's 51st birthday, it so happened—the governor was in high spirits and approved the speech prospectus.[459]

At the ceremony in the rotunda, Governor Engler said the following in honor of President Ford:

I have a simple test for assessing an American president. Would our founders have smiled on his leadership? Would they be proud to admit him into the circle of their own? Would they say: Now there is a chief executive who selflessly served the American people—who was a steward of our great experiment in ordered freedom—who discharged his duties with courage, integrity, and respect for the Constitution.

To my mind, President Ford passes the test of the founders. He left a special mark on the American presidency—a mark we recognized at the time, back in the '70s, but that becomes even more valuable with the passing of the years. That mark is integrity.

Men and women on both sides of the aisle always felt they could trust him. He has that Midwestern decency and common sense that are the trademarks of American political culture. Consider the observation of a prominent Democrat, former Michigan Congresswoman Martha Griffiths, who said this about her colleague: "In all the years I sat in the House, I never knew Mr. Ford to make a dishonest statement nor a statement part-true.... He never attempted to shade a statement, and I never heard him utter an unkind word."[460]

I recently had the opportunity to re-read the words President Ford spoke to reassure our nation back in 1974, shortly after assuming the presidency. He said: "I believe that truth is the glue that holds government together, not only our government but civilization itself.... In all my public and private acts as your president, I expect to follow my instincts of openness and candor with full confidence that honesty is always the best policy in the end."

Thank you, Mr. President, for that great and timely sentiment that lives on in our hearts.[461]

What else happened at the ceremony?

A couple of weeks later, when I saw Bryan Roosa in our Washington office, he was grinning ear-to-ear. I asked why he looked so satisfied. He told me about

[459] *GW, personal papers, November 1999.*

[460] *Martha Griffiths quoted in William A. Degregorio,* The Complete Book of U.S. Presidents, *3rd ed., (New York: Wings Books, 1991), p. 614.*

[461] *John Engler, speech for President Ford's Congressional Gold Medal Ceremony, Washington, DC, October 27, 1999.*

the event in the rotunda. Ford seemed very pleased by the governor's remarks—and Clinton seemed very displeased.

"When Engler started talking about the integrity of the founders," Bryan said, "Clinton appeared visibly annoyed. He stiffened and clinched his teeth."[462]

A few minutes after this report, Engler and I were standing outside of the Hall of States, waiting for our ride to the evening event.

"How do you think your remarks in the rotunda went?" I asked. "Were you at all uncomfortable damning Clinton by praising Ford?"

"Not at all," the governor answered. "If he was uncomfortable with the message, that was his problem."[463]

*

Environment

During his first years as governor, John Engler was incessantly criticized by the environmental lobby; they were loathed to acknowledge even a single achievement of the governor's. They fostered the perception that the governor did not care about Michigan's environmental beauty and protection. Symptomatic of the problem: the state's premier university press published a history of conservation in Michigan so unbalanced that not one positive comment about the Engler administration can be found in its 266 pages.[464] G. Tracy Mehan, director of the Office of the Great Lakes, reflects on the problem.

Republicans generally have a tin ear when it comes to the environment. The GOP is the commercial party, the free-market party. They get nervous when they have to talk about the importance of protecting the environment and natural resources. And yet Republicans need to reach out to the swing vote, and clearly the environment is very important to swing voters. It's perhaps not always their paramount concern, but people want to know that politicians care about the environment; the voters want the park at the end of the road to be clean, and they care about their drinking water.

Early on John Engler found himself surrounded by some very powerful advisors who have been very persuasive with him—people like Dan Pero and Rusty Hills. We've all heard Rusty say, "The environment is not going to be one of our top four issues." That was Rusty's mantra.

[462] *Bryan Roosa, interview with GW, November 5, 1999.*

[463] *GW, personal papers, November 1999.*

[464] *Dave Dempsey,* Ruin and Recovery: Michigan's Rise as a Conservation Leader *(Ann Arbor: University of Michigan Press, 2001).*

Engler himself seemed to have a tin ear when it came to the environment. Environmental issues just didn't resonate with him the way economic development, education, and welfare reform did. This was especially true in the first years of the administration.

But I think that changed with the Clean Michigan Initiative (1998). That was a stroke of genius. John Engler got it right with CMI and many other environmental issues over the years—from water diversion and exotics to brownfields and sound science. It turns out that John Engler is extremely knowledgeable about the environment. No joking, he's probably forgotten more about Great Lakes issues than most other governors in this region ever knew in the first place.

Just look at brownfields legislation—one of John Engler's biggest triumphs. Think heavy industry, the old rustbelt, areas just crying for cleanup. The governor has showed great leadership here, and Michigan has some of the best laws in the nation.

He has also made some tough decisions—splitting the old DNR into a new DNR and Department of Environmental Quality. There is merit in the argument that the system was broken and needed fixing. The old system had a rabbit warren of boards and commissions. It took too long to get permits. Right off the bat, the governor won the litigation and the power to use executive orders to split the DNR, and this seminal event set the tone of this administration.

Related to that, the governor expanded the Office of the Great Lakes by executive order in 1993. He made it cabinet level and reinforced my position with a number of appointments that have given the office a strong standing in interstate and binational policy debates.

The governor has also been supportive when it comes to fighting exotics (biological threats), diversions of Great Lakes water, and pollution prevention.

In terms of chemical pollution, Michigan is better off now than we were in 1991. The level of contaminants in fish tissue is down. Phosphorus is down. The toxic relief inventory, a list of hundreds of chemicals, is down some 40 percent since the 1980s. We have made tremendous progress in reducing chemical pollution.

The governor has made good progress on the non-point pollution issue (runoff). This is very important in a state that has a multi-billion dollar sport fishing industry.

John Engler is a leader in so many other environmental initiatives. He is the only governor to veto a Great Lakes diversion. His leadership has brought us a sea lamprey control program. As early as 1994, the governor spoke on the exotic species issue at the State of the Great Lakes report. That was the first time I heard an elected official speak on exotics.

And we are fishing in Lake Erie again. It was a dead lake, and now it is the walleye fishing capital of the world, if you believe our Ohio friends.

In short, John Engler has been good for the environment in Michigan.[465]

Note: In 2002 (after the above interview with Tracy Mehan) Governor Engler announced his NextEnergy initiative, targeting clean fuel-cell technology as the foundation for economic growth and stability. Many environmentalists praised NextEnergy since it would "green the economy."[466]

*

Civilization of Life

Michigan's remarkably strong Right to Life organization has been a key to many electoral success stories since the 1980s, John Engler's included. John Miller of National Review *interviewed the governor for this article:*

BABY STEPS

MAKING ABORTION RARE. REALLY.

Pro-life activist Helen Alvare has traveled to all 50 states as a speaker and fundraiser. She finds that she often has to try to energize pro-lifers discouraged at the plight of their cause—except in Michigan. "I remember going there once and seeing 'Respect Life' on the marquee of a major hotel chain. I called home and told my husband, 'I'm on another planet.' Michigan has done it so right for so long—they're famous for being good."

Measuring success isn't hard for pro-lifers: They look at a state's abortion rate. And by this standard, Michigan is a national model. After holding steady throughout most of the 1980s, the abortion rate there has taken a nosedive, falling by more than 40 percent since 1987, compared with a national decline of roughly 12 percent. "Over 100,000 lives have been saved," boasts a report by Right to Life of Michigan.

For all the high-volume arguing among Republicans over abortion politics—how the Republican National Committee should fund candidates, what the GOP platform ought to say, whether a pro-choice vice-presidential nominee is acceptable—the neglected success story in Michigan shows that abortion politics needn't be a matter of haggling over symbols or an inevitably losing proposition. President Clinton has long said he would like abortion to be

[465] *G. Tracy Mehan, interview with GW, May 21, 2001.*

[466] *See, e.g., Michigan Environmental Council,* Michigan's Environmental History, *"Greening the Economy," p 57.*

"rare." In Michigan, what for Clinton is only a rhetorical flourish is a matter of some seriousness.

The pro-life movement enjoys several natural advantages in Michigan, from the large Catholic population around Detroit to strong Protestant churches in the western half of the state. "An overall pro-life ethic pervades Michigan politics," says Republican governor John Engler. Many of the state's voters are Reagan Democrats—union members who blend economic liberalism with cultural conservatism. Of the ten Democrats in Michigan's congressional delegation, three are strongly pro-life (James Barcia, Dale Kildeee, and Bart Stupack). A fourth, David Bonior, was too, until he joined his party's House leadership and moved left. Frank Kelley, another pro-life Democrat, was attorney general for 37 years until his retirement last year. In fact, Michigan is one of just a few states with a statute outlawing abortion (after 24 weeks) still on the books.

For many years, however, pro-lifers struggled in Michigan. Until Engler's election in 1990, a pair of pro-choice governors, Republican William Milliken and Democrat James Blanchard, reigned in the post-Roe period. Pro-lifers had a majority in the statehouse, but their bills were routinely vetoed. Then, in 1988, they performed an end run around Blanchard by winning a ballot question to bar Medicaid funding of abortions. "That vote energized the grassroots for Engler's election two years later," says state GOP executive director Greg Brock.

The Medicaid cutoff had an enormous impact. Michigan's abortion rate dropped by nearly 25 percent within a year. Data from other states show that bans on funding typically lead to a 20-40 percent decline in abortions among Medicaid-eligible women. Not only are there more live births among these women, but also fewer pregnancies—suggesting that the law affects behavior in addition to the decision whether to abort.

Parental-consent laws have a similar effect. The abortion rate among minors has fallen by 42 percent in Michigan since the state enacted a parental-consent law in 1990. Sometime in May, U.S. district judge Nancy G. Edmunds is expected to rule on whether to allow Michigan's informed-consent law, which includes a 24-hour waiting period, to go into effect. If it does, the rate will probably decline further. The state has also started to teach abstinence in the public schools. "We eliminated the mixed message kids were getting," says Engler, who takes credit for a 26 percent drop in teen pregnancies since 1991.

The force behind many of these changes has been Right to Life of Michigan, a Grand Rapids-based organization with an annual budget of about $4 million. In a 1995 survey of legislators and lobbyists in Lansing, the group was rated the state's second-most-influential organization, behind the Chamber of

Commerce. "Some people would argue that they're even more powerful than the Chamber," says Betsy DeVos, the Republican State party chairman. The same survey, in fact, named Right to Life the state's best get-out-the-vote organization. "Right to Life has become what the labor unions used to be. It can deliver votes, and lots of them," said Bill Ballenger, the publisher of Michigan's most important political newsletter, last October.[467]

*

Struggle for control of the GOP

Greg McNeilly, a close associate of Betsy DeVos, summarizes.

In 1998 and 1999 there was a struggle for the control of the Republican Party. Who was going to call the shots, John Engler or Betsy DeVos?

Clearly the governor had been in charge of the party for years. He had masterminded the takeover of State Party following the 1982 defeat of gubernatorial candidate Dick Headlee. The Milliken machine was breaking down. The Engler machine was revving up, and it was impressive. He had a thorough understanding of the hard work and resources it takes to position the Republican Party to be the majority party in the state. The Michigan Republican Party John Engler built is one of the most powerful in the nation—a model for other states.

All the party chairs during this time—Spence Abraham (1983-1990), Dave Doyle (1990-1994), Susy Heinz (1995-1996)—really functioned as executive directors; John Engler was the real chair. He was not just a titular or ceremonial leader; he was intimately involved in candidate recruitment, fundraising, staff hiring decisions, and vendor selection.

When Susy left in May of '96 to run for Congress [against David Bonior], the governor asked Betsy DeVos to serve the remainder of Susy's term. Betsy did so, and in January of '97 she decided to run to keep her chair another term. She had the governor's blessing and was unanimously selected. Betsy was also on a mission to demonstrate her political and tactical acumen. The reason? The party had gotten trounced in the 1996 elections: we lost our majority in the state House, lost key university races, and got massacred in the U.S. Senate race and presidential race: Michigan's electoral votes went to Clinton.

Lansing pundits blamed Betsy for the debacle. Bill Ballenger in his publication *Inside Michigan Politics* savaged her performance, calling her a lightweight,

[467] *John J. Miller, "Baby Steps: Making Abortion Rare. Really."* National Review, *May 17, 1999, pp. 44-45.*

a socialite not up to the challenge of running the state Republican Party.

So the first thing Betsy did after being elected to serve a full term as State Party chairman was clean house—unilaterally. All the top directors were told to find other work, and all vendor contracts were suspended. Betsy had a list of people she wanted in State Party—and Engler had his list. Betsy hired only one person from the governor's list, Greg Brock. That's when the problems started. Betsy regarded the governor's input as good advice, not an order. Clearly she was going to be her own chairman, not just the governor's executive director.

The next friction point arose over policy. I remember it was the spring of '97. I was in Betsy's office working on a speech. She and the governor got into a heated phone exchange over the gasoline tax. Betsy believed the Republican Party should not be saddled with a tax hike—not going into the '98 elections. But he was pressuring her to use State Party resources to promote the gas tax. At one point in the conversation, I remember her getting very frustrated. She had been holding her ground, disagreeing with the governor. Finally she relented and said, "Fine, John, we will do it." She would allow State Party to promote the gas tax in its publications. But from the tone of her voice I could tell that she was frustrated. This was the first time I saw that there was friction between the two of them. She had never said anything disparaging about the governor.

Yet another friction point was over vendor selection. Betsy required that all vendor projects be competitively bid, which was a new practice at State Party. It had been a good old boys' network. But Betsy wanted State Party to establish sound business practices. Every decision over vendors was a cause of increasing tension between the governor and his team on the one side, and Betsy and State Party on the other.

Then, in late April or early May of '98, the governor called a meeting at his campaign headquarters on Capitol Avenue in Lansing. I remember vividly the governor sitting at the head of his conference table. Along one side were Tim Ward, Dave Doyle, Tom Shields. Along the other side were Betsy DeVos, Greg Brock, and myself. The governor had a yellow legal pad and he began to write down various key races around the state, and he also wrote down the vendors involved in each of these races. And then he wrote his own name, with a question mark. We were brought there to discuss who would be the State Party vendor producing TV ads for his race.

As he worked through the list, he asked Betsy what criteria she would use to select a vendor. She mentioned creativity, speed, and price. Then the governor asked Tom Shields about his creativity, speed, and price. Tom answered, and the governor concluded the meeting by saying, "I've heard all I need to hear. Are there any questions?" Betsy had reservations but decided to keep them to herself. Against her own judgment, she hired Tom Shields and Marketing Resource Group [MRG] to do a political ad and a convention video. We were so unhappy with the results that we terminated the contract with MRG within three weeks. This was a major turning point. When she fired MRG, Betsy was drawing her line in the sand as if to say, "I am not just going to be your executive director. I am chairman of the party. We have to work together at least as co-chairmen."

Betsy and the governor seemed able to work through this. They worked well together during the '98 elections. In fact, 1998 was the best election year for Michigan Republicans in 50 years. The governor was brilliant and Betsy appreciated all the ideas he brought to the table—recruiting new donors, experimenting with new voter contact programs, detailing specific strategies for specific races. In retrospect, it appeared that these two strong-willed people had finally worked out their differences and could work as a yin-and-yang team. That is why, the morning after the election, Engler encouraged Betsy to run for RNC chair; he called on the GOP establishment to abandon the existing chairman, Jim Nicholson, and give their support to Betsy.

For a number of reasons, Betsy decided to remain State Party chairman and was re-elected in February of 1999. The next friction point arose over vouchers. Dick and Betsy had asked for the governor's support of vouchers back in '98, but he thought that it was not a good issue when he was trying to run for re-election. There seemed to be an understanding that he would support some kind of voucher proposal on the ballot in 2000. So the Kids First! Yes! coalition was formed in August of '99 to kick off their petition drive. Dick and Betsy DeVos along with Jim Barrett and Sister Monica were the among the top proponents of vouchers at this time.

At the September leadership conference on Mackinac Island, the State Party issues committee approved a resolution in favor of vouchers. It was pretty generic. But when the governor was later asked about the resolution—at Steve Markman's press conference—he thoroughly trashed vouchers. He seemed to do so 100 percent for political reasons, not policy reasons. This was the first communication the coalition had received on the governor's position. Imagine the reporters now. They were all trying to get comments from coalition leaders Dick DeVos, Betsy DeVos, and Jim Barrett. Dick gave a very politic response, and Betsy made no comments on the record. But, given all the media scrutiny, a wedge had been driven between the anti-voucher Engler party and the pro-voucher DeVos party by the end of the weekend.

Now fast forward to November: the Republican state committee meeting in Detroit. Betsy surprised us all when she stood before the committee and asked that the voucher proposal be tabled indefinitely. Two-thirds of the committee—probably about 70 people—supported the proposal. So here was Betsy backing down from a position of strength. She took a lot of heat for that from voucher supporters. But at that point the thinking was, State Party would steer clear of the issue. It would be neutral and go about focusing on the other races in 2000. Within 60 days, though, a number of donors were calling up Betsy and saying that the governor was encouraging them to donate not to State Party but to a separate fund to help with the 2000 races. Betsy immediately began to assess her ability to raise funds in direct competition with the governor. By the start of 2000, Betsy decided that she would step down as State Party Chair. Very few people knew about her decision at that point.

Within a few weeks, the governor and Betsy had further problems, this time over the Calvin College presidential debate between George W. Bush and a half dozen other contenders. Betsy saw the debate as a great way to build up the party prior to the election in November. But Engler wanted to scrap the event because he did not want his candidate, George W., to lose a debate in Michigan. Here was yet another instance where Betsy did something independently of the governor, and he apparently didn't like it. The governor still did not know that Betsy was going to resign.

Betsy picked a date to make her announcement public when she knew Engler would be in Washington, DC. I think the day was February 2, 2000. She informed staff at 8:00 a.m. At 9:00 a.m. she left a message with the governor to call her. The lieutenant governor was the first person she got hold of, and he was shocked to learn that she would be resigning. She held a 1:00 p.m. press conference in the State Capitol. Of course, in the meantime, the governor found out what was happening, changed his itinerary, and called for an impromptu press conference at 6:00 p.m. in the Romney Building. In public everybody involved did a good job saving face.

Vouchers were a controversial issue for the Republican Party, but not because the governor is anti-voucher. He refuses to criticize vouchers in principle. He only questions vouchers as a viable political issue.

An interesting anecdote: Lansing reporter Tim Skubick asked the first lady how she voted on vouchers, Proposal 1, in November of 2000. Smiling, she said something like, "John's vote and mine cancelled each other's out." Apparently even the Englers disagreed over vouchers. So it doesn't have to be personal.

If there is a moral to this long story, it's that building a strong party takes the leadership John Engler has. He has been brilliant in creating a formidable party. But he should have been able to work more cooperatively with someone as strong-willed and powerful as Betsy. His strength proved, in the end, ironically, to be his Achilles heal. If they had worked better together, the outcome in 2000 might have been as satisfying as in 1998, when Republicans did so well.

To this day, I honestly believe that the struggle to control the party was not as personal as some people want to make it out to be. The break was not the result of a grudge. It was more impersonal than that. It was a dispassionate disagreement over who was the functional state chair. I can still say that I've never heard Betsy disparage John Engler, and I assume he doesn't disparage her. They are adults. They get along well to this day.[468]

*

Engler: Michigan is not ready to have a debate over vouchers

Lucille Taylor

John Engler honestly believes that Proposal 1—the school voucher proposal on the 2000 ballot—could be very beneficial for the state. But he doesn't want to waste four, six, or eight years in litigation trying to determine whether the U.S. Constitution will accommodate vouchers. At this point he thinks, "When we have done as much as we can with education reform, charter schools, public school choice, and performance, then ask me about vouchers."[469]

*

George W.

Michelle Engler

We usually go to San Antonio for the holidays, since that's my home. When he was governor of Texas, George W. and Laura would usually invite us to Austin for dinner. In 1998 George W. was talking to John and said, "You definitely have to come for dinner this year, John, and bring Michelle. I want to talk with both of you."

John was pretty sure that he knew what George W. was up to, that he wanted to announce he'd be running for president. But we weren't just going to jump on the bandwagon. We had some serious questions to put to him. At this point, we didn't expect George to answer all our questions or address all our concerns.

[468] *Greg McNeilly, interview with GW, July 10, 2002.*
[469] *Lucille Taylor, interview with GW, September 27, 1999.*

John was especially interested in George W's view of judicial appointments. On the drive to Austin, we resolved that we would not be easily swayed or impressed.

During the course of our dinner, however, George W. laid out his vision for our country. The more John and I listened, the more we were impressed. We also believed that he had the tenacity to go through a tough campaign. He has that wonderful combination—the kindness of his dad and the steel resolve of his mother.

Later that evening, on our way back to San Antonio, all we could talk about was George W. for president. We were on board and truly excited.[470]

*

Governor Engler enjoying an informal moment with President George W. Bush. CREDIT: *White House*

Mike Huckabee, a Republican, is governor of Arkansas.

At an RGA breakfast meeting (governors only, the staff had been dismissed), we discussed the upcoming presidential election and our enthusiasm for one of our own—George W. Bush, a fellow colleague—who was going to be our

[470] *Michelle Engler, interview with GW, January 26, 2001.*

Republican nominee. And I remember remarking that one of the things we could do for our candidate was rally behind him in unity. Since in 2000 governors represented some 70 to 75 percent of the nation's population, we might have the ability to significantly influence the election. So we decided in that meeting that Republican governors would be unified, that we would devote time in our schedules, that we would travel together in the "barnstorm for reform." Every single Republican governor would travel across America campaigning for George W. Bush. And we all decided that as governors we were in a position to put our colleague on our shoulders and carry him to the winning margin. We all believe that it was one of the best decisions we ever made, because not only did he win the election, but he's proven to be a great president.[471]

*

Jim Brandell

It was amazing to watch John Engler work on Bush's behalf. In February 1999, at the NGA meeting Governor Engler and Governor Bush chatted about the upcoming presidential race. Soon after that Karl Rove, the chief strategist, and Joe Allbaugh, the campaign manager, came up to Michigan for a follow-up meeting. They wanted to discuss Engler's role and to get his advice. Over dinner they said, "We've been sent up here to listen. We were told to listen to John Engler and take notes. We want to hear what he has to say. We want to hear his ideas."

On March 7, 1999, Bush announced the exploratory committee. John Engler was the only governor on that committee. He was serving with George Schultz, Condoleezza Rice, Colin Powell, and others.

Not only was Engler the only governor on Bush's exploratory committee. He was one of the lead governors making calls to other governors to engage their support. Engler the political animal was involved in the politics, constantly strategizing and identifing specific constituents to reach out to: "We really need to court the auto industry, or the farmers, or the homebuilders." Engler was one of the only governors involved in policy. He was constantly offering suggestions on issues like welfare and taxes and federalism. Engler was out there fundraising—really he was a lead fundraiser. And Engler was involved in communications. He was willing to appear anywhere and everywhere on the candidate's behalf.

[471]*Mike Huckabee, interview with GW, October 23, 2002.*

You could find lots of Republican governors involved in one or two of these areas—but not in all of them at once. Very few people saw everything Engler was doing. I don't think any governor worked harder to elect Bush president.

Normally when the Bush campaign was planning an event in Michigan, we would do what we called a "countdown conference call" to take care of last minute logistics. This call was to be on February 15, exactly one week before the Michigan primary.

The Bush campaign had already given me the call-in numbers and passwords. I checked in with them earlier in the day to see if there was anything that we should research and be ready for. They told me no; in fact, they didn't even need us on that conference call. They said that they were going to be talking about something different, so there was really no need for the governor or me to be in on the call.

I told this to the governor and he got this little grin on his face. "You still have the number, don't you?" he asked.

"Yes, governor," I answered. I knew what he was thinking, so I warned him, "I'll dial this number only on two conditions. You have to promise me that we will keep the phone on mute at all times. And under no circumstances will you pick up the phone. If you violate either of these two conditions, I will quit." I was 90 percent serious. If Engler jumped into that call, it would destroy the confidence that the Bush campaign had in me.

You have to understand: one of the issues between the two staffs was that the Bush campaign was extremely protective of then-Governor Bush. We wanted Bush to be doing early morning radio calls and plant gates, where he would shake hands with plant workers. They didn't want him doing those things, because you had to get up very early in the morning. We got around Bush's staff by scheduling Engler to do plant gates and radio calls. And of course we would have Engler stay at the same hotel as Bush the night before. Before turning in, Engler would tell Bush that he was going to be doing a plant gate or radio call. Would Bush like to join him? Great, there will be a knock on the door early in the morning.

That made Bush's staff furious—they would just have fits. Bush was fine with it, but not the staff, who were overprotective.

Because of this tension between the two staffs, this time we told them, "Just so you know, Engler is going to be doing a plant gate at American Axle, and Good Morning America is going to be broadcasting live from there. Just so you know." And we just kind of rolled them.

I mean, since Good Morning America was going to be there, they felt they had to go—it would look stupid if they were in Michigan and didn't show up.

So that's the background to this conference call, when I made Engler promise that he would maintain "radio silence"—or I'd quit. Sure enough, during the call we heard all of Bush's advance people bitching about us: "They want us to do a plant gate.... They want to do this.... We can't do that.... They're basically forcing us to do something else.... What a stupid idea." And on and on.

After listening to the Bush people talk like this for a while, Engler reached for the phone.

"Don't you dare," I warned. "Don't you even dare. You promised." He restrained himself, but you could see how much he wanted to pick that phone up. He was muttering and talking back at the receiver.

Eventually they stopped complaining about us and went on to discuss an event later that day. The advance people were talking about an event that the candidate was going to do. They were talking about a rope and stanchion, and how they needed to do a rope line.

Engler was agitated—"No rope lines," he said to the phone. "We need to have Bush with the people. He's not president of the United States yet. Gore needs to have rope lines and more security, but we don't. That's our advantage. We need to make the most of it. We need him to be with the people." His words were falling on deaf ears because the Bush people couldn't hear us.

Now, at that time Bush's national field director, Ken Mehlman, and the regional political director were in our Michigan headquarters. I called the office on my cell phone and told one of our staffers, "Please take a note into Ken. Write, 'The governor says NO ROPE LINES at the events that day.'"

The Bush people had no idea that we were listening. I told the staffer that we were listening but warned her not to tell Ken. Just give him the message and walk out.

So the staffer handed him the note, and I could hear Ken on the conference call say, "Thanks ... Uh ... What? ... No rope lines? ... Uh ... Just a second...." Then Ken called me on my cell. "Jim ... uh ... I don't ... what's going on?"

I said, "The governor and I have been talking, and I just wanted to let you know how he felt about rope lines."

"Uh ... well ... I'm on a conference call ... I'll have to call you later," Ken stammered.

We took him totally off guard. Through it all Engler kept his promise. They never knew he was listening in on their entire conversation.[472]

[472] *Jim Brandell, interview with GW, February 1, 2001.*

*

John Truscott

Engler would be riding on the bus with Bush. It was right before the primary and we needed all the press we could get. And yet the Bush staff would not agree to do morning radio calls.

Engler said, "Go ahead and set them up."

So I scheduled about 20 radio calls for that morning on the way from American Axle to Jimi's Restaurant in Royal Oak. We passed the word along to the Bush staff and figured that if Bush didn't want to do the radio calls, we'd just have Engler do them alone.

The morning came. On the bus, there's no way that Engler could pick up the phone and do all those radio calls and have Bush just sit there. The candidate joined right in. We were just rotating cell phones. I'd call in and hand the phone to Engler, he'd do the introduction, then hand the phone to Bush, who was phenomenal. Bush just blew their socks off. He had a great time and dominated statewide media that day. It was the largest bloc of calls that he had made in one morning anywhere in the country.

The interesting thing is that it wasn't the most senior staff that were giving us a hard time. I showed Karen Hughes what we had planned and she said, "That's fine. Go with it." It was the mid-level staff that didn't seem to want to do anything.[473]

*

VP candidate? Cabinet post?

National Review *reporter John Miller interviewed Engler when speculation arose that he was being considered as George W. Bush's running mate or for a Bush administration cabinet post.*

W's MAN IN MICHIGAN
THE STORY OF JOHN ENGLER

On January 13, Michigan governor John Engler rose early in Lansing and caught a private jet to Washington, D.C. His State of the State speech was less than a week away, and he spent part of the day holed up in an office working on it. But the American Enterprise Institute had invited him to a forum on "How Would George W. Bush Govern?" That was worth the hassle.

The organizers knew they had a prize panelist in Engler. He's mentioned as a possible cabinet secretary, White House chief of staff—and maybe even vice

[473]*John Truscott, interview with GW, February 1, 2001.*

president. When a moderator asked Engler how much a President Bush would rely on Republican governors for policy advice, Engler, who has had weight problems his whole life, replied: "Well, I would suggest heavily—that he would rely on heavy governors."

It was a witty remark, but perhaps a meaningful one too. Although neither Engler nor any of his staff has talked about jobs in the Bush administration—"I can honestly say we've never had that discussion," says a top aide—it is impossible to suppress that speculation. Four years ago, Engler was short-listed by Bob Dole for the GOP's vice-presidential slot. Last year, the Bush campaign registered "bushengler.com" as a web domain name. It's easy to see why. As a longtime Bush loyalist—backing the father in 1980, doing so again in 1988, and endorsing the son early in the current cycle—Engler is a known commodity in Austin. As a tax cutting Republican governor from a labor-union state in the Midwest, he brings experience to the ticket and helps deliver contested electoral votes. And as a pro-life Catholic conservative, he simultaneously satisfies the party base and reaches out to Reagan Democrats.

Engler, now 51, got his start in politics in 1970, when the 21-year-old beat an incumbent Republican for a seat in the Michigan legislature. He was generally considered a rural conservative and even wound up with Russell Kirk as a constituent and a mentor. Kirk, a philosopher and one of the most important conservatives of the century, adored Engler; the last book the older man ever inscribed was made out to the governor. "Russell used to say that John has an ability to reform with a disposition to preserve," recalls Kirk's widow, Annette.

But the governor didn't act like a conservative at all times. In 1980, he supported Howard Baker in the GOP presidential primaries. When Baker bowed out, Engler switched to George Bush—and voted for him on the day Ronald Reagan clinched the nomination. He had more influence on local races, such as when he helped organize the 1983 recall elections of two tax-hiking state senators, both Democrats. Their defeats catapulted him to the post of state senate majority leader.

In 1990, he challenged Gov. James Blanchard and, running a crack campaign, beat him in an upset. Democrats still complain that lousy weather on Election Day depressed their turnout.

Engler is an unlikely success in the era of blow-dried politics. He's more a cloakroom arm-twister than a telegenic bully-pulpit man. In Lansing, he is known as a bruiser. "Win or lose, he will always take a pound of flesh from you," says one Michigan Republican. Yet there's very little turnover on his staff, and he can be strikingly loyal. When his chief of staff's mother died in 1991, the governor had been scheduled to throw out the first pitch at Tiger Stadium on Opening Day; Engler cancelled the appearance and went to the funeral instead.

... His record through nine years is impressive: some 26-tax cuts, saving the public some $11 billion; fewer state employees; and a plummeting abortion rate. Engler has also reshaped the state judiciary: Michigan may have the most conservative state supreme court in the nation. When the Cato Institute released its biennial report card on governors two years ago, it declared that "there is almost nothing not to admire" about Engler's work.

He's no compassionate conservative, either. In one of his first acts as governor, Engler tossed 80,000 able-bodied adults off the dole. The media savaged him daily. A tent city dubbed "Englerville" sprouted on the lawn of the capitol. Leftwing activists tried to blame several wintertime deaths on the new policy. Engler's approval rating sank to about 30 percent, making him look like a one-termer. The state teachers' union distributed a nasty bumper sticker: "John Engler has no kids and he hates yours."

Engler took care of that problem in 1994; his wife gave birth to triplets (all girls). The state's Rust Belt economy also started to improve. The unemployment rate has been below the national average for six years. Engler also earned a national reputation as a welfare-reform leader, trimming the state rolls by two-thirds. He coasted to re-election in 1994 on the heels of a voter-approved school-financing package that included a major property-tax rollback. He won again four years later, easily besting Geoffrey Fieger, a foul-mouthed trial lawyer who once represented Jack Kevorkian.

If future historians write about a Republican revolution during the 1990s, they'll be referring to the GOP's strength outside Washington as much as to the 1994 takeover of Congress. In 1990, there were just 21 Republican governors. Today, there are 30. Engler, who is now third in seniority, has championed this group for years. Following the Dole debacle, he made it known to anybody who would listen that the next Republican nominee should be one of the governors. Shortly after the 1998 races, he decided that Bush was his man.

Since then, Engler has been a tireless Bush advocate. He joined Bush's 10-member exploratory committee last year and locked up endorsements from virtually every member of Michigan's GOP establishment. He also turned on the state's money spigot. Some $3 million of Bush's campaign treasury has come from Michigan, in large part because of Engler. The state party moved its primary forward to February 22. "We're the firewall," explains John Truscott, Engler's press secretary. "Bush either stops bleeding here or gets the big-state momentum he needs to pick up the nomination." Engler also sent at least one member of his staff to Iowa to help Bush in the caucuses, and his office is in regular contact with Austin on everything from speech drafts to issues research.

The governor has even come out against a school-choice initiative that will probably appear on the state ballot in November. He believes that a high-profile campaign over vouchers would boost Democratic turnout and thereby imperil the re-election of Sen. Spencer Abraham, endanger GOP control of the state House of Representatives right before congressional redistricting (watch out, David Bonior!), and make it harder for the GOP presidential nominee to carry Michigan. Engler certainly isn't against competition in education; Michigan students and parents now have extensive public-school choice, and more than 50,000 students attend charter schools. So his iron-fisted assaults on the initiatives have puzzled some longtime backers. But the fallout probably won't be great. "A lot of conservatives are willing to give him a pass on this one," says Lawrence Reed, president of the Mackinac Center, a Midland-based think tank that supports the initiative.

And it surely won't hurt his standing in the Bush camp. Which raises the obvious question: Who should get the vice-presidential nomination? "There's less of a need for Bush to go to the governors because he is one," says Engler. "He has our support. We view him as one of our own." Engler says there are many good choices in Congress or the states—he names John McCain and Pennsylvania governor Tom Ridge as possibilities—and then mentions a third category: former officeholders with extensive government experience but now in the private sector. He describes Dick Cheney without using the name.

Would he take the job himself? "I'll wait until somebody asks before I respond to that question," he says. The consensus among friends and colleagues is that he doesn't want the job as much as he did four years ago. His wife is said to be reluctant to leave Michigan. And Engler probably wouldn't settle for anything less than veep. "There is no cabinet post that would give him more satisfaction than being governor of Michigan," says Richard McLellan, a Lansing lawyer and one of Engler's closest friends.

Perhaps the Mackinac Center's Reed puts it best: "It used to be you could tell Engler was getting serious about a campaign when he dropped weight. He did that in 1990 and then in 1996. He's not doing it now."

If Bush wants Engler to join him in Washington, he may just have to draft him.[474]

[474]*John J. Miller, "W.'s Man in Michigan: The Story of John Engler,"* National Review, *February 21, 2000, pp. 18, 20. Copyright 2000 by National Review, Inc., 215 Lexington Avenue, New York, NY 10016. Reprinted by permission.*

*

Darkness at noon—the Michigan primary

John Engler drew a line in the sand. He said that Michigan would be George W. Bush's "firewall" in the presidential primary season: Michigan would stop John McCain in his campaign for the GOP nomination. It turned out that McCain was stopped, but not because of Michigan. February 22, 2000, would prove to be one of Engler's lowest points in office. From the Detroit Free Press*:*

CAMPAIGN HEATS UP, TIME RUNS DOWN
BUSH, MCCAIN RACE TO WOO VOTERS
BEFORE TODAY'S CRUCIAL VOTE

The close race could attract an unusually large number of voters. Secretary of State Candice Miller has predicted 950,000 voters, or 40 percent more than voted in the 1996 presidential primary.

How many of those voters are independents or Democrats could determine the outcome, according to several polls. A WDIV-TV poll taken after the South Carolina primary showed the Michigan race a virtual dead heat....

Engler predicted a Bush victory by 4 or 5 percentage points.

"I think our biggest challenge is just getting out the vote," Engler said.[475]

*

Sharon Rothwell

The day before the February 22, 2000, primary, my heart just ached for John. He read the writing on the wall and kept asking himself, "What did I do wrong? What could I have done?" He was agonizing over what he could have done to help George Bush win.

I didn't know how to answer him and simply said, "I don't know—I just do not know." Who could have known?[476]

*

Rachel Siglow recounts three dramatic moments from primary day:

The governor called about 2:00 or 3:00 in the afternoon.

"It doesn't look good," he said.

"I know, governor."

"Did you vote?"

"Yes, I did."

[475] *Chris Christoff, "Campaign Heats Up, Time Runs Down,"* Detroit Free Press, *February 22, 2000, p. 1A.*
[476] *Sharon Rothwell, interview with GW, March 16, 2001.*

"Did all your family vote?"
"I think so.
"Just in case, call everybody you know and make sure they've voted."
It was the first time I'd ever heard desperation in the governor's voice.

We got the call in the afternoon. A law firm told us they had received a phone threat from a man who said he was going to do damage to the law firm and get the governor, too. Somehow the law firm got the death threat on tape. They shared it with [security] detail, and they went straight into action. They traced the call to a man in Indiana. Dave Peltomaa [in charge of detail] assigned extra people to the girls' school. Every available member of detail was with the Englers at the Southfield event where the governor and first lady were watching the returns. With everything else going on, they had to deal with this.

That evening, when it was clear that George W. Bush would lose the primary, the governor gave his speech down in Southfield. There must have been 50 or 60 news cameras, more than I've ever seen before. Then he went on CNN live and really showed the kind of leader he is. On national news he said, in effect, "This is not George Bush's loss. This is John Engler's loss. The votes *for* McCain were votes *against* me."

On national TV, the governor took all the blame. He emphasized that Bush was a great candidate who deserved to win, but that his [Engler's] enemies had come out and voted for McCain just to spite him.[477]

*

Michelle Engler

I think John's worst political moment was when George W. lost the primary. When we were driving home that night, John said to me, "I let my friend down. I should have anticipated this."

I told him, "You couldn't have anticipated 280,000 Democrats coming out to the polls!"

Friends have told me this was the only day they have ever seen him shaken. A few days later, John was still questioning himself. He took the whole weight of the loss onto his shoulders.[478]

*

[477] *Rachel Siglow, interview with GW, July 29, 2002.*
[478] *Michelle Engler, interview with GW, January 26, 2001.*

From the Detroit News

ROAD ONLY GETS ROUGHER
INDEPENDENT MINDSET IN MICHIGAN SENDS MCCAIN STEAMING TOWARD SUPER TUESDAY

In the end, the message sent out by Michigan voters in Tuesday's Republican primary was not about tax cuts or the national debt; maybe not even about the character of one candidate over another.

In this largest of all states to hold primaries and caucuses so far, it was about Democratic and independent voters seizing an opportunity to make a political statement about a maverick Republican candidate they like or a GOP governor they don't....

Engler and Bush were severely tested in the open primary here, which allowed McCain-friendly and Democratic voters to cast ballots....

"It's a unique system where people can come into our primary if they feel like it," Bush said during a radio interview that he conducted from Jimi's Restaurant in Royal Oak.

During his final morning of campaigning before leaving the state, Bush complained loudly about two factors that could sway the vote towards McCain: an anti-Engler sentiment among Democrats and a telephone campaign on election eve by the McCain campaign that criticized Bush's speech in South Carolina at Bob Jones University, which espouses racial and anti-Catholic bigotry.

Catholics were expected to make up about 35 percent of the voter turnout.

Confronting reporters at the start of election day, Bush complained the McCain campaign was calling him an "anti-Catholic bigot" in the taped telephone messages to voters....

Engler also blamed Detroit-area Democrats, who he said set up a massive phone bank in one of the party's congressional district headquarters, on behalf of McCain.

"The Democratic Party and the Democratic district officials were running the phones, working for Sen. McCain. It's extraordinary," Engler said.[479]

*

[479] *Gebe Martinez, "Road Only Gets Rougher,"* Detroit News, *February 23, 2000.*

From the Detroit Free Press

MICHIGAN'S VOTE

BUSH, ENGLER MACHINES HAVE REASON TO BE WORRIED

There are many ways to read John McCain's victory in Tuesday's Republican presidential primary, and none of them bode well for George Bush.

Gov. John Engler, who staked so much of his political capital on delivering Michigan as a Bush "fire wall" against McCain, suddenly isn't looking so hot either. With many big-state primaries yet to come, this race is far from over, but Republicans who lined up early and shelled out often for Bush have to be wondering if the Texas governor is really ready for prime time.

Bush did win handily among card-carrying GOPers in Michigan, but ought to be very worried about polls showing about 20 percent of Republicans have a generally unfavorable impression of him. He also showed little pull among independent voters, who will decide which way Michigan swings in November....

As for Engler, he's peerless at working the power levers in Lansing, where Republicans now control everything. But this setback, and recent fractious events in the state GOP leadership, call into question the existence of an Engler "machine" and really ought to inspire Democrats for fall.[480]

*

Michelle Engler

During the primary, John had taken a lot of abuse from the press about his underlying motives concerning George W. The press twisted John's loyalty to George W. They were so cynical of every step John took to help him in the election. The media were saying, "John Engler is doing this because he wants to be in the cabinet. John Engler is doing this because he wants to have access to the president."

John believes strongly in good government, and he felt that George W. was the man for the job, and his confidence in George W. has only grown with time.[481]

*

Dawson Bell

Some people think McCain's victory was Engler's personal failure. I don't

[480]*"Michigan's Vote: Bush, Engler Machines Have Reason to Be Worried," editorial,* Detroit Free Press, *February 23, 2000, p. 12A.*

[481]*Michelle Engler, interview with GW, January 26, 2001.*

agree. Looking back, I don't think that John Engler made any serious miscalculations. He couldn't control an open primary, and he couldn't control Mike Murphy, who made Michigan a major part of McCain's strategy.

But February 22 was made out by Engler's enemies to be his personal failure. That story had a life of its own—John Engler had no power to control it.[482]

*

Vouchers and the 2000 elections

John Engler kept warning the GOP and education reformers that Michigan was not ready to have the "voucher debate" in 2000.

Mark my words: Proposal 1 won't even be close. It will be crushed. And that will set back the voucher movement in this state at least a decade. More than that, it could hurt Republican candidates in many close elections.[483]

*

Jef Mallett, an editorial cartoonist, had this take on John Engler's thinking:

I drew a cartoon on October 30th, 2000, just before the election. I titled it "The Real Michigan Swing Vote." And it shows a crane with a wrecking ball. The crane is labeled "Voucher Turnout Demolition and Mayhem Company." And it is swinging the wrecking ball toward George W. Bush. I think it kind of sums up exactly what the governor was concerned about with the voucher proposal.

The governor was very keen on George W. Bush and wanted to make sure that Bush was elected with Michigan's help. Unfortunately it didn't turn out that way. That was probably not one of the high points of the governor's career. I think he was embarrassed by the result. (Now I am speculating as to his emotions.)

I think there are two different reasons for the defeat. In the primary, I think a large part of the problem was how the primary was set up; Democrats could vote for McCain, not so much because they favored McCain, but because they didn't like George W. Bush. And I have no doubt that there were a lot of Democrats causing that kind of trouble, working within the system.

But Proposal 1 [the voucher proposal] was another huge factor in why George W. Bush didn't win Michigan in the general election. That brought a lot of people to the polls who may not have shown up otherwise. They wouldn't have come out to vote for Gore, but as long as they were there to vote against

[482] *Dawson Bell, interview with GW, February 27, 2001.*
[483] *JE, comment to staff on several occasions during the fall of 2000, before the November 2000 election.*

Proposal 1, they figured they'd cast a vote for Gore while they were at it.

And I think, if I am guessing right, that that was the governor's fear with Proposal 1. If I want to go out even farther on a limb, I would say that he opposed Proposal 1 more for political reasons than for ideological reasons. I get the impression that, at the right time and written correctly, the governor probably would support a good voucher proposal for schools. But timing is everything.[484]

*

Gary Wolfram

I don't think Engler handled Proposal 1 very well. If he had come out actively in opposition before the signatures, that's one thing. Once there were the signatures and it was on the ballot, things were already set in their course.

I was on Mackinac Island at a leadership conference when Dick DeVos approached me and asked me to meet with him after lunch. At 10:30 that morning Engler had announced that he was not supporting Proposal 1. Then I met with DeVos and he asked me to help him with the Kids First! Yes! plan, and I agreed.

I didn't talk to Engler about it, but I told Dick Posthumus that I thought the proposal was right for Michigan.

The lieutenant governor said, "I don't think John would have thought you'd do anything different."

I didn't think then, and I don't think now, that it was a problem. John Engler doesn't expect you to be different from who you are.[485]

*

Supreme Court races

Jef Mallett discusses another cartoon he produced.

Of all the races in 2000, the nastiest by far were for the Michigan Supreme Court. It got ugly. And these were the races that were supposed to be civil. They were supposed to be nonpartisan. They were supposed to be the high road all the way.

Here is one case where the governor didn't get a complimentary cartoon from me. The cartoon shows Governor Engler at his desk with three puppets. One puppet is Justice Markman; one puppet is Justice Young; one puppet is

[484]*Jef Mallet, interview with GW, March 29, 2001.*
[485]*Gary Wolfram, interview with GW, February 13, 2001.*

Justice Taylor. Governor Engler is holding one puppet on each of his hands and one on his foot. The puppets are talking to each other. Justice Markman asks Justice Young, "How did the Supreme Court race become so politicized?"

"I don't know," answers Justice Taylor.

The implication, of course, is that since all three justices were appointed by Engler, they not surprisingly followed Engler's line of thinking, and Engler's thinking naturally made its way into the contest. I was happy with that cartoon—it is one of my favorites.[486]

*

Bush-Engler?

Detroit Free Press *reporter Chris Christoff tells of the time Engler had to be cagey to keep a secret.*

John Engler is an intensely private man. He can keep a secret as well as anybody we've ever covered. The Connie Binsfeld announcement back in 1990 was as good as it gets. But there was another time he kept a secret from just about everybody.

In July of 2000, during the presidential campaign, somebody at a press conference asked Engler if he were being considered for vice president. Had he been vetted like several other candidates we were aware of?

Engler's answer was, "No." What he meant was, he hadn't gone through exactly the same vetting process that other potential VP candidates had gone through. Engler was being cagey—he can sometimes be cagey to a fault—and he gets into these parsing games with reporters.

So I wrote an article that ran July 25, 2000, reporting that John Engler had never been considered seriously by the Bush camp. Right after the story ran, Peter Secchia and I talked—he and Dick Cheney are close. Secchia told me that Engler was being considered; that he was on the short list in fact; and that Cheney had asked Engler for background information. The governor was definitely being considered.

I called John Truscott to ask what was going on. He said he didn't know. He called back later and apologized and said that Engler hadn't even told him that Bush was considering him for VP. My article the next day ran under the headline: "Engler Finally Admits He Was on the VP Shortlist."[487]

[486]*Jef Mallet, interview with GW, March 29, 2001.*

[487]*Chris Christoff, interview with GW, July 11, 2002; see Chris Christoff, "Engler Finally Admits He Was on the VP Shortlist,"* Detroit Free Press, *July 26, 2000, p. 6A.*

*

The first lady reflects on what it was like for her husband to be considered as a potential vice-presidential candidate in 2000.

2000 was different from 1996. When Dick Cheney called prior to the 2000 election, asking John to send in his information for consideration for the vice presidency, John said, "You know, Dick, you don't have to do this for me. You don't have to flatter me. I've been considered before."

Cheney answered, "I assure you that this isn't flattery. Send me your stuff." So John sent information to him.

Later, when George W. made his decision, he called us that morning to tell us he had chosen Dick Cheney to be his running mate. He had the courtesy to call and tell us.

We knew that it wasn't going to happen. I never thought they would pick another governor. I wasn't worried this time. But we appreciated the call.[488]

*

2000 elections

Election Day 2000 will go down as one of the most contentious in U.S. history. George W. Bush's contest with Al Gore in the Electoral College remained unsettled until five weeks after the polls had closed, and only after the U.S. Supreme Court's decision cleared the way for Florida's 25 electoral votes to go to Bush. John Engler was thrilled that his friend won, but disappointed that it wasn't because of Michigan. In the Great Lakes State, Gore garnered 51 percent of the vote, Bush 47 percent, and Green Party candidate Ralph Nader 2 percent.

Engler believed that the voucher campaign hurt not just George W. Bush, but Republican candidates throughout the state. True, the Michigan House remained secure, with 58 Republicans and 52 Democrats, but several GOP representatives reported having to work harder than anticipated to keep their seats. And the state board of education, which had been tied at 4 Republicans and Democrats apiece, swung 5 to 3 in favor of the Democrats.

As Engler had predicted, vouchers were resoundingly rejected by Michigan voters. Despite having a $15 million war chest, the Kids First! Yes! coalition could not deliver on Proposal 1, which went down 69 percent to 31 percent statewide, and lost 61 percent to 39 percent in conservative Ottawa County on the west side of the state.[489]

Engler was extremely pleased with the Supreme Court races. All three of his recent

[488] *Michelle Engler, interview with GW, January 26, 2001.*
[489] *Steven Harmon, "Voucher Proposal Hurt GOP, Critics Say," November 8, 2000.*

appointees to the court won. Justices Clifford Taylor, Stephen Markman, and Robert Young added great depth to what was already the best Supreme Court in the United States.

Engler's greatest personal disappointment on November 7 was voters' rejection of his friend, Spencer Abraham. The one-term U.S. Senator narrowly lost his seat to Democratic Congresswoman Debbie Stabenow. Andrea Fischer Newman observes:

In all the years I've known John, one of the lowest points was Spence losing the Senate race. They are friends—it was personal. The night Spence lost, I was talking to John, and he just refused to believe the numbers the RNC had. He held out hope to the end.[490]

*

Inauguration of President George W. Bush

Michelle Engler

When we were packing to go to Washington, I saw John getting out his big, beige Stetson. Now I'm a Texan, born and raised. But I try to play it down outside of Texas. I know John can wear his Stetson legitimately because he's from a farming family. He grew up where people wear hats like that. But I said, "John, you shouldn't take that hat. It just looks like you're trying too hard around all those Texans."

"But it's my hat! I like it!" he said. He is a lot less self-conscious about these things than I am.

"But more practically," I said, "if you wear that big hat in a crowd, somebody behind you is going to be really mad."

The practical argument won out, so he put his Stetson back and got a smaller black hat.

But I'll tell you, when we were in Washington and he saw Donny Evans wearing his big hat that looks just like John's, he said, "See? See?"[491]

*

Flashback from Linda Gobler

John just loves that hat—I wondered if he was going to take it to the Inaugural. I remember the night he came home with it. It was a few years ago, and he had been in Oklahoma, I think. Michelle and I were in the kitchen yucking it up. John came in, pushing the swinging doors open, saying with a big

[490] *Andrea Fischer Newman, interview with GW, August 3, 2002.*
[491] *Michelle Engler, interview with GW, January 26, 2001.*

smile, "Look what I got!" And he's got that Stetson hat on.

Well, Michelle took one look and started howling with laughter because it just looked—you know, so out of context. And I had the exact Siamese-twin reaction that Michelle did.

Poor John was like, "Well, I don't care. I like it and I think that it looks good and I'm wearing it."

I wanted to tease him: "And are the cattle waiting in the front yard? Did you have a hard day on the trail?"

Actually, it's a beautiful hat. It looks good on him. But it was funny because he leaves the GQ governor, and he comes home—Rowdy Yates.[492]

*

Michelle Engler

In our hotel room on the morning of Inauguration Day, John lamented the fact that we would not be sitting together to share the occasion. It was so momentous.

We left for the Capitol at 8:30. For the swearing in ceremony, the first ladies were seated directly below the main platform. I know that during the ceremony several of us got tears in our eyes. I am sure John got tears in his eyes. This moment represented such a restoration for our nation. As the ceremony came to a conclusion, Linda Graves and I couldn't help but let out a barely restrained "*Yes!*"

The weather wasn't great. But later in the day, when John was talking to a reporter, he said, "It might as well be 80 degrees and sunny for how we feel!"

Toward the end of the Inaugural parade, John and I were still in the viewing stand with a few other governors and cabinet members, and President Bush looked our way and said, "Come on over," so a few of us went over to see him. We gave him and Laura big hugs. The Cheneys and a few members of the Bush family were standing there with the president and first lady.

I said, "It's so great to call you 'Mr. President.'"

He said, "We did it. Thanks so much for your help. You know, we're gonna do all right."

Going with John to the Bush Inaugural was like going with a rock star. Because of his achievements as governor, we were invited to all the A-list par-

[492]*Linda Gobler, interview with GW, January 26, 2001.*

ties. At these parties everybody knew John. People would come up and say, "I'm from California, and you're my hero." People kept saying they thought of him as a real star in the party.[493]

*

Dick Posthumus

At the Inauguration of President Bush, I saw a foreshadowing of the closeness the state of Michigan is going to have with this presidency. I saw the president standing and watching the parade. Right next to him were Governor John Engler and First Lady Michelle. They were standing right next to each other, and I realized that was symbolic of the close and important role that our governor was going to play in George W. Bush's administration.[494]

*

Michelle on her husband's strong convictions and inner peace

I read an article the other day that talked about Ronald Reagan. The premise was that so-called simple souls, like Reagan, had great leadership qualities built on strong convictions and an inner tranquility. I was reading this article and said to myself, "This is *so* John."

And I said to John, "This is you! This is really you!"

John has such strong convictions along with that searing intellect. He's also at peace with himself. He knows who he is, what he believes in, and where he is going. No matter what's happening around him, he knows the right thing to do and he's very comfortable with that. It comes from his inner tranquility. And I think that is the most important quality of a leader. Because then the leader doesn't get caught up in polling and opinions and in what the popular thing to do is. John has avoided getting caught up in that from the beginning.[495]

*

Heinz Prechter, RIP

In a distressing phone call on Friday, July 6, 2001, Governor Engler learned of the death of his cherished friend, Heinz Prechter. The German-born Prechter had battled depression for more than three decades and had received extensive treatment at the

[493] *Michelle Engler, interview with GW, January 26, 2001.*
[494] *Dick Posthumus, interview with GW, February 7, 2001.*
[495] *Michelle Engler, interview with GW, January 26, 2001.*

University of Michigan. He succumbed to the disease, however, and took his life at the age of 59. He left behind an amazing story. As a foreign exchange student, he turned a $764 business out of his garage into a successful international company. He touched the lives of many, including the governor who regarded Prechter like an older brother.

Shortly after hearing about the death of his friend, Engler wrote the following statement in his own hand:

Governor Engler with his friend Heinz Prechter (middle) and White House Chief of Staff Andrew Card, spring 2001. SOURCE: *John Engler*

Michigan has lost a generous and caring citizen and Michelle and I have lost a dear friend. The death of Heinz Prechter is a profound loss for all of us. Heinz loved Michigan and lived life to the fullest. His countless contributions, his leadership, his philanthropy, and his optimism will be sorely missed. Heinz leaves a legacy of good deeds that reflected his pride in being an American.[496]

*

[496] *JE, personal papers, July 6, 2001.*

Gleaves Whitney

On Monday, July 9, our staff assembled to have a surprise party for one of our colleagues. At the end of the party, the governor, Sharon Rothwell, and I found ourselves talking about Heinz's death and the tragedy of suicide. I had never seen the governor so sad. Every few minutes of the conversation his eyes would tear up. Just looking at him made a lump rise in my throat.

The Prechter eulogy was one of the toughest speeches I ever worked on. The funeral was scheduled for Wednesday, July 11.

On the night before the interment, the governor was in his Capitol office, working with legislators to get some bills passed. He sat at the table in the parlor, receiving legislators. As always, he was masterful in his strategizing and people would express delight with his ideas and say, "Absolutely brilliant, governor! You've done it again!" Then the lawmakers would leave his office for a while to go back to their caucus, and the parlor would become quiet.

These interludes gave the governor and me a few windows of opportunity to work on the eulogy. It was work that had to be done, but it was hard on the governor. Every time he would redirect his attention to Heinz, he had to hold back his grief. I could tell that he was struggling.

I had composed a draft that had some well-crafted sentiments, but there was a huge gap in the message. I said, "Governor, I need a couple of personal stories to make the eulogy complete." But the governor wouldn't tell me personal stories. He kept telling me how Heinz did this for the Republican Party, did that for the auto industry, did such-and-such for the community. Every word of it true—but.

After this had gone on awhile, I said, "Governor, we still don't have a eulogy. You are giving me a resume. I don't think people want to hear you talk about Heinz's business and political achievements, considerable as they are. I think they want to hear you talk about your friendship, what he meant to you. I need something from the heart."

He seemed to look absent-mindedly at the speech. Given the limited time left, I ventured: "Do you think Michelle would have any stories?"

"Yes, let's call Michelle," he said decisively, rising from his chair.

We walked over to his desk, and he called Michelle and put her on the speaker-phone so that the three of us could talk. I remember looking at my watch. It was after 9:30 p.m. and I wondered if she were feeling too tired to talk. Heinz's loss was hard on her, too.

Michelle was just right for what John needed. She knew exactly the feelings the eulogy should convey. In no time she and the governor began to reminisce about their trips to Germany with Heinz, and to recall some of the wonderful and humorous times they had together. They enjoyed the memories and even laughed a few times.

About five minutes into the conversation, the governor was called out of the room for more huddling with legislators. Michelle and I continued the conversation alone. She was calling up wonderful memories, and I wrote them down as fast as possible. I was pleased—I knew the governor had his eulogy. I said something to that effect, and she said, "You know, this is so hard. Heinz is like a brother...." Her voice broke off to a whisper.

I never felt so bad for her and John. It was as if they had lost one of their own family.

About five hours later, at 2:30 a.m., the eulogy was finished.[497]

*

Rachel Siglow

It's the saddest I've ever seen the governor. Working on the speech took a long time. There seemed to be many drafts. It was a struggle, but it helped him go through the grieving process. Also, he wanted that speech to be perfect—he wanted the right words to console Mrs. Prechter and the employees.

About a week after the funeral, a letter came. It had been signed by Heinz personally, and there was a personal note in his own hand. For some reason, the letter had been delayed in reaching our office. It was dated just a day or two before his passing. I laid it down on my desk where the governor would see it. He picked it up and said, "How about that—something from good old Heinz." I could tell that he was calling up memories of his friend.

The governor seemed down all month. All during July he was distracted. Even six months later he would say, "You know, if only Heinz were here, we could call him...."[498]

*

John Engler: Visionary

Weeks before September 11th, John Engler was thinking strategically about how to wean America and the Middle West from the oil in the Middle East. He was also thinking about ways to help Michigan's marquis industry—the auto industry—position itself on the cutting edge of America's economic future. Doug Rothwell, president and CEO of

[497] *GW, personal papers, July 2001.*
[498] *Rachel Siglow, interview with GW, July 29, 2002.*

the Michigan Economic Development Corporation, helped the governor develop numerous initiatives to make the state more economically competitive.

As the governor would be hosting President George W. Bush in Michigan on Labor Day, he seized the opportunity to put his ideas about the "hydrogen economy" into the president's hands. On August 30, he compiled a notebook that included the following speech for the president's consideration. John Nevin reports that Engler composed much of the speech himself, sitting at Rachel Siglow's computer outside his office. The text of the speech follows.

A little more than 40 years ago—in May of 1961—President John F. Kennedy set forth a vision for America that shaped not just the next decade but the next generation. In his first speech to a joint session of Congress, Kennedy said:

"I believe that this nation should commit itself to achieving the goal, before this decade is out, of landing a man on the moon and returning him safely to the earth."

Kennedy called this bold plan a "great new American enterprise {that} may-hold the key to our future on Earth."

Today, I propose the next great new American enterprise—one that may hold the key to our future on Earth. By the year 2012, America's best and brightest scientists and engineers must achieve the equivalent of sending a man to the moon. We must build a hydrogen economy—an environmentally sustainable future based on a renewable, clean, and abundant supply of energy.

My vision is to tear down the barriers that hold American industry back and speed the development of hydrogen fuel-cell technology. This breakthrough will end our dependence on foreign oil, create a surge of economic growth, make the U.S. a global technology leader, and provide for the most dramatic gains in environmental quality since the beginning of the Industrial Age.

The promise of hydrogen fuel-cell technology is within our reach and the benefits will be extraordinary. Fuel cells running on hydrogen can produce electrical power for homes, workplaces, and vehicles that is vastly more efficient and free of pollution. Within ten years, hydrogen fuel-cell technology can change the world and America can lead the way—to cleaner air, stronger economies, and a better quality of life for everyone.

We must focus every effort and all available resources on achieving this goal. To engage every able hand in our crusade, we will offer a 10-year safe harbor from increased federal CAFE requirements as well as a full exemption from a growing proliferation of state regulations to companies willing to take up this challenge.

Regulations that mandate specific, incremental changes to the petroleum-based internal combustion engine restrain America's ability to step outside the box and lead. My vision unshackles our creative genius by calling for bold action to accelerate the pace of innovation and achieve an unlimited future.

More than two years ago, when I announced that I was a candidate for president, I pledged to "set goals worthy of a great nation." Sending a man to the moon was such a goal. Transforming the way we power our nation is such a goal.

The time is right.

The potential is real.

We must act.

For more than two centuries, when Americans faced a challenge—from forging a nation, to spanning a continent, to conquering space—our can-do spirit triumphed.

I am confident that this challenge will be no different. American ingenuity and engineering expertise will find the key to unlock the hydrogen economy. Our bold vision will produce a boundless source of energy that will power a revolution in the quality of our lives here in America and for people around the globe.[499]

*

September 11th

Rachel Siglow

It was Tuesday morning, so we were having our monthly staff meeting. But since the governor was coming in, I stayed at my desk. He came in about 8:50. A few minutes after nine, he asked me to get Dan Wyant on the phone and I did so. A few minutes after that, Bobby Grubbs [with security detail] walked up to my desk. "I need to talk to the governor." He sounded very serious.

"As soon as the governor is off the phone, I'll let you into his office."

Then I got the call from one of our colleagues about the World Trade Center. Immediately I got up, went straight into the governor's office, and turned on the TV. "Governor, you've got to see this." The image on the screen was of the second plane hitting the WTC. It was a replay of what had happened just moments before. I remember a man on MSNBC saying, "Moments ago a second plane hit the other World Trade Center tower."

Bobby, who was right behind me, said, "Governor, we have been notified by

[499] *John Nevin, personal papers and interview with GW, August 30, 2001.*

Central Command that two planes have crashed into the World Trade Center."

The governor, still on the phone with Dan, said, "Oh my gosh, Dan! Do you know what's going on? Rachel just turned on the TV, and we're looking at New York City. Two planes have just hit the twin towers. It's unbelievable."

He kept talking to Dan, describing everything he was seeing on TV.

Bobby continued to stay with the governor and monitor the situation. We did not know at that point whether other places were being targeted.

Then the Pentagon was hit. From my desk I heard Sharon [Rothwell] screaming, "Oh, my God! Oh, my God, no!" She was yelling into the phone, telling LeAnne, in our Washington office, "Get out of there! Get out of there right now!"

Later I went into the office: "Governor, do you want me to cancel the rest of the day?"

He didn't really answer. But he kept procrastinating going to his morning meeting. So I cancelled the meeting.

Later, he met with Dan DeGrow at 1:00 p.m. in his conference room and they had the TV on during the entire meeting.

The next morning when the governor came in, he looked tired from staying up late into the night. He had been listening to all the gruesome details of September 11th. He said, "It's just awful, just awful."[500]

*

On Thursday, September 13, the White House called on each of the states to hold a "National Day of Prayer and Remembrance for the Victims of the Terrorist Attacks on September 11, 2001." Our office had only 24 hours to prepare. Susy Avery coordinated the effort on behalf of the Engler administration. On September 14th, in an ecumenical service at St. Mary Cathedral in downtown Lansing, the governor gave these remarks:

We come from many different faiths—Jewish, Christian, Muslim—but we are all Americans. And as Americans, when we are tested, we close ranks. *By the grace of God, we will renew our national purpose under God.*

Just 76 hours ago, America was at peace. Now we are at war—at war with enemies of civilization and freedom—at war with evildoers who devised and exe-

[500]*Rachel Siglow, interview with GW, July 29, 2002.*

cuted the most savage attacks ever on our soil. Our generation, regrettably, has its own "date that will live in infamy." These acts of mass murder have seared our hearts. *But by the grace of God, these acts have also strengthened our resilience and steeled our resolve.*

Throughout our history, Americans have turned to God in times of war. During the American Revolution, the Continental Congress asked patriots in the Thirteen Colonies to pray for wisdom in *forming* a nation. During the Civil War, President Lincoln asked Americans to pray for wisdom in *preserving* a nation. Now President Bush calls on Americans to pray for wisdom in *defending* our nation. *By the grace of God, justice will be done.*

The losses due to the terrorists and those who've harbored them are beyond comprehension. It is not just the New York City skyline that is emptier. It is thousands of families that have lost one or more loved ones. It is hundreds of organizations that have lost one or more colleagues. It is scores of communities that have lost a Little League baseball coach, a Brownie Troop leader, a school volunteer. Their names have begun to be broadcast, names like ours. They were David, Barbara, and Peter; Julie, Chris, and Ruth; John, Daniel, and Lauren; and many, many others too numerous to name. On this "National Day of Prayer and Remembrance," we pray for the victims, their families, and the heroic rescue workers. *By the grace of God, we will help them bear this tragic burden.*

In the face of such horrific carnage and suffering, words seem inadequate. Yet we should take comfort in a passage from St. Paul's Letter to the Romans, in which he assures us that "The Spirit helps us in our weakness. We do not know what we ought to pray for, but the Spirit Himself intercedes for us with groans that are too deep for words." *By the grace of God, our deep wounds will begin to heal.*

In our nation's first great test, the American Revolution, Samuel Adams urged fellow patriots: "Contemplate the mangled bodies of your countrymen, and then say, What should be the reward of such sacrifices?"

For more than two centuries, America has had an answer to that question—an answer that has inspired millions of people around the world. The answer is freedom—America stands for freedom. To be an American means to be free. *By the grace of God, America shall remain free.*

The victims of the September Massacres did not choose to become casualties in a war with the enemies of freedom. So today, as our nation mourns, our solemn obligation to the victims is that we shall never forget. Likewise, as survivors, our duty is to ensure that our generation and those that follow shall live in an America that remains a beacon of liberty and justice for all. *May God in his grace continue to bless America.*[501]

*

Can History Repeat Itself?

After September 11th, John Engler pursued the idea of the hydrogen economy more aggressively than ever. Gleaves Whitney observes:

John Engler wants history to repeat itself. He wants Michigan history to repeat itself.

When we were working on the 2002 State of the State Address, he became fascinated with the early auto industry. One Saturday evening before speech practice, he pulled documents off the Internet that told the story of the great auto pioneers and their early prototypes. He came into the conference room and handed me a veritable notebook on the history of the industry.

What Engler was pulling together in his own mind was a comparison of Michigan in 2002 and Michigan in 1902. The state faces the same fundamental challenge today that it did one hundred years earlier: to become the preeminent place in the nation where new ideas and visionary entrepreneurs and smart workers and abundant capital all concentrate.

A century ago, this concentration was precisely what Michigan experienced. But it was hardly inevitable, hardly a given that the auto industry would develop most spectacularly in Michigan or even to the United States. In Germany Karl Benz and Gottlieb Daimler had been developing automobile prototypes since the 1880s, at least a decade before anything similar was happening in Detroit. By the turn of the century France, too, was a thriving automobile center, and Paris was the world capital of the industry. Its pantheon included Louis Renault, Rene Panhard, Emile Lavassor, and the Peugeot brothers. Clearly the U.S. was forced to play catch-up with the Europeans.

On this side of the Atlantic, moreover, there was keen competition among numerous communities to become *the* Motor City. At the start of the twentieth century, Detroit had not yet earned the title. No Michigan community could even claim to be the birthplace of the automobile. That bragging right was reserved to Springfield, Massachusetts, where the Duryea brothers had developed the first horseless carriage back in 1893. The first Michigan automobile was built and driven three years later, when Charles King ventured onto

[501] *JE, remarks for "The National Day of Prayer and Remembrance...," Lansing, September 14, 2001.*

the streets of Detroit with a "horseless carriage" that the *Detroit Free Press* called a "most unusual machine."

Detroit was not inevitable. Since 1893, more than 3,000 manufacturers throughout the US have made cars. Only about one-tenth of them were located in Michigan. Most of these companies never produced more than a prototype. Most survived only a few years. Despite that competition, or rather because of that competition, Detroit rose to the top. By 1914 it was recognized as the Motor City. Detroit succeeded because of an unusual mix of ingredients in the entrepreneurial stew: bold innovators clustered in the region; the city's marine-engine makers were already refining internal combustion engines; stove manufacturers could mold metals; machine shops could tool precision parts; wealthy entrepreneurs could make plenty of capital available; and the nation's earliest unions were relatively weak in the Detroit area. For all these reasons, Detroit had the right mix to succeed and earn the title "Motor City." Engler wants to make sure the same basic ingredients are in today's economic stew.

Another thing about Engler's preoccupation with the automobile industry struck me. He was preparing to use the 2002 State of the State address to roll out his vision of the new "hydrogen economy." He seemed to be making an intrinsic comparison between the development of the auto industry a century ago and the potential development of the hydrogen economy today. At first I thought the comparison was over the top. But then I read these words:

"It could be argued that since the development of agriculture about 12,000 years ago, the invention which has had the most profound effect on the way we live has been the automobile. There have been many advances in technology which have had important and far-reaching effects, but few have changed the way we actually live as completely and as rapidly as the automobile....

"The automobile is, like no other machine, part of us."[502]

As I scanned the Web documents the governor gave me, it all became so obvious, so clear. John Engler wanted Michigan history to repeat itself. We had to encourage the same things to happen now that had happened a century ago. We had to be in the vanguard of the economic frontier.

When you understand that, you go right to the heart of John Engler's economic agenda. It involves so much more than tinkering to achieve mere incremental improvements. At base it is not evolutionary; it is revolutionary.

[502] *Source: http://www.aaca.org/autohistory/01.html. Quotation from Richard A. Wright, Department of Communications, Wayne State University.*

The tax cuts, the reformation of state government, the reduction in regulations, the renaissance zones, and grants to lure new and innovative industries; the life sciences corridor, clusters of innovation, and the hydrogen economy—they are all of a piece. It's John Engler's back-to-the-future vision of this state. He passionately wants Michigan to become the cool place to be in the hot economy of the future. He wants to cultivate Michigan talent, foster Michigan creativity, encourage Michigan ingenuity. He seeks to attract capital and people from other parts of the nation to the Great Lakes State so that Michigan becomes the Austin, the Silicon Valley, the Research Triangle of the North.

Ambitious, but Michigan has seen it happen before. And John Engler is doing everything possible to set the stage for it to happen again.[503]

*

Judicial Philosophy

One of the most important duties of a governor is to appoint judges when vacancies arise on the bench. Engler delivered his defining statement on the topic to the Michigan Supreme Court Historical Society upon receiving their first legal history award. In the address he fleshed out his judicial philosophy, making a key distinction between judicial conservatism and political conservatism. The luncheon ceremony took place on April 18, 2002, at the Detroit Athletic Club. The speech was later placed in a time capsule at the dedication ceremony for the Michigan Hall of Justice, for safe keeping until October 8, 2102. Excerpts from the text of the speech that was posted on the governor's Web site follows:

Our current Michigan Supreme Court is simply stellar. It's one of the greatest things to be proud of in our state. Just last Friday Gene Meyer, president of the Federalist Society in Washington, DC, told one of my aides that the Michigan Supreme Court is, bar none, the best state court in America. In decision after decision after decision, our High Court adheres to legal principles consistent with the Founders' understanding of the role of the judiciary in our constitutional republic.

Over the past 11 plus years, I've made 183 judicial appointments. But even more important than the number of judges are their quality and independence and competence to sit on the bench. When it comes to judicial appointments—as in much else—my critics miss the point. They charge that I want a "Republican

[503]*GW, personal papers, February 2002. See the same theme expressed 11 years earlier, in the First Inaugural Address, January 1, 1991 (pp. 175-79, above).*

court." Or a "*politically* conservative court." Or a "John Engler court."

That's sophistry. I've said it a thousand times, and I'll say it again. I want jurists on the Michigan bench who understand that it is legislators, not judges, who make the law; who believe that the people should govern through their elected representatives; who comprehend that the burden of policy-making is on the legislative not the judicial branch; who render decisions based on the text of the Constitution or statute rather than on somebody's social agenda. In short: Give me a few good men and women who can read our Constitution!

In Michigan, we are blessed to have more than a few who are making their mark, and I am proud of their achievement. Gene Meyer is absolutely right—you are the very best. In historical perspective, it is certainly fair to compare our current Supreme Court with the greatest court in Michigan history, when the "Big Four"—Justices Cooley, Campbell, Graves, and Christiancy—served on the bench. The two courts are similar because of the integrity of their judicial method—which is textual and restrained. Again, the aim is to seek out the original meaning of a statute or the Constitution, and to be guided by the words that are in the law, not by some "penumbra" or social agenda.

That is consistent with the thinking of Hamilton, Madison, and the framers of our U.S. Constitution. Recall that at the Constitutional Convention of 1787, the framers rejected proposals to set up an activist judiciary three separate times. Later, in *Marbury v. Madison*, Chief Justice Marshall opined that the act of judicial review would be—and by implication should be—rare. He was correct: judicial review would be rare in America for a long time. Justices Holmes and Brandeis and others carried the banner of judicial restraint for later generations.

Unfortunately, a creeping activism crept into the judiciary at the federal and the state level, and it was reinforced by trendy professors in the law schools. By the late 1960s, the judiciary was usurping legislatures' authority and veritably dictating public policy on issues ranging from bussing to abortion.

One of the key achievements of the Reagan Revolution was to bring the idea of judicial restraint back into public discourse, and to ratify the idea with the appointment of outstanding jurists like Antonin Scalia and, later, Clarence Thomas. Chief Justice Rehnquist has also been solid. Even the contentious Bork hearings in the fall of 1987 gave our nation a much-needed tutorial in competing judicial philosophies.

I go through this all-too-brief historical recap to make the point that we cannot take the ideal of judicial restraint for granted. It is absolutely vital to the health of our constitutional republic. It transcends partisan politics, but needs protection by and within our political process.

For the record, the current Michigan Supreme Court has rendered decisions that in some cases run counter to my policies or social philosophy, but they are nevertheless excellent decisions.

Why? Precisely because they stick to interpreting the law as *written*. They are fulfilling the duty our Founders envisioned for the judiciary.

Now, if that is the definition of a "judicial conservative," then I seek judicial conservatives for the High Court. It is important to understand that a judicial conservative is not the same thing as a political conservative. Political conservatives are advocates of certain public policy or social outcomes. Not the judicial conservative. Judicial conservatives liken their role to that of an umpire. Others play the game; the judge calls the balls and strikes.[504]

*

Budget crisis

What a pair of bookends—budget bookends, that is. John Engler's first year as governor was marked by a budget crisis and actual deficit. Engler's last year as governor was marked by a budget crisis and potential deficit. 2002 and 2003 would be extremely difficult years for state budget planners because revenues were down from projections and cuts were necessary. Michigan did not face the challenge alone. By the end of the '02 fiscal year, 45 other states were also facing deficits, to the collective tune of $40 billion. In the '03 fiscal year, deficits nationwide were projected to balloon to more than $50 billion.[505]

Every year that he was governor, Engler's negotiating skills paid off (literally) when it came time to finalize the budget. Every year, people from inside and outside the administration and from both sides of the aisle would shake their heads in wonder. Usually late on the previous night, Engler would craft a deal that would pay for public schools and cut taxes, avoid a deficit and bad press. Predictably, the next morning, word of Engler's negotiating skills would spread through the Capitol. Speechwriter Bill Nowling observed:

He did it again. But, then, he always does—year after year after year. John Engler must have an infinite number of rabbits to pull out of his hat.[506]

*

[504] *JE, "Michigan's Conservative Judiciary," speech to the Michigan Supreme Court Historical Society, at the Detroit Athletic Club, Detroit, April 18, 2002.*
[505] *Sources: National Governors Association and National Conference of State Legislatures, August 2002.*
[506] *Bill Nowling, interview with GW, July 3, 2002.*

Education

Rusty Hills

It's always struck me as strange that so many in the education establishment hate John Engler. They should give him more credit. From 1990 on, Engler said that he intended to be the education governor, and he has certainly earned the right to that title. Michigan children in 2002 are receiving a better education than Michigan children in 1990 did. The test scores prove it.

Also look at education funding during Engler's tenure. The Michigan Education Association does not want you to know this, but Michigan public schools have more money than public schools in just about every other state, and they have more real dollars now than at any time in the past. I'd challenge every lobbyist at the MEA to look at a little history. From 1837 [the year Michigan became a state] to 1990, our K-12 budget went from $0 to $7.9 billion. From 1990 to 2002, our K-12 budget went from $7.9 billion to $14 billion. Look at those numbers again. It took 150 years to reach the $7 billion mark—and just 12 years to hit the $14 billion mark. On Engler's watch, education spending almost doubled. It's time the education lobby quit whining.[507]

*

Lucille Taylor

I think one issue that continues to be foremost in the governor's mind is education. He gets a bad rap for education, which is very unfair. He thinks about it all of the time. He is like a parent who has provoked a child into performing better, rather than coddling the child. As a result, the public school system is performing better every year. It is a huge bureaucracy that needed a kick in the pants. John Engler was willing to give it that kick in the pants. That's one of his greatest achievements.[508]

*

12 Years of Achievement

During his last months in office, this document served as John Engler's official biography posted on the www.michigan.gov Web site.

First elected in 1990 as Michigan's 46th governor, Governor John Engler is now America's most senior governor. Engler was elected chairman of the National Governors Association in August 2001.

[507] *Rusty Hills, interview with GW, May 24, 2002.*
[508] *Lucille Taylor, interview with GW, September 27, 1999.*

A common sense Midwestern conservative who believes strongly that every child should have the chance to succeed, Engler has made improving education Michigan's number one priority. With boldness and vision for the future, Governor Engler also cut taxes, reformed welfare, right-sized government and implemented the biggest road repair and rebuilding plan in state history. Under his watch, the quality of Michigan's water, land, and air resources has steadily improved.

In 1994, Engler led the fight to enact Proposal A—a ballot proposal overwhelmingly approved by voters to fund schools fairly and cut property taxes. Now, all children have a foundation grant that follows them to the public schools of their choice, including more than 180 charter public schools. With funding issues resolved, high standards and rigorous assessments have helped improve student performance. To encourage academic achievement, Governor Engler created the Michigan Merit Award—a $2,500 scholarship for college or training—that is awarded to high school students who pass their proficiency tests in reading, writing, science, and math.

Governor Engler has signed 32 tax cuts into law, saving taxpayers nearly $32 billion. The state inheritance tax and capital gains taxes have been eliminated. Personal exemptions for children, seniors, and the disabled have been increased. The personal income tax rate is being reduced to 3.9 percent—the lowest level in a quarter century—and Michigan's main tax on business is being phased out completely.

Engler's economic policies have helped to create more than 800,000 jobs in Michigan, cutting the state's unemployment rate from over 9 percent the year he took office to 3.4 percent in 2000—the lowest annual level ever recorded. For an unprecedented five years in a row, Michigan has led the nation with the most new factories and expansion projects. As part of the nation's most forward-looking economic development strategy, $1 billion is being invested in a "Life Sciences Corridor" from Ann Arbor to Grand Rapids, and a high-tech cybercourt to hear business disputes is also in the works. In addition, Governor Engler's NextEnergy initiative is positioning Michigan to be an international cluster of innovation in the development and commercialization of alternative energy technologies, including hydrogen fuel cells.

Governor Engler has strengthened Michigan's role as guardian of the Great Lakes, fought water diversions, and invested more in clean water than any governor. Thanks to reforms of environmental laws, Michigan leads the nation in reclaiming contaminated brownfield sites while preserving green space and farmland.

Other highlights of the Engler administration include:

- passing the $675 million Clean Michigan Initiative to reduce pollution, fix up state parks, improve water quality, and clean up contaminated sites;
- trimming state government personnel by more than 20 percent (excluding state troopers, prison guards, and other public safety workers);
- transforming the $1.8 billion deficit he inherited to a $1.3 billion surplus;
- restoring Michigan's AAA credit rating [on Wall Street];
- helping nearly 300,000 families achieve independence from cash welfare, and reducing welfare rolls by nearly 70 percent;
- restructuring the regulation of energy and telecommunications industries to increase consumer choice and reduce rates;
- investing a record-high $1.54 billion to fix our roads in 2001 alone—more than four times the amount spent in 1990;
- reducing violent crime by more than 25 percent;
- serving an additional 45,000 patients annually with mental health services;
- giving Detroit's mayor authority to appoint the local school board and speed up the pace of reform;
- increasing K-12 education spending by 84 percent; and,
- dramatically improving student reading and math test scores.

Engler, 53, is a graduate of Michigan State University with a degree in agricultural economics and earned a law degree from the Thomas M. Cooley Law School. He was recently elected to the Board of Trustees of the Gerald R. Ford Foundation and named a Public Official of the Year by *Governing Magazine*.[509]

*

GLEAVES: Given all the achievements of the past 12 years, what was your most satisfying moment as governor?

ENGLER: The night Proposal A won.[510]

*

Farewell

Engler's twelfth and final State of the State Address, delivered January 23, 2002, in the Michigan House, was warmly received even by a number of Democrats. There were frequent interruptions by applause as the governor discussed the hydrogen economy and other visionary initiatives. Particularly striking to listeners was the conclusion, which

[509] *From the Engler administration Web site, accessed October 9, 2002.*

[510] *GW, personal papers, September 2002.*

served as John Engler's farewell to the legislature and to politics. Many people in the chamber and the TV audience had never seen the governor so emotional. Following is the conclusion of the speech.

My fellow citizens: You have given me one of the greatest privileges a citizen can ever hope for: to serve you and our state. Over the last three decades, it has been my honor to serve as a member of the House, a member of the Senate and Senate majority leader, and, since 1991, as your governor.

Each of us who serves here is greatly changed by the experience. My appreciation for public service has grown with each office I have held.

I believe with all my heart that public service remains an important and noble calling. I love this beautifully restored state Capitol. This Capitol is our seat of government and the symbol of a great ideal, the ideal that we are capable of self-government under the rule of law. Look at this fabulous ceiling, at the seals of 50 sovereign states. They remind us that we are, first and foremost, a nation of states—strong, vigorous, independent states. That's what makes America great.

Tonight, as I complete my final State of the State message, I have many, many memories. My career began 31 years ago this month when I took the oath of office in this chamber.

I see Chief Justice Tom Brennan, who administered that oath and went on to found the Thomas Cooley Law School, which also became an important part of my life. Judge Brennan recently announced his retirement after a marvelous and distinguished career in public service. Tom, we wish you godspeed and congratulations!

I see Carol Viventi, who is now the Secretary of the Senate. Thirty-one years ago, she was my first and only legislative employee. A little later on, Carol actually became my classmate and my savior in getting through law school. Carol, thanks for sharing all the notes!

Dick Posthumus is here, my first campaign manager and my successor as Senate majority leader. Dick, thank you for your friendship. Sometimes I think, if only everybody in East Shaw Hall could see us now.

I see Senator Harry Gast, my freshman classmate, and the last member serving from the class of '71. Harry's 19-year chairmanship of the Senate Appropriations Committee is a record that will never, ever be matched. I am fond of telling folks that Harry and I have gone to work together every day for 31 years. Harry, of course, is fond of saying: "John, I'll never let you forget where you came from." Harry, thanks!

I see my mother, my family, nieces and nephews. This family has been through a lot—campaigns, the ups and downs, and the loss of their privacy.

Governor Engler at the annual troop review, Camp Grayling. SOURCE: *Engler administration*

Their support has never wavered. I love them and I am very proud of them.

So many colleagues, so many friends, so many, many memories. We all came to this Capitol because we shared a goal—we wanted a better Michigan. We came from across our state, from all walks of life, converging under this dome to stand up for what we believe in. Over the years, we waged many a lively battle, the rough and tumble of democracy. No matter what the outcome, we were always fighting for a better Michigan.

I will always, always treasure my memories and cherish my friends. I thank you all. God bless you, and God bless the great state of Michigan.[511]

*

Gleaves Whitney

It was a tearful farewell. The governor's voice faltered several times. Everybody but the most hardened critics must have felt a lump in the throat. Moments after the address, as I began to circulate on the House floor, Sharon Rothwell and I eyed each other.

[511] *JE, final State of the State Address, January 23, 2002.*

She raised a hand to her forehead. "There's no way he could come back and do a farewell address," she said. "It would tear him up—he would never get through it."[512]

[512] *GW, personal papers, January 23, 2002.*

PART III

What Kind of Legacy?

Sometimes party loyalty asks too much.
JOHN F. KENNEDY

★

Chapter Sixteen
Democrats and Opponents

The experience of interviewing more than 150 people for this documentary biography revealed strikingly different perceptions of John Engler. In the next three chapters, assessments—of Engler as a man, politician, and party leader—are grouped according to the vocation or perspective of the speaker. It obviously makes a difference whether the person is a Democrat (Chapter Sixteen) or Republican (Chapter Eighteen), or a journalist or analyst (Chapter Seventeen). Not surprisingly, there are quite different perceptions even within each group. Following are the perspectives of 10 Democrats.

Frank Kelley was Michigan's attorney general from 1961 to 1998, the longest-serving AG in the United States.

I served as attorney general for 37 years, so I had the opportunity to work with five governors—and 27 of those years were with Republican governors. I was their attorney.

John Engler was a very strong governor. He used the office and its powers to the maximum. He was adroit at knowing what he could do politically. He completely understood government, having been in the legislature for 20 years. And he was the first governor to fully use the executive powers given to the office by the Constitution of 1963.

Because of his knowledge, experience, and courage, he had some remarkable successes in accomplishing his agenda.[513]

[513]*Frank Kelley, interview with GW, October 1, 2002.*

*

Gary Owen was Democratic speaker of the House from 1982-1988, when Engler presided over the Senate as minority then majority leader.

What has made John Engler a dangerous politician was that he was tenacious; he was persistent; he was a survivor. He wouldn't give up on any issue that he felt strongly about. Best example: his campaign against Blanchard. The polls showed he would lose big. But he had the tenacity to stay in there and convince people he was a viable candidate. I give John a lot of credit for that.

In many ways John Engler has been extremely successful. He came into politics when the Republican Party was very weak. His construction of the Republican Party will never be rivaled in our lifetime, or maybe in Michigan history. No one but John could have made it the partisan machine it is today. When John started out, all he had were a few votes in the Senate. But look at state government today—the Supreme Court, the House, the Senate. They are Republican. That did not happen by accident. John Engler made it happen.

As governor, John has done a relatively good job. His major accomplishment was Proposal A. That took a lot of tenacity. It made sense to shift taxation from the income tax to the sales tax.

But in other areas I don't think John did enough. He delayed the road tax too long because of his flirtation with national politics in 1996. I think you'd have a hard time arguing that other areas are much better today than they were when he took over. Look at the state budget, at our school systems, at the cost of higher education, and at the services state government provides. Is it *substantially* better today than 12 years ago?[514]

*

Lew Dodak was Democratic speaker of the House from 1989 to 1992, when Engler was Senate majority leader and then a new governor.

John Engler was a tough negotiator. At times he beat me up pretty good. But I liked him—always have. I never lost respect for him. He is strong. He knows that if he holds the line on an issue, he will win.

John was elected governor when people were against incumbents. I give him credit. He not only got himself elected; he got himself re-elected. He was successful because he was tough; he made bold stands. The people of Michigan wanted a leader who had the intestinal fortitude to make tough decisions, even if they didn't agree with the decisions. That is why John was so successful. He

[514]*Gary Owen, interview with GW, July 8, 2002.*

had the guts to make tough decisions. People admired him for that. Legislators in my own caucus admired him for that.

What is John Engler's legacy? Well, he had a good economy for 10 years. A governor can do a lot with a good economy. John once told me he wanted to be the education governor. I don't think he has been—or will be. It's true that he has had an impact because of Proposal A. But only time will tell if kids are really smarter and schools are truly better. John has also had an impact on welfare reform—but then Clinton was able to steal some of the Republicans' thunder on that issue. John has definitely downsized government—but that was made possible by Ronald Reagan years before. John did cut regulations—but don't people want regulations after there has been abuse? Look at what is happening on Wall Street today: Enron, WorldCom, Arthur Anderson, and all the rest. People are justified in calling for more regulations. These are the ordinary peaks and valleys of politics.

I think John Engler will be remembered as one of Michigan's stronger governors. He will be remembered as a governor who was willing to make tough stands and fight for them to the finish. I think history will treat him well.[515]

*

David Hollister, proudly liberal, represented Lansing in the Michigan House from 1974-1993.

John Engler is a complex person. On the one hand, he called me this morning to ask about my health. He didn't have to do that. I was flattered. It was a nice gesture, very touching. On the other hand, I don't consider him a personal friend. He's helped the city of Lansing out in a lot of ways, but always behind the scenes. If I were to say, "Governor, if you were to help us with this performing arts center, we will name it the Engler Performing Arts Center." He would laugh and turn down the offer to name it after him. But—he would still help.

Engler has an extraordinary ability: it's to polarize and then to position himself on the side of the majority. He's got the best political radar of anybody I've ever met. He makes issues black and white. If you look at the big issues Engler won on, he won by being brutal, by being determined, by polarizing, and by running over his enemies.

[515] *Lew Dodak, interview with GW, July 10, 2002.*

I was probably Engler's biggest antagonist in his early years. He made what I thought were ideological decisions, not pragmatic decisions. John went about governing in a way that was brutal, and I took him on. He was considered a maverick among the old-style Republicans. They resented him and thought he was a wild man.

Ironically, because of that we shared similar traits, which is probably why we didn't get along back then. Now that I am mayor and John is governor, we have a good relationship.

In fact, I think if you went across the street [to the Romney Building, where the governor's office is] and asked John Engler what he thought about Dave Hollister, he'd say, "I think he is crazy as hell, but he's smart, loyal, and gets his job done." And I feel the same way about him.

I look at Engler from lots of angles. As a politician, he is tough and has the ability to get things done. In this sense, he has been successful by any criteria. I admire him for that. But as a leader, he doesn't inspire people. You won't find many people who want their kids to grow up and be like him. He commands respect. But he is not warm. He does not connect on an emotional level.

Every president since Lyndon Johnson has run against the government. People don't see the government as a partner. They see the government not as an agent of good but as something that has to be controlled and downsized. Even Clinton talked this way. Engler has always been a master at playing on that kind of visceral distrust in government.[516]

*

Lana Pollack was a liberal Democratic senator from Ann Arbor.

I think John Engler lacks soul. While he compensates brilliantly with his political agility, and has been recognized for his support of the arts, I doubt that he has the capacity to be moved by nature or human artistic creativity. His prodigious political accomplishments are achieved without ever really connecting to the God-given beauty of this splendid state or to the souls of the people who live here. Life for John Engler must be seen through some amazing three-dimensional chessboard with every element a potential political move, and none of them a reflection of nature's grace.

[516] *David Hollister, interview with GW, March 29, 2001.*

I think John Engler has a love of power. He must have long ago recognized and appreciated his own extraordinary capacities for political gamesmanship. Like a great artist who discovers he's better than the rest of his peers, John Engler knows he's a star. He is not hesitant to test the boundaries between his will and the weakness of his opponents. He takes full advantage of his own political prowess.

John Engler always had a way to get what he wanted. He's just that smart and just that ballsy to take any advantage he conceives of, with or without the constraints of ideology, tradition, or honor.

Success in opposing John Engler had to be realized on his own terms. He was a masterful negotiator. After Gary Owen left, Engler never had a match on the Democratic side. My caucus, which could have withheld "immediate effect" on bills as negotiating chips, never had the discipline to do so, leaving us pretty emasculated as negotiators. Engler could always reach enough Democratic senators to put them on his side when needed.

A largely lazy, understaffed, and compliant press corps removed much possibility that he'd be subjected to public censure for his actions either as majority leader or governor. As majority leader and governor, he often outworked and outsmarted his opposition, and once his power was consolidated (after Speaker Owen retired and gifted the speakership to an inept successor), Engler added threats of retribution. Together this was a powerful cocktail that tended to render his opposition almost inert. I think it must have almost become too easy, even boring for John Engler to run state politics. I assume that only Ed McNamara was left to challenge him, and eventually even that challenge was removed when the governor and Ed found it in their interests to carve up the spoils and call a truce.

I spent seven years building a coalition and a grass roots movement to pass the "polluter pay" bills. I always thought Engler, as majority leader, felt that he could ignore my efforts, and that I'd never be able to pull it off. I think he gave it little thought until the coalition and the momentum (and Governor Blanchard's rather late-blooming enthusiasm) made it apparent that we were going to pull it together. Then Engler simply made the legislation his own, cutting his deals with the ever up-for-grabs House Democratic committee chairman, and throwing in an opportunity for a Republican committee chairman to steal and seal the legislation I'd introduced seven years earlier. So the polluter pay bills passed without my sponsorship. But five years later, when Engler pushed for the law's repeal, the now-rejected legislation magically became mine again.

On a superficial level at least, John Engler had good manners. I believe he seldom raised his voice (in my presence at least), and he wrote nice condolence notes when people were suffering personal losses. But his character was lacking an apparent capacity to feel the pain of people hurt, or nature damaged, by his actions. Did he ever lose sleep over the mental patients that were tossed out on the street or, more accurately, into obviously substandard group homes? Did he feel anguish that the children of poor single mothers suffered the consequences of going untended in bad daycare situations? Did he ever grieve the lasting damage his political favorites were able to inflict on Michigan's environment? I doubt it.

John Engler consolidated the power of the executive beyond the scope of anyone's imagination (other than his). It will be interesting to see if his successors manage to hang on to that legacy.

I think his best legacy was to break the back of the property tax base as an increasingly uneven funder of Michigan public schools.

On the negative side, he diminished, if not decimated, a nationally respected professional cadre of civil servants. His outsourcing and downsizing of government leaves gaping holes in essential services. My friends in the children's advocacy, public health, and mental health fields were previously unpolitical but now highly critical of the loss of services and the dismantling of systems that, while imperfect, saved many lives and improved the quality of lives of the mentally and physically ill.

As for the environment and natural resources, John Engler brought down a department that was largely led by people of education and integrity, driving many of them to early retirement and replacing the leadership with political hacks. He reduced important decisions to political equations, cost future generations thousands of acres of wetlands, stalled out the clean up of Great Lakes hot spots, initiated a brownfield cleanup program with so many compromises that the public health of the poor is damaged and the middle class is reluctant to move back into the cites. Our water is dirtier, our air less healthy, and our sand dunes and landscape damaged in ways that simple straightforward enforcement of existing state and federal legislation would have precluded. Engler's environmental legacy is a sad reflection of what I call his soullessness, his apparent inability to connect with the intangible magnificence of the land and water which fell under his control.[517]

[517]*Lana Pollack, interview with GW, July 30, 2002.*

*

Art Miller, a fairly conservative Democrat from Macomb County—home of the "Reagan Democrats"—served in the Senate from 1977-2002 and was minority leader during Proposal A.

Before John became governor, the top two questions people in Macomb County wanted answers to were: When are you going to lower our property taxes? And when are you going to cut welfare rolls? As governor John tackled both of those problems—very well from this Democrat's perspective. Because of Proposal A, there has been a tremendous housing boom. And thousands of people across the state have a lower monthly house payment, largely because of John Engler.

Proposal A also helped level the playing field in our schools. I think Proposal A was one of the best pieces of legislation this state has ever seen. It has helped a lot of people and restored a lot of confidence. The governor was a big engineer in putting it together. In terms of legacy, that will be regarded as one of the best pieces of legislation he ever signed.

After his welfare reforms were in place, there were no mass demonstrations and people weren't starving. Because of John Engler, people who had been on welfare gained confidence because they went to work.

I give John credit. In the 1980s he saved the Republican Party, which in the 1970s had been on the verge of collapse. He was visionary and understood that times were changing. He is one of Michigan's better governors.[518]

*

Alma Wheeler Smith, a Democratic senator, attracted a reporter's attention.

State Sen. Alma Wheeler Smith, D-Salem Township, one of the more liberal Democrats in the race for governor, put a surprise twist on a recent speech to students at the University of Michigan-Dearborn.

She held up Republican Gov. John Engler as a role model—sort of.

"One of the things that made John Engler so successful is that he knew the legislative process," she says. "He knew how to move money, he knew the system...."

She also borrows the Engler model in responding to skeptics in the audience, acknowledging that her candidacy is barely registering in the polls and that her resources are limited....

[518] *Art Miller, interviews with GW, September 19 and 25, 2002.*

"If John Engler had listened to the polls in 1989, 1990," Smith says, borrowing a quote from [Dave] Bonior, "he'd be milking cows in Beal City."[519]

*

Al Short has long been a part of the leadership at the Michigan Education Association.

John is the most pragmatic politician I've ever come into contact with. He is not a hard-line person to the right; he is not a libertarian. He does what he needs to do to respond to a particular situation. If he has to be hard-nosed, he will be; if he can be soft, he will be. He is not ideological at all.

John is what I call a divide-and-conquer politician. He will look at the situation and say, "Where is the wedge in the opposition that I can use to get this particular thing through." He is very skillful at that. He'll take people of like beliefs and play one against the other and get them fighting. Then he'll slip in between and get his way. He is a master at that.

There were two major instances in John's time in Lansing when he took advantage of the Democrats' mistakes and was able to propel his political career forward. One occurred in 1983 when he made the shrewdest political move of his career. He took advantage of the backlash against Blanchard's income tax increase and the recall of two Democratic senators. This led to Republicans gaining the majority in the Senate, which set him up to run for governor in 1990.

Then in 1993 he took advantage of the opportunity presented by Debbie Stabenow in the Senate. She didn't even understand what she was doing when she introduced an amendment to wipe out the *ad valorem* [property] tax for schools. John Engler said to his caucus, "Go for it," and caught all of us off guard. I give him tremendous credit for it.[520]

*

Carolyn Stieber, the professor who graded that term paper back in 1970, confessed (with a smile) that she is a Democrat and has never voted for her former student. But she had this to say about John Engler and his career:

I am a Democrat. I did not vote for John when he ran for governor. However, in the last election, I could not bring myself to vote for Fieger either, so I suppose my not voting for the Democrat was a vote for John. I have by no means

[519]*Darcy McConnell, "Underdog Democrat Relies on Know-How,"* Detroit News, *March 5, 2002, p. D1.*
[520]*Al Short, interview with GW, February 26, 2001.*

agreed with everything John has done. But if I had to grade his 32 years in government, I would give him an "A."

John has done a number of things that have been very affirmative for the state of Michigan. One of them is Proposal A, regarding school funding. It has been nationally recognized. Without John's leadership, it would never have been adopted.

Also, we are much less dependent on the automotive industry than we were in the past. When I first came to Michigan, I noticed how dependent the state was on the success of the auto industry. When there was a downturn in the industry the whole state felt it, and during those times it was awful to live here. But in recent years John has worked hard with others to decrease our state's dependence on the auto industry.

I also think he has shown some independence from his supporters—for example, in his recent stance on vouchers. The way he stood up and said that vouchers would not play well in 2000 must have disappointed many Republicans. That took courage. I also thought the way he stood up and led welfare reform was crucial; reform were needed in that area.

John has certainly risen to a national leadership role. He is currently one of the best known, articulate governors in the country. When there was much talk about his possible nomination to the vice-presidential ticket of Bob Dole in 1996, I was prepared to go to Sotheby's to auction off the term paper that I had been hanging on to! In all seriousness, my view of John Engler is that he has been at the forefront of the fifty governors of the United States; other governors have recognized his leadership role. He became a prominent figure nationally.

*

Jim Hunt was the Democratic governor of North Carolina from 1977-1985, and from 1993-2000.

John and I served together on many NGA [National Governors Association] panels and education summits. He was one of the brightest governors in the land. He also was one of the most energetic, dynamic, passionate governors—always looking for ways to improve his state, especially when it came to education. At our meetings he showed great curiosity and wanted to learn how other states were improving. He was always wondering what reforms would work back in Michigan. He himself had very good ideas on how to improve education, and he possessed great zeal and energy in pushing education reform forward. I especially admired John's leadership and courage in changing school finance back in 1993 and '94.

In 1996, I thought John had all the qualities to be a terrific vice president. People knew that he knew what he was talking about—he had a grasp of all the issues from the ground up. John had a tremendous impact on the debates in Washington in the mid '90s.

John is a man of strong ideas and he is willing to fight for his ideas. He would push hard when he thought he was right. But—he was always personable with the other governors, always open to new ideas, always willing to work with both parties. John was a great representative of all the governors in the United States. I hope that he will continue to provide leadership in education, where he has done so much good. [521]

[521] *James Hunt, interview with GW, September 30, 2002.*

Whenever the press quits abusing me I know I'm in the wrong pew.
I don't mind it because when they throw bricks at me—
I'm a pretty good shot myself and I usually throw 'em back at 'em.
HARRY S. TRUMAN

★

Chapter Seventeen
Journalists and Analysts

What is the assessment of John Engler by those who have covered him for many years in newspapers, magazines, and journals of opinion?

David Broder, columnist for the Washington Post, *interviewed Engler during his last summer in office and wrote this article.*

CONSERVATIVE LEAVES PROGRESSIVE LEGACY
MICHIGAN GOVERNOR LED SCHOOL FINANCE REFORM
SEEN AS MODEL OF EQUITY, INNOVATION

As John Engler approaches the end of his 12 years as governor of Michigan, the great paradox is that this Republican, described by both friend and foe as the most conservative governor in a half-century, should leave as the centerpiece of his legacy a progressive reform in school finance that has become a national model of equity and innovation.

Interviews with Democrats and Republicans here confirm that Engler, who just stepped down as chairman of the National Governors Association and leaves office at the end of the year, also has, like his hero Ronald Reagan, set a model of strong executive leadership his successor may find it difficult to match....

That leadership has helped reshape the Michigan economy from its dependence on the auto industry to a much more diverse and growing mix, and it has brought significant change—much of it still controversial—in urban, welfare and environmental policies.

But Engler himself and almost all his allies and critics agree that nothing the 53-year-old farmer's son has done will be of greater significance to his state than the conversion of the Michigan school system....

The basic change was made eight years ago, but Engler has pushed for higher school spending each year and for reforms in the system that have created 190 charter schools and a process of inter-district transfers, making public school choice a reality for about 100,000 pupils. Engler and his allies also claim that the reduction in property taxes has been a major factor in a pattern of economic growth that kept Michigan's unemployment rate below the national average for most of the past decade—though it is climbing in the current industrial recession.

The job growth has not been evenly spread, and cities such as Flint and Detroit still face serious problems. But former Detroit mayor Dennis Archer, a Democrat, who backed Engler on the state's controversial ouster of the city's elected school board, said that the governor was "very forceful in getting help" for the city's efforts to clean up polluted "brownfields" sites and allow new employers to come in without assuming liability for past contamination. Even though Detroit is overwhelmingly Democratic, Archer said, "Engler understands he is governor of the whole state, and if its largest city does not do well, the state will not do well."

State Sen. Robert L. Emerson (D), who comes from Flint, has alternately battled and compromised with Engler, and he has come to think of the governor as "a tireless worker who is determined to change both his party and his state."

"He has difficulty dealing with people who oppose him," Emerson said, "but he's as tough on his [GOP] friends as he is on us. And in the end, it hasn't cost him much. People see the results, and they mostly like what they see."

Republican pollster Robert Teeter confirms that view and adds, "He has run over a lot of people, but that's because if there is a tough problem, he takes it on. There is plenty of legitimate disagreement, but no one could argue he has not been very competent and very strong."

When Engler was asked how a self-described conservative could have brought so much change—along with controversy—his answer was indirect. "All those years I spent in the minority in the legislature, I could see that Michigan was being stymied by its refusal to change. But I could also see what was possible—if we did change."

His model was clear, he said. "Ronald Reagan had the best attitude. He approached each issue in terms of what was achievable. But he never forgot—or let anyone else forget—the direction he knew we had to move. I've tried to do that here."[522]

[522]*David S. Broder, "Conservative Leaves Progressive Legacy: Michigan Governor Led School Finance Reform Seen as Model of Equity, Innovation,"* Washington Post, *July 28, 2002, p. A4.*

*

Tom Bray, former editorial page editor and current columnist for the Detroit News, *said in an interview:*

John Engler is, on balance, a terrific governor and one of the nation's premier politicians. Michigan is a lot better off because of his leadership. He is one of the rare politicians who actually has a vision and also the political skills to get there.

If he has a weakness, it's that he doesn't suffer fools gladly. (On second thought, perhaps this is not a weakness.) I think he has sometimes offended people by treating them brusquely.[523]

*

Bray's July 14, 2002, column in the Detroit News *summed up Engler's legacy this way:*

The conventional wisdom about this year's gubernatorial race in Michigan seems to be that the electorate is tired of John Engler and looking for a change....

Meanwhile, the three Democratic contenders—former Gov. James Blanchard, Congressman David Bonior and Attorney General Jennifer Granholm—regularly criticize the Engler record and say the time has come to return to a kinder, gentler politics.

It's possible, though, that voters will have a different view. If you stand back from the immediate political fray and consider the overall Engler record, as well as the character of the man who has dominated Michigan politics for 12 years—and, in some ways, for far more than 12 years—the real problem for the candidates may be to prove that they are worthy of inheriting the Engler mantle.

Quite a mantle it is.

John Engler came into office facing a budget deficit of well more than $1 billion, but he delivered on his promise of tax cuts. And he has kept on delivering—[more than] 30 tax cuts in all. Many of those cuts were small, incremental affairs. And much of their impact has been offset by hikes in sales taxes, gas taxes and now the cigarette tax. A portion of the rollback in the Single Business Tax has been placed on hold because of the current economic slowdown.

But by the time Engler leaves office, the individual income tax will stand at 4 percent, down from 4.4 percent when he took office in 1990—and peaked at 6.3 percent.

[523]*Tom Bray, interview with GW, July 3, 2002.*

Engler took office pledging welfare reform—and again he delivered, first ending Michigan's General Assistance program for able-bodied adults and then leading the national effort to require work in return for welfare checks. Critics predicted social catastrophe. Instead, more Michiganians than ever were soon at work, and welfare rolls, which used to grow in good times and bad, have been cut to a fraction of their former level.

Engler came into office promising educational reform—and once more he delivered, most notably with Proposal A in 1994. Through a legislative masterstroke (in which Lt. Gov. Posthumus, then the Senate majority leader, played a key role), Engler achieved something that had eluded Lansing for decades: a sharp reduction in property taxes in return for a two-cent increase in sales taxes. Proposal A also went far to reducing gross disparities in school funding across the state.

And unlike many chief executives who seem to burn out after a few years, Engler has been the Energizer Bunny of Michigan politics right up to the end. He reorganized much of state government, brought it into the Internet age, placed a sizeable bet on Michigan's future as a leader in bio-sciences, appointed large numbers of very able people to the state judiciary, axed thousands of needless and unproductive regulations, and brought long-overdue reform to Detroit's public schools.

Yes, he was often confrontational. And, yes, he could be very partisan—he worked hard to produce a Republican legislature and Republican-dominated Supreme Court that would be sure to approve a Republican redistricting plan.

But you always knew where you stood with Engler. And there is a reason that Democrats had so much difficulty fielding challengers to Engler: Voters may not have found him very warm and fuzzy, but they saw in him a tough politician willing to take on the tough issues. They said he lacked charisma, but that wasn't true either: His charisma derived from the fact that he was a consequential man.

The story isn't over quite yet, of course. But so far there are lessons aplenty in the Engler legacy for his would-be successors.[524]

*

Craig Ruff is the president of Public Sector Consultants, a private firm in Lansing.

John Engler is an historic figure, and I don't use that phrase lightly. Probably 50 to 100 years from now, those who write textbooks about Michigan politics and history will list only a few individuals as being our strongest governors:

[524] *Tom Bray, "How Engler's Legacy Influences Campaign,"* Detroit News, *July 14, 2002.*

Stevens T. Mason, Alex Groesbeck, Soapy Williams, and John Engler. They are the top four.

Engler was transformed by, and transformed, Michigan politics. He led public opinion far more than most politicians, which is a hallmark of leadership. Leaders change the landscape. Like Margaret Thatcher, Engler never took the easy way out. He was not afraid of battle. He took controversial stands and let the public come to his position.

Undeniably, Engler left a major imprint on the most revolutionary public policy change in decades: school finance reform.[525]

*

Lawrence Reed served as president of the Mackinac Center for Public Policy during the entire time John Engler was governor.

During the '80s and certainly by 1991, John Engler became increasingly committed to a consistent set of ideas—free-market ideas. That's why he was the catalyst for creating the Mackinac Center. I think in time something like the Mackinac Center would have been started by someone. But the fact is, John Engler was the man who felt strongly enough about the need for a Michigan-based think tank to approach people who had the horsepower to bring it about.

I respect John a lot for backing off after the Center was established and for letting it do its thing as an independent entity. It was wise of him. I always felt independent. I can honestly say to the press that he was never calling the shots; he was never on the board; he never told the board what it ought to issue studies on; nor did he pull any strings to steer us in any one direction or another. He never called me to ask what I thought about a particular piece of legislation.

However, because we were on the same wavelength, I think the Center contributed significantly to developing the administration's policies in such areas as privatization and welfare reform; our studies provided the intellectual ammunition to support reforms that were sorely needed.

Over the years, especially after the first term, the relationship between John Engler and the Mackinac Center went through some ups and downs. One major disagreement was over the creation of MEGA [Michigan Economic Growth Authority]. Another was over the education ballot proposal in 2000 [vouchers].

John's actions made me realize that he is less of a movement builder and more of a party builder. Party building is an important role for the governor to

[525]*Craig Ruff, interview with GW, July 3, 2002.*

play, but if he were a true movement builder, he would not have opposed needed education proposals, or he would have done so in a way that would not set the movement back. Instead, he chose to pursue his policies in a particularly hurtful way.

And yet, when I evaluate all the governors, I give John Engler an above average grade. If I only look at recent Michigan governors like Blanchard and Milliken, he would score even better. In the first term especially, John was a breath of fresh air. He made a substantial difference for the better in many areas. I have a high regard for his overall record. He will clearly go down in history as one of the best governors in the twentieth century. His three terms will be known as the "Engler era."[526]

*

Just about every year he was governor, Engler was given the grade of "B" by the Cato Institute, a free-market oriented, Washington, DC, think tank. Here was the explanation in 2000.

During the 1990s, John Engler earned a reputation as one of the nation's preeminent policy pioneers at the state level in areas ranging from welfare reform, to charter schools, to privatization, to growth-oriented tax reduction. When Engler took over the statehouse in 1991, Michigan was in a spiral of economic decline. The unemployment rate was about twice the national average. The state budget had a $1.5 billion deficit. Michigan was considered the epicenter of America's rust belt. Businesses were leaving the state for more capital-friendly environments. Engler initiated many policies that turned the state around, but tax cuts and welfare reform were by far the most significant. Engler was one of the first governors to impose work requirements for welfare and to end general welfare assistance for 80,000 employable adults. The Michigan welfare rolls fell by 70 percent in the 1990s under Engler—making this state number two in the success of welfare reform efforts. To create more jobs, Engler has cut taxes more than 25 times for a cumulative taxpayer savings of $12 billion. The income tax has been cut by nearly a full percentage point. The average property tax for school funding has fallen from 36 mills to 6 mills—an 80 percent decline that was accomplished in exchange for a two point increase in the state sales tax. No state has cut property taxes more than Michigan in the past decade. The tax-cutting plan seems to have worked. In 1997 and 1998 Michigan won the prestigious Governor's Cup for building the

[526]*Lawrence Reed, interview with GW, July 6, 2000.*

most new industrial plants and attracting the most new businesses, and now the unemployment rate is near 3 percent, the lowest since Ford first introduced the Mustang convertible in the mid-1960s. The budget is now running a $500 million surplus, and the state bond rating is stronger than at any time in two decades. There are only two blemishes on Engler's fiscal record. First, in recent years the economy has done so well that Engler has started to become a big spender, especially on education and unpromising economic development projects. Second, Engler has been an outspoken advocate of taxing the Internet, a curious position for such a taxpayer-friendly governor. On balance, it's hard to point to much that hasn't markedly improved during Engler's "Michigan Miracle" years.[527]

*

Tim Skubick, the dean of Lansing journalists, has covered the entire gubernatorial career of three long-serving governors—Bill Milliken (1969-1982), Jim Blanchard (1983-1990), and John Engler (1991-2002). He has long hosted public television's "Off the Record."

Let's compare John Engler with his two predecessors. Engler, by far, had the most tremendous grasp on all of the details involved in an issue. Milliken and Blanchard relied much more on advisors for the smallest of details. But Engler was his own best council on the tiniest of matters. He relished that and often knew more about budget details than the budget analysts working on them.

Engler and Milliken shared something in common: their desire for privacy. Milliken would jump in the car and head up to Traverse City every Thursday night and you wouldn't see him again until Monday afternoon. Engler was so good at it that he surprised everyone with his engagement to Michelle, and he was pretty good at keeping the triplet story out of the press for a time. On the other hand, every year that Milliken was in office, we (public TV) did a one-hour, sit-down, one-on-one that we recorded at the executive residence. When Engler came into office that stopped. We never did one "Evening with the Governor."

Milliken and Blanchard both attempted to bring Democrats into the inner office to work out differences. The so-called quadrant meetings of the four legislative leaders and governor were used by both, but to my knowledge

[527] *Stephen Moore and Stephen Slivinski, "Fiscal Policy Report Card on America's Governors: 2000,"* Policy Analysis *(Washington, DC: Cato Institute, 2000), p. 43.*

these meetings have occurred much less frequently since Engler has been in office. I don't think the hallmark of the Engler administration was molding a bipartisan working relationship—at least, not in public, the way Milliken and Blanchard did.

Engler knew when he was first elected to the House that he would run for governor—so the legend goes. While all three governors enjoyed the political game, Milliken was loathed to campaign; he found it very unappealing. Blanchard and Engler were more alike in this regard. They enjoyed working a crowd and seemed to need that fix from time to time. I remember a trooper telling the story of Engler attending an early evening event at the City Club that was over at 7:30. It was the last thing on the schedule and the troopers were ready to go home. Engler jumped in the car and announced, "Hey, there's another group meeting at the Radisson. Let's stop over there." I think Engler and Blanchard lived and breathed politics, while Milliken made a studied attempt to get away from it all.

Clearly, of the three, Engler was the one who was always several steps ahead of everyone else in a political battle. He knew the end game and how to get there, while others were still trying to figure out what the issue was. He used that to great advantage. The Stabenow property tax cut proposal is a classic illustration of Engler's skill. Democrats offered it as a lark, knowing no one would vote to eliminate school funding. Engler shocked everyone by telling Republicans, including Dick Posthumus, to go for it. It was a brilliant move which helped him get re-elected.

Engler was also a hard sell when it came to getting inside information out of him. I can recall on numerous occasions that I could get off to the side with Milliken and Blanchard and ask for some "guidance" on what was really going on, and most of the time I got it. I tried that with Engler and I consistently got the chuckle, the dodge, and a goose egg. If he didn't want you to know something, you could not get it from him. No way, no how. That made him more of a challenge to cover.

I liked and admired all three of these guys. Each had his own style and personality. I really believe under the tough exterior, John Engler is a compassionate guy with deep feelings that would surprise many if he allowed them to be seen more often in public. I have this impression that he developed an ability to build this wall around him so that the "real man" was concealed. He did it to survive the rough game of politics, where personal attacks come as frequently as ticks on a clock. His tears on election night 1990; his tears when he introduced Michelle to Connie Binsfeld and his close advisors the day after the 1990 election, and his near tears during the last State of the State Address show that those deep feelings are there, but seldom seen. I often wonder how these last 32 years might have been different had that side of John Engler been revealed more often.... He is one of a kind.[528]

*

Dawson Bell, political reporter for the Detroit Free Press, *covered Engler since his senate days.*

I've been covering John Engler for fifteen years. The first time I met him I thought, "Man, this guy really knows his shit."

For some time we journalists have been in awe of his abilities. He is so sharp on all the issues. He is always up-to-date on his information. And he is like a rock—you can't rattle him. So it is hard for the press to catch him off guard. Some may consider that to be intimidating, because unless you know everything about a given topic, you have no chance against him.

On occasion I've seen him answer a question by a reporter who really didn't know what he was talking about. Engler was brusque. His answer showed he knew the reporter didn't know what he was talking about. So the press had to be careful with the questions they asked.

Engler will also stop the press dead in their tracks if he thinks that their assumptions are incorrect. A lot of reporters are know-it-alls. They will ask a question in a way that assumes something. But if someone asks a question that is bad, he will treat it as such.

In the political arena, Engler always had a strategy. To him journalists were to be given the information needed to maximize *his* success. Engler never shared anything with me that he thought I might be able to use against him. But I never felt abused or resentful about it. I found that Engler was fun to cover because he was so damn smart and interesting.

I can say that he has never lied to me. That is what sets him apart from other politicians.

I think the best thing that Engler did for Michigan was change the mindset about the role of government. There was a time in Michigan when the assumption was that government would always get bigger and it would always tax a little more. While Engler was in office, that assumption was reversed.[529]

*

[528] *Tim Skubick, correspondence with GW, October 6, 2002.*
[529] *Dawson Bell, interview with GW, February 27, 2001.*

Chris Christoff, Lansing Bureau chief for the Detroit Free Press, *has been covering John Engler since 1987. He called Engler the "third House of the legislature."*

John Engler has set the standard for using the levers of state government to bring about change. Because of term limits, he will never be matched. He consolidated power in the executive office as no one else has. At times he was the third House of the legislature.

The seminal example is Proposal A. You go around the country to other states that have wrestled with the problem of school finance. They want to know how Michigan did it. Well, it came about in large part because of Engler's knowledge of the issues, of the legislative process, and of the members in the House and Senate.

We all know how he could twist arms and even threaten legislators when he lobbied for an outcome he was seeking. One House Republican recently described his session with Engler as "brutal." The governor wouldn't give him help with other legislation or the upcoming election if he didn't yield.

Engler will be remembered by people like me as the most effective governor —and at the same time the most disliked governor. There are people who liked what he did, but who didn't like the way he did it. They didn't like him or his style or his persona. There is a segment of the population that has regarded him as an SOB, and that perception hasn't changed. He has never lived that down. And yet, people kept voting for him. This contrasts with Soapy Williams and Bill Milliken. People had an affection for them—but not for John Engler. He always acted as if he didn't care whether he was liked or not. At least, that was journalists' perception of him.

I enjoyed covering him. In fact, one of the reasons I ended up staying in Lansing so long was because of the Engler administration. When you thought you were tired of the beat, there was always some new controversy, something around the corner that was going to blow up. Journalists thrive on conflict—I admit that—and there was plenty of conflict under John Engler.[530]

*

Matt Davis covered John Engler for the Detroit Free Press *in 1994 and 1995.*

Hunter Thompson said the media and government need each other even if they don't like each other.

Most political reporters want to cover government and public policy. But there are newspapers in Michigan—I worked for one—that have little regard

[530] *Chris Christoff, interview with GW, July 11, 2002.*

for state government because they cannot demonstrate to readers how a decision in Lansing affects readers' lives; also because the governor's views do not correspond with the editors'.

Reporters have to do a certain amount of muckraking to satisfy shareholders and bolster the bottom line. Always there is pressure to increase circulation and sell more newspapers. Reporters have to pursue questions that are not always the most germane. But John Engler understands that. He knows that they have to do some dirty work. And he accommodates them. They respect him for that.

Journalists in this town also respect John Engler because he does what he thinks is right. In his personal dealings he respects you if you're honest. Even if you disagree with him, he respects you.

However, John Engler's relationship with the media was pretty bad at first. It improved over time—he was getting much better press by the end of his first term. He didn't change; the press changed. And people's perceptions of him changed. By the end of his first term he was no longer seen as sinister. He was seen as conservative, but Michigan was doing well by 1994-1995. He was pushing policies to do good, and more and more people liked what they saw....

John Engler found his perfect conduit to the people with the Internet: here's the message, unfiltered. No reporter needed. Just think if he had had e-Michigan in 1991....

John Engler is not a slap-you-on-the-back, press-the-flesh, glad-handing politician. He keeps his personal life and even his personality private. During the time I covered him, he only joked with me once, and then with such sarcasm that I thought he was being serious. I didn't get the dry humor....

He has such a profound grasp of issues that he can speak with authority. There is nothing anybody on earth can tell John Engler about Michigan government that he doesn't already know.[531]

*

Rick Pluta has covered Engler since the late 1980s.

I arrived here in 1987 to be the full-time state Senate reporter for United Press International. John Engler was the Senate majority leader, and I had a lot of chances to watch him in action. His philosophy for running the caucus seemed to be: everyone will get to vote his or her conscience—once my desired result is ordained. The Republican caucus wasn't exactly monolithic, and

[531] *Matt Davis, interview with GW, July 9, 2002.*

Engler had his share of enemies within his own camp, but it was pretty astonishing, in retrospect, how constantly Engler got his way.[532]

*

Chris Andrews covered Engler his entire gubernatorial career and is political editor for the Lansing State Journal.

John Engler has been extraordinarily shrewd and forceful in reaching his goals. He has accomplished the vast majority of what he set out to do 12 years ago.

There is a perception, however, that he has been polarizing; that he has made enemies along the way. Teachers have been offended. State workers have been offended. Democrats have complained that they have often been ignored. There are definitely people out there who don't like him a lick.[533]

*

Henry Payne

When I give lectures and talk about my drawings, I always lead off by saying, "One of the difficulties of being an editorial cartoonist in the twenty-first century is that it's the TV age. Just about every successful, modern politician has that blow-dried look and is on a diet. The great thing about being a cartoonist in Michigan is that the governor actually looks the way a politician should look. He is fun to draw—he's been good for cartoonists."[534]

*

The Detroit Free Press *ran a three-part series at the outset of John Engler's last year as governor. This first article provides vivid insights into the man and his leadership.*

ENGLER'S MICHIGAN: A REIGN OF CHANGE

It began awkwardly and unmemorably with a hokey campaign jingle about a guy who wanted to sit at our kitchen table and listen to our troubles.

"For the future for Michigan. For me and for you.

"Just think what the right man could do.

"Just think what John Engler could do."

Music critics wanted to retch. Political analysts rolled their eyes. The general public was generally oblivious.

[532] *Rick Pluta, correspondence with GW, October 10, 2002.*
[533] *Chris Andrews, interview with GW, July 3, 2002.*
[534] *Henry Payne, interview with GW, August 5, 2002.*

That was in 1989. We weren't thinking about what John Engler could do. We didn't think he could get elected.

We had no idea.

Twelve years later, as Engler enters the final year of his final term in office, it is hard not to marvel at how wrong we were. Not about the song (former Engler campaign manager and chief of staff Dan Pero, who commissioned it, still carries a tape around in his car and remains one of its few admirers).

But about Engler.

He came into office with a mandate measured in millimeters (about one-half of 1 percent) and governed as if he had won with an FDR-like landslide.

He defied every conventional expectation Michigan held for its governors. He is not, like G. Mennen Williams or George Romney, a commanding personal presence. He has neither the charm of William Milliken nor the winsome eagerness of James Blanchard.

Even after 11 years and two landslide re-elections, Engler has never been, in the usual sense of the term, a leader beloved by the people.

But he has been incredibly busy and, for good or ill, uncommonly effective. During the Engler years, Michigan overhauled its tax and welfare systems, its schools, its finances and its governance. So much has changed that it is difficult to measure the differences against the status quo of 1990.

We found out that Engler could do things that most people thought couldn't be done.

But the question lingers: How did he do it?

The governor's vision

Grand Valley State University President Mark Murray was a top aide in the Engler administration (and before that, under Blanchard) until leaving for academic life earlier this year.

He echoed other experienced Engler watchers when he said that his old boss has a combination of skills and personal attributes rare in an elected official: smarts, a broad understanding of how government works, vision, political skill, fearlessness and resolve.

"Sometimes, there are people with great political skill and courage, but they don't have any idea where to go," Murray said. "Sometimes they know where to go but don't have any idea how to get there."

Like many who worked closely with him in times of crisis, Murray recalled Engler's utter imperturbability amid chaos. The atmosphere surrounding the overhaul of Michigan's tax structure and school reform embodied in Proposal A is a lasting memory for him.

In late 1993, following the legislature's precipitous elimination of local property taxes for school operations, Lansing's decision makers were in disarray. School lobbyists were desperate for a solution (i.e., new money from taxpayers). Special interests ferociously guarded every possible source of new revenue. School reformers wanted to expand parental choice. The politicians, with an eye on elections a year away, were trying to please all of them.

But Engler "alone had the grasp of all the political and policy implications," Murray said.

"I was in awe at how calm and focused he was throughout. He never lost his confidence that a solution could be found."

Innovative solutions

Engler's intelligence is not that of an academic or an intellectual.

He was a mostly average student. His mother, Agnes, once recalled for a reporter a run-in he had with an elderly history teacher, who tired of his smirking and repeated wisecracks in class. Her son was ordered to write a 500-word essay ... and used it to author a critique of the teacher.

Going to school part-time, the young lawmaker, who first served in the House and then the Senate, earned a law degree. Engler once said his study habits weren't stellar; he got through by cramming for exams.

But he is endlessly curious and a voracious reader. Friend and foe alike have long marveled at how comprehensively he understands a broad range of issues. In his 20 years in the legislature he soaked up knowledge about the legislative process and its arcane ground rules, learning to use them to leverage the tiniest advantage.

The result was evident in his first year as governor. When the Democrat-controlled state House balked at Engler's proposals to eliminate a billion-dollar deficit, he took them to an obscure state panel called the Administrative Board. Although authorized under an obscure provision of a 1921 state law, no governor had before exercised the power to bypass the legislature on budget matters. The Democrats howled and sued. They also returned to the negotiating table and ultimately made a deal. The lawsuit continued; Engler won.

Pero recalled watching Engler and a team of advisers put together the Administrative Board ploy and other contingencies during the post election transition of 1990. Richard McLellan, a Lansing lawyer and one of Engler's oldest friends who led the transition team, had been discussing the limits of executive authority with him for years.

"They knew the process better than anybody," Pero said.

"Their understanding of what was possible in almost every area was astounding. When they talked it was like watching Spock and the Vulcan mind meld."

Less obvious was that the stolid, conservative son of a cattle farmer also had an inventive mind.

"I was frequently surprised by his idea for a solution," Murray said.

Engler's is not a blue-sky creativity as much as a capacity to grasp an untried, but practical, solution to a vexing problem.

"He is constantly surveying the situation of Michigan and trying to find a way to make it better," Murray said.

Tenacity, self-confidence

Self-doubt has seldom been a problem for Engler.

Administration aides remember the dark, early days of his tenure as an endless siege. The budget crisis was raging out of control. Welfare advocates were camped out on the Capitol lawn. A recall campaign was under way.

Former press secretary John Truscott said he was taking 80 to 90 media calls a day, all of them negative.

"It didn't bother him," said Pero, who said his own blood would boil when he'd see welfare protesters camped on the Capitol lawn.

"He understood that it was all part of the business," Pero said of Engler. "He didn't take it personally like we did."

In his public life, Engler has seldom played defense. And he didn't then.

Amid the siege early in 1992, about the time Engler reached the nadir of his personal popularity, the Rev. Jesse Jackson came to town.

Jackson apparently thought the turmoil in Michigan would make a good backdrop for a national story about the Reagan-Bush era's tattered safety net.

Engler didn't wait in his office for Jackson to show up, however. He issued a press release saying that he looked forward to meeting Jackson so that they could discuss making Michigan a standard to which Democratic candidates for president could aspire.

Even after cutting its budget, Engler pointed out, Michigan provided more welfare benefits than the home states of that year's Democratic presidential hopefuls, including then-Arkansas Gov. Bill Clinton.

The Democrats weren't amused.

But they got used to it. Subtle, mocking sarcasm, delivered with the barest hint of irony, was an Engler trademark.

To this day, administration officials and the state GOP refer to Geoffrey Fieger—the wild man, celebrity attorney and Engler opponent whose drag on the ticket nearly handed Republicans a clean sweep in 1998—as the leader of the Michigan Democratic Party.

Of course, goading the opposition sometimes carries a price. Engler suffered perhaps the biggest setback of his career in 2000, when he failed to deliver his home state for George W. Bush in the GOP presidential primary.

Engler, described at the time by the Almanac of American Politics as the "colossus" of Michigan politics, had promised that his state would provide a "fire wall" for Bush against the insurgency of U.S. Sen. John McCain. Democrats, many of them motivated by a desire to stick it to Engler, voted in droves for McCain and handed Bush-Engler an embarrassing defeat. But stick-to-itiveness has more often served Engler well. Elected to cut property taxes, he tried and failed repeatedly before Democrats thought they could call the bluff and end the school-funding debate by offering a plan he would have to refuse. Instead, they handed him Proposal A.

Tactical skill

Almost every year-end legislative session during the Engler era culminated in an all-night debate during which 12 months' worth of thorny, intractable issues are laid on the table in a single marathon bargaining session. Exhausted lawmakers sit at their desks for hours as small groups of negotiators work behind closed doors.

The most intimidating door lies just off the entrance to each chamber on the second floor of the Capitol, tucked around a corner, and topped by a frosted glass window bearing the inscription GOVERNOR.

Engler rarely emerged from behind it during those long sessions, relying instead on his deputies to identify persuadable members and summoning them to his office.

There, he pleaded, handed out favors and, when necessary, threatened. Although the latter was often implicit, those who sat across from Engler when he wanted something did not need to be reminded of whose signature was required at the bottom of every bill and who could fix a constituent problem or create a political one with a single phone call.

Jeff McAlvey, Engler's top legislative aide for eight years, said watching his boss negotiate was a thing of wonder. Almost always, McAlvey said, Engler was better prepared. He had a more complete understanding of what was doable. And he seemed to have an unerring sense of whose votes were available to do it.

In the six years of Engler's tenure in which Democrats controlled (or shared power) in the state House (1991-94 and 1997-98), he engineered countless deals by bringing over—or buying off—a handful of moderate Democrats.

It drove the Democrats crazy. Former Rep. Pat Gagliardi, D-Drummond Island, who served as House floor leader, once tried to figure out how to lock the door to Engler's office from the outside to prevent a wavering Democrat from re-entering for another session.

Another classic Engler tactic was the misdirection play.

In late fall 1996, when Democrats were about to reassert control of the state House, he announced to the staff that they would use the lame-duck session to overhaul the state employees retirement system. Instead of a defined benefits plan, in which the state bargained for fixed benefits and wrote a check to pay for them, employees would be enrolled in a defined contributions system along the lines of a 401(k).

Although the idea was a venerable one, proposed in various forms for years and virtually certain to save taxpayers millions over the long haul, it had never gone anywhere because employee unions viewed limits on retirement benefits as a declaration of war. Further, it was next to impossible to enlist public support for an esoteric bookkeeping reform.

As McAlvey recalled, "I thought he was nuts." But neither McAlvey nor the unions reckoned with the divide-and-conquer strategy Engler had devised. First, he linked the proposal to an early retirement offer for state employees that had strong union backing.

Then, he put forward a defined contributions proposal that called for the enrollment of both state employees and public-school teachers. By doing so, he diverted the attention of the teachers unions (the most powerful labor lobby in Lansing). They invested all their energy protecting the teachers' system, and when Engler settled for state employees alone it looked like a compromise.

State Sen. Bob Emerson, D-Flint, often drafted to represent his party in negotiations with the administration, described the Engler strategy as one in which he tries to convince the opposition that they "face execution."

"Then amputation doesn't seem so bad."

Personal appeal

The notion that Engler's success can be attributed, in significant measure, to the warmth and charm of his personality is—to put it mildly—a risible one to his (many) ardent enemies. And probably even to his more dispassionate constituents. In his public persona, Engler customarily exudes all the charisma of an IRS agent stopping by to check the books.

In part, that is because he is intensely private and loathes the modern era's infatuation with the private lives of public officials. One of the most intense partisans on the planet, Engler remained largely mute over the Clinton sex scandal.

In 1989, before he actually became a full-blown public figure, Engler was asked what he wanted to share about his personal side in the upcoming gubernatorial campaign.

Nothing really, he said. "The worst thing about being in public life is the lack of privacy. Everything else is off the charts."

Nor does he seem to possess the trait so common among politicians (and distilled to its purest essence in Clinton): a need to be loved.

Truscott, in a moment of candor, said: "Most politicians really care what they look like ... how well their clothes fit.

"With John, he just doesn't seem to think about it."

Engler's political handlers always claimed his taciturnity appealed to voters. According to their theory, since most regular folks have limited charisma, the public sees Engler as one of its own.

In recent years, the Engler image also benefited from its association with his more charismatic spouse, Michelle, and their photogenic children (born days after the 1994 election).

But perhaps most telling in its effect on outcomes was Engler's ability to inspire loyalty and commitment among staff and Republican activists.

The commitment of the latter, with whom he nurtured relationships over decades, provided the core of a political operation that made it possible for a conservative Engler and an increasingly conservative Republican Party to enjoy startling electoral success in the 1990s in a state that had long leaned liberal and Democratic.

The devotion of his staff was evident as they went to war for Engler time and again.

The story of Anne Mervenne—who served Engler as an appointments aide, a liaison to southeast Michigan and, currently, as administrative assistant to Michelle Engler—is typical.

Mervenne worked herself to the brink of exhaustion in the first Engler term, then spent the last weeks before the 1994 election on the campaign trail trying to get him re-elected. At an appearance in Bay City on the eve of the election, she collapsed and ended up in the hospital.

Her physicians couldn't find any underlying ailment.

"I said to the doctor, 'I can tell you what's wrong with me. I've been working for John Engler for four years.'"

Gleaves Whitney, an Engler speechwriter working on the official history, describes an interview he had with another longtime staffer: "He said he'd take a bullet for John."

To outsiders, that attitude may sound weird. But there can't be much question that it helped Engler to get things done.

Claim to victory

As the end of his tenure nears, Engler and those who have worked with him display a sense of certainty and rectitude in interview after interview.

However it was accomplished, they express little doubt that Michigan changed a lot and for the better under Engler's stewardship.

They lay claim to a government that works better and a state where taxes are lower, individual initiative is rewarded, and business and opportunity thrive.

In the year ahead, Posthumus, who hopes to succeed Engler, will endlessly describe the transformation of Michigan's culture from one of hopelessness and decline in the 1980s to one of promise by the end of the '90s.

He'll talk about how he and his wife thought, back in the bad old days, that the future of their family lay elsewhere.

The skilled and articulate Democrats who seek to thwart Posthumus and put an end to the Engler era will offer a comprehensive alternative view.

Voters will be disadvantaged. It is too soon to know whether the changes enacted over the past 11 years will be lasting or good. Just as it began, the Engler era ends with a recession and a state budget bleeding red ink. The heady, boom-boom '90s may become in memory a pleasant, but not permanent, interlude in state history.

Asked to reflect on his record as the final days approach, Engler said he "doesn't look back."

After 30 years in public life—never having lost an election—he said he's looking forward to its end (without indicating what's next).

"It's turned out better than I could have imagined," he said.

But he can't resist a parting shot at those who would suggest otherwise and those who tried repeatedly and in vain to end it prematurely.

Showing off the smirk that got him into the soup back in history class, he quipped, "I take great satisfaction in knowing that there are thousands of Democrats out there tormented by the fact that I got out undefeated."[535]

[535]*Dawson Bell, "Engler's Michigan: A Reign of Change,"* Detroit Free Press, *January 14, 2002; see also Chris Christoff, "Engler's Michigan: Gamble on Proposal A Pays Off for Governor,"* Detroit Free Press, *January 15, 2002; and Wendy Wendland-Bowyer, "Engler's Michigan: New System Touts Work Ethic, Not Entitlement,"* Detroit Free Press, *January 16, 2002.*

Winston Churchill had a debate in the House of Commons with Stanley Baldwin, the British prime minister. History will say, "The right honorable gentleman was wrong in this matter," Churchill said. "I know, because I will write the history."

★

Chapter Eighteen
Republicans and Supporters

Dennis Schornack, a long-time friend of and senior aide to John Engler:

This is a man I would die for—I'd take a bullet for him.[536]

Campaign manager and first-term chief of staff Dan Pero spoke these deeply personal words in a tribute to the governor. They were delivered in September 2001, at the Republican leadership conference on Mackinac Island:

I've known John Engler for almost 30 years. He's like a big brother to me. Some of you may have known him longer; perhaps a handful of you shook his hand this weekend for the first time. But for me, for all of us who have known John, who have worked with him, he is a remarkable human being.

He didn't hesitate to skip opening day at Tiger Stadium in April, 1991, to attend the funeral of the mother of a friend. John, I will never forget how you cared and the strength you provided not only to me, but to my entire family during our time of grief.

When anyone is ever asked to describe John Engler, they generally don't comment about this kind of compassion. They almost always first describe his incredible intellect, his work ethic. And he does work harder and know more politics than just about anyone.

But there is so much more to John Engler. He is a very private man. A confident man. A man with purpose and resolve. He is someone who keeps his own

[536]*Dennis Schornack, interview with GW, November 15, 1999.*

counsel. He isn't flamboyant. He doesn't wear his emotions on his sleeves. His first instinct isn't to go to the camera.

Most Michiganians have not really come to know him, to understand him, to appreciate him—his thoughtfulness, his kindness, his humor, his passion for all things green and white, his love for Michigan and America, and above all his love for and devotion to Michelle and Maggie and Madeleine and Hannah, the four ladies in his life he cherishes more than life itself.

Ladies and gentlemen, as we finish this wonderful conference, we do so knowing this will be the last time John Engler will sit here as our governor.... [There are] memories we have pasted in our own mental scrapbooks ... of the John Engler we know.

The John Engler we call friend.

The John Engler we love.[537]

*

On another occasion, Dan Pero observed:

In Michigan, John is the tide upon which all Republican ships have risen. He gained control of the Senate. We have control of the House of Representatives. And we have control of the Supreme Court. He's a living legacy.[538]

*

President Gerald R. Ford

I recognized John in the early days of his career in the legislature, and I watched him progress step-by-step. What impressed me the most was how he moved from one office to the next with such strength. He rose up the political ladder on the basis of hard work, knowledge, and merit.

The true test of a successful governor is his ability to get things done. That ability is a natural, inbred characteristic of John Engler. He is a door. And what he has done in Michigan has made him a shining light among the governors.

I lived through the Soapy Williams era, and I think John Engler's name will be at the top of everyone's list as one of Michigan's very best governors. Just look at the record, his elections, his re-elections, his achievements. The public believes it and the facts justify it. Among all the public servants I have known, John Engler is a favorite of mine.[539]

[537] *Dan Pero, tribute to John Engler, September 2001.*
[538] *Dan Pero, interview with GW, February 3, 2001.*
[539] *Gerald R. Ford, interview with GW, October 4, 2002.*

John Engler on Air Force I with President George H. W. Bush, President Gerald Ford, James Baker, III, and an unidentified aide to Ford, 1992. CREDIT: *White House*

*

David Willetts is a Conservative MP in the British Parliament.

John Engler has a devoted international following—he is an inspiration everywhere. Certainly he is one of my heroes.[540]

*

Lieutenant Governor Dick Posthumus

All of the battles John Engler faced in the House and Senate groomed him to be the great leader he is today. The years he spent in the wilderness as a member of the minority party helped him bloom into the powerful leader he is.

I was more impressed with John after he became governor than before he became governor. There are very few leaders who could have done what John did in the 1990s. He had to make some very tough decisions, and it takes someone who is as strong as John, who has fought the battles he has fought, to make

[540] *David Willetts, interview with GW, April 29, 2000.*

the right decisions in those situations. As a matter of fact, I think I told everyone on a monthly basis in the 1990s that I was more impressed with John every day.

John was a late bloomer who blossomed as a governor. He was a good legislator, but he wasn't great. He was a good Senate majority leader, but it wasn't his best work. But as governor, I think he has been great.[541]

*

Ambassador Peter Secchia

John Engler has done more for this state than any two governors combined have. He did not get into politics to be governor. He became governor because he did a good job as a leader in politics....

John never quits giving to others. Here he is, in his last summer in office, and what's he doing? Steeping himself in the state budget mess. Working hard to get Dick Posthumus elected. Meeting with other governors at the NGA. Sharing his political war chest with others. And he doesn't try to take credit for any of it. I have never seen a less selfish man in politics.

John Engler has outstanding executive and administrative skills. He knows how to make tough decisions. When you make tough decisions to achieve a worthy goal, you can appear hard. People think John is hard and uncaring. They are dead wrong. Deep down, he is a warm-and-fuzzy kind of guy. Family is important to him, and he cares about his friends.[542]

*

Betsy DeVos

John is gifted with many natural leadership skills and a love of service. It was natural for him to devote his life to serving his state and his country in a way that he could bring together leadership skills with the things he loves to do—debate, strategize, legislate. All of these skills and experiences bore fruit when he became governor. In his first year in office, John won over most of his opponents. He gained respect from people on both sides of the aisle.

Then came Proposal A, which changed Michigan's political landscape. It was certainly the riskiest legislative move of John's career. Someone without John's intelligence and character could not have taken that original Senate bill and turned it into far-reaching school finance and education reforms. There are not

[541]*Dick Posthumus, interview with GW, February 7, 2001.*
[542]*Peter Secchia, interview with GW, July 12, 2002.*

many people besides John Engler who could have pulled it off the way he did.

John is a very straightforward and decisive person, and his positive characteristics have been a benefit to the Republican Party and to the state. His bold, decisive leadership style was successfully translated into a variety of policies that have put Michigan on a better course. In the 1980s, this state was headed rapidly downward by any measure; in the 1990s we experienced positive growth. With focused determination, he improved the public policy of our state. What he has accomplished over the years has been phenomenal.

I am very curious as to what the governor will do next. I have a hard time envisioning him doing something unrelated to government or politics. He loves politics, and he definitely is the CEO type. Whatever role he is in, he really needs to be captain of the ship. He would have a hard time being a first mate even on the largest ship in the world. I think he'd sooner be captain of a smaller boat than the first mate on a much bigger ship.[543]

*

Cliff Taylor

John is a vintage product of the Midwest. I remember at Matt Engler's funeral, there was a poem that was read. That poem gave me a real understanding of how John grew up. He was raised with strong nineteenth-century values.

Ever since John has been governor, he has understood that as governor he is expected to have a sense of propriety and good judgment. In all circumstances, John is appropriate and measured.

John is always the quietest person in the group; he takes in a lot more than he gives out.

In the 1990s John started to become more philosophical. John's conservatism would be reflected, for example, in the pages of *National Review*.

John is not vindictive. He goes to fundraisers and takes a thrashing from judges whom he has appointed and never says anything to them and never tries to badger them.

On the bench, I have decided in many cases in a way that John does not like, and not once has he said anything. He just doesn't hold a grudge—he is not vin-

[543]*Betsy DeVos, interview with GW, July 31, 2002.*

dictive. In fact, he will come up to me and say something complimentary like, "I guess that statute was poorly written."

What I have seen is that John is quick to recognize loyalty and steadfastness. He is quick to honor that with praise.[544]

*

Andrea Fischer Newman

I know a lot of politicians, and I've known John Engler since 1984, and John Engler is the best political strategist in the nation. He is a great politician. Because he's been on stage all his life, he rarely lets his guard down. He doesn't show any vulnerability to the public.

Dad reading to (from left) Madeleine, Maggie, and Hannah, at the governor's residence, Lansing, summer 1996. SOURCE: *John Engler*

But—John has this soft, this sweet side of him, a vulnerable side that hardly anybody knows about. He can be very domestic. He likes to putter around the kitchen, making sandwiches for his kids, and he likes reading to them. I'll call him on the weekend and he'll say to me, "I'm reading to the girls. Can I call you back?" He will call back—but always at 11:00 p.m. God forbid that he would call back earlier! It's just that he wants to make sure his girls are happy and safe

[544]*Cliff Taylor, interview with GW, June 16, 2000.*

and tucked in for the evening. He really enjoys being a husband and dad and spending time with his family.

If John had a problem during his first years as governor, it was that no one around him effectively portrayed this softer side. Mike Murphy certainly tried. The ads of John with his mother and later with Michelle were powerful.

Part of the problem is that John is hard for people to read. He doesn't often tell you what he's thinking or what he wants to do. If you need his help and make a pitch, and John doesn't think your idea is feasible, he'll tell you no. Quickly. But if he thinks there is something good in your pitch, he will listen. Rarely, though, will he tell you yes right away. He wants to keep his options open and think it through. If your idea has to do with legislation, he'll go back and reread the bills involved. He'll come up with his own way of how all the pieces fit together. Only when he is ready will he commit to you. And when he does, it is often amazing how he repackages what you want. It's often better than what you originally asked for.

John likes to buy gifts for his friends. He buys his friends beautiful gifts, thoughtful gifts. At Christmas in 1989, he went to a gallery and bought me a handmade ceramic picture by Israeli artist Ruth Faktor. Since I'm Jewish, it was obviously a thoughtful gift. It's beautiful and I treasure it.

For a wedding present, he gave me a drawing of a vase with flowers. How many people give art when you get married? It was unusual. When I called to thank him, he was tickled that I liked it so much (but also a little embarrassed because I was thanking him). He said, "I really thought you'd like it. It just reminded me of you."[545]

*

Chief of Staff Sharon Rothwell

John has a different kind of charisma. It is the antithesis of Bill Clinton's charisma. Bill Clinton oozes charm; John Engler inspires awe.

People are in awe of John's ability and his vision. That makes people want to protect and defend him, because he doesn't defend himself. He doesn't get all upset about the negative press he gets. His feeling is, if that's what people want to think, then they can go ahead and think it. But his staff want to defend him....

[545] *Andrea Fischer Newman, interview with GW, August 3, 2002.*

In comparing John with all the governors I have known, he's at the top. I have often had to remind him that other governors are not like him. Whether it was things that he wanted RGA or NGA to do, he would get so excited and I would have to remind him—and LeAnne Wilson would have to do the same thing—we would tell him, "Governor, other governors are not like you. They are not as bright as you are; they don't have the intellectual curiosity you have; they don't care about these things the way that you do."

Shortly after I had started working in the Office of the State Employer, a difficult issue came up regarding health insurance. Denny Schornack said, "Sharon, I think you should tell him, rather than me." Denny commented on how John sometimes respects opinion from women more than from men. He said, "If it is a high-level or competent woman who tells him something, it will be more meaningful."

I told him, "Good grief, Denny, I don't think that's true." And yet, the governor and I have talked about that, especially in the second and third terms. He has gotten national recognition from women's groups for having so many women at key spots in his administration. Many women have done well with the governor because I think he thinks most women work harder. I do not want to overgeneralize, but I think that has been his experience....

There is a great distance between the media image of John Engler and the real man. He is far more complex than anyone knows. The teachers' union tells teachers that he hates them. The media have tried to make him out as this scheming political machine who doesn't care about anyone. Nothing could be further from the truth.

Just last week, he handed me a letter from an elderly woman up on Mackinac Island. She was appealing for his help on a domestic issue. I told the governor, "It is not appropriate for us to get involved in family lawsuits."

The governor replied, "This is so sad. She is old and doesn't know what to do." He doesn't know this woman, yet he felt so much empathy for her. He really felt she was being victimized and wanted to help her. Eventually we asked our legal department to investigate and see what could be done.

A cold-hearted person would not have given that letter a second thought—and this was not an isolated incident. John Engler is a man who has true compassion.[546]

*

[546]*Sharon Rothwell, interview with GW, March 16, 2001.*

Bill Gnodtke

John Engler is one of Michigan's great governors. He put an enduring footprint on the state—through tax cuts, welfare reform, Proposal A, charter schools, and court appointments that have changed the attitude toward litigation. He probably has done more, in more areas, than any other governor. He was never a lame duck or caretaker. He is working till the end.

John Engler is also one of Michigan's great political leaders. Canvass the 50 states and find me another governor who has hosted 12 consecutive galas—and not kept the money for himself. He's given it all to state party. Most governors keep the money to build a war chest for the next race. John could have said to hell with public funding. But he didn't, and that was smart. Because he has a Republican House, a conservative court, and strong majority in the Senate.

John remembers how lean it was when the GOP was not in the majority. I hope up-and-coming Republicans don't squander his achievement.[547]

*

L. Brooks Patterson, Oakland County executive:

I think John Engler is one of the savviest politicians that I have ever had the pleasure of working with. He is a good tactician. He can see problems and figure out how to get to the solution. He has changed the face of state government in Michigan.

We were going to Washington once to meet with Jim Baker, who wanted to know where we were with the '92 campaign. So on the airplane, John Engler, Spencer Abraham, Pete Secchia, and I laid out our campaign plan on the back of an envelope. Pete was holding the envelope, and we brainstormed the whole way there. When we got to DC, Jim Baker asked, "What do you have?" We handed him the envelope.

It was clear to me from that exercise that John Engler is one of the best campaigners around. He also has an in-depth grasp of a whole range of issues—it just boggles most people's minds. You ask him a question about a specific issue, and he can answer you in such detail that you would think he had studied it all his life.[548]

*

[547] *William Gnodtke, interview with GW, August 2, 2002.*
[548] *L. Brooks Patterson, interview with Josh Nunez, July 22, 2002.*

Mary Ellen Brandell

John Engler has made a difference in many lives. He has touched and will touch all our lives for many years to come.... We will never know the many hours he has spent talking and listening to people.... We will never have a way to measure the lives he has affected in so many ways.[549]

*

Elroy Sailor has told his story to audiences many times. He was 21 when Engler hired him, giving him a second chance.

At age 19 I made a terrible decision. I had a federal conviction and spent a year incarcerated in Michigan.

In prison I read the newspapers about John Engler when he was running for governor. I felt a kinship with what a white male from Beal City was saying to this African-American from Detroit. I had been raised by my mom and dad and grandparents to appreciate Republican values. I found myself being inspired by what John Engler was trying to do. So when I got out, I worked at Pizza Hut at night so that I could volunteer with the Engler campaign during the day.

Then I decided to pursue my dream and I applied for a job with the governor. I was turned down twice. But I was persistent. On the third occasion, I met with Lucille Taylor in her office and told her my story. It was a very humbling and frightening experience. After a half hour, she told me to step out of the room while she made a phone call. I later learned she called either John Engler or Dan Pero. They would have to make the decision. At the same time she was on the phone, I was on the phone with my mom and we prayed. We prayed because not many people in Detroit thought the Engler administration would hire me. I was from the inner city and had no political connections with the Republican Party. Besides, it would be too risky to hire an African-American with my background. All I had was hope.

After a few minutes, Lucille came back and told me that it would be all right; I felt that I would be hired. Sure enough, a couple of days later, the Engler administration made me an offer to work in constituent services, answering the phones. They would hire a 21-year-old African-American from Detroit, who had had a federal conviction, who had been incarcerated, and who wondered if he would get a second chance.

[549] *Mary Ellen Brandell, "Introduction of 1991 Outstanding Citizen," speech to Mt. Pleasant Area Chamber of Commerce, February 16, 1991, pp. 1-2, 5.*

That was a turning point in my life. I wanted a second chance, and John Engler provided the opportunity. The governor saw something in me that people even in my own community either refused to see or couldn't see. In my eight years with the administration, I learned about politics, writing, public policy, and leadership. I went from answering the phones to being Engler's senior advisor on urban affairs.

Now I'm in Washington. Last May, I had the opportunity to sit in a meeting in the Oval Office with President George W. Bush and Congressman J. C. Watts. I pinched myself and realized how much John Engler made that moment possible. He is a cornerstone of my foundation—right there with Jessie (grandfather) and Nancy (grandmother), Clarence (father) and Deanna (mother), and the Reverend Wendell Anthony (pastor). John Engler has greatly affected how I view the world. He has become a part of my values and belief system. I have never found the words to adequately express how deeply indebted I am to him.[550]

*

Gleaves Whitney describes an encounter with an admirer of John Engler's.

Mansfield Morris, the African-American shoeshine man in Kositchek's department store, is about 70 years old. A former sharecropper from Mississippi, he has been in Lansing since 1940. Mansfield is a voracious reader of excellent history books. I've seen him reading James MacPherson's *Civil War*, David McCullough's *Truman*, and many other serious books. This morning I went in and saw him sitting in his usual spot. A paperback dictionary was under his chair. This time he was hunched over a big book on his lap and underlining lengthy passages. When he saw me, he said, "Look at this." It was David McCullough's new biography of John Adams.

Manchester turned to the title page. There was a substantial inscription by John Engler to Mansfield, dated June 28, 2001, and saying he hoped, since Mansfield enjoyed this particular author, that he would enjoy this wonderful new book. The inscription ended, "Thanks for always being so helpful."

"The governor gave this to me a week ago." Mansfield had already closely read more than 100 pages.

Mansfield then started talking about how he had known Engler from the days when he was a young representative—"practically a boy," he cracked.

[550] *Elroy Sailor, interview with GW, July 9, 2002.*

"I've always enjoyed John. It's the way he treats me, man to man. He knows how to listen. We can talk about all kinds of things." And then Mansfield proceeded to tell me how they had talked about immigration, the economic backdrop to the Civil War, Truman. "Now we'll talk about John Adams," he laughed.[551]

*

Dave Peltomaa headed Engler's security detail.

In the early years we did a lot of late-night driving—16 to 18 hour days. Often we would be short staffed and dead tired. In these situations the governor would always offer to drive. Of course we never took him up on his offer. (The governor still offers to drive. In the summer of 1999, we were driving to the NGA meeting in St. Louis. He said, "Just let me know if you get tired and want me to drive.")

We've had some interesting experiences over the years. For instance, twice we've had flat tires on the primary car. The first flat occurred on the drive back from Mackinac Island after a 4th of July weekend. Traffic was extremely heavy, and I didn't want to make him wait while I changed the tire. I wanted to get him into a new car and get him safely back home.

But the governor got out of the car and said, "I don't want to leave this car. Let's just change the tire."

While I got the spare tire out of the trunk, the governor began jacking up the car himself. Two state troopers from the Ithaca post arrived. They were shocked to see the governor of the state down on his knees, with a tire iron, taking the tire off. It just surprised them that he would roll up his sleeves and help.

The same thing happened when we had a flat tire on I-96. He pitched right in and helped change the tire. I don't think the media ever saw this side of him.[552]

*

Paul Hillegonds

John Engler will go down as one of Michigan's greatest governors. Of all the people I've worked with in politics, he is unique in a great way: he combines principles and pragmatism; he is strategic and the master of detail. It is such a rare combination.

If there has been any weakness in his leadership, it is that he's been so driven to get the job done that he hasn't cared what people think of him. As a result,

[551] *Mansfield Morris, interview with GW, July 6, 2001.*
[552] *Dave Peltomaa, interview with GW, October 22, 1999.*

people haven't seen the whole man. They do not understand that he cares about people. If I have any sadness about his 32 years of public service, it's that people don't know him better.[553]

*

Bart LaBelle is a businessman from Mount Pleasant.

I have supported John since the day in 1970 when he approached me at my dad's hamburg stand and asked me to support him. I liked what he said and have supported him ever since. Today he is one of the top three or four political strategists in the country.

John is scrupulously honest. He never feathered his own bed. The power never corrupted him. He always remained focused on the goal, which was to serve and make government better. He never let polls, criticism, public opinion, or celebrity deter him from where he was going. He always followed the compass direction he had set.[554]

*

William Bennett served in the Reagan and Bush administrations. The author of The Book of Virtues *said this about John Engler at a Catholic Campaign for America event in southeast Michigan in 1999.*

John Engler is not only one of the best governors in our time; he is among the best Catholic leaders in America. He knows what he is about. He stands firm, absolutely true to his principles, yet at the same time knows how to forge majorities and get things done through the democratic process.

John is as pro-life as they come. Catholics in Michigan and around the country are indebted to him because of his ability to articulate and defend what John Paul II calls a "civilization of life." Michigan in the 1990s has a pro-life record second to none, and that is due to John Engler. He has stood up to Dr. Death himself, Jack Kevorkian, and to his ambitious lawyer. In a tough state politically, he has consistently defended the dignity of the human person from the moment of conception to life's natural end.

John has championed far-reaching education reforms because he knows that our children must have greater opportunities to grow in knowledge and virtue. They are our nation's future. The improvements he seeks in education may be his greatest, his most lasting, legacy.

[553]*Paul Hillegonds, interview with GW, September 27, 2002.*
[554]*Bart LaBelle, interview with GW, October 18, 2002.*

John is part of a generation of Catholic leaders and governors who are changing politics in America. They are a courageous group, challenging the status quo, building new coalitions, and pushing through impressive reforms. Among these leaders, John is in the vanguard. And he is not yet finished.[555]

*

Rusty Hills and John Nevin

John Engler is like a rock. His strength and composure in the face of criticism are amazing. I think that strength comes from his family and faith. His ability not to lash back at critics or respond in kind is unlike any other politician I know. At all times he conducts himself with grace, which is rare among people in his profession. Remember, he went through attacks not just on himself, but also on his wife and his family. Yet his strength and composure remained constant. He maintained grace and aplomb. All the criticism bounced off of him like BBs off a battleship.[556]

*

Jack Wheatley

I have worked inside two of the greatest organizations in the world, General Motors (the greatest corporation in the world) and Michigan state government (under John Engler, the best state government in the nation). Over the course of my career, I have worked with many leaders. But I have to say, my years with John Engler have been the high point of my working life.

What impresses me about John is that he does not abandon his principles. In times of stress, many politicians and executives abandon their principles for short-term gain. I've seen that happen time and again. Not John Engler. During the first and second year of the administration, he was looking at terrible poll numbers. It must have been tempting to abandon his agenda for short-term gain. But he didn't.

Such commitment to principle is rare. John Engler is one of the most successful governors not just that Michigan has ever had, but that the United States has ever had.[557]

*

[555] *William J. Bennett, keynote address, Catholic Campaign for America Gala Banquet, October 28, 1999.*
[556] *Rusty Hills and John Nevin, interview with GW, February 12, 2001.*
[557] *Jack Wheatley, interview with GW, July 3, 2002; Jack Wheatley, letter to JE, June 28, 2002.*

John Engler at the beginning of the third term.
SOURCE: *Engler administration*

George H. W. Bush

John Engler has been an outstanding governor. He is a true leader.[558]

*

Pat Laughlin

Because of term limits, there will never be another John Engler. Not in Michigan. He is one of a kind.[559]

*

Lucille Taylor

John Engler would rather listen than speak. He would rather serve than be served. He is the kind of person who made a career of public service because he believes in his ideas. He believes that ideas have consequences.

I think the improvements in Michigan during the last decade have generated an admiration for the governor, but I'm not sure that there is genuine fondness yet. However, I believe that as time goes by there will be genuine fondness, too.

We will never again see a governor like John Engler—he will go down as one of the great governors.[560]

[558] *George H. W. Bush, interview with GW, November 18, 2002.*
[559] *Pat Laughlin, interview with GW, July 3, 2002.*
[560] *Lucille Taylor, interviews with GW, September 27, 1999, and October 20, 1999.*